A Companion to the Works of Stefan George

Studies in German Literature, Linguistics, and Culture

Edited by James Hardin
(South Carolina)

Camden House Companion Volumes

The Camden House Companions provide well-informed and up-to-date critical commentary on the most significant aspects of major works, periods, or literary figures. The Companions may be read profitably by the reader with a general interest in the subject. For the benefit of student and scholar, quotations are provided in the original language.

Profile of George, ca. 1893.
Photograph by K. Bauer, Munich.
Courtesy of the Stefan George-Stiftung.

A Companion to the Works of Stefan George

Edited by
Jens Rieckmann

CAMDEN HOUSE

First published 2005 by Camden House
Reprinted in paperback and transferred to digital printing 2010

Camden House is an imprint of Boydell & Brewer Inc.
668 Mt. Hope Avenue, Rochester, NY 14620, USA
www.camden-house.com
and of Boydell & Brewer Limited
PO Box 9, Woodbridge, Suffolk IP12 3DF, UK
www.boydellandbrewer.com

Paperback ISBN-13: 978-1-57113-456-1
Paperback ISBN-10: 1-57113-456-5
Hardback ISBN-13: 978-1-57113-214-7
Hardback ISBN-10: 1-57113-214-7

Library of Congress Cataloging-in-Publication Data

A companion to the works of Stefan George / edited by Jens Rieckmann.
        p. cm. — (Studies in German literature, linguistics, and culture)
Includes bibliographical references and index.
ISBN 1-57113-214-7 (hardcover: alk. paper)
    1. George, Stefan Anton, 1868–1933 — Criticism and interpretation.
I. Rieckmann, Jens, 1944– II. Title. III. Series: Studies in German
literature, linguistics, and culture (Unnumbered)

PT2613.E47Z593 2004
831'.8—dc22

                                                        2004017491

A catalogue record for this title is available from the British Library.

Cover image: *Feier-Abend,* by Alexander Zschokke.

Contents

List of Illustrations   ix

Acknowledgments   xi

Standard Editions and References to the   xiii
Works of Stefan George

List of Principal Works of Stefan George   xv

Introduction   1
    Jens Rieckmann

The Poetry

Stefan George's Poetics   25
    William Waters

Stefan George's Early Works 1890–1895   51
    Robert Vilain

In Praise of Illusion: *Das Jahr der Seele* and *Der Teppich*   79
des Lebens: Analysis and Historical Perspective
    Karla Schultz

In Zeiten der Wirren: Stefan George's Later Works   99
    Michael M. Metzger

Contexts

Stefan George and Two Types of Aestheticism   127
    Jeffrey D. Todd

Master and Disciples: The George Circle   145
    Michael Winkler

Stefan George and the Munich Cosmologists   161
    Paul Bishop

George, Nietzsche, and Nazism   189
        Ritchie Robertson

Stefan George's Concept of Love and the   207
Gay Emancipation Movement
        Marita Keilson-Lauritz

Works Cited   231
Notes on the Contributors   245
Index   247

Illustrations

Profile of George, ca. 1893.   iv

Title page of *Das Jahr der Seele,* 1897, designed by   78
Melchior Lechter.

Title page of Max Kommerell's *Der Dichter als*   144
Führer in der deutschen Klassik, 1928.

George, Verwey and the Cosmologists,   160
Munich, April 1902.

George and a friend, 1896.   206

Acknowledgments

First and foremost I want to thank the contributors to this volume for their dedication and patience. I would also like to thank James Hardin for initiating this project and for his support throughout the work. In the final stages of getting the manuscript ready for print James Walker provided supportive guidance and advice.

The photographs in this book are reproduced by permission of the Stefan George-Stiftung.

Special thanks are due to Ute Oelmann, the director of the Stefan George-Archiv in the Württembergische Landesbibliothek and to Bertram Schefold, the director of the Stefan-George-Gesellschaft, for their interest in this project and for their advice.

J. R.
Amherst, NH
July 2004

Standard Editions and References
to the Works of Stefan George

THERE ARE THREE EDITIONS of the collected works of Stefan George. The eighteen-volume *Gesamt-Ausgabe der Werke, endgültige Fassung* was arranged by George himself, published by the Georg Bondi Verlag in Berlin between 1927 and 1934, and reprinted in a reduced format by the Küpper Verlag between 1964 and 1969. In 1958 the Küpper Verlag in Munich and Düsseldorf published the *Werke. Ausgabe in zwei Bänden*, edited by Robert Boehringer. This two-volume edition contains all the texts of the eighteen-volume edition, but not the illustrations and appendices of the original edition. The two-volume edition was reprinted with additional texts from George's literary estate (*Nachlaß*) in 1968, 1976, and, edited by Georg Peter Landmann, in 1984 by the Klett-Cotta Verlag in Stuttgart. Since the *Werke: Ausgabe in zwei Bänden* is the most accessible edition, references (by volume and page number) in this *Companion*, unless otherwise noted, are to this edition. Since 1982 the Klett-Cotta Verlag has been publishing a new edition with appendices, *Sämtliche Werke in 18 Bänden*, edited by Georg Peter Landmann and Ute Oelmann. To date, thirteen volumes have been published.

Unless otherwise noted, translations of the titles of George's volumes of poetry and of individual poems are taken from Olga Marx and Ernst Morwitz, trans., *The Works of Stefan George: Rendered into English*. 2nd, revised and enlarged edition (Chapel Hill, NC: U of North Carolina P, 1974).

George's journal *Blätter für die Kunst*, whose nominal editor was C. A. Klein, was published between 1892 and 1919 in twelve volumes. Küpper Verlag published a complete reprint in six volumes with an introduction by Robert Boehringer in 1968. Unless otherwise noted, references in this Companion are to this edition and will be abbreviated *BfdK*, followed by volume number (and, where appropriate, issue number) and page number.

Principal Works of Stefan George

Listed by year of first appearance. When available in translation, English title and date of appearance are given.

1889   *Zeichnungen in Grau* (Drawings in Grey, 1974)
1890   *Hymnen* (Odes, 1949)
1891   *Pilgerfahrten* (Pilgrimages, 1949)
1892   *Algabal* (Algabal, 1949)
1895   *Die Bücher der Hirten- und Preisgedichte, der Sagen und Sänge, und der hängenden Gärten* (The Books of Eclogues and Eulogies, of Legends and Lays, and of the Hanging Gardens, 1949)
1897   *Das Jahr der Seele* (The Year of the Soul, 1949)
1899   *Der Teppich des Lebens und die Lieder von Traum und Tod mit einem Vorspiel* (The Tapestry of Life and the Songs of Dream and Death with a Prelude, 1949)
1901   *Die Fibel, Auswahl erster Verse* (The Primer [excerpts], 1974)
1903   *Tage und Taten, Aufzeichnungen und Skizzen*
1906   *Maximin, ein Gedenkbuch*
1907   *Der siebente Ring* (The Seventh Ring, 1949)
1913   *Der Stern des Bundes* (The Star of the Covenant, 1949)
1917   *Der Krieg, Dichtung* ("The War," 1949)
1921   *Drei Gesänge* (An die Toten. Der Dichter in Zeiten der Wirren. Einem jungen Führer im ersten Weltkrieg.) ("Verses for the Dead," "The Poet in Times of Confusion," "To a Young Leader in the First World War," 1949)
1928   *Das neue Reich* (The Kingdom Come, 1949)

Translations by Stefan George

1891   *Charles Baudelaire's Blumen des Bösen,* umgedichtet von Stefan George
1905   *Übertragungen aus den Werken von Albert Verwey*
        Übertragungen aus den Werken von Waclaw Lieder
        Stéphane Mallarmé. Herodias. Umdichtung von Stefan George
        Zeitgenössische Dichter, Übertragen von Stefan George
1909   *Shakespeare: Sonnette, Umdichtung von Stefan George*
1912   *Dante: Göttliche Komödie, Übertragung von Stefan George*

Introduction

Jens Rieckmann

STEFAN GEORGE (1868–1933) is one of the three pre-eminent German poets of his time. Together with Hugo von Hofmannsthal and Rainer Maria Rilke, he initiated the revival of German poetry at the turn of the century and put an end to the "Sing-Sang Mode" of post-Romantic German poetry (Glöckner 81) written by poets such as Friedrich Bodenstedt (1819–1892), Adolf von Schack (1815–1894), Paul Heyse (1830–1914), and Emanuel Geibel (1815–1884), poets who were popular at the time, though they are now mostly forgotten. At age twenty-two, Rilke referred to George as "Meister Stephan [*sic*] George" (*Zeittafel* 74). Hofmannsthal was a lifelong admirer of George's poetic achievements; in a 1903 note he called him "der große Dichter unserer Zeit" (*Sämtliche Werke* 31: 235). Neither the personal and artistic differences between Hofmannsthal and George, nor the rupture of their relations in 1906 diminished in any way Hofmannsthal's high regard for the "Größe seines Werkes [. . .] die Einzigkeit seines Schöpferischen u. Prophetischen in der Sprache" (Hofmannsthal/Pannwitz 22).

George played an equally important, albeit controversial and provocative role in German cultural and political history. Although George is often linked with the *l'art pour l'art* movement, and although his artistic consciousness and the poetry he wrote in the 1890s bear the imprint of European aestheticism, his post turn-of-the-century poetry and the writings that emerged from the poets and intellectuals he gathered around him in the *George-Kreis* constitute above all a scathing commentary on the political, social, and cultural situation in Wilhelmine Germany. In the decades immediately following the Second World War his memory was kept alive primarily by memoirs and reminiscences of those who had joined his circle and by the journal *Castrum Peregrini* (Encampment in Exile) founded in 1951 by German emigrants in the Netherlands. For reasons I will discuss below, the general public as well as much of the literary and scholarly establishment in Germany did not and could not approach George with the same impartiality as it did other writers who had achieved fame before the Second World War. Criticism centering on the aesthetic aspects of George's works rather than on his person or his works in relation to political events in Germany before and after 1933 was primarily the work of non-German scholars such as Claude David.

In recent years, however, there has been renewed awareness of George in the German-speaking world. Although the *Rhein-Main-Presse* referred to George as an almost forgotten poet as recently as 1993, three years later, on the occasion of the opening of the Stefan George Museum in his home-town of Bingen on the Rhine, the *Allgemeine Zeitung* (10 August 1996), registered a growing interest in George. This is evident in the recent pro-liferation of studies devoted wholly or in part to George and the *George-Kreis*;[1] in the publication of the *George-Jahrbuch* (established in 1996), and of the annotated eighteen-volume edition of his works begun in 1982. And although the Gay Emancipation Movement had claimed George as one of their own as early as 1914, critics later averted their eyes from this aspect of George's person and poetry until Marita Keilson-Lauritz pub-lished in 1987 her pioneering study, *Von der Liebe die Freundschaft heißt: Zur Homoerotik im Werk Stefan Georges*. For the past decade George has been omnipresent in gay anthologies, encyclopedias, and literary histories, representing, as Gregory Woods put it, the spiritual rather than the physi-cal element in gay literature (184).

Some attention has also been paid in recent years to George as a writer who anticipates some of the concerns voiced by the environmental move-ment. The poem most often referred to in this context is "Der Mensch und der Drud" (Man and Faun) from his last collection of poetry *Das Neue Reich*.[2] In this dialogic poem man points proudly to the achieve-ments of civilization, but the faun warns him that the harm man has done to the environment will result in the destruction of the source from which all life springs. This aspect of George's writings calls for further discussion.

Despite renewed critical interest in George and his Circle and his rediscovery as a gay writer, his reputation has lagged in the Anglo-Saxon world. This may be due in part to the lack of a congenial translation of George's works. Some of George's poems were translated into English as early as 1902, and individual poems subsequently found their way into anthologies of modern poetry, of German poetry in English translation, and into literary journals. Cyril M. Scott (1879–1970), who belonged to the Berlin circle of George's friends, published a selection from George's works in 1910.[3] The only complete English translation of George's poems was made by Ernst Morwitz and Olga Marx [Carol North Valhope] and published in 1949.[4] George's relative obscurity can also be attributed in part to Rilke's reputation in the Anglo-Saxon world as the pre-eminent modern German poet, an opinion that has hindered the reputation of both Hofmannsthal and George. A sign that this state of affairs may be chang-ing is the recent publication of Robert Norton's monumental George biography *Secret Germany: Stefan George and His Circle* (2002). A com-prehensive account of the European and American reception of George's works and those of the members of his circle is yet to be written.[5] The wide-ranging and original essays in this book will, I hope, contribute to a rekindling of interest in this crucial, albeit controversial writer among scholars, students, and readers generally interested in German culture in the Anglo-Saxon world and beyond.

Stefan George was born on July 12, 1868 in Büdesheim, a village near the small town of Bingen on the Rhine. George's paternal grandfather grew up in the French duchy of Lorraine. He eventually followed his uncle to Büdesheim where he worked as a cooper and later acquired and ran a *Weinstube*. George's father, the easy-going Stephan George, kept a tavern in Büdesheim and became a successful wine merchant after the family moved to Bingen in 1873. His mother, née Eva Schmitt, a devout Catholic, was emotionally withdrawn from her husband and children. George's French ancestry and the pervasive French cultural influence in the Rhineland may account in part for the disdain with which George looked upon all things Prussian in later years and for his plans, as expressed in a 1889 conversation with Albert Saint-Paul (1861–1946), to "écrire en français" (*Zeittafel* 12). His religious upbringing, particularly the rituals of the Catholic church, made a lasting impression on him and exerted, as Braungart has shown, a profound influence on George's poetry.

Before entering the Ludwig-Georgs-Gymnasium in Darmstadt at the age of fourteen, George attended the parochial school in Bingen. He started writing while still a schoolboy; his first extant poem, "Prinz Indra," and fragments of three dramas (*Manuel, Phraortes, Graf Bothwell*) date from his school years. The short verses written in 1886 and 1887 were later published in a volume called *Die Fibel: Auswahl erster Verse*. None of these are remarkable; they neither foreshadow the originality of George's later works nor do they differ thematically from the kind of poetry most teenagers tend to write. Some of the beginning lines and titles, such as "Ich wandelte auf öden düstren bahnen" (I wandered along bleak dark paths), "Vernunft! du legtest deine kalten hände" (Reason! You laid your cold hands), "Gräber" (Graves), and "Es heulet der Dezemberwind" (The December winds howl) are indicative of the weltschmerz, melancholy, and despair typically experienced by sensitive adolescents. Despite their conventionality, George saw in these early poems "ungestalte puppen aus denen später die falter leuchtender gesänge fliegen," as he wrote in his 1901 preface to *Die Fibel* (2: 467).

During his Darmstadt years George also first engaged in another life-long activity: translation. Soon after he had seen a performance of Ibsen's *The Pillars of Society*, he embarked on rendering parts of Ibsen's early tragedies into German. His later translations or rather adaptations of Shakespeare's sonnets, Baudelaire's *Les fleurs du mal*, portions of Dante's *Commedia*, and poems by contemporary English, French, Italian, Danish, Dutch, Belgian, and Polish writers form as much a part of his poetic oeuvre as his own poems. A third endeavor of these years, the publication in 1887 of *Rosen und Disteln* (Roses and Thistles), anticipates another of

George's later interests — assembling the works of like-minded writers in a literary review. Although *Rosen und Disteln,* a literary journal containing works by George and a few of his schoolmates, was short-lived (only one issue appeared), its programmatic statement prefigures George's later, highly influential literary enterprise *Blätter für die Kunst* (Pages for Art, 1892–1919): "Artikel religiösen und politischen Inhalts streng ausscheidend, wird sie [die Zeitschrift] [. . .] ihre Leser zu unterhalten und zu belehren suchen."[6] Similarly, the first issue of the *Blätter* stated: "Der name dieser veröffentlichung sagt schon zum teil was sie soll: der kunst [. . .] dienen, alles staatliche und gesellschaftliche ausscheidend" (*Einleitungen* 7). Yet another of George's plans, dating back to the months immediately following his graduation from the *Gymnasium* in Darmstadt, foretokens the cosmopolitan character of the early volumes of the *Blätter.* With Arthur Stahl (1869–1929) and Carl Rouge, two of his fellow students and collaborators on *Rosen und Disteln,* he discussed the so-called "Mappeplan," a continuation of the *Rosen und Disteln* project under international auspices. George had traveled to London and Montreux after his graduation, and through the connections he established had hoped to win French and English writers for this undertaking. Although it was never brought to fruition, the plan illustrates George's opposition to German nationalism and his advocacy of cosmopolitanism, positions he adhered to throughout his life. In 1889 he stated: "Berührung mit andern völkern andern sitten anderer weisheit [. . .] ist das beste mittel zur ausrottung aller steifheit aller verblendung alles stumpsinns aller knechtschaft kurz alles schlimmen im geschicke der völker" (Boehringer 30).

Finally, as another portent of things to come, there is the frequently cited "Amhara"-episode from George's childhood, in which the nine-year-old George, together with a playmate, founded the imaginary kingdom of Amhara and declared himself its king; the playmate was relegated to the role of prime minister. Several commentators see in this episode a preconfiguration of the structure of the George Circle; its hierarchical nature — with George as the "Master" and members of the Circle as "disciples" — best captured in the title of Friedrich Wolters's essay *Herrschaft und Dienst* (Sovereignty and Service, 1909). The episode also figures prominently in two of George's poems, "Kindliches Königtum" (A Child's Kingdom 1: 101) and "Ursprünge" (Origins 1: 294–95).

The last stanza of "Ursprünge" expresses, as Peter von Matt has shown (265), George's narcissistic and erotically charged remembrance of the boy he once was:

> Doch an dem flusse im schilfpalaste
> Trieb uns der wollust erhabenster schwall:
> In einem sange den keiner erfasste
> Waren wir heischer und herrscher vom All.

According to von Matt, this relation remained the lodestar guiding George's later search for the young man who would resemble the boy George remembered. After he had vainly hoped to have encountered him in the seventeen-year-old Hugo von Hofmannsthal in 1891, and later in the nineteen-year-old Friedrich Gundolf in 1899, George believed to have finally found him in the thirteen-year-old Maximilian Kronberger (1888–1904) who died at the age of sixteen, two years after George's first encounter with him (von Matt 267–68).

It is not known when George first became aware of his sexual orientation, but, as Norton has pointed out, the poem "Der Schüler" (The Pupil 2: 516–18), written in 1888, testifies to "an undeniable certainty" and ensuing anxiety (34).[7] The poem's speaker, a novice monk, ponders what has undermined "die friedlichkeit der frommen" that characterized his ascetic life in the monastery:

> Was bringt nun diese wandlung? Doch nicht einzig
> Mein schweifen in den unbetretenen erkern
> Wo ich bei manchem seltsamen gerät
> Den spiegel glänzenden metalls entdeckt
> Vor dem ich meines eigenen leibs geheimnis
> Und anderer zuerst bedenken lernte.
> Auch wäre frevel länger noch zu glauben
> Dass jenes blonde kind der jüngste schüler
> Das oft mich mit den grossen augen sucht
> So gänzlich meinen sinn erschüttern könne.

A sojourn in the south, contact with a land and a people whose pagan past still permeates the present, results in a transformation of the self:

> Ich fühlte innres rasen . . meine glieder
> Als drängten sie zu neuen diensten bebten
> Und schauerten . . es drang in mich ein hauch
> Und wuchs zu solchem brausen so gewaltig
> Und schmerzlich dass ich selbst mich nicht mehr kannte.

Returned to the monastery, he endeavors to restore his former self, to "bannen was vielleicht versuchung war . .," but in vain:

> Doch es treibt mich auf
> Der alten toten weisheit zu entraten
> Bis ich die lebende erkannt: der leiber
> Der blumen und der wolken und der wellen.

Before George enrolled as a student at the Friedrich-Wilhelm University in Berlin in the fall of 1889, he spent the spring and summer in Paris, the one place in the world, as he was to say later, "wo man enthusiasmiert war für Dichtung" (Edith Landmann 76). Here he was introduced to the French

Symbolists, among them Paul Verlaine, and took part in Mallarmés *mardis soirs.* In 1907 George recalled the formative impact these contacts had on him in his poem "Franken" (Frankish Lands):

> Und in der heitren anmut stadt · der gärten
> Wehmütigem reiz · bei nachtbestrahlten türmen
> Verzauberten gewölbs umgab mich jugend
> Im taumel aller dinge die mir teuer -
> Da schirmten held und sänger das Geheimnis:
> VILLIERS sich hoch genug für einen thron ·
> VERLAINE in fall und busse fromm und kindlich
> Und für sein denkbild blutend: MALLARMÉ. (1: 235)

Albert Saint-Paul, who had introduced George to the French Symbolist poets, persuaded him to return to Germany, promulgate the Symbolist poetics, and revolutionize the epigenous German poetry of the late nineteenth century. In a conversation with Albert Mockel (1866–1945), the editor of the Belgian Symbolist journal *La Wallonie,* George accordingly spoke of the task he was confronting: "il nous faut développer d'abord la plastique du langage; nous devons créer nos instruments de travail, enseigner aux poètes leur métier d'artisan, — leur rappeler que le mot est musique, [. . .] qu'il a un contour, un volume, une masse, une couleur, une saveur."[8] He endeavored to realize this program in his first slim volume of poetry *Hymnen,* which, according to Saint-Paul, established his credentials as the "poète symboliste de l'Allemagne" (Zeller 51), a verdict confirmed by none other than Mallarmé who wrote to George: "J'ai été ravi par le jet ingénu et fier, en de l'éclat et la rêverie, de ces <u>Hymnes</u> (nul titre qui soit plus beau); mais aussi, mon cher exilé [. . .] que vous soyez par votre main d'oeuvre, si fine et rare, un des nôtres et d'aujourd'hui" (*Zeittafel,* 18).

Both *Hymnen* and George's subsequent volumes of early poetry (*Pilgerfahrten, Algabal,* and *Die Bücher der Hirten- und Preis-Gedichte · der Sagen und Sänge und der hängenden Gärten*) were printed privately in limited editions of one hundred copies (two hundred in the case of the latter), distributed to friends and fellow poets, and displayed in a few carefully selected bookstores in Berlin, Munich, Darmstadt, and Leipzig. The procedure is indicative of George's lifelong contempt for the masses, for the marketing strategies of large publishing houses, and of his desire to be read and appreciated only by those already initiated into the esoteric poetic rites of the Symbolist credo. He followed a similar procedure when he launched his journal *Blätter für die Kunst* in 1892. Subscriptions to the journal were not made available to the public, but rather its readers were carefully selected and invited to subscribe. It was not until 1898, when he met Georg Bondi, owner of a small and refined publishing house, that he entertained the idea of making his works available to a larger, yet still discriminating public. As Dieter Mettler has shown, George's conscious decision to strictly limit the number of copies of his first four collections of poetry and of the *Blätter* was strategically designed to emphasize the exclusive character of his publications as harbingers of a new art. Their very exclusivity guaranteed a growing demand for them by those who considered themselves and wanted to be considered part of the intellectual elite. In addition to these strategic concerns, George's anti-capitalist, anti-democratic, and anti-bourgeois views also account for his initial insistence on limiting the editions of his own works and of the *Blätter*. He blamed capitalism, democracy, and the bourgeoisie for what he perceived as the commercialized character of the arts in Wilhelmine Germany.

George's first four volumes of poetry combine many of the elements that were to characterize his subsequent works. Written in a stylized language, distinguished by a predilection for the rare and the precious, they deploy archaic and esoteric words, neologisms, and complex syntactical and grammatical constructions. These stratagems were devised to create barriers for the uninitiated reader, as were the idiosyncratic spelling, punctuation (or lack thereof), and typography. The love poems contained in *Hymnen* and *Pilgerfahrten* make exclusive use of the gender-neutral second person in addressing the beloved, as do most of the love poems in George's later works. It was a strategy, as Marita Keilson-Lauritz has shown, employed to camouflage the expression of same sex love.[9]

These first volumes of poetry found enthusiastic reception in the journals of the Symbolist movement, most notably in Belgium, but also in France, Holland, Flanders, and, to a lesser extent, in England and Scandinavia. The Symbolist writers welcomed them as signs that they had found an ally in their battle against naturalism, noted the affinity of George's poetry with their own endeavors, and dated the renaissance of German letters from the publication of the first issues of the *Blätter*.[10] However, in the German-speaking world George's first publications were met either with silence or ridicule. *Stern's Literarisches Bulletin der Schweiz,* for example, objected to the "verschrobene Orthographie" in the *Blätter* (Landmann, *George und sein Kreis* 18). Julius Hart (1859–1930) conceded in the *Freie Bühne für den Entwicklungskampf der Zeit* that the proponents of art for art's sake — "Richard [*sic*] George" is mentioned only in passing — are capable of technical innovations and enriching the means of expression, but ultimately their poetry would only appeal to those who "etwas für Zucker und süßen Schaum schwärmen."[11] As early as 1895, Oskar Panizza (1853–1921) insinuated that George and other Symbolist writers were adherents of the "love that dare not speak its name."[12] The first positive reviews of George's poetry and of the writers he published in the *Blätter* did not appear in Germany until 1894, when the *Allgemeine Kunstchronik* devoted two issues to the Symbolist movement in Germany.

After writing his first two volumes of poetry, George abandoned his studies at the Friedrich-Wilhelm University and enrolled pro forma at the University of Vienna. In Vienna he began translating Baudelaire's *Les fleurs du mal* and worked on his third volume of poetry *Algabal*. This cycle of poems, dedicated in 1898 to the "verhöhnte[n] dulderkönig" Ludwig the Second of Bavaria (1: 44), an icon of the homosexual movement, is set in an artificial realm, conceived as an alternate reality to that of the hated and despised Wilhelmine Germany and centered on the late Roman boy emperor Heliogabalus, who was destined to haunt the decadent imagination. *Algabal* became one of the canonical works of decadence.

For *Pilgerfahrten* George chose the "Aufschrift" or motto "ALSO BRACH ICH AUF / UND EIN FREMDLING WARD ICH / UND ICH SUCHTE EINEN / DER MIT MIR TRAUERTE / UND KEINER WAR (1: 26). This captures George's increasing sense of loneliness and isolation at this time. In Paris he had found in Mallarmé and his circle (*le Maître et le cénacle*) what he had previously envisioned as the ideal community of poets. The search for his own cenacle had up to this point been in vain. True, at the university in Berlin he had met Carl August Klein (1867–1952) who shared his enthusiasm for the Symbolist movement and his homoerotic feelings, but Klein, who later served for many years as the nominal editor of the *Blätter,* was hardly his intellectual equal. With *Algabal* George seemed to have reached a dead end in his poetic career. It was at this impasse that in late 1891 he met the then seventeen-year-old Hugo von Hofmannsthal, an encounter that was to have a lasting impact on both writers.[13] In one of his great confessional letters to Hofmannsthal, written in early January 1892, George said:

> Schon lange im leben sehnte ich mich nach jenem wesen von einer verachtenden durchdringenden und überfeinen verstandeskraft die alles verzeiht begreift würdigt [. . .]. Jenes wesen hätte mir neue triebe und hoffnungen gegeben (denn was ich nach Halgabal noch schreiben soll ist mir unfasslich) und mich im weg aufgehalten der schnurgerad zum nichts führt. [. . .] Diesen übermenschen habe ich rastlos gesucht niemals gefunden [. . .]. Und endlich! Wie? Ja? Ein hoffen — ein ahnen — ein zucken — ein schwanken — o mein zwillingsbruder —.
> (*Briefwechsel zwischen George und Hofmannsthal* 12–13)

Initially Hofmannsthal shared this sense of a personal and artistic affinity — at least in part. Recalling the meeting with George, he was to say shortly before his death in 1929 that it had been for him "die Bestätigung dessen, was in mir lag, die Bekräftigung, daß ich kein ganz vereinzelter Sonderling war, wenn ich es für möglich hielt, in der deutschen Sprache etwas zu geben" (*Briefwechsel zwischen George und Hofmannsthal* 236). The two writers were united in their opposition to Naturalism, their desire to overcome the stagnation of German post-Romantic poetry, their modernist tendency to consider the work of a poet as a craft, and their admiration of

Baudelaire, Mallarmé, Verlaine, Poe, Shelley, Rossetti, and Swinburne. Several factors put a sudden end to the "Tage schöner Begeisterung,"[14] which almost culminated in a duel between the two poets: Hofmannsthal's increasing fear of becoming captive to George's charismatic and dictatorial personality; George's advances, which Hofmannsthal interpreted as sexual in nature; and Hofmannsthal's anxiety about his own latent homoerotic feelings stirred by the encounter with George. Although Hofmannsthal later contributed intermittently to George's *Blätter* until 1904, their personal relations remained tense and crisis-ridden. Increasingly disenchanted with Hofmannsthal's turn toward drama and opera, a development George viewed as a kind of devil's pact with commercial art, George finally broke with Hofmannsthal in 1906.

Yet the failed relationship had a lasting impact on both writers. As early as 1899, when his relations with Hofmannsthal were at a particularly low point, George had included a poem entitled "Der Verworfene" (The Outcast) in his sixth volume of poetry, *Der Teppich des Lebens und die Lieder von Traum und Tod · Mit einem Vorspiel*. It indicates the direction that George's criticism of Hofmannsthal was to take, culminating in a *Merkspruch* published in the *Blätter* in 1910. In it George summarized — without naming Hofmannsthal — everything that, from his point of view and that of his circle, separated him from the "Ästheten": Hofmannsthal's chameleon-like nature, his journalistic prostitution, his insincerity, his mercantile spirit, and his failure to engage in the task of cultural renewal, which George had first pursued in the realm of poetry, and, since the turn of the century, increasingly in the public sphere (*BfdK* 9: 7). George's comments on Hofmannsthal in conversations, his veiled attacks on Hofmannsthal in poems such as "Helfer von damals! Richttag rückt heran" (Helpers of yesterday, the judgment nears, 1: 364) or the short essay "Die Untergehenden," published in the second edition of George's only volume of prose *Tage und Taten* (1926), leave no doubt that he considered Hofmannsthal's later career as a betrayal of the hopes sparked by those "Tage schöner Begeisterung." Hofmannsthal, for his part, continued his futile attempts to come to terms with the personal and artistic conflicts triggered by his relationship with George. His ambivalent attitude towards George is reflected in many of his works, among them the drama *Das gerettete Venedig* (Venice Preserved, 1904), the novel fragment *Andreas* (1932), and the lecture "Das Schrifttum als geistiger Raum der Nation" (1926).

In 1892 George had left Vienna frustrated and embittered. "Vorläufig aber lockt mich Paris," he wrote to the Austrian critic and translator Marie Herzfeld (1855–1940) in February 1892, adding that for him Paris, not Vienna, was the home of true artists: "Ich gedeihe nicht unter jenen (grösstenteils) zeitungsschreibern ohne jedes musikalische oder malerische interesse. Dort aber leben dichter, die wahre künstler zugleich sind" (*Zeittafel* 25). And thus began George's incessant wanderings between Paris,

Bingen, Berlin, Munich, Darmstadt, Marburg, Heidelberg and, towards the end of his life, Minusio on the Lago Maggiore. He never settled permanently anywhere — yet another expression of the contempt he harbored for a bourgeois existence.

The 1890s were marked by George's indefatigable engagement with the *Blätter,* the publication of his fifth and most widely read volume of poetry *Das Jahr der Seele,* and his growing fame. The *Blätter,* modeled on such Symbolist journals as *La Plume, Le Mercure de France, L'Ermitage,* and *Floréal,* started out rather modestly with contributions by George, Hofmannsthal (the two pillars of the first issues), George's school friend Carl Rouge, who had already collaborated on *Rosen und Disteln,* and the Flemish writer Paul Gérardy (1870–1933), who wrote with equal ease in German and French. In order to create the impression that the adherents of the "kunst für die kunst" were more numerous than they were, George published one of his poems under the pseudonym Edmund Lorm — the preface ended with a an exalted claim: "In der kunst glauben wir an eine glänzende wiedergeburt" (*Einleitungen* 7).

The appeal of *Das Jahr der Seele,* unsurpassed by any of George's previous or subsequent volumes of poetry,[15] can be attributed in part to the evocation of landscapes symbolizing states of the soul and in part to George's avoidance of some of the linguistic and Symbolist excesses of his earlier collections of poetry. George had originally planned to dedicate the volume to Ida Coblenz (1870–1942), the only woman with whom he entered into a close personal relationship. He first met Coblenz in March 1892, shortly after the disastrous turn in his relations with Hofmannsthal, and several of the poems in *Das Jahr der Seele* were written with her in mind. Particularly the poem "Die du ein glück vermehrst auch nicht es teilend ·" (You who enhance a joy you never tasted) seems to be addressed to Coblenz and to allude to the helping hand she lent after the "schiffbruch" of George's relationship with Hofmannsthal (1: 146). However, this intimate friendship too failed when Coblenz first unwittingly committed the faux pas of suggesting as a potential contributor to the *Blätter* Richard Dehmel (1863–1920), a poet whom George absolutely despised because of his proximity to the Berlin Naturalists, and subsequently, despite her knowledge of these tensions, of knowingly falling in love with Dehmel. In his last letter to Coblenz, dated November 1896, George wrote that friendship "schwindet dann ganz wenn dem einen etwas gross und edel scheint was dem andren roh und niedrig ist" (63). In the end George dedicated *Das Jahr der Seele* to his sister Anna Maria Ottilie.

Marie von Bunsen's statement in 1898 in the *Vossische Zeitung* that even among connoisseurs of modern literature George was largely unknown does not necessarily reflect the true state of affairs, but must be seen in the context of yet another strategy George employed to establish his reputation in the influential circles of the *Bildungsbürgertum,* a strategy we would now refer to as "net-working."[16] Von Bunsen was present at a reading George had given in November 1897 at the salon of the painters Richard (1857–1922) and Sabine Lepsius (1864–1942). Von Bunsen's assertion that George was known and admired only in a small circle was of course intended to draw the attention of a broader public to the poet. George had made the acquaintance of the Lepsiuses in November 1896. In their salon George held readings of his poetry and met artists, writers, academics, and entrepreneurs who in their turn spread George's name among Berlin's cognoscenti. It was in the Lepsius salon that Georg Bondi first heard of George and it was here that Richard M. Meyer, a professor of German literature, met George on numerous occasions. These meetings led to the publication in 1897 of Meyer's article "Ein neuer Dichterkreis" in the *Preußische Jahrbücher,* one of the most widely read and influential journals of the time. Word of mouth and articles like those mentioned here secured a growing demand for George's works, a demand George met "reluctantly" by allowing limited public editions to be printed (Mettler 40–42). Similarly, the salon of Karl (1869–1948) and Hanna Wolfskehl (1878–1946) in Munich was instrumental in spreading George's reputation among artists and intellectuals in this second cultural center of Wilhelmine Germany. Wolfskehl had been among George's earliest admirers, became a regular contributor to the *Blätter,* and was for several years part of the circle around the Munich cosmologists Ludwig Klages (1872–1956) and Alfred Schuler (1865–1923). George was initially drawn to Klages and Schuler because of their radically anti-bourgeois views and the contempt in which they held their own age, but he broke with them in the winter of 1903/1904 partly because of Klages' and Schuler's anti-Semitism which became so virulent that Wolfskehl, who had never wavered in his identification with his Jewish ancestry, felt personally threatened by them.

The end of the 1890s was marked by the publication of George's sixth volume of poetry *Der Teppich des Lebens,* generally considered both as a summation of George's artistic endeavors in the preceding decade and a turning point in George's career, punctuating, as Max Weber put it, George's exodus from the aesthetic monastery "um, ein Asket mit ästhetischen Vorzeichen nach dem Vorbild so mancher anderer Asketen, die Welt, die er zuerst geflohen hat, zu erneuern und zu beherrschen" (500). This reorientation is also evident in the gradual transformation of the *Blätter* circle of mostly minor poets of the first generation into the elitist *George-Kreis* of the second generation at the beginning of the twentieth century. In 1899 George met the nineteen-year-old Friedrich Gundolf (1880–1931), his first and most important disciple. Gundolf possessed all the qualities that were to be requisite for admission of new members to the *Kreis* in future years: he was young, handsome, and intellectually and artistically gifted. Some of those admitted to the *Kreis* experienced their first encounter with George as a kind of rebirth and recalled it in terms that are both erotically and religiously charged. Ernst Glöckner (1885–1934) spoke of his first meeting with George in the spring of 1913 as "ein furcht-bares, ein unsägliches, glückseliges, verruchtes und hohes Erlebnis" (23). Overcome by the seductive power of George's charismatic personality he "küßte die dargebotene Hand und [. . .] flüsterte [. . .]: 'Meister, was soll ich tun?'" (Glöckner 26) August Husmann, a farmer's son, who had been introduced to George by Klages, waxed poetical:

> Ich preise Deinen Namen Du hast mir
> In meiner Nacht tröstenden Stern enthüllt
> Ich baute Dir einen Hausaltar
> Da trete ich zum Morgenopfer hin
> Und bringe freudig meinen Dank Dir dar
> Und lege meinen Mund zu langem Kusse
> An jene Säule die Dein Bildnis trägt.[17]

The male-bonded *Kreis* was conceived and perceived by George and his disciples as an aesthetic state with the "Dichter als Führer" — to quote the title of Max Kommerell's (1902–1944) influential book on German classicism (1928) — as a state within a state. It was, as Max Scheler lauded, an "erotisch-religiöse hocharistokratische gnostische Sekte," born "aus dem Geist der schärfsten Opposition zur Vermassung des Lebens."[18] In its exclusively male composition, it was based on the classical concept of male eros as "Staatsschöpfer," as Thomas Mann, clearly alluding to the *George-Kreis,* said in his speech "Von deutscher Republik" (1922). Women were excluded from the *Kreis* or at best played marginal roles. They were con-sidered to be "bünde zerstörend," as George said in a conversation with Boehringer (1884–1974).[19] Educating the carefully chosen young male disciples as harbingers of an intellectual and cultural renewal of Germany, a "Neues Reich," created in the spirit of ancient Greece, was the foremost goal of the *Kreis:*

> Eine kleine schar zieht stille bahnen
> Stolz entfernt vom wirkenden getriebe
> Und als losung steht auf ihren fahnen:
> Hellas ewig unsre liebe. (1: 176)

Since most members of the second generation of the *Kreis* were academics whose literary criticism and historiography were widely read in the 1920s — by 1930 more than 46,000 copies of Gundolf's *Goethe* had been printed — and since they had a ready-made audience in the student body, from which most members of the third generation were recruited, the *Kreis* exerted considerable influence on the intellectual culture of the Weimar Republic. The *Jahrbuch für die geistige Bewegung* (1910–12), nominally edited by Gundolf and Wolters (1876–1930), but virtually directed by George's invisible hand, was conceived as a mouthpiece of the *Kreis* to promulgate the ideas of an intellectual avantgarde; the purpose was to renew and revolutionize the practices of academics in the humanities and to put its stamp on German culture. A fourth volume of the *Jahrbuch,* planned for 1914 and then for 1920 never saw print, a first effect of the divergent political views of the *Kreis* members during and after the First World War. The *Kreis* was after all not a monolithic group; it would be more accurate, as Michael Winkler has pointed out, to refer to circles rather than *a* circle (1). When George died in 1933, the *Kreis,* for all practical purposes, ceased to exist. Its charismatic center gone, the fissures, already apparent in the 1920s, became visible. Some of George's disciples, convinced or hoping that the Third Reich was or would become the realization of George's "Neues Reich," joined the National-Socialist Party or sympathized with the Nazi movement, some only initially. Others opposed the regime, and went into exile or saw themselves as part of the *innere Emigration.*[20]

I come now to George's encounter with the precocious thirteen-year-old Maximilian Kronberger in 1902, Kronberger's premature death from meningitis in 1904, and George's subsequent deification of the youth as "Maximin," first in the privately printed *Maximin, Ein Gedenkbuch.* This was addressed primarily to the *Kreis* ("Preist eure stadt die einen gott geboren! / Preist eure zeit in der ein gott gelebt!" [1: 284]), and was then reprised publicly in "Maximin," the central part of George's next volume of poetry, *Der Siebente Ring.*[21] Interpretation of these poems has been contentious. They can be read, as Michael and Erika Metzger have argued, within the context of the poetic tradition of mourning a poet who has died young (38). At the time of their publication, however, some saw in the proclamation of the boy's divinity and in the erotic and pious language in which it was couched — "Dass ich dich erbete — begehre" (1: 282) — a sacrilege, particularly in the comparison of Kronberger to Christ in poems such as "Erwiderungen: Die Verkennung" (Responses: The Mistaking 1: 281–82) and "Das Zweite: Wallfahrt" (The Second: Pilgrimage 1: 284–85). The relationship between the poet in his mid-thirties and the teenager struck others as scandalous; George's comments in the preface to his *Umdichtung* of Shakespeare's sonnets may well have been directed against such attacks. Pointing out that Shakespeare's passionate devotion to his friend is central to the sonnets, he stated: "Zumal verstofflichte und verhirnlichte zeitalter haben kein recht an diesem punkt worte zu machen da sie nicht einmal etwas ahnen können von der weltschaffenden kraft der übergeschlechtlichen Liebe" (2: 149). Not his devotion to Kronberger, he seems to argue indirectly, was scandalous, but rather the incomprehension and prurience of his bourgeois contemporaries.

The "Zeitgedichte" (Poems of Our Times) which open *Der Siebente Ring* contained George's most outspoken critique of contemporary Germany to date. His opposition to his age — its bourgeois values, its capitalist economy, worship of mammon, nationalist hubris, democratic tendencies, and faith in industrial and technological progress — is already discernible in poems composed shortly after his graduation from the Gymnasium. As early as 1888 he associated his cosmopolitan tendencies with anarchism (Norton 39) and in 1889 he characterized himself as a "Socialist, Communard, Atheist."[22] These rebellious attitudes were reinforced, as Norton has shown, through his contacts with the French Symbolists. Like many a young person since then George demonstrated his disdain for bourgeois conventions by a carefully chosen wardrobe designed to *étaper le bourgeois:* dressed in tight fitting black suits, silk top hats, and brocade ties, he wore a square monocle and put a speck of incense on the tip of his burning cigarette. As his subsequent comments on politics and the First World War indicate, however, his protest against bourgeois society and all it represented was not merely a phase typically associated with youth. This protest was presumably influenced as much by his sexual as his aesthetic orientation.

Nothing captures George's enduring opposition better than his attitude toward the First World War. Far from sharing the nationalist fervor and the optimism that gripped some of his disciples, most of his fellow German writers, and much of Europe at the outbreak of the war, he did not believe that this was the war to end all wars or that it was a panacea ushering in a better future. In his poem "Der Krieg" (1: 410–15), written between 1914 and 1917, the "Siedler auf dem berg," is a thinly disguised mouthpiece for George's views who distances himself from the all-pervasive patriotism ("Er kann nicht schwärmen / Von heimischer tugend und welscher tücke"), warns against the blandishments and false rhetorical flourishes of the instigators and supporters of the war ("Wie faulige frucht / Schmeckt das gered von hoh-zeit auferstehung"), and accuses those responsible for the advances of technological warfare of having created, as Frankenstein did, a monster: "Des schöpfers hand entwischt rast eigenmächtig / Unform von blei und blech · gestäng und rohr." For him the war is not a sign of "auferstehung," but rather yet another symptom of the sickness that had infected not only Wilhelmine Germany but the entire bourgeois-capitalist world: "Erkrankte welten fiebern sich zu ende." Salvation is only possible if a spiritually (*geistig*) transformed younger generation, and here George is obviously thinking of his *Kreis,* determines the future: "Und Herr der zukunft [bleibt] wer sich wandeln kann." In this regard, too, George remained consistent. In a conversation with Edith Landmann in 1919 he declared that it would be illusionary to place one's faith either in the political Right or the Left. A "friedliche Durchdringung vom Geistigen her, eine Erneuerung von innen heraus" was the only answer, the only alternative to a total apocalyptic collapse (70).

In the first of the "Zeitgedichte" George wrote, referring to the reception of his poetical works: "Ihr sehet wechsel · doch ich tat das gleiche"

(1: 228). He made this claim because he was convinced of the continuity between his aestheticist poetry of the 1890s and his later, vatic poetry of "lob und fem" (1: 411). And, indeed, if one accepts George's premises, such a claim is not unjustified. In the 1890s he defined his poetic task as contributing to the transformation of aesthetic taste as a prerequisite for a renascence in the arts (*Einleitungen* 16–17). Amidst the chaotic beginnings of the Weimar Republic he argued in the introduction to the last issue of the *Blätter* that only later generations would recognize "die gemeinsamen wurzeln der übel" that had caused not only the war but the decline of political and social culture in Germany. The task of preparing these future generations must determine the "haltung des geistigen menschen in den staatlichen und gesellschaftlichen dingen" in the present. And poetry once again — but now George's vatic poetry and his pedagogical endeavors in the *Kreis* — plays a central role in this process: "Nur den wenigen dürfte es einleuchten, dass in der dichtung eines volkes sich seine lezten schicksale enthüllen" (*Einleitungen* 58).

George had devoted the years between the publication of *Der Siebente Ring* and the demise of Wilhelmine Germany increasingly to the formation of the *Kreis* — his "geheimes Deutschland"[23] — and its cultural mission. His translations of Shakespeare's sonnets and parts of Dante's *Commedia* formed an integral part of his cultural-political work. On the eve of the First World War he published his penultimate collection of poetry *Der Stern des Bundes*. The *Bund* of the title refers to George's *Kreis* and the volume is addressed primarily to it. In the preface written in 1928 for volume 8 of the *Gesamtausgabe*, George refers to it as a "buch das noch jahrelang ein geheimbuch hätte bleiben können." George's explanation for why he nevertheless published it ("dass ein verborgen-halten von einmal ausgesprochenem heut kaum mehr möglich ist" [1: 347]) strikes one as farfetched and may once again reveal his desire to be considered the spokesperson for an exclusive elite even as he sought broader public appeal. The book was widely read during the war; but its reception as a breviary for the soldiers in the field was a misunderstanding, as George argues in the 1928 preface (1: 347).

George's fame had grown steadily during the first decade of the twentieth century and reached its zenith in the Weimar period. In 1927 he became the first recipient of Frankfurt's prestigious Goethepreis. Sales of his works were at their highest between 1919 and 1921 and again in 1928, the year of his sixtieth birthday (Petrow 14). On this occasion newspapers proclaimed him to be the judge and prophet of his time. In 1929 George was celebrated together with Woodrow Wilson, Georges Clemenceau, Hindenburg, Gandhi, and Lenin as a contemporary figure who had become a legend (Norton ix). The publication in 1930 of Friedrich Wolters's biased George biography, *Stefan George und die Blätter für die Kunst: Deutsche Geistesgeschichte seit 1890* marks a turning point in the reception of George's works. Wolters presented George as the spiritual father of the imminent renewal of Germany (Petrow 17). Up to this point he had usually been read by the political Right and Left not so much as a writer who subscribed to a certain political agenda but more as a representative poet of modernism. In the aftermath of Wolters's biography and in the increasingly radicalized political climate of the agony of the Weimar Republic, the political Right claimed him as one of their own and hailed George's last volume of poetry, *Das Neue Reich,* published in 1928 as a prophetic vision of the Third Reich and its *Führer.* Actually, some of the poems published in this volume were written as early as 1905, most of them no later than 1924, and only two, non-political poems ("Das Licht" [The Light] and "In stillste ruh" [Through deepest rest]), as late as 1928.

George's reaction to Hitler's ascension to power has given rise to various and contradictory interpretations.[24] In the winter of 1933 George was staying in Minusio, Switzerland where he had spent previous winters and where he was to die in December of the same year following a brief summer sojourn to Germany. His return to Switzerland was interpreted by some as going into exile. He had refused the Nazis' offer to assume an honorable post and stipend in the Preussische Dichterakademie. It would certainly have been a coup for the Nazis if such a prominent poet as George had accepted the offer, all the more so because other famous writers had either been expelled from the academy or had resigned, some under pressure. In his letter of refusal he pointed out that in his entire life he had never belonged to any writers' association, but he added that he acknowledged the "geistige ahnherrschaft der neuen nationalen bewegung."[25] This phrase has been seized upon by those who see an affinity between George and National Socialism. Certainly Bernhard Rust (1883–1945), the Prussian Minister of Culture, who had issued the invitation, made the most of it. In the telegram of condolence he sent to George's sister, he either changed the adjective "national" to "nationalsozialistisch" or else the newspapers that printed the telegram made this crucial change. Whichever the case may be, three different versions of the text appeared in the newspapers: some spoke of the "nationale Bewegung," others of the "nationalsozialistische Bewegung," and yet others replaced "nationale bewegung" with "jetzige Regierung."[26]

The Nazi's claim that George had been a "Herold des Dritten Reiches," thus the title of Ferdinand Bechtold's obituary in the *Wiesbadener Zeitung* of 6 December 1933 (quoted in Petrow 22), was immediately challenged by Werner Vordtriede in a letter to the editor of the *Weltwoche.* He rejected those obituaries that praised George exclusively as a prophet of National Socialism and stressed instead the pure and timeless character of George's poetry.[27] On the basis of his analysis of thirty-two articles and obituaries published in 1933 on the occasions of George's sixty-fifth birthday and his death, Michael Petrow concluded that more than half of these did not consider George a precursor of the National-Socialist regime (22). The Nazis' embrace of George was short-lived: as early as 1936 the "Stefan George Preis" Joseph Goebbels had announced in December 1933 was renamed "Nationaler Buchpreis." In 1938, on the fifth anniversary of George's death and the year that would have marked his seventieth birthday, the by-now thoroughly cowed or outright sympathetic press took hardly any notice of the two anniversaries. In 1943, Adolf Bartels, a Germanist favored by the Nazis, dismissed George and Hofmannsthal as mere aesthetes and décadents in the nineteenth edition of his *Geschichte der deutschen Literatur:* "die Lyrik [. . .] Stephan [*sic*] Georges [. . .] und Hugo von Hofmannsthals [wurde] als die Höhe der modernen Kunst hingestellt. In Wirklichkeit haben wir hier die ausgesprochenste l'art pour l'art - Poesie, [. . .] eine wahre Artisten-Kunst, die [. . .] nur noch Selbstberauschung ist."

George, who was imbued with the idea of the poet as a prophet, visionary, priest, and educator, saw himself as the Messiah of a New Hellenism and a New Reich led by an intellectual and aesthetic elite consisting exclusively of males bonded together through their allegiance to a charismatic leader. Initially, the German fascists seized upon some of the themes George articulated in his later works, particularly in *Der Stern des Bundes* and *Das Neue Reich,* among them a glorification of heroism, self-sacrifice, and the envisioning of a leader who would restore the "Secret Germany," for the present Germany had almost succumbed to the onslaught of modernity. Subsequently George's writings and those of his circle were considered to be protofascist by some, most notably by Georg Lukács, who saw in George an ideological precursor of Hitler (34), a view apparently shared by George's recent biographer Norton. Conceding and emphasizing that George's "Secret Germany" was not identical with Nazi Germany, he argues nevertheless that it would be "dishonest or naïve not to recognize the preparatory role [George] played" in helping to make the crimes committed by the Nazis "thinkable" (Norton xvii). Others denied any affinity between George and fascism. In 1938 Klaus Mann wrote in his essay "Das Schweigen Stefan Georges": "Hitler — und Stefan George: das sind zwei Welten, die niemals zueinander finden können. Das sind zwei Arten Deutschland."[28] Sixty-two years later Martin Roos came to similar conclusions: "Im Blick auf George und den Nationalsozialismus steht fest: Die politische Realität des Dritten Reiches hatte nichts mit dem Neuen Reich gemein." Roos adds, however, that George either was not aware or became aware too late of the political reality and thus failed to protect his poetry from ideological usurpation (186). Most recently Ulrich Raulff, in his review of Norton's biography, asserted that George's works, particularly the volumes of poetry that are most critical of conditions in the Wilhelmine Empire must be read, like the poetry of Virgil and Dante, in the context of the European tradition of prophetic and visionary poetry, and, one may add, that George himself certainly wanted to be seen in this tradition.[29] Not to do so, Raulff contends, is to follow in the footsteps of the Nazis who considered themselves the fulfillment of all prophecies. Thus the controversy surrounding George — in his time he was equally admired by the political left (Rosa Luxemburg, Erich Mühsam [1878–1934], and Klaus Mann) and by the political right (Ernst Bertram [1884–1957], Hans Naumann [1886–1951], and Friedrich Wolters) — continues to this day.[30] The multifaceted and contradictory image of George that ultimately emerges from the critical, polemical, and hagiographic George criticism was perhaps best summarized by Georg Peter Landmann in his 1974 George lectures:

> Der grösste deutsche Dichter nach Goethe, unser grösster Mystiker, der Erneuerer der deutschen Sprache, der Bringer einer Weltenwende — ein Symbolist, ein Ästhet mit Lilien, Kerzen und violetter Krawatte, ein exklusiver Artist und Formalist, l'art pour l'art, Neuromantik, Neuheidentum, ein Dichter des Jugendstils, ein Dichter der Jugendbewegung, ein Prophet des Dritten Reichs, ein Nationalist, ein Religionsstifter und ein Magier, nur ein Schauspiel, ein Aristokrat, ein raffinierter Erfolgssucher, beweihräuchert von einem schwärmerischen Kreis blinder Anhänger, ein Skandalon. (8–9)

The essays written for this volume address the issues raised above in far greater detail and depth than it was possible to do in the introduction. The first series of essays is devoted to George's poetic theory and to his works. William Waters bases his discussion of George's theory on George's poems themselves rather than on the relatively few and well-known statements published in the *Blätter für die Kunst*. Robert Vilain's analysis of George's early works questions the labeling of the young George as aesthete, dandy, or decadent. Karla Schultz's essay focuses on George's two most popular works and further illuminates George's place in the history of twentieth-century Germany based on an analysis of Adorno's essays on George. Michael Metzger traces the complex evolution of George's ethos in his last three volumes of poetry. The second series of essays views George in the contexts of European aestheticism, the George Circle, and the Munich Cosmologists. Jeffrey Todd argues that the centrality of a new religion founded through the power of poetry constitutes the unity of George's works. Michael Winkler contextualizes the concept of bildung in the George Circle, and discusses the unique contributions members of the Circle made to scholarship and their affinities with the nationalist conservatives in the Weimar Republic. Paul Bishop stresses that although George was not one of the Munich Cosmologists, they provided him with a model for his Circle and had a lasting impact on his poetry. The two concluding essays address the most controversial issues in George criticism: George's sexuality and his relation to Nazism. Ritchie Robertson examines the triangular relationship between George, Nietzsche, and Nazism and cautions against employing metaphors of ancestry and forerunner in interpreting this relationship. Marita Keilson-Lauritz explores both the complexity of George's sexuality and its ramifications for his revolutionary concept of love. With these essays we may hope that a new and wider circle of readers will find their way to George.

A Note on Resources for Further Research

The standard George bibliography of primary texts, translations, and secondary literature is Georg Peter Landmann, *Stefan George und sein Kreis* (Hamburg: Hauswedell, 1960). A second updated edition was published by Hauswedell in 1976. The most recent bibliography is Lore Frank and Sabine Ribbeck, eds. *Stefan George-Bibliographie 1976–1997. Mit Nachträgen bis 1976.* (Tübingen: Niemeyer, 2000). The most comprehensive bibliography of translations of George's works is Georg Peter Landmann, *Stefan George in fremden Sprachen: Übersetzungen seiner Gedichte in die europäischen Sprachen außer den slawischen* (Düsseldorf: Küpper, vormals Bondi, 1971).

For information about George's library see Gisela Eidemüller, *Die nachgelassene Bibliothek des Dichters Stefan George: der in Bingen aufbewahrte Teil* (Heidelberg: Lothar Stiehm, 1987). Archival materials are housed in the Stefan George-Archiv in the Württembergische Landesbibliothek, Stuttgart and in the Stefan George-Museum, Bingen.

Notes

[1] Since 1995 the following major studies have appeared: Stefan Breuer, *Ästhetischer Fundamentalismus: Stefan George und der deutsche Antimodernismus* (Darmstadt: Wissenschaftliche Buchgesellschaft, 1997); Michael Petrow, *Der Dichter als Führer? Zur Wirkung Stefan Georges im "Dritten Reich"* (Marburg: Tectum, 1995); Carola Groppe, *Die Macht der Bildung. Das deutsche Bürgertum und der George-Kreis 1890–1933* (Cologne, Weimar, Vienna: Böhlau, 1997); Wolfgang Braungart, *Ästhetischer Katholizismus. Stefan Georges Rituale der Literatur* (Tübingen: Niemeyer, 1997); Jens Rieckmann, *Hugo von Hofmannsthal und Stefan George. Signifikanz einer "Episode" aus der Jahrhundertwende* (Tübingen/Basel: Francke, 1997); Rainer Kolk, *Literarische Gruppenbildung: Am Beispiel des George-Kreises 1890–1945* (Tübingen: Niemeyer, 1998); Martin Roos, *Stefan Georges Rhetorik der Selbstinszenierung* (Düsseldorf: Grupello Verlag, 2000); Wolfgang Braungart, Ute Oelmann, and Bernhard Böschenstein, eds., *Stefan George. Werk und Wirkung seit dem 'Siebenten Ring'* (Tübingen: Niemeyer, 2001); Jan Steinhaussen, *"Aristokraten aus Not" und ihre "Philosophie der zu hoch hängenden Trauben": Nietzsche-Rezeption*

*und literarische Produktion von Homosexuellen in den ersten Jahrzehnten des 20.
Jahrhunderts: Thomas Mann, Stefan George, Ernst Bertram, Hugo von Hofmannsthal
u.a.* (Würzburg: Königshausen & Neumann, 2001); Robert E. Norton, *Secret
Germany. Stefan George and His Circle* (Ithaca/London: Cornell UP, 2002).

[2] See, for example, Petrow 220–21.

[3] Cyril M. Scott, *Stefan George. Selection from his Works* (London: Elkin Mathews,
1910).

[4] Ernst Morwitz and Olga Marx, trans., *The Works of Stefan George* (U of North
Carolina P, 1949). It was reprinted in 1966 by AMS Press and in 1974 by U of
North Carolina P. It does not contain George's juvenilia, early dramatic sketches,
and prose pieces. This edition was preceded by a translation of ninety-nine George
poems by Morwitz and Marx, *Stefan George. Poems in German and English*
(New York: Pantheon and London: Routledge & Kegan Paul, 1944).

[5] For the early reception see Jörg-Ulrich Fechner, *"L'âpre gloire du silence"...
Europäische Dokumente zur Rezeption der Frühwerke Stefan Georges und der Blätter
für die Kunst 1890–1898* (Heidelberg: Carl Winter, 1998).

[6] Quoted in Franz Schonauer. *Stefan George mit Selbstzeugnissen und Bilddokumenten.* (Reinbek bei Hamburg: Rowohlt, 1992), 12.

[7] The homoerotic constellations in the poem were first pointed out by Marita
Keilson-Lauritz, *Von der Liebe die Freundschaft heißt. Zur Homoerotik im Werk
Stefan Georges.* (Berlin: Verlag rosa Winkel, 1987), 67, 79.

[8] Quoted in Guido Glur. *Kunstlehre und Kunstanschauung des Georgekreises und
die Aesthetik Oscar Wildes.* (Bern: Paul Haupt, 1957), 16.

[9] See Marita Keilson-Lauritz, *Von der Liebe,* 75–82 and *passim.* The first to call attention to this strategy was Oskar Panizza in an article "Die deutschen Symbolisten,"
published by *Die Gegenwart* in 1895.

[10] The early George reception in France, Belgium, and Holland is well documented
in Fechner.

[11] Quoted in Fechner, 62. Hart's article appeared in December 1892.

[12] See the above mentioned article by Oskar Panizza reprinted in Fechner, 118–25.

[13] For a detailed discussion of the encounter and the lasting impact it had see
Rieckmann, *Hugo von Hofmannsthal und Stefan George.*

[14] George dedicated the first public edition of *Pilgerfahrten* "dem Dichter Hugo
von Hofmannsthal im Gedenken an die Tage schöner Begeisterung Wien
MDCCCXCI" (1: 26).

[15] Georg Bondi published *Das Jahr der Seele* in 1898 after Otto von Holten had
issued a private printing of 206 copies in 1897. By 1922 the tenth edition had
appeared.

[16] For a detailed discussion of George's relations with the *Bildungsbürgertum* and
that of his Circle see Groppe.

[17] Quoted in Boehringer, 94.

[18] Quoted in Max Rychner, "Stefan George." *Zur europäischen Literatur* (Zurich:
Atlantis, 1943), 79.

[19] Robert Boehringer, *Ewiger Augenblick* (Düsseldorf/Munich: Küpper vormals Georg Bondi, 1965), 31.

[20] For a detailed discussion of the attitudes of individual members of the *Kreis* toward the events of 1933 and beyond see Groppe, 651–76 and Peter Hoffmann, *Claus Graf Schenk von Stauffenberg und seine Brüder* (Stuttgart: Deutsche Verlagsanstalt, 1992).

[21] In addition to George's Maximin poems the *Gedenkbuch* also contained poems by Kronberger and tributes by, among others, Gundolf and Wolfskehl.

[22] Letter to Arthur Stahl, dated beginning of January 1889; quoted in *Zeittafel*, 10.

[23] The term was coined in 1910 by Karl Wolfskehl, a member of the George Circle, to denote George's "staat," the constellation of George and his disciples who opposed not only the "barbaric" Wilhelmine Empire and the Weimar Republic but modernity as such. See: Karl Wolfskehl, *Jahrbuch für die geistige Bewegung* 1 (1910), 14.

[24] For the most recent discussion of George's reaction to the events of 1933 see Norton, 723–37.

[25] Quoted in Franz-Karl von Stockert, "Stefan George und sein Kreis. Wirkungsgeschichte vor und nach dem 30. Januar 1933." *Literatur und Germanistik nach der "Machtübernahme."* Ed. Beda Allemann. (Bonn: Bouvier, 1983), 75.

[26] See Petrow, 37–38 and Klaus-Jürgen Grün, "Politisches Schweigen. Stefan Georges Einschätzung des gesellschaftlichen Geschehens vom Ende des Kaiserreiches bis zum Ende der Weimarer Republik." *Zeitschrift für Geschichtswissenschaft* 42 (1994), 505–6.

[27] The letter is quoted in Petrow, 40. According to Petrow it was published either in the *Weltwoche* of 22 or 29 December 1933.

[28] See Ralph-Rainer Wuthenow, *Stefan George und die Nachwelt. Dokumente zur Wirkungsgeschichte Band 2.* (Stuttgart: Klett-Cotta, 1981), 12.

[29] *Süddeutsche Zeitung,* no. 132, 16 June 2002.

[30] For a more detailed discussion, see Petrow, 12–20.

Works Cited

Boehringer, Robert. *Mein Bild von Stefan George.* Munich/Düsseldorf: Helmut Küpper vormals Georg Bondi, 1951.

Braungart, Wolfgang. *Ästhetischer Katholizismus: Stefan Georges Rituale der Literatur.* Tübingen: Niemeyer, 1997.

Briefwechsel zwischen George und Hofmannsthal. 2nd edition. Ed. Robert Boehringer. Munich/Düsseldorf: Helmut Küpper vormals Georg Bondi, 1953.

George, Stefan. *Einleitungen und Merksprüche der Blätter für die Kunst.* Ed. G. P. Landmann. Düsseldorf: Küpper vormals Georg Bondi, 1964.

George, Stefan, and Ida Coblenz. *Briefwechsel.* Eds. Georg Peter Landmann and Elisabeth Höpker-Herberg. Stuttgart: Klett-Cotta, 1983.

Glöckner, Ernst. *Begegnung mit Stefan George: Auszüge aus Briefen und Tagebüchern, 1913–1934.* Ed. Friedrich Adam. Heidelberg: Lothar Stiehm, 1972.

Hofmannsthal, Hugo von. *Sämtliche Werke.* Vol. 31. Ed. Ellen Ritter. Frankfurt a.M.: S. Fischer, 1991.

Hofmannsthal, Hugo von, und Rudolf Pannwitz. *Briefwechsel 1907–1926.* Ed. Gerhard Schuster. Frankfurt a.M.: S. Fischer, 1994.

Keilson-Lauritz, Marita. *Von der Liebe die Freundschaft heißt: Zur Homoerotik im Werk Stefan Georges.* Berlin: Verlag rosa Winkel, 1987.

Landmann, Edith. *Gespräche mit Stefan George.* Düsseldorf/Munich: Helmut Küpper vormals Georg Bondi, 1963.

Landmann, Georg Peter. *Vorträge über Stefan George.* Düsseldorf/Munich: Helmut Küpper vormals Georg Bondi, 1974.

Landmann, Georg Peter, ed. *Stefan George und sein Kreis.* 2nd ed. Hamburg: Hauswedell, 1976.

Lukács, Georg. *Die Zerstörung der Vernunft. Vol.1 Irrationalismus zwischen den Revolutionen.* Darmsatdt/Neuwied: Luchterhand, 1983.

Matt, Peter von. "Der geliebte Doppelgänger. Die Struktur des Narzißmus bei Stefan George." *Das Schicksal der Phantasie: Studien zur deutschen Literatur.* Munich/Vienna: Carl Hanser, 1994. 257–76.

Mettler, Dieter. *Stefan Georges Publikationspolitik: Buchkonzeption und verlegerisches Engagement.* Munich/New York/London/Paris: Saur, 1979.

Norton, Robert E. *Secret Germany: Stefan George and His Circle.* Ithaca/London: Cornell UP, 2002.

Petrow, Michael. *Der Dichter als Führer? Zur Wirkung Stefan Georges im "Dritten Reich."* Marburg: Tectum, 1995.

Roos, Martin. *Stefan Georges Rhetorik der Selbstinszenierung.* Düsseldorf: Grupello Verlag, 2000.

Seekamp, H[ans].-J[ürgen]., R[aymond]. C[urtis]. Ockenden, and M[arita]. Keilson[-Lauritz]. *Stefan George / Leben und Werk. Eine Zeittafel.* Amsterdam: Castrum Peregrini, 1972.

Weber, Marianne. *Max Weber: Ein Lebensbild.* Heidelberg: L. Schneider, 1950.

Winkler, Michael. *George-Kreis.* Stuttgart: Metzler, 1972.

Woods, Gregory. *A History of Gay Literature: The Male Tradition.* New Haven/London: Yale UP, 1998.

Zeller, Bernhard, ed. *Stefan George 1868–1968: Der Dichter und sein Kreis: Eine Ausstellung des Deutschen Literaturarchives im Schiller-Nationalmuseum Marbach a.N.* Munich: Kösel Verlag, 1968.

The Poetry

Stefan George's Poetics

William Waters

"WIR HALTEN ES FÜR EINEN VORTEIL," observes the first issue (1892) of George's journal *Blätter für die Kunst*, "dass wir nicht mit lehrsätzen beginnen sondern mit werken die unser wollen behellen und an denen man später die regeln ableite" (*Einleitungen* 7). The advantage has been imperfectly maintained. The tenets concerning poetry and art that George himself set forth — even in this same introduction, implying a precept in the act of disclaiming such a thing — have become as well known as most of his verse. But George's published poems (including his translations) occupy more than 1,000 pages in the two-volume *Werke,* while the maxims on poetry he chose to reprint in book form occupy all of a page and a half (1: 530–31). To preserve more of them, he wrote in the foreword to the second edition of *Tage und Taten* (1925), his selected prose writings, "würde [. . .] eine ungebührende beladung sein für dieses im wesentlichen dichterische werk" (1: 473). The first principle of his poetics is the reticence of art.

In deference to that design, this essay will take up George's thinking about poetics — his view of the poetic calling, of the nature of poetry, and of his own poetic practice — chiefly as his own poems on the topic formulate and explore it. Poems occupied with such concerns appeared in almost every one of his books. In keeping with this intent, the aim will be to approach these poems as expressive forms rather than, as sometimes has been done, as paraphrasable content only. Several of them number among George's most familiar works, but they still have much to offer and appear here alongside others, perhaps less well known and still to be enjoyed.

The first unmistakably poetological poem George published, "Die Spange" (The Clasp), appears deliberately placed at the close of his second book of poems, *Pilgerfahrten* (1891), and is as richly suggestive a poem about poetry as anything George wrote:

DIE SPANGE

Ich wollte sie aus kühlem eisen
Und wie ein glatter fester streif ·
Doch war im schacht auf allen gleisen
So kein metall zum gusse reif.

> Nun aber soll sie also sein:
> Wie eine grosse fremde dolde
> Geformt aus feuerrotem golde
> Und reichem blitzendem gestein. (1: 40)

This poem's title is also its label: the eight lines about a clasp themselves form a clasp, a poem for holding things together. Anaphora (in the linguistic sense of a pronoun's reference "backward") links the verses to the title with unusual necessity, since the body of the poem is missing an identifier for the first line's feminine pronoun "it" (*sie*); and the poem is organized as a bracketing together of two contrastive images of that titular "clasp." The poem also links this volume's conclusion to George's subsequent volume, the famously extreme *Algabal*, published in the following year: *Algabal* pursues motifs of opulent artifice and excess to the point where it will indeed stand out in George's oeuvre like a "grosse fremde dolde." This form of anticipatory comment is of itself metapoetic, making "Die Spange" summarize before the fact the poetic intentions shaping the poet's next collection of verse.

The speaker's handicraft was first meant to be of common and functional iron, plain ("ein glatter [. . .] streif") and "cool" or unprovocative. But (as "doch" marks the first of the two adversative moments structuring the poem) no such metal could be found in the mine "auf allen gleisen" — where a *gleis* or rail track is itself a good example of a "glatter fester streif" that attracts no attention to itself but is instead employed in pursuit of other purposes. More precisely, the poem says that no appropriate metal could be found "zum gusse reif" — that is, ripe or mature enough for casting. The surprising word "reif" suggests organic life, and similarly implies that time may "ripen" the metal in the mine after all, allowing the clasp to be forged — some day — in the simple iron form originally intended.

But neither waiting nor *not* making a clasp is an option in this poem. Rather, the second stanza asserts a compensatory substitute: the clasp that could not be cast from abundant iron will instead be wrought in rare gold and gems. The most peculiar aspect of "Die Spange" is this unexpected turn of reasoning (though it frequently goes unremarked). One could plausibly say, "I wanted fancy gold, but had to settle for plain iron"; but George's poem runs that thought backward, so that the speaker who wanted rudimentary functionality, unable to find the right material for it, therefore "makes do" with exotic, costly splendor. This resolution put forward by the second stanza is out of all possible proportion to the problem framed by the first stanza. To put it differently, the inability to find the right *material* for making something useful and inconspicuous does not prompt the speaker (as we would ordinarily expect) to seek out another means of making or acquiring the same modest object. Instead, he turns his attention from the problem of material to the choice of the thing (surely there are materials between iron and gold? surely even with gold one could make a "glatter fester streif"?). The switch gives the impression that the unreadiness of ripe iron becomes a pretext, rather than an inescapable cause, for the decision announced by the second stanza.

Yet another way to put this would be to say that the second stanza of "Die Spange" sounds like a retort to the impasse of the first stanza, rather than a mere response. The trochee forced by the opening word "Nun," the phonetic resonances (especially the seven o-sounds in lines 5–7, after which line 8's "ei / i / ei" comes out, as someone has said, like a fanfare), and the altered rhyme-scheme that piles "golde" unexpectedly on "dolde" — everything speaks of a sensual relish and an assertion of desire that surpasses, even as the flower itself surpasses, the original intention to make an iron buckle. The poem's careful pairing of elements across the two stanzas serves, in each case, to emphasize the excess. "Aus kühlem eisen" is answered not merely by warmth, but by the fire of "aus feuer-rotem golde"; and "glatter fester streif" contrasts in pointed alliteration with "grosse fremde dolde," transforming smoothness into obtrusive size, solidity into alienness, and the strip of metal into not just a flower, but an umbel (a composite, umbrella-shaped flower cluster). Instead of being cast (4), the clasp will now be wrought (7). Structurally too the second stanza shows an "excess" over the first: the "wie" comparison of a single line (2) is met by a "wie" comparison of three lines (6–8). Line 8 stands out as having no parallel in the first stanza, as if the foregoing line's image had overflowed its bounds, adding to the fiery-red gold a surplus of "reichem blitzendem gestein." *Blitzend* becomes a second, additional answer to *kühl,* though the compound *feuerrot* in itself already answered one image (coolness) with two (heat and color). A multiplicatory momentum seems to have entered the poem — its emblem is the countless small flowers of the great alien umbel — with the proclamatory counterstatement of "Nun aber."

This excess charge comes across as defiantly, or at least unabashedly, transgressive. The poet's choice is gaudy and of reduced usefulness; it draws attention to its own immoderacy and artificiality. That is to say, there is in this conception not just the fundamental Georgean principle that art is a matter of "mache," *technē,* workmanship, but also a view of aesthetic making, and perhaps of the aesthetic object, as always doubled. The sight of the strange red-gold blossom gives no hint of the artist's desire to make a plain iron link; and yet, by the poem's own account, without that original "ich wollte" there would have been no "nun aber soll." The "grosse fremde dolde" conceals its secret history even as it conceals its own (vestigial) functionality. But this poem exists to make it clear that to know only the gem-encrusted umbel is not really to know the object at all.

George's works comprise a poetry of opposition, everywhere self-conscious of their imperative to evade, resist, correct, and redirect the culture and language surrounding them. This is one sense in which his poetry is double: it carries within itself this effort to oppose. The "dolde" is like a pose willfully struck, just as the poem's own inverted reasoning is willful in its very pose of necessity. In this way the golden blossom becomes an emblem of theatricality (one is reminded of the popularity of the mask motif in the fin de siècle, and of several photographs of George and his friends in costume or in affectedly stylized poses).[1] Artifice here decadently announces its estrangement (*fremd*) from naturalness, in the vein of Charles Baudelaire's essay "Le peintre de la vie moderne" (1863).

The iron band would have been nonrepresentational. The golden flower, by contrast, is a pointedly artificial imitation of a natural object. It refers to nature while simultaneously contrasting itself with it ("fremd," "aus [. . .] golde"). The flower, in other words, clasps nature — while at the same time estranging itself from nature — in a way the iron band would not have. The two versions of the clasp, then, clasp different things. This thought is in accord with the earlier suggestion, too, that the poem shows a shift in intention between the two stanzas, a change of purpose in the object (from utility to flamboyance) rather than, as the text claims, the response to a shortage of the raw materials with which to fashion it.

Several of these features of "Die Spange" recur in George's later poetological poems: the difficult logic; the indirection that leaves crucial forces in the poem to be inferred; and especially the poetry's opposition to its surroundings together with the related theme of representation (as the "fremde dolde" refers to real flowers in order to distance itself from them). Other recurrent concerns follow from these, such as uneasiness about the ineluctable question of the value of poetry in contradistinction to its usefulness. Rare, beautiful, and scornfully set apart from mere function, poetry nevertheless occupies the center of a cultural program that George espoused throughout his life. The tension between poetry as something above mere deed and poetry as allied to noble doing persists throughout his career.

"Die Spange" may also be seen as an anticipation of George's third book of poems, *Algabal,* where the motif of precious materials, the look underground into the mineshaft, and especially the emphasis on willed making as against nature predominate. *Algabal* assembles an account, at times in the third person and at times in the first, of an ultra-aesthete emperor in an underground realm. This figure, named Algabal, is as unnatural in his cruelty and hyper-refinement as his kingdom is in construction. While Algabal is not to be equated with George, we may look to this cycle for insight into George's poetics if, as "Die Spange" suggested, the extravagant surface contains or conceals a discrepant intention.

One poem in *Algabal* reads like a gloss on the second stanza of "Die Spange" as it reflects on the simulacrum of nature crafted from inorganic materials:

> Mein garten bedarf nicht luft und nicht wärme ·
> Der garten den ich mir selber erbaut
> Und seiner vögel leblose schwärme
> Haben noch nie einen frühling geschaut.
>
> Von kohle die stämme · von kohle die äste
> Und düstere felder am düsteren rain ·
> Der früchte nimmer gebrochene läste
> Glänzen wie lava im pinien-hain.
>
> Ein grauer schein aus verborgener höhle
> Verrät nicht wann morgen wann abend naht
> Und staubige dünste der mandel-öle
> Schweben auf beeten und anger und saat.
>
> Wie zeug ich dich aber im heiligtume
> — So fragt ich wenn ich es sinnend durchmass
> In kühnen gespinsten der sorge vergass —
> Dunkle grosse schwarze blume? (1: 47)

The verb "erbauen" in the second line means to construct or erect an edifice; Algabal's lifeless black garden is a technical or engineering feat not subject to the natural cycles of growth and decay. The gray artificial light source of the third stanza goes unexplained, but it stands in for morning and evening just as the ubiquitous "dusty haze" of almond-oils (incense?) replaces the varied scents of earth and vegetation in the open air. The poem's second stanza, which by reason of rhythm, sound, and word repetition is as immediately memorable as any quatrain in George's work, reveals a similar monotony of color in this garden. The point, again, is not that these are failed efforts at creating the pervasive illusion of nature. The imitations of natural objects in Algabal's grotto, like the "grosse fremde dolde" in "Die Spange," could never be mistaken for their originals in nature: the resistance to and distance from what is represented is the point. Expressing that resistance, that palpable discrepancy, is the raison d'être for "Mein garten."

Still looking back at "Die Spange" as an anticipatory summary of *Algabal,* we might look for an analogue to the other gap to which "Die Spange" drew our attention, that between original motive and eventual result. This would suggest that Algabal and his kingdom are a retort to something, a retort savored by the poet ("Nun aber soll sie also sein") but not fully comprehensible without reference to the frustration of the first and now superseded creative intention to make something simple and "coolly" classical. The causes of that frustration are not spelled out, and any answer will remain a biographical conjecture: why write *Algabal,* if one had meant to write something "wie ein glatter fester streif" instead? Especially in the context of biographical interpretations of "Die Spange," this question has generated several proposed solutions. Some commentators assume that George felt himself unready, not yet master of his craft, though this explanation inadequately accounts for the tensions in "Die Spange." Others have suggested that the German language seemed unfit to him, corrupted by his era and more suited to showy decadence than to noble simplicity. In a third view, George is saying that his cultural surroundings in Germany prevented him from adopting a simple, straightforward aesthetic, since to value a plain style requires a sophistication that (George felt) German letters lacked. This seems to me the most satisfactory proposal. Or again, George may have feared being overlooked, as implied by one of the maxims in the *Blätter für die Kunst* of 1896 (vol. 3, no. 2):

> Praerafaeliten und ähnliche: das gewollte hervortretenlassen gewisser wesentlicher eigentümlichkeiten für beschauer die das genaue sehen verlernt und für die man schon sehr stark auftragen muss um bemerkt zu werden. (*Einleitungen* 16)[2]

A dull audience requires that artists demonstrate or even highlight "peculiarities." Again, though, this idea only goes so far as a gloss on "Die Spange," since it offers no correlate for the decisive first intention, the frustrated search for a "metall zum gusse reif."

Whatever the plausibility of these interpretations, the poetry exceeds them. Most noticeably, none of these suggestions captures the enthusiasm with which *Algabal,* like the second stanza of "Die Spange," lingers over its evocations of artifice, useless ornament, and other offenses to prudent bourgeois values. The poet's enjoyment of the shock value of his creation is manifest in the most extreme of the *Algabal* poems (such as "Mein garten"; "Wenn um der zinnen" [When ramparts tipped with copper, 1: 48]; "O mutter meiner mutter" [O mother of my mother, 1: 49–50]; "Becher am boden" [Cups on the ground, 1: 50–51]; or "Ich will mir jener stunden lauf erzählen" [And now I shall evoke those hours, 1: 57]). For all of George's solemnity of tone, this enjoyment is cognate to Joris-Karl Huysmans's gleeful evocations of the decadent antics of his hero des Esseintes in *À rebours* (1884) or to the mixture of wit and radical aesthetic philosophy in Oscar Wilde's essay "The Decay of Lying" (1889). As "Die Spange" suggested, the poet's handiwork is charged with a superfluous energy, born of contradicting the world, that goes emphatically beyond the explanatory facts that purportedly gave rise to it.

The mention of Huysmans and Wilde also brings out another aspect of *Algabal* that is sometimes missed: like *À rebours,* like Wilde's *Picture of Dorian Gray* (1891), and like the supposedly aestheticist works of the young Hofmannsthal, George's *Algabal* is a moralistic work. In these other writings, as life reasserts its demands on the aesthete protagonist, he is forced to relinquish his philosophy of life or is punished by death for not having done so. In *Algabal* there is no narrative resolution, but the figure's own amoral extremism is sufficient to undercut him from the reader's point of view, even without the reminder in "Die Spange" that the fantastic forms the poet puts forward must be understood in light of very different motive principles.[3]

Moreover, the final stanza of "Mein garten" turns to question the premises that have informed the construction of this perfectly timeless black garden. The turn is not explicitly moralizing, but it unsettles the consistency of the speaker's vision and may undermine it fatally:

> Wie zeug ich dich aber im heiligtume
> — So fragt ich wenn ich es sinnend durchmass
> In kühnen gespinsten der sorge vergass —
> Dunkle grosse schwarze blume?

With the words "wie zeug ich dich," the poem accomplishes two startling things at once. First, it apostrophizes some familiar "you," which after an extended interruption will be identified in the vocative of the last line. Second, more radically, it asks an impossible question: how shall I beget you? Even among poetic apostrophes, which are notoriously improbable speech acts (addressing the age, one's pen, an urn, and so on), the address to a specific not-yet-existent entity is an exotic trope, as the entity here in question is exotic. *Zeugen* 'to beget, engender' (stressed by the meter) is not *ziehen* 'to cultivate': George's verb implies, however peculiarly, that the speaker speaks to the black flower as to his own as yet unconceived bodily offspring. In the question, "Wie zeug ich dich aber im heiligtume," the point seems to lie in the last word: how, within this holy — and therefore, as the poem's implicit logic has it, unsexed — shrine or sanctuary, is begetting to occur? Along with the garden's lifeless minerality, the patent reason to doubt that a real flower can be "engendered" there, comes an assertion of the place's holiness and an implied incompatibility between this sanctity and sexual (or even asexual) reproduction. Perfection, as the poem's first three stanzas have evoked it, is limited by the same lifelessness that first enabled it.[4]

The uncertain question at the poem's end — emphasized by the way dactylic tetrameter falls abruptly into four heavy trochees (with all short syllables schwa) — wishes to overcome infertility itself by artifice, engendering a real "fleur du mal," a ghastly "dunkle grosse schwarze blume" both designed and alive.[5] Here the poem has come not just to a nub of uncertainty in the otherwise assured perfection of the garden, but to the thought that exposes the poem's latent contradictions. Like its blue antecedent in Novalis's *Heinrich von Ofterdingen*, this black flower stands also for the poet's own work, but as a poetic reflection, the unanswered question finds no resolution here.

The separate precinct of art, as "Mein garten" has evoked it, does not "need" (1) the real world, except as something to declare itself against. But the poem cannot hold firmly to this view. Some unseen pressure, not "in" the poem unless it is as that same resistance to nature, pushes into the last stanza with the verb *zeugen* and the question it leaves unanswered. Consequently, at some cost to its own unity as a harmonious "garden" of form, "Mein garten" acknowledges a subterranean need for exchange with the same air and warmth that this subterranean kingdom was defiantly intended to exclude. Again, this is the moralistic streak in *décadence*. As George leaves *Algabal* behind he will also return to a more consistent and ultimately more sympathetic exploration of the ways in which poetry is framed by the world.

The sharpest statement of the poetic loneliness that dominates George's work in these early volumes appears in the blank-verse "Der Herr der Insel" (The Lord of the Island, written 1893 or before and published as part of the "Hirtengedichte"). Here a fantastic, giant purple bird is ruler (and sole inhabitant?) of his exotic southern island but in that same measure drastically ill-suited for the larger world and its practical concerns. Commentators have pointed to Baudelaire's poem about the poet as albatross, ungainly and abused on the ground but glorious once aloft ("L'albatros," 1857), but George's bird represents a conception of the poet more individual to him:

DER HERR DER INSEL

Die fischer überliefern dass im süden
Auf einer insel reich an zimmt und öl
Und edlen steinen die im sande glitzern
Ein vogel war der wenn am boden fussend
Mit seinem schnabel hoher stämme krone
Zerpflücken konnte · wenn er seine flügel
Gefärbt wie mit dem saft der Tyrer-schnecke
Zu schwerem niedrem flug erhoben: habe
Er einer dunklen wolke gleichgesehn.
Des tages sei er im gehölz verschwunden ·
Des abends aber an den strand gekommen ·
Im kühlen windeshauch von salz und tang
Die süsse stimme hebend dass delfine
Die freunde des gesanges näher schwammen
Im meer voll goldner federn goldner funken.
So habe er seit urbeginn gelebt ·
Gescheiterte nur hätten ihn erblickt.
Denn als zum erstenmal die weissen segel
Der menschen sich mit günstigem geleit

Dem eiland zugedreht sei er zum hügel
Die ganze teure stätte zu beschaun gestiegen ·
Verbreitet habe er die grossen schwingen
Verscheidend in gedämpften schmerzeslauten. (1: 69–70)

When the bird, shunning daylight, appears with the evening breeze of salt and seaweed to sing, lifting up not his body in flight but his voice, the poem does not tell us whether the listeners who appear — the dolphins, "freunde des gesanges" in the myth of Arion — are intended or even noticed as an audience. What the poet's song establishes is not a relationship between singer and audience, merely a proximity. Or rather, the dolphins, "im meer voll goldner federn goldner funken," become superbly aestheticized themselves, being in a sense absorbed as part of the song. The sparkling sea at sunset appears to be adorned with, or made of, golden feathers or fire; and sea, sparks, bird, and dolphins unite in one evening glory. The art is sublime; but it remains uncompanionable and uncommunicative by thus absorbing a potential audience into (finally lifeless) golden décor. A reminiscence of Algabal's inorganic garden may also be found in the great bird's presence on the island, alone, "seit urbeginn" ("depuis le commencement des temps," runs George's own French translation).[6] This too is a timeless and infertile world, separated from all change and growth.

What brings the self-enclosed marvel to an end is not so much the bird's being accidentally glimpsed — earlier, the shipwrecked sailors seem not to have troubled him — as the express intent of outsiders to approach his domain. It is an exquisitely fragile paradise. This fragility is signaled even by the poem's own manner of transmitting its report. At first glance, such transmission might seem to be bringing the bird's domain into communication with our own. But it is not so. The whole of the poem is a legend, a tale at second hand, introduced by the words "Die fischer überliefern dass [. . .]." By the eighth line the report of the bird accordingly enters the German "quotative" subjunctive, refusing to authenticate the truth of what is related. And by the poem's own account, no one *could* have reported this tale as an eyewitness; the shipwrecked do not return, and those who arrive in ships arrive too late. The unverifiable account is thus in some sense impossible, inadmissible, fabricated: but appropriately so, since the realm of fantasy or myth is the domain proper to the lord of this island. Even in the manner of its narration, then, this exotic place cannot admit communication with the outside world: the news that travels from there to here (like the news that reaches the waiting "you" at the end of Kafka's parable "Eine kaiserliche Botschaft" [An Imperial Message, 1920], a tale likewise called "eine Sage" or legend) must always be news that is "erträumt," news created, dreamed, or imagined by the recipient.

The "Buch der Hängenden Gärten" offers another image of royal and exotic birds that varies this recurring picture of a painful and insuperable divide between art and life. The poem speaks of caged and dreaming macaws:

> Meine weissen ara haben safrangelbe kronen ·
> Hinterm gitter wo sie wohnen
> Nicken sie in schlanken ringen
> Ohne ruf ohne sang ·
> Schlummern lang ·
> Breiten niemals ihre schwingen —
> Meine weissen ara träumen
> Von den fernen dattelbäumen. (1: 102)

Rare, isolated from the world, crowned, and arranged "in schlanken rin-gen," the parrots epitomize a realm of formal aesthetics, but in a different way from the great bird of "Der Herr der Insel." The macaws are captive "hinterm gitter" and neither sing nor extend their wings, but dozing, they nod, as if assenting to their confinement for beauty's sake. Even the poem's rhyme scheme *aabccbdd* is concentric, as if enclosing the sleep of the caged birds. The final couplet puts the melancholy point on the poem and simul-taneously relates it to the epistemological impasse of the legend (transmit-ted without having been found out) in "Der Herr der Insel." In "Meine weissen ara," the poet speaks in place of his birds, who are "ohne ruf ohne sang," and ascribes to them dreams of faraway freedom — dreams for which he, as the birds' captor, was already in a certain sense responsible. As the subjunctive of indirect speech in "Der Herr der Insel" signaled the ulti-mately imaginary character of its own report, this mediation of the macaws' vision conveys something that originates with the speaker himself (or "was caused by" him, or "is merely imagined by" him, or, strangely, both).

Like *Algabal*'s "Mein garten," each of these two bird poems depicts an aesthetic entity shielded from an external world that would jeopardize it. But more, in both texts the relation of the self-contained emblem of art to the world outside is simultaneously essential — it is against that greater world that the willed limitation of aesthetic circumscription is defined — and at the same time elusive, unreliable, groundless. The lines that purport to connect what is imagined or dreamed with what is known and verifiable instead curve back to the fantasy world bewilderingly.

George's two "middle" volumes, *Das Jahr der Seele* and *Der Teppich des Lebens,* mark a turn in the way the poems themselves reflect on the posi-tion of art in the world to which it is, as it always remains in George's work, opposed. In these volumes, considered by many to be his best, the paths between art and life are repeatedly proposed, tested, rescinded, reversed — but they are now everywhere a central concern, and the poems no longer figure the disappearance or failure of sustained relation between aesthetic figures and the natural or social world.

The change is evident in the famous opening poem of *Das Jahr der Seele:*

> Komm in den totgesagten park und schau:
> Der schimmer ferner lächelnder gestade ·
> Der reinen wolken unverhofftes blau
> Erhellt die weiher und die bunten pfade.
>
> Dort nimm das tiefe gelb · das weiche grau
> Von birken und von buchs · der wind ist lau ·
> Die späten rosen welkten noch nicht ganz ·
> Erlese küsse sie und flicht den kranz ·
>
> Vergiss auch diese letzten astern nicht ·
> Den purpur um die ranken wilder reben
> Und auch was übrig blieb von grünem leben
> Verwinde leicht im herbstlichen gesicht. (1: 121)

Rather than dreaming a scene of beauty divorced from the world as it is given, this poem asks what sources for the aesthetic may be found in this (until now) dead-seeming world. In the perspective of George's earlier poems, "totgesagt" could apply less to what others have said about the park than to what he himself, shunning it, has implied. The invitation to enter the park and look cannot help being also the book's own *invitatio,* an appeal to the reader to recognize "was übrig blieb von grünem leben" in the weary world of fin-de-siècle culture. Where the earlier poems *began* with a vision, "Komm in den totgesagten park" works toward assembling one, as the poem culminates in its final word "gesicht." The poem asks its addressee to "take" yellow and gray from the trees and weave these together with other colors and flowers — "flicht den kranz" (8); "verwinde" (12) — and as it does so, demonstrates a weaving of its own by employing three rhyme-schemes in succession: *abab aacc deed.* It is especially noteworthy that the wreath or vision is to be assembled from things in decline, since the fact of time and change so fundamental to this scenery was so stringently excluded from the earlier poems discussed here.

The scene is, however, a park — almost certainly a private one — and not open countryside, much less wilderness. Parks of this kind cannot be entered *except* by invitation ("Komm"); and a park is ordered, beautified nature, nature aesthetically selected and arranged. In this respect, what George's poem urges is a second-order aesthetic filtering, concentrating art out of art. George has no use for raw or unprocessed nature, or for insufficiently cultivated language.

In the case of language, there is a potential problem for a writer in the fact that to refine words means to estrange them from communicative norms, or indeed from communication at all. In its extreme form this dilemma threatens to become a kind of analogue, in linguistic terms, of the closed fantasy realm everywhere meaningfully set against, but nowhere able to form a bridge to, things as they are.

A later poem in *Das Jahr der Seele* revisits these questions about language, privacy, and exclusion — invoking a familiar landscape of "fabelwesen" at home "in einem seltnen reiche ernst und einsam," serenaded by "des tempels saitenspiel und heilge zunge" — but now with a crucial self-reflective distance, even doubt:

> Des sehers wort ist wenigen gemeinsam:
> Schon als die ersten kühnen wünsche kamen
> In einem seltnen reiche ernst und einsam
> Erfand er für die dinge eigne namen —
>
> DIE hier erdonnerten von ungeheuern
> Befelten oder lispelten wie bitten ·
> DIE wie Paktolen in rubinenfeuern
> Und bald wie linde frühlingsbäche glitten ·
>
> An deren kraft und klang er sich ergezte ·
> Sie waren wenn er sich im höchsten schwunge
> Der welt entfliehend unter träume sezte
> Des tempels saitenspiel und heilge zunge.
>
> Nur sie — und nicht der sanften lehre lallen ·
> Das mütterliche — hat er sich erlesen
> Als er im rausch von mai und nachtigallen
> Sann über erster sehnsucht fabelwesen ·
>
> Als er zum lenker seiner lebensfrühe
> Im beten rief ob die verheissung löge . .
> Erflehend dass aus zagen busens mühe
> Das denkbild sich zur sonne heben möge. (1: 137)

The poem concerns a seer or *vates,* from Virgil onward the Latin word came to mean both "prophet" and "poet," and it was in the tradition of such visionary rhapsodes (with Klopstock and Hölderlin as his German forebears) that George wished to find his place. But a seer is not a higher order of poet; prophecy concerns itself with history, with the fate of communities or states more than with that of the individual man or woman. The first line's assertion, then, poses the prophet's quandary even as it exalts him: "wenigen gemeinsam," the word of the seer may not be received or understood, though it would be better if it were. This much may be regarded as a hazard of prophecy throughout its history. But George's next lines indicate what seems like a necessarily disabling revision of that old motif. It is said of this "seher" that in childhood he invented "für die dinge eigne namen," a private language that by necessity implies a refusal of communication: private names are not common to few, but common — by definition — to none.

The primary sense of the fourth line is that, serious and lonely in his rare "empire" of the mind, the child invented his own names for things, re-naming the world like a second Adam and feeling the power ("kraft" 9) of creation in so doing. But this line could also carry a different, secondary sense: that the names he invented were, like the names the first Adam bestowed in Eden, the *things'* own names. The poet as re-namer of the world finds that each arbitrary name he has made up turns out afterward to be identical to the true or inmost name of the object in question, the name of its essence. Such names of power, spoken properly, are the names to which things cannot help giving themselves up. The words shape the world by commanding or petitioning it (5–6), but also by forming their own landscapes in the sheer expressiveness of their sound, running now in rivers like the legendary Pactolus, ablaze with sands of gold, now gently like spring streams.

But the child's private language — and the relevance to George's own invented childhood languages is unmistakable[7] — is expressly said to be potent and sacred away from the world, when the boy, "der welt entfliehend," sits down under dreams (*Träume*) as if they were sheltering trees (*Bäume*). Power and beauty discovered in drawing back from the world need not be escapism, but the vocabulary of private dreams and loneliness in these middle stanzas is hard to square with the societal obligations announced by the word "seher."

The fourth stanza names a more specific background in opposition to which the boy's private language is constructed: he has "chosen" it for himself ("sich erlesen") in preference to "der sanften lehre lallen / Das mütterliche" (13–14). The lines imply that the mother tongue is inadequate for an unexpected reason: it is partly or wholly unintelligible ("lallen"), which strictly speaking one's mother tongue cannot be; at the same time, in apparent contradiction, it delivers instruction or even a doctrine ("lehre"). In this difficult image there may lie something analogous to the willful logic of "Die Spange." There the budding artist leaves behind the plan of making a sensible iron clasp; here he leaves behind maternal instruction (or perhaps the Catholic doctrine so cherished by George's own mother). In both cases, the thing left behind is refused vehemently, with an excess of feeling that burgeons forth in what he chooses instead. The language of the mother (the matrix of meaning) is perversely experienced as a mere stream of nonsense by comparison with the intensity of significance found in the (male) invented language. A made-up language is a pure system, a "fremde dolde" of artifice pointedly independent of the personal and societal sediments of culture in which every natural language is, for each of its speakers, impurely rooted.[8]

What marks "Des sehers wort" as a crucial departure from the earlier work, however, is principally its last stanza. Praying to an indeterminate (masculine) power, the young linguist is assailed "zagen busens" by doubt "ob die verheissung löge." The promise concerns the new language, as the echo of *heißen* in "verheissung" confirms (recalling the element of *lesen* in "erlesen" a few lines before). The new idea here is that the concept of falsehood could be applied to the realms of the imagination so precious to George. These invented "eigne namen," a language proper to its inventor that also seemed proper to the things themselves, may not be adequate to the real world. Private ecstasies, compared to which the instruments of everyday sense seemed like mere babble, themselves run the double risk of incommunicability and — worse — deception (both deceiving and being deceived). It is a fraught conclusion.

In the trajectory of George's reflections on the calling and powers of the poet, "Des sehers wort" marks a vital new direction of attention, a concern with verifiability and referentiality. Earlier, in "Der Herr der Insel," the impossible conditions of transmission of the fishermen's report, and so the unreliability of all that it contained, did not trouble the poem's images; but here, the speaker has become profoundly concerned with the ability of his language, and of the scenes of his inner life, to refer to the preexisting world.

A poem from the "Vorspiel" (Prelude) to George's next volume, *Der Teppich des Lebens*, proposes, probably in the voice of the angel whose visitation began the first poem of that book, not only a new relation to the public world but also a new model of poetry's purview and its origins in experience:

> Dem markt und ufer gelte dein besuch
> Der starken und der schlanken sehne schnellen
> Der menge stürmen jauchzen lied und spruch
> Der nackten glieder gleiten in den wellen.
>
> Zu neuer form und farbe wird gedeihn
> Der streit von mensch mit mensch und tier und erde
> Der knaben sprung der mädchen ringelreihn
> Und gang und tanz und zierliche geberde.
>
> Doch ist wo du um tiefste schätze freist
> Der freunde nächtiger raum · schon schweigt geplauder
> Da bebt ein ton und eine miene kreist
> Und schütteln mit der offenbarung schauder.
>
> Da steigt das mächtige wort — ein grosses heil —
> Ein stern der auf verborgenen furchen glimmert
> Das wort von neuer lust und pein: ein pfeil
> Der in die seele bricht und zuckt und flimmert. (1: 182)

The first two stanzas urge the addressee, whom I take to be the poet, to get out into a noisy and vigorously alive world, one both of work ("markt") and of play ("ufer"). The first stanza even makes a point of including the crowd ("menge") in a not immediately pejorative sense (this is rare in George; see Beck). Dance, youth, and conflict will flourish "zu neuer form und farbe" when, witnessed by the poet, they become material for his art. This otherwise banal conception — that artists draw on and transform their experiences in the world — becomes noteworthy when we realize it has been absent from the other poems examined so far. Up until now, poetry and art have been almost an absolute; at most, in "Komm in den totgesagten park," the artist's work has consisted of locating and filtering the few aesthetically promising aspects of a scene, not in drawing the world into the alchemy of imagination.

The third and fourth stanzas withdraw indoors, but here too there is a change from the scenery of all the poems discussed before: other people are included. Intensity is found in discussion, or readings, with friends in the evening.[9] For George, this is a setting "wo du um tiefste schätze freist"; the juxtaposition of the last two words conveys, oddly but suggestively, a petitioning of the inorganic. Inspiration is not digging for treasure, but wooing it; yet what one is wooing is by definition not present and apparent (it lies *tief*). When the courtship is successful, the depths rise up (*steigen*) to become revelation ("der offenbarung schauder"), and revelation becomes poetry ("das mächtige wort"). The collection of impressions of human activity that opened the poem, then, is absorbed first into the "geplauder" of a closed circle, which falls silent and yields to a non-linguistic expression ("ton," "miene," "schütteln") and then into a single "wort." That word has, in return, a message and value that go beyond the poet and by implication return to other people (whether of the narrow circle or the broad populace). This too is a new note in these poems: the idea that the poet's word is "mächtig" in any dimension other than that of the choice empires of solitude that it itself creates. The phrase "ein grosses heil" underlines the fact that in this case, the word changes something. The word that is simultaneously star and seed, the flaming arrow lodged in the soul is the poem itself, as Hart Crane would later agree: "It is as though a poem gave the reader as he left it a single, new *word,* never before spoken and impossible to actually enunciate, but self-evident as an active principle in the reader's consciousness henceforward."[10]

In one way the word ("das wort von neuer lust und pein") recalls the private languages referred to in "Des sehers wort," and both poems assert the poet's visionary authority.[11] But "Dem markt und ufer" urges and depicts a vision and a language that include others: in the poem's first half by collecting impressions from the busy outside world and activities of the "menge," and then in the second by acknowledging that circle of friends who had long figured so importantly in George's life.

By contrast, the celebrated poem "Der Teppich" (The Tapestry), which leads off the main section of *Der Teppich des Lebens,* seems at first to be withdrawing again into isolated meditation on the work of art, and it is true that this kind of lonely rapture is never completely abandoned in

George's work. But in this case the poem neatly suggests a double reading that helps it to accord with the angelic announcement of "Dem markt und ufer." "Der Teppich" runs as follows:

Der Teppich

Hier schlingen menschen mit gewächsen tieren
Sich fremd zum bund umrahmt von seidner franze
Und blaue sicheln weisse sterne zieren
Und queren sie in dem erstarrten tanze.

Und kahle linien ziehn in reich-gestickten
Und teil um teil ist wirr und gegenwendig
Und keiner ahnt das rätsel der verstrickten . .
Da eines abends wird das werk lebendig.

Da regen schauernd sich die toten äste
Die wesen eng von strich und kreis umspannet
Und treten klar vor die geknüpften quäste
Die lösung bringend über die ihr sannet!

Sie ist nach willen nicht: ist nicht für jede
Gewohne stunde: ist kein schatz der gilde.
Sie wird den vielen nie und nie durch rede
Sie wird den seltnen selten im gebilde. (1: 190)

With the deictic or "pointing" adverb "Hier" the poem signals that it constitutes an instance of ekphrasis, a verbal evocation of a work of visual art. What the tapestry (or carpet; *Teppich* means either) depicts is a confused "alliance" of people, plants, and animals. (In this poem, George's habitual omission of punctuation between items in a series acts to make syntax imitate the difficult muddle — "wirr" [6] — of "gewächsen tieren," "blaue sicheln weisse sterne," and so on.) These figures "schlingen [. . .] / sich fremd zum bund": the figures in the carpet are alien to one another and alien in the total effect produced by their interlacing, while at the same time and in contradictory fashion, they also form a bond or league with one another. In what this alliance consists, or what end it serves, is perhaps the "rätsel der verstrickten," impenetrable to viewers.

The tapestry's coming to life begins, appropriately, not in a new and separate stanza; rather, beginning in line 8 it links together the stanzas of riddle (stanzas 1 and 2) and solution (stanza 3). The moment of magic is akin to resurrection (as *tot* [9] indicates), and it brings not just motion within the pattern but also motion out of it, as the images of human, plant, and animal "treten klar vor die geknüpften quäste." Like the artwork in Rilke's poem "Archaïscher Torso Apollos," George's tapestry reaches beyond itself in unleashing its aesthetic power upon the beholder. "Die lösung [. . .] über die ihr sannet" is in this sense not only the answer to the "rätsel" posed by the figures themselves but also in equal measure the viewers' sense that something in themselves has been resolved. It is a moment of revelation whose limits are never firmly drawn, and which is always also a resolution ("lösung") that unbinds psychic energy in the beholder.

The poem's final stanza is retrospective, summarizing and didacticizing this experience of uncanny animation and revelation ("sie" refers back to "die lösung"). The magic moment is not under conscious control, is necessarily ephemeral, and — if one can take the phrase "ist kein schatz der gilde" in this way — cannot be made the secret or the possession of an institution, nor perhaps can it even be shared among the members of a group. In this case, the resolution also lies outside the power of language even to trigger, a fact that marks a striking concession and a departure from the exaltation of poetic speech in "Des sehers wort" and "Dem markt und ufer." Instead, the poem concludes, "Sie wird den seltnen selten im gebilde." That last word recalls the poem's opening word "hier": although the work steps forward out of itself as it comes to life, the ingredients of the mystery continue to be found not in the answer, but in the knotted question; not in explanatory "rede," but in the seemingly dead tangle of the tapestry's "gebilde."[12]

I suggested in introducing this poem that it permits another reading, too, one that makes it less of a withdrawal from the outward-looking spirit of "Dem markt und ufer." This reading consists of taking the tapestry as already a metaphor for life. In this sense, the frozen dance and confusion of forms are the alien (*fremd*) aspect of the everyday world, which always remained uncongenial to George. But for this "tapestry," too, there are moments where the whole is seen as it were aesthetically, life coming to life in a way that makes its meaning and value available to the surprised spectator. For a writer like George, such a view of "Der Teppich" is secondary: his loyalty and love are for the silent artwork. But as his evocation of the poet as seer or prophet indicated ("Des sehers wort"), the silken frame of the artistic image does not, in the end, mark the boundary of his concerns.

"Hehre Harfe" (Sublime Harp), a poem from George's 1907 volume *Der Siebente Ring*, addresses what I am calling George's steady and chief concern — the relation of the poet and poetry to the world outside — in a familiar-sounding trochaic tetrameter. Here the poem engages the opposition of self and world by making to dissolve it altogether:

HEHRE HARFE

Sucht ihr neben noch das übel
Greift ihr aussen nach dem heile:
Giesst ihr noch in lecke kübel ·
Müht ihr euch noch um das feile.

Alles seid ihr selbst und drinne:
Des gebets entzückter laut
Schmilzt in eins mit jeder minne ·
Nennt sie Gott und freund und braut!

Keine zeiten können borgen . .
Fegt der sturm die erde sauber:
Tretet ihr in euren morgen ·
Werfet euren blick voll zauber

Auf die euch verliehnen gaue
Auf das volk das euch umfahet
Und das land das dämmergraue
Das ihr früh im brunnen sahet.

Hegt den wahn nicht: mehr zu lernen
Als aus staunen überschwang
Holden blumen hohen sternen
EINEN sonnigen lobgesang. (1: 307)

Trochaic tetrameter as a vehicle for dispensing wisdom to an unnamed "ihr" makes this poem George's variation played upon Goethe's celebrated poem "Selige Sehnsucht" from the *West-Östlicher Divan* (The Parliament of West and East, 1819), a poem that incidentally opens with a sentiment George must have found sympathetic: "Sagt es niemand, nur den Weisen, / weil die Menge gleich verhöhnet."[13] The theme of "Hehre Harfe" is self-sufficiency; good or evil is to be found neither "neben" (1) nor "aussen" (2), but rather "drinne" (5). Even love is wholly interiorized, as religious devotion, friendship, and marriage melt together or become interchangeable. And ironically, given the poem's own indebtedness to Goethe, "Hehre Harfe" urges independence from tradition and the past: "keine zeiten können borgen." Or, perhaps, more in keeping with the absolutism of the poem's thought, the claim is that in some sense there *are* no other ages to borrow from: everything we do now is shaped out of the world as we now receive it and returns to that world as well.

The second half of "Hehre Harfe" elaborates the idea of *making* in a world thus "swept clean" (10) of any presences, powers, or history external to the sovereign autonomous self. One's gaze is itself "voll zauber," bestowing magic upon the world at the same time as it meets a landscape "bestowed" upon it (*verliehen*) in turn. This unaccountable reciprocity may recall the bestowing of names in "Des sehers wort," discussed earlier; and the close of the fourth stanza reaffirms the visionary or projecting character of this gaze as well as the way this projection unexpectedly appears as a reflection and a return. The lines in question urge us to cast our gaze "[auf] das land das dämmergraue / Das ihr früh im brunnen sahet" (15–16). As in George's earlier poetry, poetic making begins with a vision, but here the vision comes to fruition when it is beheld in real life. Gone is any sense of captivity in the visionary world (as in "Meine weissen ara" or "Der Herr der Insel"), and gone too is the anxiety of "Des sehers wort" that what is newly invented could turn out to be inauthentic or lying. "Hehre Harfe" is a poem of confidence, even an almost mystical trust in the sufficiency of the mind. What is beheld in the well of the self — a vessel opposed to the first stanza's leaky buckets — is destined to return in the outside world.

The last stanza of "Hehre Harfe" culminates with an increasing complexity the motif of a mysterious reciprocity between world and self. As the speaker had earlier asserted that no era can borrow from another, here he advises his listeners that it would be delusion to think that one can learn more than what is ordained as, it is implied, the natural or fitting limit. This limit, however, is not something given, but rather something one must make oneself: "aus staunen überschwang / Holden blumen hohen sternen / EINEN sonnigen lobgesang" (18–20). It is easy to take these lines as if they spoke of *making* a "lobgesang" that would unify inner ("staunen überschwang") and outer ("holden blumen hohen sternen"); indeed that is in one way their necessary sense; but the verb "lernen" styles this making as itself a process of taking in, or recognizing, or mastering, something preexisting and external. Poetry is in this conception an act of creation that responds to and reshapes the sublime (*hehr*) moments of nature and the emotional response to nature, while poetry is also a thing to be discovered and accepted as ultimate and, in the manner of a law, given.

In George's final volume, the collection *Das Neue Reich,* two very different poems show the views of poetry that mark the last station in this career of preoccupation with the relative powers of art and the social world.[14] The first is a long poem, "Der Dichter in Zeiten der Wirren" (The Poet in Times of Confusion), divided into three thirty-line sections (1: 416–18). The poem begins with three lines describing the poet's reputation in peaceful times, an image that the rest of the poem will throw into relief:

> Der Dichter heisst im stillern gang der zeit
> Beflügelt kind das holde träume tönt
> Und schönheit bringt ins tätige getrieb.

The bringing of beauty into the busy world forms a late complement to the poet's willingness, in "Dem markt und ufer," to let the world's activity inspire his verse. Dreams, song ("tönt"), and ethereal childlikeness all signal a distance, however, between poet and society. The verb "heisst" assigns this picture to general opinion, leaving its accuracy an open question.[15]

In what follows, the speaker drops any attribution to others. A series of six "if-then" constructions (the third and fourth of these, sentences beginning with "dann," are structured by an "even though-nevertheless" logic) repeatedly invokes an antithesis between the poet's words or activities "in Zeiten der Wirren" and those of the uncomprehending crowd. The poet is Cassandra or Jeremiah, a "seher" (7) and "mahner" (16) ignored or imprisoned by the "tollgewordne menge" (10) and aware of the people's degradation as they themselves are not: "Er fernab fühlt allein / Das ganze elend und die ganze schmach" (29–30).

The second stanza concerns principally the frivolity, dullness, and unbelief of the many, promising a break in the clouds of delusion only "wenn alles / Was eine sprache spricht die hand sich reicht / Um sich zu wappnen wider den verderb" (55–57). The line remains suspended between two rather different meanings, "all who speak a language" and "all who speak one language." The first, perhaps less likely reading connects (and converts) speakers by the sign or power of language *tout court,* and so continues a string of words having to do with voice and speech as fostering enlightenment or confusion ("spruch der löse / Aus dieser trübsal" [32–33], "himmels stimme" [34], "rede / Von geiste" [35–36], "fabeln" [40], "raten" [42], "lügen" [47]). The second reading would see the alliance "wider den verderb" as built on the more specific foundation of one shared language, which could be taken literally or as a figure for some common understanding. The sentiment evades simple nationalism, however, in the stanza's final image of shaking off "gleichviel ob rot ob blau ob schwarz die fahlen / Verschlissnen fahnenfetzen" (58–59).

The third section of "Der Dichter in Zeiten der Wirren" shifts the emphasis to the life-tending work of the poet ("der Sänger," a rare capitalized noun) and then, by two unexpected and crucial turns, first to a "jung geschlecht" (75) growing up around the poet and then to a savior figure, whom the poem calls "den einzigen der hilft" and, simply, "den Mann" (82), and who is himself the offspring (physically or spiritually) of the "jung geschlecht."

To this messianism George joins an evocation of Prometheus that combines two separate motifs of the titan's myth: "Er schürt die heilige glut die über-springt / Und sich die leiber formt" (63–64). Prometheus was both the fire-bringer and the shaper of man out of clay; if the poet, in George's vision, does not himself exercise the making powers of the demiurge, nevertheless the flame that he keeps does. "In zeiten der wirren" the sacred potency with which the poet is charged so dwarfs his reputed role in peaceful times — "Beflügelt kind das holde träume tönt / Und schönheit bringt ins tätige getrieb" (2–3) — as to expose it as a ridiculous caricature.

The complement to this primordial creative fire is the poet's work as the keeper of lore, the inert or dormant inheritance from the past: "er holt aus büchern / Der ahnen die verheissung die nicht trügt" (64–65), a prophecy namely that the weary march of those chosen for the highest aim must go before so that "the heart of the continent" may redeem the world.

The messianic politics of the visionary future spring, by the poet's efforts, from the prophecy that purported merely to refer to them. Rescuing this promise from the archives ("aus büchern / Der ahnen"), the poet finds in it also a tardy answer to the doubt voiced in "Des sehers wort" (1897), amid the "eigne namen" of the poet's invented private language of vision and power, "ob die verheissung löge." Where that earlier poem called into question the reliable applicability of the imagined world to the world of time and history, so undermining the poem's own view of the poet as prophet ("seher"), "Der Dichter in Zeiten der Wirren" solves the problem by identifying the "Sänger" as the custodian of energies and visions not original with him, promises that "do not deceive." The fact that this poem of grand poetic vocation and mystic knowledge also alludes to a geopolitical destiny for the state of Germany ("des erdteils herz") enmeshes the work of poetry with its social context in a way that, however vague it remains here, would have been unthinkable for the younger poet of "Der Herr der Insel," "Der Teppich," or "Hehre Harfe."

But the poets are not themselves the saviors. The end of this poem describes a curious relay instead. Of the singer it is said, "Ihm wuchs schon heran / Unangetastet von dem geilen markt / [. . .] / Ein jung geschlecht das wieder mensch und ding / Mit echten maassen misst" (71–76). The passivity of the image ("ihm wuchs heran") is notable, and even the poet's influence over the fact that his followers remain untouched by the despised market is a matter of surmise, implied but not asserted. Nor are these followers the ones who inaugurate the new age; rather they are said to be a race

> Das aus geweihten träumen tun und dulden
> Den einzigen der hilft den Mann gebiert . .
> Der sprengt die ketten fegt auf trümmerstätten
> Die ordnung · geisselt die verlaufnen heim
> Ins ewige recht wo grosses wiederum gross ist
> Herr wiederum herr · zucht wiederum zucht · (81–86)

This nonbiological birth of "the man" out of the consecrated dreams, deeds, and suffering (or acquiescence) of a group is the poem's explicitly millenarian conclusion; this man, it is said, goes on to affix "the true symbol" to the people's flag and leads the mass of those loyal to him ("seiner treuen schar") through storm and dread fanfares of dawn "zum werk / Des wachen tags und pflanzt das Neue Reich" (89–90).

With this stirring fulfillment at two removes from the poet's own labors, it is nevertheless manifest that the place of art is still found in opposition to social realities, no less in this late poem than in, say, *Algabal's* "Mein garten" or in "Komm in den totgesagten park." What changes, through the diverse periods of George's writing, is the articulation of this underlying constant opposedness: the domain of art may take shape as a fantastic retort to the philistine sensibilities of the age, or it may be a selection and refinement of the world's fading loveliness. Or, as in "Der Dichter in Zeiten der Wirren," it may be the matrix of revolutionary war and the founding of utopia.

One final poem from *Das neue Reich,* celebrated especially since Heidegger's discussions of it in "Das Wesen der Sprache" (The Nature of Language, 1957) and in "Das Wort" (The Word, 1958), styles poetic making as a literal translation, an importation that remains nevertheless dependent on the finite resources of the poet's native tongue:

DAS WORT

Wunder von ferne oder traum
Bracht ich an meines landes saum

Und harrte bis die graue norn
Den namen fand in ihrem born —

Drauf konnt ichs greifen dicht und stark
Nun blüht und glänzt es durch die mark . . .

Einst langt ich an nach guter fahrt
Mit einem kleinod reich und zart

Sie suchte lang und gab mir kund:
»So schläft hier nichts auf tiefem grund«

Worauf es meiner hand entrann
Und nie mein land den schatz gewann . . .

So lernt ich traurig den verzicht:
Kein ding sei wo das wort gebricht. (1: 466–67)

Actually, less than half the poem is concerned with the poetic "finding" that converts a "wunder von ferne oder traum" into something "dicht" that will bloom and shine throughout poetry's borderlands. The last four couplets are instead about the failure of poetry to become a "thing" when the customs books list no equivalent for it: the new treasure must paradoxically already exist (even if "asleep") in the land's vocabulary in order to be added to that vocabulary. Otherwise the outcome is the sad learning of the "verzicht" that consents to the loss of whatever cannot be put into words. The loss is framed in public terms: "und nie mein land den schatz gewann," writes the poet, whereas in an earlier poem like "Des sehers wort," it seemed like a personal failure when naming went awry. As Heidegger points out (222), renunciation at the limits of language — the acceptance of those limits — may itself be the condition of poetry. Poetry's force, for a poet like George, is felt in its restraint. This poem belongs to the class of those works (like Hopkins's "To R. B.") that make themselves out of their own negativity, describing in poetic arcs the absence of poetry.

It also recalls "Die Spange" as a two-part poem that evokes poetic making by setting an instance of failure or frustration against an instance of success.

Why does the gray Norn find a name for the "wunder von ferne oder traum," but none for the "kleinod reich und zart"? The first term is intangible or elusive four times over. It is a miracle; it retains the aspect of distance; no, perhaps it is something else ("oder"); perhaps it is a dream. A rich jewel held in the hand, by contrast, seems altogether "dicht" and "greif[bar]." Yet it is to the airy nothings of uncertain identity that the Norn gives a name and a habitation in the "mark" or border country of language, while the already definite "kleinod" awakens no word in her deep well and so — startlingly — it slips away from the poet's grasp as if it were itself a dream. Poetry ("das wort"), in other words, veers away from the real.[16] The thought goes deeper than "Komm in den totgesagten park," to say nothing of "Mein garten": instead of poetry as defiant artificiality or as a choice recombination of gathered colors, "Das Wort" shows poetry as the dense and blossoming radiance of what can only barely be believed ("wunder") or communicated ("traum"), while the solidity of the real world runs out of poems like melting snow.

"Das Wort," in sum, describes the workings and condition of poetry in terms of two different kinds of "thing." Insubstantial or unreal things (like the "fremde dolde" of "Die Spange"?) can be spoken into being, "dicht und stark." But for a thing that is already in the hand, nothing sleeps in the well of art; and because the poem will not stick to reality, even the thing itself is then lost (or at least lost to the enduring realm of poetry). Instead of *Gedicht* one is left only with *Verzicht,* words about the absence of a thing instead of the thing made word.[17]

George's poems about poetry are marked, as George's life was marked, by a ceaseless effort to negotiate his place and the place of art in an era he felt to be hostile or indifferent. Rather than, as is sometimes said, mounting a monumental critique of his age and its views, George constantly tacks back and forth, trying out now an extravagant pose of defiance, now a reconciliation, now a cry of doubt. On the whole, the early work, from at least "Die Spange" on, dramatizes the resistance that is for George the starting-place of poetry. The two chief collections of George's middle period, *Das Jahr der Seele* and *Der Teppich des Lebens,* explore the possibility of a mediation that would bring the worlds of imagination and social reality into communication; these poems turn towards the world, and sometimes away again. Finally, in the last collections, George creates works that proceed to new extremes, erasing (as in "Hehre Harfe") the troublesome boundaries between self and world; affirming (as in "Das Wort") the social benefit of poetry while simultaneously suggesting a radical metaphysical incompatibility between language and the world; or making the poet (as in "Der Dichter in Zeiten der Wirren") a true prophet whose words and work will conquer history. Far from being a battery of *idées fixes,* then, George's poetics as the poems embody them describe a durative struggle to house aesthetic value and aesthetic labor opposite, or in, or over the common activities of human society and of human life. The cultural climate of Wilhelmine Germany and the early Weimar republic may have seemed to George the specific obstacle with which he had to contend in his endeavor, but the effort to protect or assert the claims of art against a dull world resonates beyond his time in ways that suggest that George's struggles remain, as well, perennial ones.

Notes

[1] See Mattenklott, esp. chap. 3, "Das Bild Stefan Georges" 175-317.

[2] Durzak also cites this passage in connection with "Die Spange" (52).

[3] Metzger and Metzger also underline the moralism implicit in *Algabal* (63).

[4] Tiedemann-Bartels argues that sterility, a notion less worrisome to George than to writers who cherish a view of art as organic, is not at issue in this final stanza: "Vielmehr öffnet sich in der Frage nach der 'dunklen großen schwarzen Blume' die nach der Vollkommenheit der Kunst selber" (82).

[5] The vocative phrase of the poem's last line is separated from the question to which it belongs (line 13) by a distracting two-line interpolation, and the rhyme scheme, as in "Die Spange," changes in this last stanza from alternating rhyme (*abab*) to envelope rhyme (*abba*). The effect is to delay, by two different means, the full sense of the question "Wie zeug ich dich aber im heiligtume" until the poem's last word, "blume." Both of these are means by which the final stanza concentrates attention on itself, and especially on its last line.

[6] *Sämtliche Werke* 3: 118–19. I am indebted to Gerhard Kaiser's reading of this poem (138-45).

[7] See for example Norton 21–23, 55, 61.

[8] See also Kaiser 238.

[9] On the rituals of such readings in George's circle see Braungart 154–75.

[10] "General Aims and Theories." *Complete Poems and Selected Letters and Prose of Hart Crane,* ed. Brom Weber (New York: Anchor, 1966). Reprinted in Gibbons 182.

[11] "Lust und Pein" are what Johann Wolfgang von Goethe, in the *West-Östlicher Divan,* proposes to share with his "twin," the medieval Persian poet Hafiz (see the poem "Unbegrenzt" [Unbounded] in the section "Hafis Nameh"). Annette von Droste-Hülshoff's "Das Wort" (The Word) also compares the poetic word to arrow, seed, and spark — though Droste might seem an unlikely forebear for George.

[12] Also, these last lines, opposing "rede" and "gebilde," again allude to Goethe: "Bilde, Künstler! Rede nicht! / Nur ein Hauch sei dein Gedicht" (Goethe 1: 325).

[13] Goethe 2: 18–19. Goethe's poem switches after the first stanza into the singular *du*-form, as if illustrating and taking further the narrowing-down of the audience that the first lines urged.

[14] I omit from consideration George's 1914 volume *Der Stern des Bundes*. It is an anomalous book in many ways, one of which is that it contains comparatively little poetological reflection of the kind I am discussing.

[15] Compare the report of the fishermen in "Der Herr der Insel" and the unverifiable promise of "Des sehers wort."

[16] The final couplet pertains to the second half of the poem and even represents only the second step, so to speak, of the story about the jewel: not the Norn's failure to find its name but only the results of that failure ("worauf es meiner hand entrann"). The last line, "Kein ding sei wo das wort gebricht," spells out a different renunciation from the inverse or chiastic relation between name and thing illustrated by the contrasting fates of "wunder" and "kleinod."

[17] This is the negative side of George's recurrent thought that the power of language is to invent things that are also already there (as in "Des sehers wort," "Hehre Harfe," or "Der Dichter in Zeiten der Wirren").

Works Cited

Beck, Claus Victor. *Wort-Konkordanz zur Dichtung Stefan Georges.* Amsterdam: Castrum Peregrini, 1964.

Braungart, Wolfgang, *Ästhetischer Katholizismus: Stefan Georges Rituale der Literatur.* Tübingen: Niemeyer, 1997.

Durzak, Manfred. *Zwischen Symbolismus und Expressionismus: Stefan George.* Stuttgart: Kohlhammer, 1974.

George, Stefan. *Einleitungen und Merksprüche der Blätter für die Kunst.* Ed. G. P. Landmann. Düsseldorf: Küpper-Bondi, 1964.

———. *Sämtliche Werke in 18 Bänden.* Stuttgart: Klett-Cotta, 1982–.

———. *Werke in zwei Bänden.* Stuttgart: Klett-Cotta, 1984.

Gibbons, Reginald, ed. *The Poet's Work.* Chicago: U of Chicago P, 1979.

Goethe, Johann Wolfgang von. *Goethes Werke.* Ed. Erich Trunz. 11th ed. Hamburger Ausgabe. Munich: Beck, 1978.

Heidegger, Martin. *Unterwegs zur Sprache.* Pfullingen: Neske, 1959.

Kaiser, Gerhard. *Die deutsche Lyrik von Heine bis zur Gegenwart.* Frankfurt a.M.: Suhrkamp, 1991.

Mattenklott, Gert. *Bilderdienst: Ästhetische Opposition bei Beardsley und George.* 2nd ed. Frankfurt a.M.: Syndikat, 1985.

Metzger, Michael M., and Erika A. Metzger. *Stefan George.* New York: Twayne, 1972.

Norton, Robert E. *Secret Germany: Stefan George and his Circle.* Ithaca/London: Cornell UP, 2002.

Tiedemann-Bartels, Hella. *Versuch über das artistische Gedicht: Baudelaire, Mallarmé, George.* Munich: Edition text + kritik, 1990.

Stefan George's Early Works 1890–1895

Robert Vilain

FOR POETRY THAT IS SO WELL KNOWN, so canonical, George's early work is surprisingly difficult. Many attempts have been made to explicate the early cycles, sometimes in the manner of a decoding,[1] but the characteristic Georgean combination of extreme formal rigor, compelling semantic condensation and a dense network of allusive or symbolic imagery often makes individual poems strangely limpid yet at the same time highly resistant to simple understanding, let alone paraphrase. Their difficulty, and their subtlety, derives to an extent from George's insistent use of paradox, from the frequent conjunction of assertiveness and doubt, and from the overlaying or interweaving of apparently personal emotion with apersonal poetological reflection such that comprehension is sometimes more intuitive than rational. The paradoxes are integral to the central themes of his early writing — dominance and dependence, ruling and serving, desire and self-denial, the spiritual and the material, isolation and belonging.

For a poet whose reputation is one of self-sufficiency, with an autocratic, even arrogant persona, there is discernable a remarkable degree of under-confidence. When first meeting the artist Melchior Lechter (1865–1937), George pretended to be the editor of his journal *Blätter für die Kunst,* Carl August Klein, and only revealed his true identity after he was certain that Lechter was an admirer of his work. He tolerated few fellow poets in the circle he gathered around him and was often secretive about his movements. This manifests itself in his writing from the earliest years. George's insecurity as a poet in German led to a crisis in 1889 when he appears to have been uncertain whether to write in French or German (see Curtius 154). He emerged from this crisis partly as a result of a form of linguistic apprenticeship, the translation of Baudelaire's *Les fleurs du mal.* This was undertaken because of "[die] ursprünglich reine freude am formen" (2: 233), and because it offered him the opportunity to explore and discover German by immersing himself in the formal, technical, rhythmic, and phonetic aspects necessary to render Baudelaire's French in a manner that does not simply imitate or transfer but uses the new form to recreate or renew the content for German. His dictum was "strengstes maass ist zugleich höchste freiheit" (1: 530), but in order to achieve that freedom he needed a fuller understanding of the way in which his own language could be "measured."

The French Alexandrine line dominated Baudelaire's originals (thirty-four of the first forty poems that George translated used that form), but was uncommon and epigonal in German after the Baroque, so George experimented with various alternatives. The obvious equivalent, a six-foot iambic line, was in fact hardly ever used; he preferred instead the five-foot iambic, which, as the verse form of much German classical drama, possessed not only a strong pedigree commensurate with that of the Alexandrine but also considerable vitality and flexibility. Shortening the line also meant compressing the language, and his Baudelaire translations became the proving ground for what would later emerge as characteristic linguistic features of George's verse. Articles and auxiliaries are omitted and condensed nouns created by joining two others, participles replace finite verbs, conjunctions are removed and with them the complexities of hypotactic language. As an example, the opening lines of Baudelaire's programmatic sonnet "Correspondances" and George's translation as "Einklänge" are as follows:

> La Nature est un temple où de vivants piliers
> Laissent parfois sortir de confuses paroles;
> L'homme y passe à travers des forêts de symboles
> Qui l'observent avec des regards familiers.
>
> Comme de longs échos qui de loin se confondent
> Dans une ténébreuse et profonde unité,
> Vaste comme la nuit et comme la clarté,
> Les parfums, les couleurs et les sons se répondent.
> (Baudelaire 1: 11)

> Aus der natur belebten tempelbaun
> Oft unverständlich wirre worte weichen ·
> Dort geht der mensch durch einen wald von zeichen
> Die mit vertrauten Blicken ihn beschaun.
>
> Wie lange echo fern zusammenrauschen
> In tiefer finsterer geselligkeit ·
> Weit wie die nacht und wie die helligkeit
> Parfüme farben töne rede tauschen. (2: 239)

Lines three and four are simple translations, but the first two lines conflate Baudelaire's two clauses. The main clause verb disappears and its subject, nature, becomes the genitive qualifier of the temple (typically placed before that noun), itself the prepositional object of a verb originally in the subordinate clause. The transitive action "laissent sortir" becomes the intransitive "weichen," and the main verb is placed at the end of the sentence. The pillars of the temple disappear but their qualifying adjective, "vivants," is transferred to the temple itself. George binds the whole image together with dense alliteration. A subordinate clause is again suppressed in the first line of the second stanza, but most radically line eight omits all the articles and the conjunction so that the sense is distilled into four nouns and a verb, the last four words all disyllabic, the break between subject and predicate occurring after the third word. None of these changes significantly alters the basic meaning of the original, but the richly expansive and reflective diction of the French has ceded to a distanced, tenser, sparer, brachylogic style that is George's own, his "neue fühlweise und mache" (*BfdK* 1,1: 1), enhanced in its idiosyncrasies by a fondness for exotic or archaic vocabulary, little-used alternative nominal and verbal forms, and eloquent neologisms.

An important aspect of the new aesthetic was the physical appearance and presentation of his work, and this concern began with the very earliest volumes. The *Hymnen* appeared in October 1890 in Berlin in an edition of one hundred copies on good quality paper, printed in plain Antiqua type, the nouns without initial capital letters. Punctuation was sparing, the usual comma eschewed in favor of the Greek comma, a point set at the mid-height of the lower-case letters. Similar care was taken with *Pilgerfahrten,* another edition of a hundred copies printed in Vienna in December 1891, and *Algabal,* published in Paris in two editions: the first a mere ten copies in September, the second a further ninety copies at the end of November 1892. Carl August Klein suggested as early as December 1892 that these three volumes "scheinen als eine trilogie aufgefasst" (*BfdK* 1,2: 49), yet it was not until nearly a decade later that they were united in a single volume, dated 1899, but issued in October 1898 by the Berlin publisher Georg Bondi, in whom George had at last found someone who would devote the unique care and attention to the physical appearance of his work that he demanded.

Hymnen was the first collection of original verse that George published and the meaning of its title is the subject of some debate. Some read it as a reference to church hymns, albeit in a secularized form, as songs of praise; others see instead a reference to Greek Hymns, now usually called Odes, celebrating the deeds of the gods and later of mortal heroes.[2] Both suggest a tone of respect or reverence as well as celebration, and both imply a quasi-religious function. In poems such as the "Neuländische Liebesmahle" (Love Feasts in New Terrains) there is an almost cultic dimension to the tone of high solemnity, with incense, used in the Christian church, and myrtle leaves, used in antiquity for purification and commemoration.[3] George's art in *Hymnen* is one of images and impressions, not of feeling, experience, or confession. Life is not seized and depicted in its colorful variety; the reflections, the shadows cast, and the seismic ripples that its events cause in the soul of the poet are registered and absorbed. The poet is lonely, distanced both from the world and from himself, the world often that of art, fantasy or memory. The poems are an artistically constructed refuge for which renunciation and self-denial are prerequisite to achieving the ecstasy of poetic creation. And yet throughout this collection, which treats of loss, farewells, retrospection, and evanescent moments of contact, there is a tension between strong currents of sensuous desire and an ascetic dedication to the poet's high calling.

The first poem, "Weihe" (Initiation, but also Consecration or Ordination, 1: 9) sets the high religious tone, evoking the circumstances in which the poet can achieve the blessing of the muse. An injunction to travel out towards solitude by the noble river is followed by advice to rest and "dich betäuben / An starkem urduft · ohne denkerstörung" whilst awaiting poetic elevation. The primal breeze, once seized, will replace what George calls "die fremden hauche," or the distracting echoes and influences of others' works ("Hauch" is the equivalent of the French "souffle," often used by the Symbolists as a synonym for creative inspiration and thus for poetry itself). Once this pure condition has been reached, nature will be tamed: the reeds by the river will sway rhythmically, the haze over the water solidify into a "nebelmauer" and then shatter, so that the magic of poetry, the "elfenlied zum elfentanz" can be heard (brief references like this to the supernatural world of fairies, nymphs, and fauns are common in George's early work). In the mind's eye, the world outside will yield to intimations of higher realms and cities in the stars as reality is transfigured: "Der zeiten flug verliert die alten namen / Und raum und dasein bleiben nur im bilde" — time and space and human existence are suspended, meaningful only in the poetic image. Only when the senses usually attuned to the sights and scents of the real world are ecstatically heightened to perceive a higher realm is the poet ready for a blessing in the form of a kiss from the Muse, the "herrin" of the poem, who is in reality a projected component of the poet himself. This matchless moment in fact slips right through the poem almost as if there are lines missing. From the consistent present tense of stanzas one to five there is a shift in stanza six to the past; this stanza consists of a series of subordinate clauses beginning with "indem," but there is no main verb at the end of the fifth stanza on which "indem" can depend. That stanza ended with the trembling image of the muse, "Halboffen ihre traumesschweren lider / Zu dir geneigt die segnung zu vollbringen:" — the colon virtually promising that the main verb will appear in the next stanza. The moment of consecration when the projection of the poet's inspiration blesses the poet himself is ineffable, an almost erotic climax at a point when the poet is paradoxically at his most pure, "rein und geheiligt."

The collection thus opens with a poem celebrating the successful attainment of poetic grace, but the rest of the collection exposes the poet to temptation and underlines the difficulties and pain in the poetic process. It will end with some uncertainty, the evocation of the closing of gardens at summer's end, and the thoughtful questions "Ward dein hoffen deine habe? / Baust du immer noch auf ihre worte / Pilger mit der hand am stabe?" (1: 22). Whether the poet's hopes have been realized, and whether he is relying still too much on other poets' words are questions that remain to be answered in the collection to which the last image here points, the *Pilgerfahrten* of 1891. Between "Weihe" and "Die Gärten schliessen" (The Gardens Close), George exposes his poetic self to pain and temptation, often in the form of a female figure, the Muse and thus the incarnation of the poetic calling, or worldly temptation itself. "Nachthymne" (Serenade) comes close to renouncing the poetic path for the sake of a single, searing glance from this figure: "Nach deinem preise schlöss ich meinen psalter / Und spottete dem schatten einer ehre / Und stürbe wertlos wie ein abend-falter" (1: 17). The last image, recalling Goethe's "Selige Sehnsucht" (Blessed Longing), suggests that the abandonment of the *Psalter*, or the books of poetry, is not so much a renunciation as a fulfillment; it is not real-ized, however, and the poet must continue in his lonely calling. "Nachmittag" (Afternoon) powerfully suggests the almost masochistic pain to which the poet subjects himself: the sun's rays beat down on him, "Und dem Einsamen der mit entzücken sie fühlt / Der des gemaches duftender kühle entfloh / Gegenglut für zerstörende gluten suchend" (1: 12). The relentless torture is suggested in the repetitions of the first line in the mid-dle and at the end, as if to suggest an endless circle. A similarly cyclical structure articulates the three incarnations of the imagined companion in "Verwandlungen" (Transformation), where she first appears "Auf einem goldenen Wagen [. . .] mit mildem lächeln / Und linderndem hauche!" (1: 14), then on a silver chariot, "Mit frohem lächeln / Und kosendem hauche" only to end on a chariot of steel, smiling wildly, "[mit] sengendem hauche!" (1: 15). George is implacable in his conception of the rigor of poetic inspiration. "Im Park" suggests how, in the Baudelaire-inspired beauty of the fountain and the shady trees, the poet perceives the same sound that fans the passions of lovers: "Die jenen wonnetag erwachen sahen / Empfinden heiss von weichem klang berauscht · / Es schmachtet leib und leib sich zu umfahen" (1: 10). There is a pause between stanzas, and the sensuous verse shifts to a calmer, more controlled statement, "Der dichter auch der töne lockung lauscht," more solemn for the characteristic late positioning of the main verb. He is able to resist and remain in noble isolation because he is communing with his spirits and can write despite the recalcitrance of words: "Er hat den griffel der sich sträubt zu führen."

Hymnen is in many respects a demonstration of Mallarmé's dictum, "le monde est fait pour aboutir à un beau livre" (Mallarmé 872). The outside world is consistently absorbed and transmuted into art.[4] Nature simply enjoyed, as by the woman in "Einladung" (Invitation), is superficial, "tiefer gefühle auch arm" (1: 11), and several poems are set in unreal or imagined worlds, like "seiner wünsche wunderlande" in "Ein Hingang" (Parting, 1: 16).[5] Even where the setting is natural, the artistic predominates. The fountain in the poem "Im Park" sprays droplets of pearls and rubies into the silken green carpet, and the shelter of the trees forms a "schattensaal" (1: 10); the blue eye of "Nachthymne" is a turquoise (1: 16); the hills seen from a terrace "schütten / Den glatten guss von himmelgrünem glase" (1: 19), and the scents of dahlias, stock, and roses rise "in erzwungenem orchester" (1: 22). The opposite gesture, the anthropomorphization of nature — as when "die grauen buchen sich die hände reichen" (1: 15) or when "junger wellen schmeichelchore" (1: 9) caress the river banks — is no less a means of appropriating the world for art. Even when the possibility of communion with a kindred spirit is intimated, as in "Von einer Begegnung" (An Encounter), the woman is not described directly, but only in terms of his unanswered glances towards her. She is left only as an image in his mind, his tears dampening that recollected and recreated form: "ein steter regen bittrer lauge / Benezt und bleicht was mühevoll ich male" (1: 13). Indirectness of this kind characterizes many of the *Hymnen*. The subject of the first of the "Bilder" (Pictures, 1: 20–21) is Don Baltasar Carlos, approached via the painting in the Panthéon de los Infantes, as its twin, the poet's imagined memories of his childhood playing with his silken ball more alive and precious than the real lives of those who lived to adulthood. The "glorreich grosse tat" (1: 21) in Fra Angelico's *Coronation of the Virgin* in the Louvre which is the subject of "Ein Angelico" (Fra Angelico), is less the coronation itself than its miraculous transformation by the artist. The colors he uses are as if sucked from life, "er nahm das gold von heiligen pokalen · / Zu hellem haar das reife weizenstroh · / Das rosa kindern die mit schiefer malen · / Der wäscherin am bach den indigo."[6]

The second cycle, *Pilgerfahrten*, takes as its central figure the image of the pilgrim that closed the *Hymnen*. The poet there was shut out of the garden at a bleak moment when mist obscured the already contradictory symbolism of statues of the sun-god Apollo and the moon-goddess Diana and when the harmony of flower-scents was "erzwungen" rather than natural; since his hopes have not been realized he becomes a wayfaring pilgrim. The nature of the quest in the second volume is complex: on one level the central figure seeks deeper understanding of himself and his calling, and to this end sometimes needs a companion or a lover; on another level, the companion-figures, usually women, represent seductive distractions from or corruptions of his poetic mission or spiritual journey. A sense of the seasonality or timeliness is often what determines the rightness or wrongness of any given bond, and sometimes it is less that the pilgrim or the figures he meets and imagines are themselves problematic than that they are existentially "out of tune" or "out of time" with each other. The strong tensions between spirit and flesh and between experience and memory are never fully resolved.

Something of the multi-layered nature of the dilemmas in this collection is evident from the opening poem, "Siedlergang" (The Recluse Goes

Forth), as the hermit emerges from sheltered isolation into the brightness of spring, to be confronted (either in reality or in his memory) with the seductive dance of "die roten frauen" (1: 28). He is bewildered by the vigor of the natural world, by the women's passionate intensity; he is torn by conflicting emotions about something he has hitherto scorned but at the same time passionately desired — "Ich hasse sie und brenne sie zu greifen" — and anxious about the discrepancy between true living human-ity and the creatures of his imagination, the "lichtgestalten" that now dance on the crest of the hill, too remote even to hear his call. The last two stanzas suggest that the hermit has been fatally drawn into the world of their dance and may no longer have the determination to return to the consolations of his "treue pergamente" and the life of the mind. The fol-lowing poem, "Mühle lass die arme still" (Stop your turning vanes, O mill), though its subject matter is ostensibly quite different, is a macabre account of how a group of girls returning from their first communion are drowned as the ice breaks beneath them, and reenacts the same themes on a more mystical, almost supernatural plane. The arrival of spring triggers the crack-ing of the ice, and with an evocative fourfold echo of the previous line's rhyming vowel-sound ("Alle lampen flackern bang," 1: 28), the "brides of Christ" fall into the lake, claimed by "schwarze knaben" who represent demonic forces of nature threatening the life of spiritual devotion.[7]

In both these poems, the seasons symbolize the power of natural change. Elsewhere they are used to mark the pilgrim's readiness — or unpreparedness — for commitment and love. In the simple-sounding bal-lad "Lass deine tränen" (Why do you squander your tears) he is exhorted to cease his fruitless pining, to watch for the melting of the snows, the warming of the ground, and then the achievement of summer's full matu-rity before the time will be ripe to see the woman he desires "ohne schleier" (1: 29), with her true self unveiled. The yellow tea-rose that "In alte lande laden bogenhallen" (To ancient lands the vaulted passage calls) evokes is another image of a strong, perfect woman, "ohne weissen tadel · / mächtige mildelose" (1: 30–31), whose very perfection wounds the unready poet-pilgrim who attempts to enter the garden that is her domain "zu früh noch." His immaturity and her inaccessibility are further symbol-ized by his search for the scent of early violets, which — "zu früh noch" — he cannot find growing wild and must seek in hot-houses. Not ready either for the elegant, cultivated rose, too soon for the simple violet, his emotions are out of kilter with the proper cycle of love.

The flowers evoked in this sixth poem of the cycle also have delicate poetological overtones, and the bringing on of the wild violet beloved of Goethe under glass in Maeterlinckian *serres chaudes* is indicative of a form of poetry that wills its independence of Romantic nature because it is not properly integrated into it.[8] Similar suggestions, anticipating the aesthetic of *Algabal*, are evident in "Mahnung" (Warning) as the pilgrim imagines himself an imperial conqueror before whom defeated peoples, women in particular, prostrate themselves: "Entführte weiber weinen ihren gram / Und eine · wirr im schrecken · ohne scham / Zerreisst vor deinem herrenblick ihr kleid" (1: 32–33). The shameless depravity of such displays is paralleled by a more dignified offer as "Die priesterin in züchtigem talar / Verneigt sich grüssend: siehe deine magd," but this is no less threatening, for to be tempted is to sink lower than the animals, to the level of the dirt in which the beasts scrape their claws. The stance of the all-powerful autocrat represents the condition of the isolated artist, associated imagistically with the aesthetic loftiness of Symbolism (the throne is "aus grellem gelbem seidenstoff / Und rohem gold das oft von blute troff" and "Koralle perle demant und smaragd" are strewn before him), although at this point, prior to *Algabal,* the pilgrim rejects this vision of the nature of his vocation — indeed he condemns it in "Ihr alten bilder" (My early visions!) as "verderbnisvolle pracht" (1: 36).

At the same time he rejects the temptation to use his own suffering as the yardstick against which to measure his progress — "sag nicht dass dein leid dein führer sei" (1: 33) — an idea developed more fully in the following few poems, notably in "Schweige die klage!" (Silence despair) where the pilgrim's staff and habit are buried in the earth and the flood of pent-up emotions and sensations released by this symbolic act divorcing past suffering from the future self also prompt him to wonder whether he should not smash his lyre, too, and thereby the very instrument of his poetry. In "Mächtiger traum dem ich zugetraut" (Sovereign dream I trusted at heart) he speculated that pleasure in the ordinary world outside may indeed offer the seeds of a new life: "Läg im vergnügen an fasslichen tönen / Die mir seit monden im munde dröhnen / Zu neuer erscheinung ein keim? / Kehr ich nun zu wahren auen heim?" (1: 34). Here "erscheinung" might be the manifestation of the self in his poetry, just as the phonetic diffraction of the crucial word "keim" into "*k*ehr" and "h*eim*" enclosing and embracing the last line poetically enacts the potential growth and fruit from the seed. The Muse in "Lass der trauer kleid und miene" (Doff your mourning mien and vesture) encourages the abandonment of the topos of suffering but promises no alternative consolation. Again the imagery of the seasons is enlisted to show how untimely is the pilgrim's wresting with his pent-up anger whilst the world outside is joyful, and that the raging of winter storms does not mean that roses will never blossom and corn will never ripen.

While waiting for his own seasoned maturity, the poet's task is to prevent the lyre's strings from rusting and to sing not of present sorrow but of past journeys reaching back as far as childhood — the subject of the next group of poems. Initially, however, there is some doubt concerning the poet's capacity to reinvigorate "Ihr alten bilder." Caught between a present he cannot celebrate and a past he cannot reach, he is anxious about resorting to a damaging artificial aesthetic, "verderbnisvolle pracht" (1: 36). Here and in "Dass er auf fernem felsenpfade" (Would that on mountain walks alone) he is haunted by "the phantoms of autonomous images [. . .] images unrelated to his actual experience, mere romantic fantasies" (Metzger and Metzger 54), which fascinate and tempt him into dangerous territory. The swamp is home to a seductive white lily, akin to the Romantics' Blue Flower, but for George's aesthetic a "Böser engel · verführender engel!" (1: 37). Art must be purer, less concerned with the triumph over personal suffering or with Romantic subjectivity, and the final poem of the collection, "Die Spange" (The Clasp, 1: 40), returns once more to the ideal of Symbolist art despite the poet's fears of "verderbnisvolle pracht." The poet's artistic ideal is simplicity and strength — "Ich wollte sie aus kühlem eisen / Und wie ein glatter fester streif," suggesting perhaps a new German poetic ideal — but no such material is available to him, "kein metall zum gusse reif." Instead, and regretfully, he turns to a foreign form, "eine grosse *fremde* dolde" (my emphasis), made of gold not iron, and studded with the "reiches blitzendes gestein" which is the hallmark of the Symbolist aesthetic that will be explored more thoroughly in *Algabal.* The *Pilgerfahrten* are extremely ambivalent about this, and suggest that it is attractive only because the search for love and art that properly fit the poet's own being has failed. They are dedicated to Hofmannsthal, although the poems were all written before George met him in Vienna at the end of 1891. The motto (added in 1899) certainly echoes George's feelings about his attempt to recruit Hofmannsthal to his way of writing, and about Hofmannsthal's refusal to follow: "ALSO BRACH ICH AUF / UND EIN FREMDLING WARD ICH / UND ICH SUCHTE EINEN / DER MIT MIR TRAUERTE / UND KEINER WAR" (1: 26).[9]

After the medievalizing asceticism of the pilgrim comes the decadence of the late Roman empire, although this decadence assumes a peculiarly Georgean slant. Algabal is named after Heliogabalus, the notoriously sybaritic Roman Emperor who reigned from the age of fourteen in A.D. 218 until he was murdered by his own Praetorian Guard in 222, in disgust at his cruelty and debauchery. George was aware of some of the historical sources for the life of Heliogabalus, but his reign had already become a topos of decadence for French writers such as Gautier, Verlaine, and Huysmans with whom he was certainly more familiar.[10] However, George's Algabal is not characterized by decadence in the sense of unbridled sexual indulgence or effete lassitude; he does not preside over moral collapse but displays moral indifference, subordinating ethics to aesthetics. Features derived from Heliogabalus are autarchic power, wealth, and an eye for costly beauty, as the dedication of the second edition to Ludwig II of Bavaria implicitly acknowledges. In a much less decadent manner, and with some ambivalence, George's Algabal is stylized into a hieratic figure of priestly dignity and unworldly alterity to symbolize the high calling of poetry — characteristics perhaps more appropriate to his original choice of dedicatee, Hugo von Hofmannsthal.[11]

The first four of the twenty-two poems in *Algabal* form the section "Im Unterreich" (The Realm Below). They evoke a subterranean world of anti-nature and luxurious artificiality, the product of its creator's will alone, with "häuser und höfe wie er sie ersonnen" (1: 45), conjured from the Master's imaginings. The garden he has made is sterile, "bedarf nicht luft und nicht wärme" (1: 47), its trees are made of charcoal, their fruit of lava, and a gray mist hides the rising and setting of the sun. And yet even though it is completely underground, the palace is ablaze with light — Heliogabalus was after all high-priest of the Syro-Phoenician cult of the sun — the third poem in particular is replete with evocations of white, brightness, and refracted luster. "Der Eine" is the only one not dazzled by all this splendor, and it is a combination of his isolation and a memory of childhood that elicits a tear from the Emperor of the Under-Realm, thus introducing an important note of vulnerability into the collection.

The rivers of garnets and rubies, fiery fountains of topaz and amber, and decorations of ivory, opals, diamonds, alabaster, and crystal (1: 45–46) all reflect George's debt to the "paradis artificiels" of Baudelaire and the landscape of his "Rêve parisien" (Parisian Dream).[12] The scents of "amber, weihrauch und zitrone" (1: 46) rising from three thousand massive urns recall Baudelaire's "Correspondances" in some detail: "[des parfums] corrompus, riches et triomphants, / Ayant l'expansion des choses infinies, / Comme l'ambre, le musc, le benjoin et l'encens, / Qui chantent les transports de l'esprit et des sens" (Baudelaire 1: 11). Crucially, George has also borrowed from Baudelaire the association of artificial landscapes and poetry. As the last stanza of the fourth poem shows, his central dilemma is to render the sterile landscape fruitful: "Wie zeug ich dich aber im heiligtume [. . .] Dunkle grosse schwarze blume?" (1: 47). The black flower, unlike the entirely black *repas de deuil* in Huysmans' *A rebours* (1884), is not designed to induce the decadent's illicit frisson of moral daring: it is a poetological provocation.[13] By deliberately negating the Romantics' symbol of longing, the Blue Flower, George rejects the Romantic tradition and the world of natural feeling, posing himself the problem of a new aesthetic for German poetry, based on the Symbolists' primacy of the word over lived experience.

The second section, "Tage" (Days), moves from depicting the underground kingdom to episodes depicting the nature and character of its absolute ruler. Algabal aspires to a life between apparently irreconcilable paradoxical opposites, crying "O lass mich ungerühmt und ungehasst / Frei in den bedingten bahnen wandeln" (1: 50), striving to transcend human emotion, enjoying freedom within patterns of constraint. This final paradox is reminiscent of Baudelaire's response to the exigencies of literary form, "les bénéfices éternels de la contrainte."[14] Warning his machiavellian grandmother not to try to disaffect his brother, Algabal suggests that it is a mistake to regard his own inaction and peaceful demeanor as manifestations of weakness; he is perfectly able to master the mysterious combination of love and violence and knows that if he sees the latter's headless corpse dripping blood onto the white marble of a staircase, he will merely pull his regal train out of the way of the gore, unmoved (1: 50). Banqueting guests are stifled in torrents of rose-petals, the gesture communicated more in terms of love than of cruelty, "liebkosen," "laben" or "segnen" (1: 51). His aim is to obviate the disillusion of a return to mundane life after the sensual excitement of the feast, so their death is an act both of murder and of transfiguration. Even in moments of tenderness, such as when the proud Algabal comforts Agathon who is anxious about the imminent loss of his youth and beauty, there is a combination of vulnerability and mastery. Agathon alone is privileged to hear the Emperor's own acceptance of his mortality; he and Algabal enjoy such nobility, of beauty or birth, that it is beneath them to lament the passing of earthly time.

There is at the root of some of these poems a belief that death or the denial of life will produce fulfillment or self-realization, which is perhaps why Algabal shows such equanimity by anticipating rebellion with plans for his own suicide. In the fifth poem, Algabal, unable to sleep, has Egyptian flautists come to play to him, and is transported, finding himself "in äthergezelten" and eating the bread of heaven. Music has the power to bring about blissful oblivion, and he sighs for more: "entrückt und tötet mich wieder / Flötenspieler vom Nil" (1: 51). Algabal's relationship with his people has something of his own dividedness; by torturing and crucifying them he inflicts on them what he feels life inflicts on him; but when he disguises himself and walks among them, far from feeling hatred for a group he cannot comprehend, he comes to see that he has never properly understood his own harshness — or, in poetic terms, doubts emerge about whether he can maintain the rigorous stance demanded by his conception of poetry. His response is another gentle, trembling moment of otherworldliness as he locks himself away from the world and suspends his will: "Ich ruhte ohne wunsch und mild und licht" (1: 52). In his mirror he sees himself almost as his own sister, androgyny here being another instance of the coexistence of opposites that characterizes this section of the cycle.

Just as in *Hymnen* and *Pilgerfahrten* the third section of *Algabal*, "Die Andenken" (Memories), is retrospective. Here Algabal enjoys a final stage of contemplation before death, lifted beyond the contingencies of life by dreams and memories of childhood and youth, when he lived in anticipation of triumph, blissfully planning, "bang vor eigener gedanken wucht" (1: 55), adored by his soldiers almost as a god. He recalls his precipitous courtship of a Vestal virgin, her stern yet confident demeanor and their sumptuous marriage, but also that he repudiated her, because "sie hatte wie die anderen ein mal" (1: 57). Arguing on the basis of George's homosexuality, some interpret this "flaw" to be her femininity, but others more plausibly see it as a reference to her capacity for human feeling, which for Algabal will always have been a weakness.[15] Their ideal condition, *au-dessus de la mêlée*, is not sustainable, unlike that of the young lovers who have fallen asleep after making love and whom he poisons so as to spare them both punishment and the disillusion of waking from perfect dream into imperfect reality (1: 57). He remembers his own sexual initiation as the destruction of a beautiful dream, causing him to crave death as a release from the distress of the loss of innocence.

The final poem, "Vogelschau" ("Augury" 1: 59) is the only one in *Algabal* to bear a title. Its first three stanzas have been mapped onto the collections *Hymnen, Algabal,* and *Pilgerfahrten,* and more plausibly onto the three sections of *Algabal* itself (in reverse, the snow-white swallows representing the unspoiled condition of the young Algabal remembered in "Die Andenken," the many-colored parrots and humming-birds in the second his glorious "Tage" as Emperor at the peak of his powers, and the black ravens and jackdaws in the third the garden of the "Unterreich"). But this neglects the complexities and ambivalences of each section, and the poem reads more satisfactorily not as a description of "phases" in Algabal's development but as a summation of the poetic challenge that George set himself by evoking the "schwarze blume." His ideal was poetry of a purity suggested by the white swallows, hovering "hell und heiss"; it consisted partly of dreams, visions and imaginings, as exotic and alien to ordinary reality as the jungle birds darting through the "wunder-bäume" in the Forest of the Tusferi, but with a component of mystery suggested by the ravens "im verzauberten gehau" and the threat implied by the snakes. The final stanza, which, unlike the previous three, is in present tense, suggests that the vision of purity is sustainable nonetheless.

George's remark in a letter to Hofmannsthal of January 1892 — "denn was ich nach Halgabal noch schreiben soll ist mir unfasslich" — is often quoted, but rarely in its context.[16] It follows a confession about the kind of soul mate George had been searching for:

> Schon lange im leben sehnte ich mich nach jenem wesen von einer verachtenden durchdringenden und überfeinen verstandeskraft die alles verzeiht begreift würdigt und die mit mir über die dinge und die erscheinungen hinflöge · und sonderbar dies wesen sollte trotzdem etwas von einem nebelüberzug haben und unter einem zwang des gewissen romantischen aufputzes von adel und ehre stehen von dem es sich nicht ganz lösen kann. (*Briefwechsel zwischen George und Hofmannsthal* 12)

There is something of Algabal in this picture, and the image of soaring over the world is as if taken from "Vogelschau." There is something of Algabal, too, in the self-doubt that George confessed to Hofmannsthal's father shortly afterwards, referring to the young Viennese poet as "die erste

person auf deutscher seite die [. . .] mein schaffen verstanden und
gewürdigt . . und das zu einer zeit wo ich auf meinem einsamen felsen zu
zittern anfing" (*Briefwechsel zwischen George und Hofmannsthal* 242).
There was indeed something of a block; during most of 1892 George
worked largely on translations, the first issue of the *Blätter,* and poems in
French. A solution to the problem of what was to follow *Algabal* came in
the winter of 1892–93, with the first poems of *Das Jahr der Seele,* and was
facilitated by a replacement for Hofmannsthal in George's affections in the
complex figure of Ida Coblenz.[17] At the same time, he had become interested in the adaptation of ancient lyric forms. This is not to say, however,
that George's work at this point suddenly became confessional, imitative
or derivative, or that he turned his back on the poetic development represented by *Hymnen, Pilgerfahrten,* and *Algabal.* On the contrary, the
*Bücher der Hirten- und Preisgedichte, der Sagen und Sänge, und der
Hängenden Gärten* demonstrate strong elements of continuity with the
earlier collections: "dans ces trois livres plus encore que [dans] mes œuvres
publiés l'âme ne voit pas directement [mais] sous un certain angle —
l'époque culturelle: le premier classique, hellénique, attique, idyllique
d'une claire tranquillité, le second moyen âge mystique et pieux, le
troisième oriental bizarre et luxurieux."[18] They are set in three historically
distant, idealized cultural contexts: Classical Antiquity, the Middle Ages,
and a temporally indeterminate Orient (a trio that parallels the three collections of the earlier 1890s), each symbolically displacing present (poetic)
concerns into one of three religiously distinct cultures as the preface states:
"Jede zeit und jeder geist rücken indem sie fremde und vergangenheit
nach eigner art gestalten ins reich des persönlichen und heutigen und von
unsren drei grossen bildungswelten ist hier nicht mehr enthalten als in eini-
gen von uns noch eben lebt" (1: 63).

There is every indication that George worked on all three books more
or less at the same time. Most of the poems for the trilogy were completed
in 1893, with some of the *Sagen* originally written in French in late 1892
or early 1893 before being rendered in German in the spring of 1893
along with the rest of that book, and some of the poems for the third book
were completed in the summer of 1894.[19] Several individual poems were
published in the *Blätter* and elsewhere before the first book edition of
1895 (by the Verlag der Blätter für die Kunst), a limited edition of two
hundred copies printed on hand-made paper. Seven of the *Sagen* appeared
in French in the December 1895 edition of the Belgian journal *Réveil* very
soon after the first German edition, and a second German edition, by
Bondi, appeared in Berlin in November 1898 (dated 1899).

Algabal made use of late Roman subject matter, but the *Hirten- und
Preisgedichte* evoke the "kühlere und reinere Luft" (Schulz 93) of the classical world, as much formally and tonally as by way of historical allusion. The
ideal pastoral world — Greek *and* Roman, certainly, although Hofmannsthal

remarked in a review of 1896 that these poems owed more "dem Tone des Tibull und Horaz als dem der Griechen" (Hofmannsthal, "Gedichte von Stefan George" 220) — is suggested in the use of unrhymed verse and classical meters or verse forms (including echoes of rare forms like the amphibrach, the choriambus or the Horatian asclepiad),[20] and above all in the epigrammatic distichs of the second part, the *Preisgedichte auf einige junge Männer und Frauen dieser Zeit* (Eulogies on Some Young Men and Women of Our Time). The symbolic world of these poems is no less dense than in the earlier cycles, but the diction enjoys a classical clarity and apparent simplicity new in George's verse.

The world of the *Hirtengedichte* is peopled with simple human types characterized by an unsophisticated faith in pastoral gods and their rituals, although simplicity is by no means always associated with happiness. In "Jahrestag" (Anniversary) two women commemorate the deaths of their husbands-to-be on the same day "in frommer wiederholung" (1: 65) by drawing water from the spring between two poplar trees and a spruce. In "Erkenntag" (Day of Recognition) each tentatively discovers how the other's hopes match her own, and in the quiet communion of mutual recognition they strike a profound bond of friendship, anchored in faith in the power of the constellations, the swan and the lyre, to bring about "das schöne wunder" (1: 65) which is love. In the third poem, "Loostag" (Day of Destiny), a threat to the bond is presaged by the resurgence of another passionate elemental force symbolized in the vines of Dionysus. The mysterious power of nature to command celebration in the form of song structures "Der Tag des Hirten" (Shepherd's Day). The spring fields call musically to the shepherd — "ihm riefen singende gelände zu" (1: 66) — but he prefers the shade of the trees and the sound of the water in the precipitous streams. Images of darkness and depth lead him and the reader to a place of eerie silence at the heart of the woods — "Im schweigen und erschauern dichter wipfel / Entschlief er während hoch die sonne stand" — before the end of the poem rises and unfolds into the light on the hilltop where the poet-shepherd crowns himself "mit heilgem laub" (1: 67), singing loudly his paeon to nature.

The god Pan seems to lurk implicitly in "Der Tag des Hirten," and the *Hirtengedichte* now turn overtly to the supernatural. The Faun complains in "Flurgottes Trauer" (Field-God's Sorrow 1: 67) that the Lord of the Harvest did not give him the beauty he needs to seduce the human girls, despite his skill with his pipes — his vexation reminding us of the fate of the artist isolated from ordinary humanity. And yet the artist may be just as far removed from the dignity of the immortals: as the Faun's attempts to write are frustrated by a beautiful nymph or nixie in "Zwiegespräch im Schilf" (Dialogue in the Reeds), he threatens to stab himself, unable to realize his desires for immortalizing life in verse.[21] Most famously "Der Herr der Insel" (The Lord of the Island) stands for the poet, cut off from "mainland" humanity on a luxurious isle rich in oils and spices, where precious stones are mixed with the sand on the beach — or so the fishermen tell, for the whole poem is clearly marked as a report by the subjunctive verbs, a device that heightens its mythic, even parabolic quality. The Lord is said to be a majestic bird (unnamed, but like the Roc from the *Arabian Nights* with huge wings that can block out the sun like a cloud): he sings sweetly to dolphins, described with an allusion to the Arion myth as an elite group of "freunde des gesanges" (1: 69), and is seen only by a few unfortunate "gescheiterte" (suggesting both shipwrecked sailors and life's miserable failures). When humanity approaches in the form of a sail on the horizon, the Lord is said to have climbed to the highest peak, spread his wings and sung, "Verscheidend in gedämpften schmerzeslauten" (1: 70) so that even his last utterances were muffled from the wider public. The poem is related, perhaps consciously, to Baudelaire's allegory of the poet in modern society, "L'albatros" (Baudelaire 1: 9–10), also a prince of the clouds with giant wings, but the crucial difference is that the albatross in the French poem is hobbled by the sailors, by common humanity — a much more straightforwardly Romantic view — whereas George's magnificent bird is a prisoner of his own vision.

Misfortune, even tragedy, is often a component in the dignity of the elect in the world of the *Hirtengedichte*. The innocent, uncomprehending children singled out in "Der Auszug der Erstlinge" (Exodus of the Firstborn) are willingly sacrificed in propitiation of a god. "Das Geheimopfer" (Secret Sacrifice) describes the ritual purification of young men who have left gracious society and are tied to pillars of bronze before being exposed to the unveiled countenance of the godhead to die, "In sprühender kraft / In zehrendem schmerz / In glühendem rausch" (1: 71).[22] They too die willingly, "[im] dienst / Des Schönen: des Höchsten und Grössten," and their ecstasy stands in sharp contrast to the despair of those *not* chosen as temple servants in "Abend des Festes" (After the Festival); rejected for not being sufficiently beautiful, they can never again tolerate the lesser life of ordinary humanity. Their counterpart in the world of action and heroism is the champion in "Das Ende des Siegers" (The End of the Victor), who withdraws, "allein sich in leiden verzehrend" (1: 74), no longer fit for public approbation. Underlying all these poems is a conception of service and devotion to an ideal of integrity in humanity and art that is implicitly shared by the whole community, the elect and the mass — the successful manifestation of which is apparent in the two favorites of the people, the Wrestler and the Lyre Player, who embody a form of art in which artist and populace are not mutually alienated. A note of tension between the private and the public only creeps in with "Erinna" (1: 73), whose song is so perfect that the trees and the very stars tremble in delight: her self-doubt is not for its public efficacy, but for whether her poetry will move the man she loves.

Integrity is what links the Eclogues to the Eulogies, eleven portraits of George's friends, disguised with Greek names and celebrated as instances of friendship, whether fully realized or not, with timeless value. Not all the relationships commemorated were plain-sailing; several poems record partings, loss, disputes or disappointment, sometimes seeming even to mock (as Ludwig Klages is teased at the end of "An Isokrates," where he is described as having the "unschuldig grausame miene des kindes" [1: 79]). The unidentifiable Apollonia is lost, married to the poet's friend, for example, and the poem to Kallimachus (the Polish poet and translator Waclaw Rolicz-Lieder [1866–1912]) seems torn between expressions of grief at their parting — "letzte segenrufe [. . .] verhaltenes weinen" (1: 77) — and frustration that he is determined to return to the "barbarenhofe" of Russian-occupied Warsaw and leave behind the friendships he has established. "An Antinous" commemorates another parting, from Edmond Rassenfosse (1874–1947), and George here seems inconsolable; his friend's suggestion that the countryside would be a comfort, "zeigt sich jetzt als trügend," and he remembers tearfully "ein lächeln [. . .] lieblicher / Als alle vogelstimmen" (1: 80).

The bond with Sidonia (whose counterpart is also unknown) emerges from unpromising beginnings, "Deine berechnende lippe · dein blauer und stählerner blick" (1: 77) into a sympathetic and symbolic holding of hands as she reveals how she had been willing to sacrifice all for a younger man who then rejected her. Similarly, "An Kotytto" (to the Munich singer Frieda Zimmer-Zerny) is ambivalently called "blume süss im duft doch herben schmackes" (1: 80). Friendship at its best, however, is celebrated in the poem to Albert Saint-Paul ("An Damon") as a condition of peace, "Sinneverklärende ruh" (1: 75), which lifts those who share it above the realm of "Sterbliche wesen," and there is a suggestion in the second poem to Menippa (published well before George's break with its dedicatee, Ida Coblenz) that their friendship has been compromised by her failure to maintain such aristocratic distance from "gespielen die du doch verachtest" (1: 76). Even the most lyrical poems are shot through with the sense that the condition of mutual happiness is fragile and temporary: "Die furcht dass augenblicke wir genössen / Wie sie spät nicht widerkämen: / Sie warfen milde schatten lang auf deine / Phaon! und auf meine wege" (1: 78, to Paul Gérardy [1870–1933]). As a whole, the *Preisgedichte* are unusually gentle and restrained, the result partly of George's fluent handling of long, unrhymed lines " 'antikischer' im Metrum als die Hirtengedichte" (without being direct imitations), and of being addressed to a "Du" figure (Schulz 110).

Like the first book of the trilogy, the *Sagen und Sänge* are divided into two distinct sections, both set in the Middle Ages, French as much as German, although largely without overt formal imitation of medieval literature. Whilst the function of each historical location is to provide a simplified canvas for modern or timeless emotions, there is a clear dissociation of sensibility between this world and George's version of classical antiquity. That was a place largely without inner turmoil and conflict in which fate or destiny, in whatever form, was unquestioningly obeyed; the noble and religious inhabitants of George's medieval world, however, are blessed or cursed with active willpower and take up personal moral and emotional struggles between physical desire and spiritual calling that the *Hymnen, Pilgerfahrten,* and *Algabal* have already explored. This is apparent from the opening poem — at forty-seven lines the longest in the trilogy — in which a young man on the threshold of adulthood and knighthood completes his "Sporenwache" (Vigil of Arms) in a church, vowing purity and devotion to God and his chivalric calling. He is encouraged by the tomb of a noble ancestor and the family coat of arms, held by a cherub, but his fervent prayers are unwittingly interrupted by a vision of a golden-haired girl, indicating the irruption of sensuality into piety.[23] He looks to the Virgin Mary and the Lord Jesus to save him from this vision of a non-spiritual virgin and prays forgiveness for faltering. This may be a momentary slip from the path of purity and self-abnegation, but a fundamental tension is nonetheless established. It is interesting that the vision of the beautiful girl emerges as the knight prays most earnestly, "bittet brünstig Den da oben / Und bricht gelernten spruches enge schranken" (1: 83), for in the last poem of this section "Das Bild" (The Image) the monk prays to the Virgin in a similar manner: "Entflossen gebete mir ohne anfang und schluss / Wie nie in den sammetenen buch ich sie ähnlich gefunden" (1: 91). Both pray desperately from the heart, breaking with conventional forms, the monk daring even to kiss the image of the Mother of God before becoming angry at her failure to grant him a sign of her love.[24] The point where the personal invades the traditional is clearly a weak spot, although the knight's steadfastness contrasts with the monk's bleak prospect.

The Legends make full use of the most evocative paraphernalia of the Middle Ages, with references to dragon-slaying adventures (1: 84 and 87), the carrying of a lady's silken favor in tournaments (1: 86), deeds of bravery (1: 52), knightly brotherhood (1: 52–53), the figure of the wandering minstrel (1: 93–98), and suggestions of the court dwarf in the "Lied des Zwergen" (Ditties of a Dwarf, 1: 97). They also evoke love with particular intensity. The knight about to leave for the wars in "Tagelied" (Aubade) tries to stem his beloved's tears with assurances that he worships her body with the devotion usually reserved for the Eucharist, "mit gesenktem lid / So wie man Gott empfängt" (1: 86), which is as powerful as Faust's similar, more famous blasphemy, and more Romantic than medieval in sentiment.[25] Even when spurned, like the young lad in "Die Tat" (The Deed), the lover in "Im unglücklichen Tone dessen von . . ." (In the Unhappy Manner of . . .) or Frauenlob himself (1: 84–85), the men of the Middle Ages maintain an almost worshipful attitude of respect, cultivating their rejection for its very intensity. A father's love for his chivalrous son is rendered all the more poignant as the young man spurns the peace and security of his parent's hermit-cell for honor and glory in the field; heaven has not accepted the father's "reiches lösegeld" (1: 91), ironically a symbol of his *renunciation* of earthly wealth. Perhaps the culminating image of rejection and ultimate redemption, however, is in "Irrende Schar" (Knights Errant), as the knights "dulden zu der andren heil" (1: 88) but are kept at the margins of society, the subject of grotesque rumors, praised for their help but soon forgotten. Their reward is in the evening of their lives, as they are led "Zur burg worin das Höchste Licht [. . .] Auf immer ihnen rast verspricht" — the Grail Castle — where "Sie werden selig unter hallen / Die unvergänglich neu und schön" (1: 88).

The *Sänge eines fahrenden Spielmanns* (Strains of a Wandering Gleeman), some of which were set to music by Karl Hallwachs (1870–1959) even before their publication,[26] lyrically develop the theme of love from the first part of the *Buch der Sagen und Sänge,* but with the emphasis on loss, on the unattainability of the object of desire. In the first eight of the Lays the minstrel has mastered a pose of intense but stylized devotion, he sings to his beloved in his imagination, so rapt in admiration that he almost hears her voice echoing his (1: 94–95). He is content to sit at her feet and gently kiss her hand (1: 94), and prefers to leave her rather than to trouble her even with the mere telling of "Menschen müh und weh" (1: 95). His song is an unreliable instrument of wooing. The first poem, "Worte trügen · worte fliehen" (Words delude and words deceive, 1: 93), aims to fix the figures of dreams in form (for the poet has the power to counteract the delusions of words by shaping them, and "Nur das Lied ergreift die seele"), but the third wonders whether the song is the best means of convincing a skeptical beloved, alongside traditional gifts of flowers or the wearing of her colors, or whether a simple declaration of love might be more efficacious. The pose is ironically undermined by lines seven and eight of the last song in this group, "Ist es neu dir was vermocht" (Have you never felt before), as the minstrel, anxiously awaiting the outcome of his suit, concedes "Ach du weisst dass du nicht stirbst / Ruft es wiederum: entsage!" (1: 96). Potentially this also undermines George's whole undertaking in the three *Bücher,* for the adoption of poetic roles and masks is thus radically divorced from the perception of existential truth, and the gesture of renunciation on which so much stress has been laid is merely rhetorical. The repetition of an unusually long refrain re-establishes the conventional song-like mold and draws us away from a glimpse into the abyss. Amongst the remaining poems of this book, "Ein edelkind sah vom balkon" (A Lord's child leaned from the sill) and "Erwachen der Braut" (Awakening of the Bride), by leaving aside the lyric persona of the minstrel (and in the former making him a character in the narrative) reinstate a sense of the seriousness of love particularly as articulated through music. The nobleman's daughter is frightened by the love song she hears and throws away her ring which has become a symbol of a bond that has disturbed her by marking the end of childhood innocence; the bride trembles with anticipation and apprehension as the horn-call announces her wedding day. The last poem reads like a prayer from either figure to the Virgin Mary, "frau der frauen" (1: 98). It shares with many in the *Sagen und Sänge* a complex personal questioning, the repeated protasis in "Wenn ich voll vertrauen / Wenn ich ohne sünde / Deine macht verkünde" preceding the simple apodosis "Schenkst du mir worum ich lange bat?" (1: 98) suggesting the all-too-human condition of one almost bargaining with the divine for human love, not as unlike the stylized calculations of the minstrel as the Christian context and prayer-form might at first suggest.[27]

Orientalism had featured in George's youthful works before the *Bücher*, notably in the moralizing poems of *Prinz Indra* and in aspects of the drama *Manuel*. Nonetheless, the shift within the *Bücher* from the medieval to the oriental is dramatic and many commentators have identified a radically different, radically modern character in *Das Buch der hängenden Gärten*. Schoenberg famously "found the poetry of Dehmel more suited to his compositional needs at the turn of the century and George's poetry [specifically the 'Semiramislieder'] a more appropriate midwife for atonality."[28] In a letter to George, Melchior Lechter concludes his response to the three books, "In den 'Gärten' steigert sich [. . .] der farbige Klang und die klingende Farbe zu erstaunlicher Modernität."[29] The subject matter itself is ancient and quasi-mythical, and the book's title refers to one of the seven wonders of the world, the hanging gardens of Babylon built, it is usually supposed, during the sixth century B.C. by Nebuchadnezzar II on the bank of the River Euphrates in honor of one of his wives. This was not Semiramis, however, whose regency was more than two hundred years earlier in circa 810–805 B.C.; the fifteen "Semiramis Poems" in the central section were so called by Ida Coblenz in letters to George, but never by George himself.[30]

In many respects *Das Buch der hängenden Gärten* echoes *Algabal*. Its central figure is a poet-king, its setting is extravagant and luxurious, richly bejewelled and scented with exotic aromatics and unguents. *Algabal*'s affinity with the poetry of the French Symbolists is similarly in evidence in this collection, and the crafted opulence of its verse is Mallarméan in inspiration. Algabal's self-doubt is modulated here into a more searching consideration of the intense nature of love and of its effects on individual selfhood and carried to a more logical conclusion. The scenario of *Das Buch der hängenden Gärten* is explicitly one recovered from an earlier time — the opening words are "Wir werden *noch einmal* zum lande fliegen / Das dir *von früh auf* eigen war" (1: 99, my emphasis). The plural pronoun almost suggests the opening of a magical storybook tale, a narrator encouraging a reader to become part of the dream-world he is about to conjure up — a world that the addressee instinctively or innately seems to belong to him. "Kindliches Königtum" (A Child's Kingdom) fills in some of this narrative, showing the poet-king as a boy selecting gems for his crown, establishing himself as a leader and enjoying the adoration of his underlings. Between the first and the second poem, however, the narrative shifts immediately to the first person as the central figure assumes control. When he approaches his world even the palm trees bow in submission and a radical transformation of sensibility — "wandel der seele" — occurs in the *Ich*-persona, who now sees "offene bahnen / Nach den ersehnten höchsten stufen" open before him (1: 99). The tension between the noble self-restraint of a ruler and the sybaritic self-indulgence of a conqueror familiar from *Algabal* and "Mahnung" in the *Pilgerfahrten* is at once apparent as a voice is heard inducing him to forget "Die würde so dir anvertraut" in favor of "Der weichen wünsche frevel" (1: 100). The first stanza of "In hohen palästen" (The palaces reared) suggests that he succumbs for a while to these physical blandishments. Its imagery and vocabulary are heavily sexualized in a way that exceeds anything in *Algabal:* naked bodies are likened first statuesquely to blue-veined white marble, then sensuously to the juicy rich yellow of perfectly ripe grapes, then evoked directly with phonetic patterns making extravagant use of licking "l" sounds — "Die leiber die hellrot wie blüten und hochrot wie blut" — and with a suggestive imagistic *Steigerung* from anticipatory pale-red blossom to full-blooded passionate intensity. Similar images are used later in "Vorbereitungen" (Preparations) as the king's chosen bride is physically bathed and anointed with oils and salves, although the state of mind being cultivated is one of "tiefer zucht" (1: 103). The images of the bud and the ripening fruit in this poem are simultaneous qualities rather than sequential, and they serve to heighten the tension between potential and fulfillment. After lingering evocations of devoted physical and mental preparation, the last line, intimating that the bride may never in fact be permitted to touch her lord, is a powerful restatement of the same theme.

In fact, the second stanza of "In hohen palästen" shows the newly returned king renouncing the orgiastic delights in favor of "Erhabnes geniessen berauschender sieges-gebräuche" (1: 100) — rather as his bride in "Vorbereitungen" is enjoined "[den] Geist in einsamkeit zu schonen" (1: 103). He still feels the threat of melancholy and wonders whether, if he chases this away with wine, the noise of his warriors arming themselves on the morrow will be sufficient to wake him. The force of arms invigorates him and, untroubled by Algabal's self-doubt, he is transfigured by a shaft of sunlight as he wanders the city he has devastated and lifts his sword to smash the idols in its ruined temple. In stark contrast to poems of such action, the remaining poems of this section are limpidly calm, the seventh,

"Halte die purpur- und goldenen gedanken im zaum" (Bridle your phantasies, golden and purple), showing the king in a state of almost transcendental meditation, his worldly thoughts banished, birds settling to a siesta, no music, military noises receding in the distance, yet transported by the complex architectural forms of a tower: "Verschlungenes gefüge / Geschnörkelte züge / Verbieten die lüge / Von wesen und welt" (1: 102). Art is the realm in which the contradictions of self and world are resolved.

This may be the sense of the last stanza of "Friedensabend" (Evening of Peace), which closes the first section of *Das Buch der hängenden Gärten:* the conquests are complete, the landscape and its inhabitants are at rest, memories of past campaigns recede, and "Im dichten dunste dringt nur dumpf und selten / Ein ton herauf aus unterworfnen welten" (1: 104). This mysterious tone from realms buried deep in the unconscious is allowed to resurface only when the mind is brought to a state of perfect rest by art. In this case the central section of the cycle, the so-called "Semiramislieder," may be conceived of as an interlude, either the projection of the king's memories or the narrative of someone else's experiences, both revelatory of the profound truths of love. This seems to be how Schoenberg thought of it when he selected these texts for his Opus 15 in 1907/1908.[31] This interlude is distinguished as a separate narrative because, almost uniquely, it is comprised of wholly celebratory poems exemplifying how fulfilling love can be, even though (as the fourth and twelfth poems hint) it is in some sense illicit — the king is an intruder "in anderer herren prächtiges gebiet" (1: 106) — and despite the fact that it will end sadly.

"Als neuling trat ich ein in dein gehege" (As a novice I was drawn into your sway, 1: 105) introduces two lovers' the first meeting, but does so only after an "up-beat" of two poems that round out the physical and emotional context of "gehege." In the first, nature and even the supernatural seem agitated in anticipation of the event, the flames of candles symbolizing incipient love; in the second the paradisiacal atmosphere in the young woman's domain is equally in tune with the young man's agitation, and is sketched in economical but highly musical four-foot trochaic lines before he dismisses it as incidental: "Doch mein traum verfolgt nur eines" (1: 105). The novice appears as an emotional blank slate without wonder or wishes until he sets eyes on the woman, nervous and vulnerable, a supplicant for the right to serve. Anticipation takes his breath away, and although he registers that he still has a chance to refuse this path, a sense that she is trying to meet his gaze seals his decision. The narrative progresses quickly: the "heute" in the fifth poem ("Saget mir auf welchem pfade / Heute sie vorüberschreite" [Tell me on what path today . . .], 1: 106) clearly marks a stage in the relationship where the lovers meet in the garden, as if by chance, only for him to shower her again with expensive gifts. Something of the acute and exquisite pain of love is conveyed in the preciously exaggerated offer of his very cheeks to cushion her feet as she walks. He is paralyzed by desire, "jedem werke [. . .] fürder tot" (1: 106), and weeps because the images of her that he allows to grow in his mind while lying awake at night prove insubstantial and melt into the cold air of morning. The alternation of opposites — "Angst und hoffen wechselnd mich beklemmen" (1: 107) — is quite distinct from the paradoxes of desire and duty that dominate the rest of the cycle and its predecessors. They are not principles wrestling for control of a man's mind but the opposite emotional poles of desire, co-present in love, indeed a necessary dynamic to produce the intensity that is evoked here. Although hardly an image or an expression in this short poem is original, it uses a variety of highly effective devices to convey the symptoms of a lover's distress — an odd number of lines and a deliberately lopsided rhyme scheme (*abbcacc*); the syntactic ambiguity of the verbs in the first two lines (placed as in subordinate clauses, meaning as in main clauses); the disruption of the apparently regular pattern of "dass"-clauses in line four, which is a foot shorter than the rest and inverts subject and object. The relationship progresses to physical contact and a brief kiss in the next two poems, but the young man's emotional state is outrunning it. The beloved is akin to a drug to which he has become addicted — "Wenn ich heut nicht deinen leib berühre / Wird der faden meiner seele reissen" (1: 107) — and the fierceness of his love paradoxically consumes the kiss on which it feeds, as burning hot desert will instantly evaporate a droplet of rain, "ungenossen" (1: 107).

Morwitz argues plausibly that the change of pace in the tenth poem, "Das schöne beet betracht ich mir im harren" (Beside the lovely flower-bed I lean, 1: 108), the shift to stanzas exclusively with even numbers of lines, a preponderance of regular rhyme schemes and longer five-foot lines suggest that the lovers have consummated their passion.[32] Yet the consummation itself is surely the subject of the eleventh poem, where the lovers, finally alone, sense "nur das eigne hauchen" and tremble like reeds whenever they gently touch each other. Here, the obvious alliteration in "Beide stumm zu beben wir begannen" and the uncertain word-order underline the trembling ecstasy of their love-making. The fact that the pair risk death if they are discovered (the sand on the beach is "Bereit [. . .] unser warmes blut zu schlürfen") is rendered even more sinister by subtle parallels in structure between the eleventh and twelfth poems: both begin with temporal conjunctions, the "als" of a single event ceding to the "wenn" of multiple meetings; the fourth line of each introduces contrasting constructions, which are then picked up in the seventh ("Ich erinnere dass [. . .] Und dass [. . .]" and "So denke nicht der ungestalten schatten [. . .] Und nicht dass [. . .]" 1: 108). The shift between a poem that uses memory to reinforce love and one that demands forgetting to protect it marks the shift in the cycle towards parting. In the following poem the lovers are playfully comfortable together, but she will not step into his boat; the penultimate poem moves to a brittle two-stress line to show the man's frustration with his beloved's talk of changing seasons and the delicate mutability of dragonflies, and thus symbolically of the waning of their love — its last word is "wandelbar." Closure is finally obtained in the fifteenth of these poignant lyrics as the lover realizes "Nun ist es wahr dass sie für immer geht" (1: 109). Many of the motifs of earlier poems reappear under more somber conditions, and nature is in decline. Winter is not far away, as the pond has ice on it — a reminder of the characteristic Georgean attention to seasonal progress. The "Semiramislieder" began in spring (the second poem speaks of "blütenwiesen" 1: 105), the heat of love reflected the high summer, talk of autumn heralded its waning, and now the cycle ends in late autumn in a faded Eden of dried-up grass, brown leaves and overcast skies. In the terms of *Pilgerfahrten,* however, the love depicted here has been timely and seasonal.

The six poems in the final section of *Das Buch der hängenden Gärten* return to the poet-king for whom the "Semiramislieder" have served to underline his own predicament: erotic love, or "heidnische verzückung" (1: 111) has entrapped and debilitated him and he has sinfully neglected his calling as a king, "seines amtes heiligkeit verlezt," to the extent of losing half his realm to invading armies. The young man in the earlier sequence seems not to have had such responsibilities. Whilst the king has succeeded in punishing the traitors, he is no longer able to exact revenge by driving out the interlopers. His only consolation is "der sänger-vogel" (1: 112), which continues to sing sweetly, oblivious of the desolation around it, an image of aesthetic perfection. The king abdicates, throwing aside his diadem, abandoning his palaces and — in a poignant, metrically foreshortened line — his throne. That the "sänger-vogel" was a form of alter ego for the king is confirmed by his new role, as a slave singing to another oriental potentate, and the sudden role reversal highlights how intimately *herrschen* and *dienen* are related for George.[33] Tempted to continue the cycle of betrayal, the former king plots to kill his new master as he returns from another military triumph, but is seized by "eine neue reue" (1: 112) — one of George's few less than euphonious phrases — and retreats to the banks of the river. The last two stanzas of "Ich warf das stirn-band" (I flung my circler) shift from first to third person narrative to enact a form of self-objectivization. Symbolically the king breaks a sycamore twig to externalize the break he has made with his past and the place itself, "wo seine seele brach" (1: 113). The verb "brechen" is used for a third time in the following poem as he flees, unrecognized, unresentful, "doch flieht er weiter / Scheu weil seine hoheit bricht" (1: 113). The overwhelming sense in these last poems is of loss, loss magnified by virtue of former grandeur, what Pascal memorably called "misères d'un roi dépossédé" (Pascal 513, no. 116), and what George qualifies here as somehow beyond merely human experience: "das den menschen fremde trauern / Des der ein königtum verlor" (1: 114). Beside the river, his head in his hands, he hears mysterious voices calling in the last poem of the volume, "Stimmen im Strom" (Voices in the River). They offer refuge and security to the "liebende klagende zagende wesen" that constitute humanity in a realm that is in some respects an aquatic image of the world the king once inhabited but one that promises "selig beschauliche ruh" instead of the anguish associated with power and love. A kiss will redeem him from the trials of "das sinnen das singen" (1: 115), thought and art, and he can dissolve his self into the very waters he is contemplating.

George's early work, six collections in two books, is remarkable for the honesty with which it explores the conditions of poetry and love, although this is not a quality usually associated with the Aesthete, the Dandy or the Decadent — labels still often stuck to the young poet. The exclusivity that he undoubtedly cultivated is not born of contempt for vulgar bourgeois morality, or at least not entirely; it derives from a conviction, tested to breaking point in these works, that aesthetic quality must be forged (to use a metaphor from "Die Spange") if it is to convey anything meaningful. The austerity that characterizes his later work is clearly present from the beginning.

Notes

[1] This is the tendency in particular of Ernst Morwitz's *Kommentar*, which, although meticulously detailed, is highly positivistic in its reliance on biographical or historical evidence to support interpretation.

[2] Contrast for example David 45–47 ("diese Hymnen sind freilich nicht griechisch"), and Morwitz 7.

[3] Cf. Morwitz 13–14.

[4] Although many of the poems have traces of the real places in which they were written or conceived (see Morwitz 7–23).

[5] See also "Neuländische Liebesmahle," whose title is glossed in a letter from George to Carl Rouge: "Neuland nannte die sprache ein ewiges traumland oder einmal werdendes wahres erdenland. Liebesmahle (griech. Agape) waren in erster Zeit der aufblühenden jesuslehre die versammlungen der auserwählten," quoted in Boehringer 39.

[6] Some of Théophile Gautier's *Guide amateur au Musée du Louvre* (1882) is detectable in this poem. See Schulz 29.

[7] Siegbert Prawer links this with the thaw in section 8 of "Von alten und neuen Tafeln" in Nietzsche's *Also sprach Zarathustra* and makes of the end of George's poem an evocation of "the demonic forces at work beneath the outward calm and prosperity of the early Wilhelmine Empire." Prawer 198–99.

[8] Maurice Maeterlinck's collection of Symbolist verse, *Serres chaudes,* was published in 1889; George transcribed seven of these, probably in 1889. See Boehringer 31–32 and 212.

[9] For a refreshingly honest account of the complex dynamics of George's relationship with Hofmannsthal in this period, see Rieckmann, esp. 17–47. On the poetic manifestations of this see also Schefold, passim.

[10] See Oswald, "The Historical Content of Stefan George's *Algabal*" and "Oscar Wilde, Stefan George, Heliogabalus"; and Meesen.

[11] According to a letter of 16 January 1892 (to Hofmannsthal's father). *Briefwechsel zwischen George und Hofmannsthal*, 243.

[12] The motifs are not limited to Baudelaire, and others are found in Villiers de l'Isle-Adam's *Contes cruels* (1883), Flaubert's *Salammbô* (1862), and Huysmans's *A rebours* (1884) for example. See David 78–81.

[13] Joris-Karl Huysmans, *A rebours* (Paris: Gallimard, 1977), 89–90, said to be inspired by Heliogabalus' banquets with food all of a single color, and a possible source for George's poem.

[14] In an article on Gautier (1859), Baudelaire, *Œuvres* 2: 119.

[15] See for example Metzger and Metzger, 67, and Durzak, 244.

[16] It is not clear why George adds an "H" to *Algaba*l here, although it clearly echoes the name of the Emperor Heliogabalus and may be a deliberate mannerism.

[17] Ida Coblenz was first married to a wealthy businessman, Leopold Auerbach, but in 1901 married Richard Dehmel, who had dedicated *Weib und Welt* (Woman and World) to her in 1896. For an investigation of her relationship with George, see Thiel.

[18] Letter to Edmond Rassenfosse, March 1894, cited by Ute Oelmann, "Anhang" in Stefan George, *Sämtliche Werke in 18 Bänden* 3: 106.

[19] See *Sämtliche Werke*, 3: 106, 126, and 140.

[20] See Arbogast, "Stefan George und die Antike" in *Versuche über George*, 21–25, and "Zwischen Alexandriner und Hexameter" in the same volume, 29–49, especially 43–47.

[21] There are echoes here of Mallarmé's "L'après-midi d'un faune" and perhaps of Verlaine's "Dans la grotte" from *Fêtes galantes*.

[22] According to Morwitz these pillars may be read as "Symbol für unabänderlichen Willen zur Künstlerschaft," Morwitz 65.

[23] Schulz 33–34, shows how many of the details in this poem — with the exception of this figure — are taken from Léon Gautier, *La chevalerie* (Paris: Victor Palmé, 1884), esp. 315–16.

[24] See a similar mixture of sacred and profane in "Neuer Auffahrtssegen" (Blessing for New Quests) from *Pilgerfahrten* 1: 36–37.

[25] "Ja, ich beneide schon den Leib des Herrn, / Wenn ihre [Gretchen's] Lippen ihn indes berühren." Goethe, *Faust I* ll. 3334–45.

[26] See *Sämtliche Werke* 3: 135. They were eventually published as *Lieder eines fahrenden Spielmanns von Stefan George*, op. 12 (Mannheim: Heckel, [1901]) and *Das Lied des Zwergen von Stefan George*, op. 27 (Berlin: Deneke, 1901).

[27] There is perhaps another echo of *Faust*, the opening line of the same scene, "Wald und Höhle," as the one cited in note 27. "Erhabner Geist, du gabst mir, gabst mir alles, / Warum ich bat," ll. 3217–18.

[28] Cross and Berman xix; see also Vilain, "Schoenberg and German Poetry" in the same volume, 1–29.

[29] 24 January 1896, Ms., cited in *Sämtliche Werke* 3: 107.

[30] 29 December 1894 and 17 October 1895; see Stefan George and Ida Coblenz, *Briefwechsel* 48 and 56.

[31] He had already set "Friedensabend" and several other George poems to music. See Vilain 20.

[32] Morwitz 100. He cites George's confirmation of this view, 97.

[33] As they are for Hofmannsthal, in fact, for whom "ein Gefühl von Herrschaftlichkeit und Abhängigkeit zugleich" is a crucial poetic and existential balance. Hugo von Hofmannsthal and Richard Beer-Hofmann, *Briefwechsel* 47–48.

Works Cited

Arbogast, Hubert. *Versuche über George*. Stuttgart: Akademie für gesprochenes Wort, 1998.

Baudelaire, Charles. *Œuvres complètes*. Ed. Claude Pichois, Bibliothèque de la Pléiade. Paris: Gallimard, 1975.

Boehringer, Robert. *Mein Bild von Stefan George*. Düsseldorf/Munich: Helmut Küpper vormals Georg Bondi, 1967.

Briefwechsel zwischen George und Hofmannsthal. 2nd edition. Munich/Düsseldorf: Helmut Küpper vormals Georg Bondi, 1953.

Cross, Charlotte M. and Russell A. Berman, eds. *Schoenberg and Words: The Modernist Years*. New York and London: Garland, 2000.

Curtius, Ernst Robert. *Kritische Essays zur europäischen Literatur*. Bern: Francke, 1950.

David, Claude. *Stefan George. Sein dichterisches Werk*. Trans. Alexa Remmen and Karl Thimer. Munich: Hanser, 1967; originally *Stefan George: Son Œuvre poétique* (Lyon/Paris: IAC, 1952).

Durzak, Manfred. *Der junge Stefan George: Kunsttheorie und Dichtung*. Munich: Fink, 1968.

George, Stefan. *Sämtliche Werke in 18 Bänden*. Vol. 3. *Die Bücher der Hirten- und Preisgedichte, der Sagen und Sänge und der Hängenden Gärten*. Stuttgart: Klett-Cotta, 1991.

George, Stefan, and Ida Coblenz. *Briefwechsel*. Eds. Georg Peter Landmann and Elisabeth Höpker-Herberg. Stuttgart: Klett-Cotta, 1983.

Hofmannsthal, Hugo von. "Gedichte von Stefan George." In *Reden und Aufsätze*. Vol. 1, *1891–1913*. Frankfurt a.M.: S. Fischer, 1979.

Hofmannsthal, Hugo von, and Richard Beer-Hofmann. *Briefwechsel*. Ed. Eugene Weber. Frankfurt a.M.: Fischer, 1972.

Mallarmé, Stéphane. *Œuvres complètes*. Ed. Henri Mondor and G. Jean-Aubry. Paris: Gallimard, 1945.

Meesen, H. J. "Stefan Georges *Algabal* und die französische *décadence.*" *Monatshefte für deutschen Unterricht* 39 (1947): 304–21.

Metzger, Michael M., and Erika A. Metzger. *Stefan George.* New York: Twayne, 1972.

Morwitz, Ernst. *Kommentar zu dem Werk Stefan Georges.* Munich/Düsseldorf: Küpper-Bondi, 1960.

Oswald, Victor A. "The Historical Content of Stefan George's *Algabal.*" *Germanic Review* 23 (1948): 193–205.

———. "Oscar Wilde, Stefan George, Heliogabalus." *Modern Language Quarterly* 10 (1949): 517–25.

Pascal, Blaise. *Pensées. Œuvres complètes.* Ed. Louis Lafuma. Paris: Seuil, 1963.

Prawer, S. S. *German Lyric Poetry: A Critical Analysis of Selected Poems from Klopstock to Rilke.* London: Routledge & Kegan Paul, 1952.

Rieckmann, Jens. *Hugo von Hofmannsthal und Stefan George: Signifikanz einer "Episode" aus der Jahrhundertwende.* Tübingen/Basel: Francke, 1997.

Schefold, Karl. *Hugo von Hofmannsthals Bild von Stefan George: Visionen des Endes, Grundsteine neuer Kultur.* Basle: Schwabe, 1998.

Schulz, H. Stefan. *Studien zur Dichtung Stefan Georges.* Heidelberg: Lothar Stiehm, 1967.

Thiel, Friedrich. *Vier sonntägliche Straßen: A Study of the Ida Coblenz Problem in the Works of Stefan George.* New York: Lang, 1988.

Vilain, Robert. "Schoenberg and German Poetry." *Schoenberg and Words: The Modernist Years.* New York and London: Garland, 2000. 1–29.

DAS·JAHR·DER
SEELE·VON
STEFAN★GEORGE
IM·VERLAGE·DER·BLAETTER·FUER·
DIE·KUNST·BERLIN·MDCCCXCVII·

Title page of Das Jahr der Seele, *1897,*
designed by Melchior Lechter.
Courtesy of the Stefan George-Stiftung.

In Praise of Illusion:*Das Jahr der Seele* and *Der Teppich des Lebens:* Analysis and Historical Perspective

Karla Schultz

THE TWO MOST POPULAR OF GEORGE'S poetry cycles appear near the midpoint of his life. *Das Jahr der Seele* appeared in 1897, and *Der Teppich des Lebens* in 1899, both in Berlin. Marking a decisive turn, they represent the two halves of George's artistry: his lyrical notations of the soul and his mythopoetic vision of a new culture. The melancholic, retrospective *Das Jahr der Seele* is followed by the programmatic, life-affirming *Der Teppich des Lebens*. It is as if two personae were changing guard: the mournful one retreats, the confident one steps forth; nature is laid to rest, art put on the banner. Even the titles, vivid in their symbolism, demonstrate the shift from introspective, seasonal mood to richly patterned, deliberate design: "der Titel 'Teppich' meint nicht den Zweck, sondern die Art des Zusammenhangs" (Gundolf 182).

The Seasons

The title of the 1897 volume, *Das Jahr der Seele,* alludes to Hölderlin's *Menons Klagen um Diotima* (Menon's Mourning of Diotima, 1800/ 1801), in which the death of the beloved inspires the utopian vision of poet and beloved some day being reunited in a place where songs are true and the beauty of spring lasts longer:

> Wo die Gesänge wahr, und länger die Frühlinge schön sind,
> Und von neuem ein Jahr unserer Seele beginnt. (1: 295)

In light of this allusion, spring is conspicuously absent from George's presentation. His cycle begins in the fall and opens with an invitation to come see the park, a landscape considered dead at this time of year if one does not know how to see. "Look," the lyrical "I" commands, and clear vistas and colors unfold:

> Komm in den totgesagten park und schau:
> Der schimmer ferner lächelnder gestade ·

> Der reinen wolken unverhofftes blau
> Erhellt die weiher und die bunten pfade.

As in the paintings of the impressionists, colors predominate over shapes. The unnamed companion is directed to pick and choose, to compose a wreath from beautiful, decaying remnants:

> Dort nimm das tiefe gelb · das weiche grau
> Von birken und von buchs · der wind ist lau
> Die späten rosen welkten noch nicht ganz ·
> Erlese sie und flicht den kranz ·

A wreath of memory, of ever-deeper colors is in the making, and the companion is urged not to forget, yet to take and bear lightly what remains of nature's display:

> Vergiss auch diese lezten astern nicht ·
> Den purpur um die ranken wilder reben ·
> Und auch was übrig blieb von grünem leben
> Verwinde leicht im herbstlichen gesicht. (1: 12)

Who is addressed? Both autumnal vision and autumnal face ("gesicht"), companion/reader and maker of wreath/cycle ("erlese sie, flicht den kranz") merge in this opening to introduce the themes of memory and melancholia. But it is an undulating memory, a memory on the wane, sinking and receding as it is written down. Only the melancholy lingers. The poem that closes the entire cycle links almost verbatim to the first ("Willst du noch länger auf den kahlen böden / Nach frühern vollen farben spähn"), only to conclude on a bitter note:

> Und sieh! die tage die wie wunden brannten
> In unsrer vorgeschichte schwinden schnell . .
> Doch alle dinge die wir blumen nannten
> Versammeln sich am toten quell. (1: 167)

While memory has lost its sting, the sense of loss and lyrical exhaustion remains. Biographically, it is the memory of George's only romantic attachment to a woman, Ida Coblenz (1870–1942), who, after four years of friendship in the early 1890s, had the audacity to become romantically involved with the poet Richard Dehmel (1863–1920), a contemporary whom George despised. As a result, he dedicated the volume to his sister and not, as he had originally intended, to Ida Coblenz. Artistically, *Das Jahr der Seele* is an experiment in personal disclosure, in painting a landscape of emotions kept in check by understated language and simple form. The plangent, intimate tone, together with a seemingly transparent story of loss, made it George's most popular collection. Of all his works, it is "the book that least runs counter to common ideas about poetry [. . .] a poetry of the heart for which the analysis of feeling is more important than sense impressions or concepts" (David 140).

Several of the poems had been previously published in George's journal, *Blätter für die Kunst*. Gathered into a cycle they now appeared in an edition lavishly illustrated by Melchior Lechter (1865–1937), whose art and friendship would accompany George for the next decade. Lechter's ornamental, sinuous lines did much to convey the lingering sense of preciousness that pervades the volume, while at the same time profiling the natural imagery employed. As Claude David points out, nature and its seasons are but a framing device for George, a parade of images, an allegory painted by and for a contemplative soul (151).

The ninety-seven poems are organized into three sections, but only the first of these adheres to the seasonal theme and is divided again into three subsections corresponding to fall, winter, and summer. In a series of vignettes, fall and winter find a pair of would-be lovers — man and woman — strolling through parks, rowing on ponds, sitting in rooms, conversing by moonlight, and generally sharing an intimate understanding of all things aesthetic. It is the man, the lyrical "I" who observes and laments his soul mate who is not also a sex mate. The chronicle of the relationship with Ida Coblenz (who remains unnamed) speaks not so much of passion as it does of missed cues, silent gestures, and hoped for yet never uttered words. Or does it? The overtly chaste relationship seems to rest on Victorian evasions and constantly stoked fires:

> Du willst am mauerbrunnen wasser schöpfen
> Und spielend in die kühlen strahlen langen ·
> Doch scheint es mir du wendest mit befangen
> Die hände von den beiden löwenköpfen. (1: 123)

And, more explicit in desire and frigid in response, a winter poem presents an interior scene of an encrypted self-offering by the "I," witnessed but not recognized by the partner. The imagery, seductive and sacred in one, remains cold and hard to the core:

> Ich trat vor dich mit einem segensspruche
> Am abend wo für dich die kerzen brannten
> Und reichte dir auf einem sammtnen tuche
> Die höchste meiner gaben: den demanten.
>
> Du aber weisst nichts von dem opferbrauche ·
> Von blanken leuchtern mit erhobnen ärmen ·
> Von schalen die mit wolkenreinem rauche
> Der strengen tempel finsternis erwärmen
>
> Von engeln die sich in den nischen sammeln
> Und sich bespiegeln am kristallnen lüster ·

> Von glühender und banger bitte stammeln
> Von halben seufzern hingehaucht im düster
>
> Und nichts von wünschen die auf untern sprossen
> Des festlichen altars vernehmlich wimmern . .
> Du fassest fragend kalt und unentschlossen
> Den edelstein aus gluten tränen schimmern. (1: 127–28)

Or is it the poem, not the carnal self which is offered here and not under-stood? Not the woman but the reader who does not know? Or — worse — the "I" who offers the sum of his experiences to his art yet cannot make his diamond poem, distilled from lava and tears, speak of what went into its making? On this level, the fall and winter series of poems, named "Nach der Lese" (After the Harvest) and "Waller im Schnee" (Journey through Snow), tell of George's frustrated courting of poetic language at the time. Whether it is with an actual woman, with the Muses or with a split self, the relationship is lacking:

> Ich schrieb es auf: nicht länger sei verhehlt
> Was als gedanken ich nicht mehr verbanne ·
> Was ich nicht sage · du nicht fühlst: uns fehlt
> Bis an das glück noch eine weite spanne. (1: 125)

The summer sequence, "Sieg des Sommers" (Triumph of Summer), leaves the woman behind. The "I" sets out to embrace a "brother" beckoning on the other shore of the divide. A new, happier adventure, a more prom-ising interval begins: "Du willst mit mir ein reich der sonne stiften" (You want to found a realm of sun with me, 1: 132). The male figure addressed provides temporary fulfillment, is part of a "sweet" life, a "hot" life spent in paradisiacal isolation, wilder and more secret than the park landscape and domestic interiors roamed with the female. Suggestively phallic symbols celebrate the memory of this new, more responsive companion:

> Gemahnt dich noch das schöne bildnis dessen
> Der nach der schluchten-rosen kühn gehascht ·
> Der über seiner jagd den tag vergessen ·
> Der von der dolden vollem seim genascht?
> [. . .]
> Und von der insel moosgekrönter steine
> Verliess der schwan das spiel des wasserfalls
> Und legte in die kinderhand die feine
> Die schmeichelnde den schlanken hals. (1: 133)

Biographers have speculated that the summer sequence commemo-rates George's liaison with the young Scottish composer Cyril Scott, or his Belgian friend, Edmond Rassenfosse. Clearly, the poetic love object Woman is replaced by images of youthful, love-inspiring masculinity

(Norton 208). Psychoanalytically, these poems project a reintegration of the self, no longer divided by opposites but, longing for a mythical childhood, made whole in primary narcissistic union. The idyllic interlude, in particular in the image of the youth caressing the swan, suggests an intimate affinity with a mirror image that unites spontaneity with meditation (Faletti 131). Paradise regained.

But this too is fleeting, although for George the artist it is a lesson in productive illusion. Addressing his readers he defends its liberating, utopian power, which, energized by bodily joy, just might set free a new and daring creativity. The illusion of paradise, of primal happiness, fuels anticipatory visions:

> Die reichsten schätze lernet frei verschwenden ·
> [. . .]
> Dass ihr in euch schon ferne bilder küsstet
> Und dass ihr niemals zu versöhnen wüsstet
> Den kuss im traum empfangen und den wahren. (1: 134)

Dedications and Dances

In a tribute to sociality, the middle section of the book groups poems dedicated to friends and fellow artists (indicated by initials). Evening gatherings, excursions into nature, intimate moments, affinities and tensions are recalled, seasonal and atmospheric motifs pursued. Yet the tone remains pensive. The poet cautions his friends that as yet he is not able to sing as he would like, his struggles for true expression are not yet over:

> Lieder wie ich gern sie sänge
> Darf ich freunde! noch nicht singen · (1: 136)

The struggle for art intimated here leads through loneliness and suffering, demanding the sacrifice of youth and spontaneity if the perfect poem is to be achieved: "Vergiss es nicht: du musst / Deine frische jugend töten" (1: 139). As if harbored on a distant island, the memory of youth — whether the poet's own or reincarnated in a young lover — is the theme of the five-poem sequence at the center of the middle section, "Nachtwachen" (Vigils). Originally written in French and published in part in 1896 in *Blätter für die Kunst,* it meditates tenderly over a sleeping youth while the elements rage and guilt feelings haunt the speaker: "Dass ich wie nie dich blass und bebend finde" (1: 145).

Perhaps the most flamboyant of the dedication poems is the one initialed M. L., referring to Melchior Lechter. It pays tribute to Lechter's graphic perfection of *Jugendstil,* to his intense palette, his stark symbolism, his sinuous lines. Sharing his commitment to craftsmanship, George considered

him a brother-in-arms in his opposition to mass production and the leveling of art for popular consumption. Artfully, the poem transposes colors
and lines into a range of emotions:

> Wie unsre glorreichen himmel — bruder im stolz!
> So breitet dein glänzendes gelb und wie ein reifender lohn ·
> Es zittern in deinem lila und wehen grün
> Gestaltlose stunden mit ihrem mühsamen rinnen
> Und lange seufzer aus kerkern ohne erhebung.
> Dein strahlendes blau umkleidet die wunschlosen götter ·
> In deinem veilchendunkel voll purpurner scheine
> Ist unser tödliches sehnen — bruder im leid! (1: 148)

The emotional spectrum, like a rainbow's band from bright yellow to pur-
plish blue, arcs from elation to exhaustion, from exuberant glory to the
longing for death.

"Traurige Tänze" (Mournful Dances) make up the third section of the
book. Where words fail the soul must dance. George's friend Friedrich
Gundolf described these poems as "Zaubersprüche" pure and simple,
where dark powers resound "als Schicksalsmächte, und wer wüßte über
diese unmittelbar etwas auszusagen!" (154). Unlike Gundolf, though,
George does address the powers directly, recognizable as his own oppres-
sive solipsism and expressed most eloquently in the following poem:

> Dies leid und diese last: zu bannen
> Was nah erst war und mein.
> Vergebliches die arme spannen
> Nach dem was nur mehr schein ·
> [. . .]
> Beklemmendes gefühl der schwere
> Auf müd gewordner pein ·
> Dann dieses dumpfe weh der leere ·
> O dies: mit mir allein! (1: 158)

To be sure, the poem's immediacy will remain singular in George's work
until *Der Siebente Ring* ten years later, but its simple expressiveness characterizes the dominant mood of the entire volume. The poet, like the
alchemist, wrestles with the task of turning the lead of memory into poetic
gold, and he finds the lonely and introspective circularity this imposes
nearly unbearable. In keeping with the dance motif the poems of this section show greater metric variety and more rhythmic musicality than the
other two. The themes of seasons and hours play loosely throughout, and
despite his grief the lyrical "I" and his companion(s) continue to roam the
landscape.

In light of the underlying theme — the quest for the poem transparent
and permanent, the struggle to distill experience into art — George's

admonishment to his readers in the foreword makes clear what his experiment has been about. Exhausted and lonely, he may be at a dead end, but the "I" and its companions, though real in actual life, have become illusory figures through his work, have become woof and weave in the fabric of his text:

> Möge man doch [. . .] bei einer dichtung vermeiden sich unweise an das menschliche oder landschaftliche urbild zu kehren: es hat durch die kunst solche umformung erfahren dass es dem schöpfer selber unbedeutend wurde und ein wissendarum für jeden andren eher verwirrt als löst [. . .] selten sind sosehr wie in diesem buch ich und du die selbe seele. (1: 119)

I do not think that George simply hoped to divert his readers from his biography with this advice, even if that was the motivating factor. *Das Jahr der Seele* is so thoroughly metaphorical, so emphatically an allegory of the endeavor to transform memory into art that the conflation of "I" and "you" — aside from veiling relationships — accentuates the effect of the process, for by force of it identity becomes illusory as well. The soul, immaterial and hence expansive, knows no borders. In this case, it is a tired, resigned soul, holding forth in soliloquies yet ceaselessly drawing attention to the shimmery textures of its making. Both resigned to and elated by illusion, this soul welcomes the breath of spirit that is its inspiration — or so we may read the penultimate stanza of the cycle:

> Bescheide dich wenn nur im schattenschleier
> Mild schimmernd du genossene fülle schaust
> Und durch die müden lüfte ein befreier
> Der wind der weiten zärtlich um uns braust. (1: 167)

The Angel Appears

And the wind blew, the spirit took a shape. George's *Teppich des Lebens,* published two years later, is a remarkable case of *Jugendstil* flaunted and eclipsed. It pulls all the registers, from programmatic vitalism to chiseled ornament, but it also charts the course of something new: a poetry of the will. This poetry subordinates mood and emotion to clarity and rigor, to the poet's decision henceforth to master his life through art alone. He will no longer be subject to his passions but celebrate the world around him for what it is — an aesthetic phenomenon. He will make palpable its texture, delineate its contours, delight in its patterns and shapes. More, he will conjure up its meaning.

The opening stanzas present the mise-en-scène. While the lyrical "I" labors in futility, a naked angel bearing armfuls of flowers steps forward and announces "das schöne Leben." Like a garden in bloom he dazzles the eye, makes pale cheeks blush:

> Ich forschte bleichen eifers nach dem horte
> Nach strofen drinnen tiefste kümmernis
> Und dinge rollten dumpf und ungewiss —
> Da trat ein nackter engel durch die pforte:
>
> Entgegen trug er dem versenkten sinn
> Der reichsten blumen last und nicht geringer
> Als mandelblüten waren seine finger
> und rosen · rosen waren um sein kinn.

The radiant apparition will be the poet's mentor and guide, indeed his double and artistic conscience. He will instruct him in the aesthetically lived life, coach him in high-minded perception. More than a momentary vision, the angel moves and talks and will be a constant companion. As he speaks in a voice that "almost" resembles the poet's, the lilies and mimosas he is carrying spill to the ground. In an intimate, erotically charged gesture he kneels beside the poet to help gather in the abundance:

> Und als ich sie zu heben mich gebückt
> Da kniet auch ER · ich badete beglückt
> Mein ganzes antlitz in den frischen rosen. (1: 172)

Both alter-ego and erotic ideal, the angel counsels the poet throughout the first section of the book. He is an allegory of the poet's will to embrace life by committing himself to his art. He bestows determination as well as serenity, self-sufficiency as well as a sensuous receptivity to all that exists around him, in particular George's rediscovered homeland along the Rhine with its history, culture, landscape, and people. On one level he is the angel of the here and now, personification of the Nietzschean "Yes!" Gone are confusion and despair:

> In meinem leben rannen schlimme tage
> Und manche töne hallten rauh und schrill.
> Nun hält ein guter geist die rechte waage
> Nun tu ich alles was der engel will. (1: 173)

On another level he is the angel of inspired discipline. Although he urges the poet to observe life up close, to mingle with ordinary people ("Dem markt und ufer gelte dein besuch," 1: 182) he insists on strict discipleship. In exchange for revealing the wonders of the world he dictates the form in which they will be expressed:

> Sind auch der dinge formen abertausend
> Ist dir nur Eine - Meine - sie zu künden. (1: 178)

Der Teppich des Lebens is George's most positive and consciously classicist work. Its balance and transparency emulate qualities that he admired in Goethe and which he felt could most beautifully tame the most deeply glowing passions. Conceived as a commemoration of his own poetic activity, the book was meant to communicate his credo to a circle of like-minded friends. Only 300 numbered copies of the first edition were printed, and after the run the plates were destroyed to preserve the book's exclusivity. George himself designed the exterior, chose the paper, the ink color, and the layout, and specified his own idiosyncratic spelling, punctuation and typeface. It was to be a special text, a sacred text. As the book was in production he inquired mockingly though not entirely in jest: "Wie geht es vorwärts mit dem tempelbau?" (Lechter-George, *Briefe* 73). The large, folio-size volume (approximately fourteen by fifteen inches) again was profusely illustrated by Lechter. It was bound in wood covered with heavy green linen on which the full title was printed in blue: *Der Teppich des Lebens und die Lieder von Traum und Tod mit einem Vorspiel*. Each of the three sections, the "Vorspiel," "Der Teppich," and "Die Lieder," had its own opulent framing design that profiled two usually antithetical poems per page, twenty-four poems per section. Subsequent, less lavish editions were dedicated to Lechter for having furnished the collection's initial magnificent ornamentation.

The style is supple and controlled, the language simple though fissured on occasion by the precious turn, the startling image. George's disciple Gundolf singled out the classic ease of this style, and characterized it as "gleichmäßiges, sicheres Schreiben, das sich nicht den Schwankungen des Gefühls unterordnet, gleichförmiger Rhythmus, der die Melodie absorbiert, ein permanenter, poetischer 'Zustand' im Gegensatz zur Inspiration der 'Gelegenheit'" (62–63). George's formal rigor allots each poem four stanzas of four lines each, most often of alternating rhyme and written in iambic pentameter. The relative monotony of meter and cadence, combined with the succinct, uniform architecture of the poems lends the collection a liturgical quality reminiscent of a prayer book. Unlike a book of prayers, however, it is secular to the core. It celebrates the artist's relationship to his art, to his environment, to his personal memories and aspirations.

The volume's tripartite, cyclical composition shows the interrelation of these spheres. The "Vorspiel" presents the poet's marshaling of his will in the form of a dialogue with the angel (the call to action), while "Der Teppich," epic in sweep, demonstrates the working of the cultural material at hand (the actual practice). "Die Lieder von Traum und Tod," finally, meditate on personal experience in expressly lyrical fashion, culminating in an apotheosis of the poetically lived life (the recollection):

> All dies stürmt reisst und schlägt blizt und brennt
> Eh für uns spät am nacht-firmament

> Sich vereint schimmernd still licht-kleinod:
> Glanz und ruhm rausch und qual traum und tod. (1: 223)

Thus, the trajectory that encircles the volume's middle and title section reaches from embarkation to achievement, from sunlit garden to starlit sky, from the angel's inspirational companionship to solitary epiphany. Within each section a corresponding trajectory is evident. The "Vorspiel" opens with the youthful appearance of the angel and, after extending his guardianship through many years of praising life ("Uns die durch viele jahre zum triumfe / Des grossen lebens unsre lieder schufen"), closes with him faithfully standing watch at the dying poet's bedside:

> Des endes schwere scheideblicke lindernd
> So stand am lager fest und hoch: der engel. (1: 187)

Likewise, the "Lieder von Traum und Tod" commence with the recollection of the waning of a single precious hour and close with the telescoped illumination of an entire life. The dynamic throughout is a process of distillation. Lived experience over time is distilled into its essence, the single precious moment recollected — letting time have its due — in the instant of its passing.

Of Tapestry, Veil, and Song

The center section presents the "tapestry" proper, introduced by the title poem. On a general level the tapestry stands for the densely woven fabric we call life. As participants, the poem suggests, we are blindly enmeshed in it; as idle observers we see only a dead artifact. Either way we remain insensitive to life's meaning. As participants we cannot perceive its rich and intricate beauty; as observers we cannot feel its pulsating, creative force. Only the chosen few, those endowed with a poetic sensibility, are granted an answer as to how these two modes might fuse, how perception and sensation might become one. When such revelations occur — and they do so only rarely — they occur not by concept but apparition, by an insight "incarnate."

The first stanza directs the gaze toward what is literally a still life, beautiful to behold but cold and inanimate until a magical transformation sets in. A richly bordered weaving depicting man and beast, plant and star is displayed:

> Hier schlingen menschen mit gewächsen tieren
> Sich fremd zum bund umrahmt von seidner franze
> Und blaue sicheln weisse sterne zieren
> Und queren sie in dem erstarrten tanze.

> Und kahle linien ziehn in reich-gestickten
> Und teil um teil ist wirr und gegenwendig
> Und keiner ahnt das rätsel der verstrickten . .
> Da eines abends wird das werk lebendig. (1: 190)

It is as if the breath of a second creation begins to blow, allowing the phenomena to escape the prison of their allotted space to begin a life on their own:

> Da regen schauernd sich die toten äste
> Die wesen eng von strich und kreis umspannet
> Und treten klar vor die geknüpften quäste
> Die lösung bringend über die ihr sannet!
>
> Sie ist nach willen nicht: ist nicht für jede
> Gewohnte stunde: ist kein schatz der gilde.
> Sie wird den vielen nie und nie durch rede
> Sie wird den seltnen selten im gebilde. (1: 190)

What is the answer incarnate to the chosen few? Let the image move, let it dance. The poem does not instruct fellow poets in mystical revelation but, just as the angel exhorted his apprentice to focus without force, it calls for an active receptivity to the phenomenal world.

On a more specific level the poem sets forth the program for George's art. He means to leave behind the static lines of his own former and his contemporaries' writing, means to give an aesthetic education to his friends, means to lead an exemplary poetic life of consequence to German culture. The poem begins by tracing the tapestry's highly ornamental texture/text deictically, "*Hier* schlingen menschen mit gewächsen tieren," a gesture that also directs the reader to this, George's, text as it unfolds. The next move intimates the author's growing distance to the beautiful but lifeless handicraft of his time. The sumptuous figuration of humans, fauna, and flora in the two-dimensional style of Art Nouveau has alienated the depicted creatures from within: they are oddly meshed, jarring in their arrested dance. In the second stanza the decorative lines of the pattern become even more abstract; they are barren, tangled, and at strife. The texture does not yield any meaning or sense. Then suddenly, dramatically, one night the fabric leaps to life. George presents his new way of seeing as a magic turn, similarly sudden and natural as the appearance of the angel. Except that now he is not alone but in the company of the rare. In the poem, the static ornamental figuration of the tapestry dissolves and becomes a collection of independent figures, who move limned and clear before the backdrop of their culture, the tapestry of *life* (the poems that follow limn figures who move and do, not states of mind). It is this stereo-scopic, dramatic vision that George commends to the readers of his text.

They are to be open to its multiple layers, to read its carefully crafted texture as process and direction.

While the imagery employed still flaunts the stylized lines of Art Nouveau, while their seemingly ineffable quickening recalls the magic of Romanticism, there is a new energy afoot. Claude David suggests that the poem marks a threshold in George's work: "was sich anbahnt, ist eine neue Auffassung der Dichtung und der Kunst, für die nicht mehr das sogenannte 'Schöne,' das schöne leben, das letzte Wort ist, sondern der Sinn. Eine Kunstbetätigung, in der es nicht mehr verwehrt ist, etwas 'sagen,' etwas 'wirken' zu wollen" ("Stefan George und der Jugendstil" 223).

"Der Teppich" also gives rise to the section's internal arc. Thematically, the center section commences by setting a fixed pattern into motion, and, after unfolding the rich cultural fabric of George's home region over the next twenty-four poems, settles on the poet asserting his power to conjure up illusions. The illusions are based on culture and myth, legend and lore, but most important, they demonstrate that he has the power to direct desire. What initially appears as an act of magic out of nowhere — the tapestry comes to life, its meaning revealed to the few — becomes the self-assured performance by a master magician who delights and manipulates the multitude.

The concluding poem, "Der Schleier" (The Veil, 1: 205), demonstrates his mastery over his material, over the thick, tightly woven texture of reality. It is as if the tapestry had thinned, had turned pliable and transparent, had become shimmery gauze so that he may cast it at will:

> Ich werf ihn so: und wundernd halten inne
> Die auf dem heimischen baumfeld früchte kosten . .
> Die ferne flammt und eine stadt vom osten
> Enttaucht im nu mit kuppel zelt und zinne.

He delights in telling his audience of the veil's capabilities, whether it is conjuring up a distant vista, a nearby atmospheric change, a pre-historic ritual or a pair of lovers, all the while demonstrating the magic as he speaks:

> Einst flog er so empor: und öde schranken
> Der häuser blinkten scheinhaft durch die nässe
> Es regte sich die welt in silberblässe -
> Am vollen mittag mondlicht der gedanken!

> Er wogt und weht: und diese sind wie hirten
> Der ersten tale · jene mädchen gleiten
> Wie sie die einst im rausch der Göttin weihten . .
> Dies paar ist wie ein schatten unter mirten.

One more display — and the audience in the scenario is hooked, their
desire putty in the hands of the impresario:

> Und so gewirbelt: ziehen sie zu zehnen
> Durch dein gewohntes tor wie sonnenkinder -
> Der langen lust · des leichten glückes finder . .
> So wie mein schleier spielt wird euer sehnen! (1: 205)

George's confidence and determination at the time of composing the
Teppich seems to crystallize in the gesture of the master illusionist. Equally
telling, however, is the lyricism of the third section. The three sections suc-
cessively adopt the persona of the eager apprentice, the savvy practitioner
and the pensive minstrel. It is this tension-laden composite that makes for
the poet's "authentic" voice. The high-minded angel, as volition personi-
fied, teaches him how to see and cast into form ("hoch vom berge / Sollst
du schaun wie sie im tale tun" 1: 176), how to gather disciples and cultivate a common vision — albeit the community will be tenuous ("Die
jünger lieben doch sind schwach und feig" 1: 186). Having made up his
mind, the apprentice-turned-master then unfurls the tapestry of the Rhine
region, telling stories — ballads really — whose settings and figures range
from primeval landscape to farming, from folk legends to historic events,
from outcasts to cultural icons (Holbein, Jean Paul, Goethe). Not coinci-
dentally, and not at all ironically, the seventh and last of the "Standbilder"
(Statues) poems presents the manipulator of the veil. In due time George
the magician will join the icons of his region.

It is in the third section, the "Lieder," where the confident tone
changes; meter and cadence loosen. The minstrel sings. And he sings as
much to himself as to others. The first twelve of the twenty-four poems
bear dedications; the remaining twelve chronicle seasonal and develop-
mental moods like a book of hours. One of the most haunting tunes is the
third movement of "Tag-Gesang" (Day Song):

> An dem wasser das uns fern klagt
> Wo die pappel sich lind wiegt
> Sizt ein vogel der uns gern fragt
> Der im laube sich dem wind schmiegt.
>
> Und der vogel spielt leis auf:
> Flur und garten sind vom blühn tot
> Jedes weiss sich schön im kreislauf . .
> Sieh die gipfel vor dir glühn rot!
>
> Nur erinnrung lässt als traumsold
> Der zu glücklichern seinen zug lenkt
> Seiner hand entrieselt traumgold
> Das er früh und nur im flug schenkt.

Heb das haupt das sich bang neigt
Ob aus tiefen ein gesicht winkt -
Und so warte bis mein sang schweigt
Und so bleibe bis das licht singt. (1: 220)

The strain's artfully simple music, together with wistful allusions to time fleeing and fear rising underscore the poet's plea to linger for the moment and to listen for just now. The gesture acknowledges *and* tries to stem the inexorable flow of time — which, in individual terms, implies the constant diminishment of a human life in its rush toward death ("Flur und garten sind vom blühn tot"). But the gesture, stirring memory, also halts time by creating the illusion that what is past is not gone ("Jedes weiss sich schön im kreislauf"). This two-fold power, reminding us that we must die and assuring us that all we have lost may be present once again, is the secret of song, is its bill and its receipt ("traumsold" and "traumgold").

Der Teppich des Lebens is rich and varied indeed. Georg Simmel described it as a book of "monumental intimacy" (quoted in Landmann 128), and it has been lauded for its rigorous composition (Aler 233), its "humane serenity" (Metzger 102), its "clarity" and "optimism of the will" (David 188, 196). It also has been criticized for its riven voice and for its ceaseless self-dramatization, all recurrent themes in George scholarship. An unlikely admirer and critic, the social philosopher and musicologist Theodor W. Adorno situates George historically in a manner worth reviewing here, not least because his reading combines a very specific kind of personal interpretation with a far-reaching cultural analysis.

Two Generations Removed

Adorno wrote two major essays on George (in 1939 and 1967), made frequent reference to him throughout his work, and set a number of his poems to music (from age eighteen to his forties). In his essay on George and Hofmannsthal (1939) Adorno describes what he calls the open secret of artists around 1900: "Geheimgehalten wird das nicht Geheime; eingeweiht wird ins Rationale die Technik selber" (10/1: 200). He cites George's program for the *Blätter für die Kunst,* which counts on the technical competency of insiders to produce what they think escapes the coarser sensibilities of the public: the transformation of sensual data into art. Priestly in demeanor, this craft is technical in practice. As George writes to his young colleague Hofmannsthal, "Und nicht einmal von den ganz kleinen will ich schweigen · den zufälligen schnörkeln und zieraten ·" (*Briefwechsel zwischen George und Hofmannsthal* 160). The vital details of the craft must not be divulged to the multitude; it would spoil the magical effect. Accordingly, the subtitle to each edition of George's journal stipulates that readership be extended only by invitation. Adorno dryly notes the course of such specialization: "Je mehr die Fragen der Dichtung in Fragen der Technik sich übersetzen, um so lieber bilden sich exklusive Zirkel" (10/1: 200).

The essay thematizes a relation of complicity and difference. George and Hofmannsthal saw eye to eye in their interest in the technical aspects of art and in the manipulability of the incommensurable with color and tone. Both criticized the cult of interiority and agreed on societal alienation and the arbitrariness of symbols. But they disagreed in their attitude (*Haltung*) toward society. George assumed an aloof, disdainful stance, cultivating a circle of like-minded artists and intellectuals. He preferred the city for its anonymity, traveled light and frequently, gave readings in private villas and salons, and paid utmost attention to the style of both his appearance and publications. He was — or wanted to be — an aristocrat of the spirit, the roving ambassador of a culture yet to come that was based on sheer will and discipline. Hofmannsthal, on the other hand — a poetic wunderkind until his break with lyric poetry shortly after 1900 — led the settled life of a country gentleman. He was equally at ease with artists and politicians, businessmen and the nobility, though inwardly torn apart by the end of a culture as he had known it. Except for brief excursions, he stayed in his home near Vienna from his mid-twenties until his death, engaged with a vast correspondence and his life-project, a socially responsive theater. In Adorno's reading, Hofmannsthal seems to prefigure the wily, adaptive half of the Odysseus figure in *Dialektik der Aufklärung* (Dialectic of Enlightenment, 1944), George its rigidly assertive other: "wo Hofmannsthal die Finte wählt, greift [George] mit Desperation zur Gewalt" (10/1: 215).

And it is George who fascinates him. Embodying the tendency of the age, George pushed this tendency to the extreme, to a self-conscious formalism that opposed society from within: "Der Trotz gegen die Gesellschaft ist einer gegen deren Sprache" (10/1: 236). While his feudal pose was anachronistic, his radical technique soon eclipsed a *Jugendstil* mired in vitalism. His chiseled language was enlightening in an objective sense. It debunked the myth of art being an ally of biological life when in actuality it served an alienated social life. However, his own secondary stylization of art into something transcendent once again (the subjective, posited aspect) simply reiterated yet another myth, the myth of "autonomous" spirit. Only in those poems, Adorno writes, "wo George ohne Vorbehalt, ohne statuarische Veranstaltung sich, im Einklang mit dem *Jugendstil*, der Vergänglichkeit des eigenen und des geschichtlichen Augenblicks überläßt, war das Glück mit ihm" (11: 533). Thus the most fortunate of George's poems yielded defiance to their material (a brittle language frozen to decor) and lovingly dissolved it, producing a lyricism that elicited the social estrangement inscribed in it. The "magic" achieved was an ascetic musicality.

Adorno marshals an array of psychological and sociological coordinates to situate George, but he turned to interpreting his technique in the concrete sense elsewhere, in his own musical compositions. Having elaborated the contradictions of subjective spirit in *Dialektik der Aufklärung,* he began setting once again several of George's poems to music. His new interpretation resulted in the Vier George-Lieder, op. 7 (1944, in *Kompositionen 1,* 76–85). In a brief commentary from 1967 he describes the technique of these compositions as searching for a certain reduction and intensification of George's musical language. All of Adorno's George compositions, whether from the 1920s or the 1940s, use sparse, folk-song type poems of an intensely lyrical, evanescent quality, not the more vision-oriented texts that draw attention to George's technical control. It is as if Adorno sought to make audible the not yet rigid George, a young apprentice not yet lost in the old master's rigor.

The terms "young" and "old" are relative, however. The poems Adorno chose in the 1940s are all from the mature George's *Der Siebente Ring* completed when George was thirty-nine. The cycle is shaped by the trauma of Maximin, a young man dead at sixteen whom George had hailed as the embodiment of an omnipotent youth "wie wir sie erträumt hatten" (Winkler 45). Adorno was especially fond of the poem "Kreuz der Strasse" (Here is the crossroads, 1: 310–11), with its multiple resonances of roads crossing and ending, of crossing over and of bearing one's cross, of meeting, leave-taking and continuing one's path alone. In a way, it is an "old" poem in that it mourns the passing of youth, yet it remains "young" by remembering the dream. Expressing the subjective and objective historical moment at once, it commemorates George's personal passion and, in hindsight, the vanished hope for a new beginning by young people and artists around 1900.

What Adorno wished to elicit through his composition — the poem's "musical continuity" — was remembrance through performance. This meant translating the verbal musicality of George's texts into the idiom he had studied when young himself, the free atonal music first developed by Arnold Schönberg. It was the art that had dissolved the key center of traditional music (its posited, imaginary foundation in chord and resolution), producing an eerily restless effect. Likewise, George's restless songs about estrangement and transience from *Das Buch der hängenden Gärten* and *Das Jahr der Seele* form the basis for his earlier compositions. Schönberg, in his revolutionary George settings (op. 15), had chosen the *hängenden Gärten* as well, setting forth, as Adorno notes in allusion to the young Lukács, "das Gepreßte, rauschhaft Schmerzliche des Innenraums, der seine Welt verloren hat" (18: 412). Mutually constitutive, this interior and its world refer to an historical subjectivity kept in check by a posited, transcendent referent — just as tonality had been constituted by the assumption of a center. Having lost its referent, "the intoxicating pain of this

subjectivity is nothing other than the shudder of freedom, of its own negativity" (Kristeva 110).

George's elliptic texts allowed Schönberg the space for expressing the
possibilities of *his* material, music. Schönberg described his break with tradition in his program notes to the first performance of the George songs:
"Now that I have set out along this path once and for all, I am conscious of
having broken through every restriction of a bygone aesthetic" (quoted in
notes to CD, Lieder op. 15). The bygone aesthetic had been tonality and,
at its pinnacle, symphony, its steadfast articulation beginning to be undone
by Wagner's chromatism, which in turn was drowned in massive orchestra-
tion. Adorno wished to elaborate the break in his own compositions in a
twofold way: by intensifying the tension buried in George's texts, and by
recalling the fling of freedom that Kandinsky, addressing the new atonality,
once greeted as *Zukunftsmusik* (Schönberg-Kandinsky, *Briefe* 229).

Historically, the configuration of new music and an ascetic *Jugendstil*
is the figure of a broken promise. The phase of trial and experiment, con-
joining free atonality with a poetry that allowed, by its fissures and breaks,
room for the moment in transition, time for dissolving the myths of the fin
de siècle (vitalism, nationalism, progressivism), was of short duration. In
tandem with the increasing rigidity of twelve-tone music superseding free
atonality came George's increasingly rigid formalism, came his cultural
vision. Every tone, every word received its assigned space. Uncannily, the
development precipitated the order of the coming age. Only a decade later,
in the political arena, radicals reviving the myths of biology/identity/
destiny shouted *"Lebensraum!"* as rallying cry for a National Socialism on
the rise.

In a radio lecture some twenty years after the fall of Nazi Germany,
Adorno imagined himself being charged with the task of editing a selection of George's poetry. Noting the changes in George's reception, from
his "official canonization" by the Nazis to the "intense revulsion" by the
post-war generation, he insisted on an art-immanent approach, singling
out the traces of unresolved tension in his work: musicality alloyed with the
imperious gesture, ready song with the subjection of something utterly
spontaneous to the will. It was this internal dissonance that Adorno considered the most authentic of George's traits; it told of forced sublimation.
Where the pain of alienation no longer resonates, Adorno writes, where
George's priestly pose prevails, where he represses, idealizes, and controls,
he unwittingly prefigures the aesthetics of fascism. He was not willing to
include much of the late George because he considered that portion objec-
tively collusive with subsequent history. But the young George had seized
the day. By radicalizing *Jugendstil,* he had saved it from being a mere stage
in an ill-omened teleology and had made it into a moment of recognition.

Unlike his contemporaries who celebrated a beauty assumed to spring
from life itself, George, in affinity to the French symbolists since Baudelaire,

cultivated beauty as an artifact. In his stringent idiom, societal alienation and the subjectivity it had produced came to self-consciousness. George's dawning horror over the hollowness of his art is addressed in the last part of Adorno's lecture, where he draws attention to the dreams George recorded in *Tage und Taten* and quotes the last dream, "Der redende Kopf" (The Talking Head), in full:

> Man hatte mir eine thönerne maske gegeben und an meiner zimmerwand aufgehängt. Ich lud meine freunde ein damit sie sähen wie ich den kopf zum reden brächte. Vernehmlich hiess ich ihn den namen dessen zu sagen auf den ich deutete und als er schwieg versuchte ich mit dem finger seine lippen zu spalten. Darauf verzog er sein gesicht und biss in meinen finger. Laut und mit äusserster anspannung wiederholte ich den befehl indem ich auf einen anderen deutete. Da nannt er den namen. Wir verliessen alle entsetzt das zimmer und ich wusste dass ich es nie mehr betreten würde. (1: 490–91)

George's art, at its outer limits, severed a form triumphant from its lived, social content — only to find that this triumph spelled living death. Like the bourgeois subject enthralled by the commodity, the dream tells of the artifact spellbinding its producer. When he makes it speak, it speaks the truth of both *its* subjection *and* his. Adorno puts it this way: "Die Gewalt, die noch einmal zum Wort zwingt, ihr Sieg und das maßlose Grauen, das dieser Sieg als selbstvernichtender bereitet — das ist Georges Rätselfigur" (11: 535).

He looked at the enigma historically. The poems he favored exhibit the tension between a rigorous technique and a brittle material made resonant, between the will to form and a receptivity to what it shapes. Yet their acute artistry turned out to be a fling: "Mit überfliegendem, musikhaft erotischem Elan gewann er der deutschen Lyrik eine utopische Spur [. . .] heute ist sie zugeschüttet" (11: 530). Reviewing George in 1967, Adorno was able to situate him in a way not yet apparent in 1939, noting a hermetic quality that was far ahead of its time: "Manchmal [. . .] läßt [seine Sprache] den faßlichen Sinn hinter sich, weit vorstoßend in ein hermetisches Bereich, das lange erst nach Georges Tod der Kunst ganz sich öffnete" (11: 529).

The essay leaves it at that. But the allusion, I think, points to yet another poet. It also suggests a history of modern German poetry lodged in extremes. Paul Celan, two generations removed from George, neither had the privilege to defy society nor the trust to envision a new culture. With the Holocaust, any meaning of dying, any hope drawn from suffering had been erased. Adorno's intimated trajectory, in light of George's adopted pose as a priest and Celan's actual life situation as a victim may seem farfetched. But it follows an insight first expressed by Walter Benjamin concerning the interpretation of history in *Ursprung des deutschen Trauerspiels*

(Origin of the German Mourning Play, 1928). It is a radically immanent, radically dialectical approach, by which "jene Elemente, deren Auslösung aus den Phänomenen Aufgabe des Begriffes ist, in den Extremen am genauesten zutage [liegen]" (17). Like art, interpretation does not synthesize a meaning but elicits a constellation.

Celan's poetry vis-à-vis George's outlines such a constellation. Like George's, it remembers the dead, but, unlike George's, does not mythologize death. It turns to matter rather than to mind. In Celan, the murdered bodies of his people, unlike the beloved body deified by George, do not testify to a sublime violence but to an abyss of human suffering. Adorno writes elsewhere that the conception of an estranged, cordoned-off poetry dates back to the period of *Jugendstil* (7: 476). The link, it seems to me, is the imposed isolation that separates both poets from their societies — an isolation born with defiance in George's time, in despair by the time of Celan. Thus, George's spare yet precious language hints of vast riches in its opposition to mass-produced art, whereas Celan's equally spare, encrypted style speaks of art's poverty and shame in the face of mass-produced death.

Works Cited

Adorno, Theodor W. *Gesammelte Schriften*. 20 Volumes. Ed. Rolf Tiedemann. Frankfurt a.M.: Suhrkamp, 1973–86.

———. *Kompositionen 1*. Ed. Heinz-Klaus Metzger and Rainer Riehn. Munich: edition text+kritik, 1980.

Aler, Jan. *Symbol und Verkündung. Studien um Stefan George*. Düsseldorf/Munich: Helmut Küpper vormals Georg Bondi, 1976.

Benjamin, Walter. *Ursprung des deutschen Trauerspiels*. Frankfurt a.M.: Suhrkamp, 1978.

Briefwechsel zwischen Stefan George und Hugo von Hofmannsthal. Munich/Düsseldorf: Helmut Küpper vormals Georg Bondi, 1953.

David, Claude. *Stefan George: Sein dichterisches Werk*. Munich: Carl Hanser, 1967.

———. "Stefan George und der Jugendstil." *Formkräfte der deutschen Dichtung vom Barock bis zur Gegenwart: Vorträge gehalten im Deutschen Haus, Paris 1961/1962*. Göttingen: Vandenhoeck & Ruprecht, 1963.

Faletti, Heidi E. *Die Jahreszeiten des Fin de siècle. Eine Studie über Stefan Georges Das Jahr der Seele*. Bern/Munich: Francke, 1983.

George, Stefan. *Werke. Ausgabe in zwei Bänden*. Ed. Robert Boehringer. Stuttgart: Klett-Cotta, 1984.

Gundolf, Friedrich. *George*. Berlin: Georg Bondi, 1930.

Hölderlin, Friedrich. *Sämtliche Werke und Briefe 1*. Ed. Michael Knaupp. Munich: Carl Hanser, 1992.

Kristeva, Julia. *Revolution in Poetic Language.* Trans. Margaret Waller. New York: Columbia UP, 1984.

Landmann, Georg Peter. *Vorträge über Stefan George.* Düsseldorf/Munich: Helmut Küpper vormals Georg Bondi, 1974.

Lechter, Melchior and Stefan George. *Briefe. Kritische Ausgabe.* Ed. Günter Heinz. Stuttgart: Hauswedell, 1991.

Metzger, Michael M. and Erika A. Metzger. *Stefan George.* New York: Twayne Publishers, 1972.

Norton, Robert E. *Secret Germany. Stefan George and His Circle.* Ithaca/London: Cornell UP, 2002.

Schönberg, Arnold. *Brettllieder, Lieder op. 2, Lieder op. 15 (15 Gedichte aus Das Buch der Hängenden Gärten von Stefan George).* Compact disk. Berkeley: Music and Arts Programs of America, 1991.

Schönberg, Arnold, and Wassily Kandinsky. *Briefe, Bilder, Dokumente einer außergewöhnlichen Begegnung.* Ed. Jelena Hahl-Koch. Salzburg: Residenz, 1980.

Winkler, Michael. *Stefan George.* Stuttgart: Metzler, 1970.

In Zeiten der Wirren: Stefan George's Later Works

Michael M. Metzger

> *Glücklicherweise bewahrt [die Geschichte] aber auch das Gedächtnis an die großen Kämpfer gegen die Geschichte, das heißt gegen die blinde Macht des Wirklichen, und stellt sich dadurch selbst an den Pranger, daß sie jene gerade als die eigentlich historischen Naturen heraushebt, die sich um das "so ist es" wenig kümmerten, um vielmehr mit heiterem Stolze einem "so soll es sein" zu folgen. Nicht ihr Geschlecht zu Grabe zu tragen, sondern ein neues Geschlecht zu begründen — das treibt sie unablässig vorwärts: und wenn sie selbst als Spätlinge geboren werden — es gibt eine Art zu leben, dies vergessen zu machen — die kommenden Geschlechter werden sie nur als Erstlinge kennen.*
>
> "Vom Nutzen und Nachteil der Historie für das Leben" (Nietzsche 1: 265)

FOR STEFAN GEORGE AND RAINER MARIA RILKE, the year 1900 was to mark the midpoint in their respective lives. Having then just achieved artistic maturity, Rilke would undergo an astonishing evolution as a thinker and writer, creating such disparate yet related works as the *Neue Gedichte* (1907), *Die Aufzeichnungen des Malte Laurids Brigge* (1910), *Duineser Elegien* (1923), and *Die Sonette an Orpheus* (1923). By contrast, remarkable constancy within a closely controlled range of ideas and styles characterizes George's three major books of poetry after 1900: *Der Siebente Ring* (1907), *Der Stern des Bundes* (1913), and *Das Neue Reich* (1928).[1] Rilke was embarking on a spiritual journey that would lead him from mastery of the aesthetics and ethics of representation to a visionary poetic philosophy that embraced the world as life and death (Brodsky 37). George, for his part, had fixed upon a new faith that divinity was immanent and potentially incarnate in the present moment. Whereas for Rilke all being yearns to be transformed, George, like Plato, insisted that ideal forms have metaphysical permanence, however changeable earthly phenomena may seem. Rilke

urged humanity to glory in mortality and affirm Earth's wisdom in grant-
ing us life and taking it away. George, on the other hand, demanded that
mankind restore archetypal social and cultural ideals to prove worthy of an
unending heroic destiny that he saw figured forth in the stars. Nietzsche's
"so soll es sein" came to dominate George's being and art after 1900. With
oracular ambiguity he laid claim to his place in history — "Ich bin ein end
und ein beginn" (I: 359) — and strove, again in the spirit of Nietzsche, to
resolve that paradox through the life he led.

George sought ceaselessly to influence the arts in Germany and ultimately thereby the nation's character. For nearly forty years, his efforts
attracted allies and later disciples, the George-*Kreis,* as well as numerous
detractors.[2] Just as integral to George's "works" during the second half of
his life as his four books of poetry — starting with *Der Teppich des Lebens* in
1899–1900 — were the eight volumes appearing in those years of *Blätter
für die Kunst,* the journal he edited between 1892 and 1919. Drawing
mainly upon poetry by George and members of the *Kreis,* the *Blätter*
sought through precept and example to elevate the content, style, and ideology of writing in Germany. Responding to wider interest and attempting
to repudiate charges of elitist exclusiveness, George published three *Blätter*
anthologies in 1899, 1904, and 1909, including selections from 1892–98,
1898–1904, and 1904–9 respectively. The preface to 1904's volume proclaimed that the "poetic and aesthetic" rebirth of the arts propagated by the
Blätter was "the only true artistic *movement*" that had succeeded in driving
saccharine bourgeois tastes and plebeian Naturalism from the scene.[3]

Claiming to guide German intellectual life more generally, Friedrich
Gundolf and Friedrich Wolters for three years issued the *Jahrbuch für die
geistige Bewegung,* whose scholarly articles presented ideas on art, philosophy, history, and critiques of cultural developments in the spirit of Stefan
George as members of the *Kreis* interpreted them. In addition, George
offered essential advice on the publication of two score of anthologies,
monographs, and original poetry with the *Blätter*'s colophon.

With Karl Wolfskehl and Friedrich Gundolf, George worked to make
Germans aware of neglected foreign authors and of German writers out of
fashion. A three-volume anthology began appearing in 1900, *Deutsche
Dichtung,* featuring Jean Paul, Goethe, and writers of "the century of
Goethe" whose poetry was nearly unknown by then: Klopstock, Schiller,
Hölderlin, Novalis, Brentano, Eichendorff, Platen, Heine, Lenau, Hebbel,
Mörike, and C. F. Meyer.[4] A two-volume collection of *Zeitgenössische
Dichter* (Contemporary Poets, 1905) followed, presenting translations by
George of poetry from England (Rossetti, Swinburne, Dowson), Denmark
(Jacobsen), Holland (Kloos, Verwey), Belgium (Verhaeren), France
(Verlaine, Mallarmé, Rimbaud, de Regnier), Italy (d'Annunzio), and
Poland (Rolicz-Lieder). George judged them "geister [. . .] denen man
das wiedererwachen der dichtung in Europa verdankt" (2: 339).

The day-by-day account of Stefan George's life reveals how intensely his mission preoccupied him.[5] While under no illusion that these authors could serve as literary models in his own time, he honored Dante, Shakespeare, and Baudelaire as beacons of the human spirit and masters of form and musicality. In 1901, his volume of German "adaptations" of Baudelaire's *Les fleurs du mal* appeared. George esteemed the verve with which Baudelaire explored new poetic spheres and "die glühende geistigkeit mit der er auch die sprödesten stoffe durchdrang" (2: 233). Between 1908 and 1915, Gundolf issued ten volumes of *Shakespeare in deutscher Sprache* (Shakespeare in the German Language), essentially a redaction of the classic Schlegel-Tieck translations. Gundolf had translated anew six dramas and, together with George, based two more on earlier versions in German. This project was associated with one of the most celebrated scholarly works to emerge from the *Kreis,* Gundolf's *Shakespeare und der deutsche Geist* (Shakespeare and the German Mind, 1911). George's own adaptation into German of Shakespeare's sonnets in 1909, while literarily impeccable, suggests a provocative thrust at social taboos. His preface says earlier readers missed the central idea of the *Sonnets:* the poet's reverence for beauty and his radiant desire for eternity. George insists that we accept Shakespeare's passionate devotion to his male friend. Even if we do not understand that, it is foolish to praise or blame what one of the greatest mortals found appropriate. Materialist, hyper-rational eras cannot conceive of a meta-erotic love capable of creating a whole world.[6]

But George's own poetic identity was bound up most closely with Dante, a prominent figure in *Der Siebente Ring,* and in whose guise George appeared at a Munich *Fasching* celebration in 1904, where he read aloud passages from his translation of the *Divine Comedy* (Boehringer 1: 116–21). Between 1901 and 1925, beginning with the fifth volume of the *Blätter,* George published selections from all three parts of the great medieval poem, in all about one fifth of the entire work. In the preface to the first book-length edition, George states that he sought only to "render fruitful" the poet's essence, "ton bewegung gestalt: alles wodurch Dante [. . .] am anfang aller Neuen Dichtung steht" (2: 7).

George added new dimensions to his own image as an artist in 1901 with *Die Fibel: Auswahl erster Verse.* It was followed by *Tage und Taten* in 1903, a collection of prose pieces, mostly lyrical and subjective, that had appeared in the *Blätter* 1893–96, superseded in 1925 by an augmented edition. At the start of a new century, George was rescuing from oblivion only certain of his writings. *Die Fibel's* preface expresses ambivalent self-confidence. George feels that a "lifetime" already lies behind him and fears that his friends will find in these poems from the late 1880s those aspects they appreciate in his recent works present, if at all, only in a distorted or muted form. Yet, "wir die dichter" see in them "die ungestalten puppen aus denen später die falter leuchtender gesänge fliegen" (2: 467). George was conceiving then the two "Zeitgedichte" (Poems of Our Times) that open and close the first cycle of *Der Siebente Ring.* The first insists that the Art Nouveau minstrel whom people saw in George in the 1890s and the combative seer who now commands their attention are identical: "Ihr sehet wechsel · doch ich tat das gleiche" (1: 228).

Stefan George was convinced that he could infuse the German nation's culture, indeed its essential being with a new spirit, purpose, and style because he believed resolutely in the special powers of great poets and their works. He shared this faith with many contemporaries and most educated Europeans of the nineteenth century. Shelley stated the ancient argument with uncompromising eloquence in 1821 in *A Defence of Poetry:*

> Poets are the hierophants of an unapprehended inspiration; the mirrors of the gigantic shadows which futurity casts upon the present; the words which express what they understand not; the trumpets which sing to battle, and feel not what they inspire; the influence which is moved not, but moves. Poets are the unacknowledged legislators of the world.
>
> (Shelley 522)

Schiller and the German Romantics had already given new life to this belief, Schiller most famously in "Die Teilung der Erde" (The Dividing of the Earth; Schiller 1: 179). The third volume of *Deutsche Dichtung* includes Schiller's elegy, "Die Sänger der Vorwelt" (The Bards of Old), whose closing verses uncannily anticipate the wishes and the grievances of George's *Kreis* concerning relations between the poet and his time:

> An der glut des gesangs entflammten des hörers gefühle ·
> An des hörers gefühl nährte der sänger die glut —
> Nährt' und reinigte sie! Der glückliche · dem in des volkes
> Stimme noch hell zurücktönte die seele des lieds ·
> Dem noch von aussen erschien · im leben · die himmlische gottheit ·
> Die der neuere kaum · kaum noch im herzen vernimmt. (29)

In essence, George's conception of the poet's extraordinary merits and privileges arose from the ideas of Plato as the Renaissance had revived them, enriched and elaborated upon in Germany by Classicism and Romanticism. Charles Baudelaire and the Symbolists who built upon the tradition that his poetry inaugurated, especially Verlaine, Rimbaud, and Mallarmé, revered the poet as the bearer of a sacred riddle, whether couched in esoteric language of flamboyant beauty or in images of repellent decadence. Like other French artists, they claimed for genius the right to a particular public attitude, a personal morality that defied prevailing ideas of good and evil, often characterized by bizarre "Bohemian" lifestyles. Post-romantic, post-revolutionary France of the late nineteenth century by tradition enjoyed a robust, adversarial cultural discourse. As synergistic forces, Symbolism and Art Nouveau stimulated and enriched it remarkably, subverting canons of conventional taste with eccentric, innovative poetry, paintings, music and architecture. This critical world might receive avant-garde poetry either with respect, as a private, sacred, cryptic message to the reader mediated by the poet from an absolute spiritual presence, or with ridicule as being pretentious, precious, and intended to dupe and amaze a gullible public.

Clearly favoring the first of these opinions, Stefan George came under the influence of the French Symbolists decisively when he visited Paris in 1889 and frequented their gatherings, especially at the home of Mallarmé. From this period stems his adoption for a time of the mildly ominous, self-confident habitus suggestive of the dandy, later modulated to a priestly demeanor. More significantly, his travels beyond his homeland established the kinship of George's thinking and poetry, so distinctive in his early works, with Art Nouveau, Symbolism, and the European avant-garde. In his 1892 tribute to Mallarmé in the first volume of the *Blätter,* reprinted in *Tage und Taten,* George defended the French master's apparent obscurantism that subordinated meaning to musicality. Mallarmé's verses have the quality of

> lieder und reime aus grauer zeit die keine rechte klärung zulassen bei deren hersagung aber weite fluten von genüssen und peinen an uns vorüberrollen und blasse erinnerungen auferstehen die wie schmerzhafte schwestern uns schmeichlerisch die hände geben. (1: 506)

During the later 1890s, George came to consider whether the destiny of a living poet like himself lay only in the realms of cosmopolitan art, culture, and society, or whether his fate was summoning him to a larger arena of the national soul, where cultural politics and metaphysical longing dwelt in volatile proximity. Reflecting changes in George's understanding of his poetic role, the melancholy artist of *Hymnen* and *Das Jahr der Seele* is succeeded first by the tormented seeker or the "Freund der Fluren" (The Friend of the Fields) of *Der Teppich des Lebens* and finally by the imperious seer of "Der Krieg." For over a century now, loyal adherents and skeptical critics alike have sought to describe and explain this evolution in light of George's complex situation within Germany's society and culture, which underwent wrenching changes during his lifetime.[7] The analytical debate continues over the roles of George, the *Kreis,* and his writings in shaping the fate of Germany in his time and beyond. Were the poet's achievements only reflections of larger artistic, social, and political currents or did he actually initiate or reinforce ideas whose consequences he could not foresee?[8]

As the nineteenth century drew to a close, a recently unified Germany was changing rapidly. The fundamental wave of secularization that had been gathering momentum for centuries accelerated with the advent of technology and free enterprise, transforming what had been a collection of essentially agricultural principalities into a modern industrial, mercantile, and military Great Power at the heart of Europe. The new nation's political, social, and religious institutions were hard pressed to change with equal speed. As they did elsewhere, the materialist, determinist theories of Darwin and Marx challenged any belief in a metaphysical teleology, whether religious or philosophical, that could endow life with purpose and meaning. Germany struggled harder with these forces than France and England due to its sheer size and complexity, its geographic, economic and social situation, and because so many long-delayed changes came at once. Especially among defenders of the old order, "reaction," opposition to modernity and democratic institutions, was widespread. From its inception, the ideology of the *Kreis* partook of this conservative, aristocratic elitism endemic to practically all German institutions of the day. This outlook was expressed not only in ideas relating to art, but also to what many members wishfully conceived of as "politics." With millions of other Germans they shared a faith that a metaphysical fatality rather than material forces ultimately moved human history (even if God was dead). Such vestigial idealism was due, in part at least, to alienation from the changes besetting society, not to mention that members of the *Kreis* came from classes adversely affected by those changes.

Schwabing, Munich's celebrated artists' quarter, where George often stayed for weeks at the home of Karl Wolfskehl around the turn of the century, was a focus of the intellectual and artistic ferment quickened by Germany's cultural turmoil. Wolfskehl's circle propagated an irrational mysticism centering on a metaphysical "Cosmos" that they believed was manifested in religious prophecy and great works of art, but especially in the heroic will of exceptional individuals. Two of the most active members of the circle, Ludwig Klages and Alfred Schuler, went even further, espousing an anti-Semitic, anti-Christian myth of Germanic supremacy strongly tinged with occultism and distilled from the ideas of Johann Jakob Bachofen, Helena Petrovna Blavatsky (1831–91), Houston Stewart Chamberlain, and a perverse reading of Nietzsche.[9] George became familiar with the notions of the Munich "Cosmics," but maintained a skeptical distance, especially in regard to the racism and bizarre occultism that some of them professed. Klages wrote a tribute to George, praising him as the exemplary mediator between the Cosmos and humankind (Klages 17). Although he broke with Klages and Schuler in January 1904 over their anti-Semitism, George's contact with the "Cosmics" reinforced his critical attitude towards contemporary events and personalities and encouraged him to trust and express his own larger intuitions about the world, just as he had earlier learned to understand and give artistic shape to his subjective responses.

The prefaces to the *Blätter für die Kunst* after 1900 reveal how George's ambitious cultural mission increasingly arises from a sweeping critique of German society, politics, and spiritual vitality. As early as 1896, arguing for German writing that is beautiful, noble, and imposing in opposition to Naturalism and the poor taste of bourgeois diversions, George links the German Reich's miserable cultural situation to its institutions: "Die thatsache dass es bei uns kein künstlerisches und dichterisches ereignis geben kann beweist dass wir uns in einem bildungsstaat zweiter ordnung befinden" (*BfdK* 3,2: 33). Tragic pride is evident in struggling to ennoble not only art for the sake of beauty and the sublime, but the nation's very soul and destiny. German culture must be brought to express a purpose and integrity akin in spirit, though surely not in form, to that which characterized the image of Greece cherished by the German *Klassik*. The only hope for prevailing in this effort lies in those who will be its beneficiaries, Germany's youth: "dass [unsre jugend] [. . .] auch ihr volkstum gross und nicht im beschränkten sinne eines stammes auffasst: darin finde man den umschwung des deutschen wesens bei der jahrhundertwende" (*BfdK* 4,1/2: 4). In the 1900s, the tone becomes more urgent, the themes more nationalistic, the language often darkly oracular: the exemplary poet, George, is termed the "urgeist," who guides his "jünger" through "rhythmus," his authority beyond question. "Preussentum" is condemned not as a state or people, but as "ein allerdings sehr wirksames aber aller kunst und kultur feindliches system." Germans need a characteristic *gestus* — "die deutsche geste" — more vitally than ten conquered provinces. At their close, these hypotactic musings warn ominously of unspecified "grosse umwälzungen und ausbrüche" of far greater magnitude than the political and economic skirmishes of the present (*BfdK* 5: 2–4).

Aggressive scorn dominates the preface to volume 7, published in early 1904. The nation, the "Volk," thanks to the "ungeheuren menschenanwüchse dieser zeit," has lost the vital "spannkräfte" needed to realize "kultur" (*BfdK* 7: 3). The closing aphorism, "Künstler und Kämpfer" (Artist and Fighter), sums up the mood of despair and defiance:

> Niemals war wie heute eine herrschaft der massen · niemals daher die tat des einzelnen so fruchtlos. wol sind zeiten und gelegenheiten denkbar wo auch der künstler es für nötig hält das schwert des kampfes zu ergreifen: über allen diesen welten- staats- und gesellschafts-wälzungen steht er aber als bewahrer des ewigen feuers. (*BfdK* 7: 11)

Four years later, in volume 8, stoic resignation reigns:

> Der künstler allein [. . .] hat noch die möglichkeit in einem Reiche zu leben wo der geist das oberste gesetz gibt. Daher seine absonderung und sein stolz. [. . .] Alle allgemeinheiten [bringen hervor und verwerten] [. . .] nur noch die schmarotzer- und zweiter-hand-leistung [. . .]: weshalb auch ihre dunkle sehnsucht nach dem Ersten hoffnungslos bleiben muss. Heut ist wirklich "die Kunst ein bruch mit der Gesellschaft." (*BfdK* 8: 2–3)

The discourse takes an unprecedented turn in volume 9 (1910). Inclusion in this issue of excerpts from Hölderlin's translation of Pindar's odes provides an opportunity to express once more a high regard for ancient Greece. Goethe and other "führende geister" of his time, instead of imitating

Hellenic poetry and sculpture, entered upon "eine Heilige Heirat" of the soul and the intellect with the highest ideals of Greek culture. Then, George boldly presents a challenging notion of what motivated the Greeks to achieve greatness: "Der Griechische Gedanke: 'der Leib · dies sinnbild der vergänglichkeit · DER LEIB SEI DER GOTT' [war] weitaus der schöpferischste und [. . .] menschenwürdigste [. . .] · dem an erhabenheit jeder andre · sogar der christliche · nachstehn muss" (*BfdK* 9: 2). An essay entitled "Über das Feststehende und die Denkformen" at the close of the volume, elaborates upon this modulation to theological myth: Creators possess the Divine (*das Göttliche*) in its primal immediacy; they are archetypes (*urtypen*), whether they carry the Divine in themselves or have received it from a god. Creators must perpetually give birth anew to the Divine, which "shepherds" then preach to the "herds." But no manifestation of the Divine can exert its power throughout all time. For ages that do not experience the Divine in a human manifestation ("das Göttliche im menschen"), God is a mere idea. The most provocative claim then follows: Germans of the century just past esteemed Jesus greatly as an exemplary human being without acknowledging that he was God. What seems "incomprehensible" today is that a man like Jesus could raise himself above the common flock to such a height at all: "der schritt von dem herdenwesen zu dem höhenwesen ist für uns der unendlich grosse · ein winzig kleiner ist uns der von dem höhenmenschen zum Gott. Drum ist es [. . .] kein opfer [. . .] wenn wir ausrufen: du bist Gottes Sohn · du bist Gott" (*BfdK* 9: 154–56). Clearly, such acclaim is no longer owed to Jesus alone, but to any mortal who can take this infinitely great step. While it is not certain that George wrote this piece, its inclusion and placement suggest that it reflects his ideas (Landmann 80; George, *Stern* 119–20).

His belief that a living person might achieve godly sublimity has complex roots in George's own emotional and ideological situation and that of the age. The triumph of pragmatic rationalism in the West was a widely felt matter of fact that established religions could not refute plausibly, even if social and political institutions changed only slowly in response. This state of ideological affairs caused many to yearn for any sign that the world has a divinely ordained purpose. By the turn of the century, this desire was lending chiliastic urgency to a Nietzschean vein of cultural pessimism, hints of which we encounter in the *Blätter*. Increasingly, too, it mingled with religious ideas stemming from Christian mysticism, Eleusinian Gnosticism, Germanic myth, and other esoteric beliefs. Ironically, the very secularization of society liberated individuals to embrace, invent, or syncretize whatever faith could offer them solace now or salvation hereafter. More than ever before they turned to philosophers, scientists, and even poets to divine the meanings behind the physical and psychic phenomena of human experience. All over the West, men and women of the educated middle class availed themselves of the new freedom of belief, which flourished most widely just prior to the First World War. The radical materialist ideologies of fascism and communism, conceived as faiths for the masses, swept away this liberty and soon divided whole continents between them.

In February 1902 in Munich, at age thirty-three, Stefan George encountered Maximilian Kronberger, a schoolboy he named "Maximin," then thirteen, from a well-to-do family. Maximin's surpassing beauty and spiritual precocity attracted George strongly, and he saw the young man often during the next two years when visiting Munich, acting, with the family's consent, as a friend and mentor in art and poetry, which Maximin was already writing. In the *Fasching* pageant of 1904, where George appeared as Dante, Maximin impersonated a Florentine page. What ultimately inspired George's unshakeable faith that the young man was a redemptive incarnation of divine power was Maximin's sudden death from meningitis on 15 April 1904, the day after his sixteenth birthday. Months later, George wrote to friends: "Ich trauere über einen unbegreiflichen und frühen tod der auch mich an die lezten klüfte hinführen wollte" (Boehringer 1: 84). George projected his grief at losing Maximin onto a plane beyond personal emotion, just as he had construed finding him as a sign that the human spirit could be rescued from depravity. Late in 1906, in the preface to *Maximin. Ein Gedenkbuch,* George described what the young man signified to him:

> Wir erkannten in [Maximin] den darsteller einer allmächtigen jugend wie wir sie erträumt hatten · [. . .] einer jugend die unser erbe nehmen und neue reiche erobern könnte. [. . .] was uns not tat war Einer der von den einfachen geschehnissen ergriffen wurde und uns die dinge zeigte wie die augen der götter sie sehen.
>
> An der helle die uns überströmte merkten wir dass er gefunden war. [. . .] Je näher wir ihn kennen lernten desto mehr erinnerte er uns an unser denkbild und ebenso verehrten wir den umfang seines ursprünglichen geistes und die regungen seiner heldenhaften seele wie deren versinnlichung in gestalt und gebärde und sprache. (1: 523)

To George, Maximin represented the forces of life in an elemental concentration; he embodied a primeval force, an Eros universally present, but only exceptionally so purely manifested. Maximin affirmed and resolved what George construed as the magnificent paradox of Greek antiquity, "DER LEIB SEI DER GOTT," as he formulated it in the *Blätter* in 1910. Maximin constituted the perfect fusion of body and mind in a self-awareness which, to George, was godlike. Although this faith provokes our skepticism, its idea can be seen in a humanistic sense, as asking that we serve the Apollonian spirit, acknowledge our own longing for the sublime, and that we open the eyes of our fellow men, so that they may learn to recognize true beauty and genuine greatness in life, embrace harmonious order as the divinely ordained goal of life, and learn to hate nothing more than destruction and chaos (Jaime-Liebig 40–41). The Maximin "experience" is pivotal in George's quest for the eternal, transcendent values that he believed had inspired Hellas. Maximin, the transfigured promise of human perfectibility, was never absent from George as the impulse to his art and his ideas. George's reverential mourning for Maximin, his burning desire to retrieve him from death, was to inspire his poetry from *Der Siebente Ring* onward; it would inevitably color the future of the *Kreis,* especially as younger members joined who were prepared to accept the disciplined reverence that George demanded.

Der Siebente Ring

Nearly two decades before Thomas Mann used it as a solemnly ironic leitmotif in *Der Zauberberg* (The Magic Mountain, 1924), Stefan George made the number seven, revered universally as magical, the unifying emblem of *Der Siebente Ring.* The richly ornamented, limited first printing appeared in 1907, the seventh collection of George's poems — following *Hymnen, Pilgerfahrten, Algabal, Die Bücher der Hirten- und Preisgedichte . . ., Das Jahr der Seele,* and *Der Teppich des Lebens* — seven years after the last of these (Landmann 69–70; George, *Ring* 189–236).[10] The number of poems, ranging from fourteen to seventy, in each of the book's seven sections is divisible by seven. The plan is to lead the reader upward through domains of the spirit, as though progressing through a cathedral's chapels to worship at the high altar, from which, then, other stations of meditation lead away. The "Zeitgedichte" initiate the excursion with multiple perspectives on Europe's spiritual bankruptcy; "Gestalten" (Pageant) demonstrates art's power to create a higher reality in myth. The third section, "Gezeiten" (Tides), celebrates the exaltations and sorrows of love. "Maximin" glorifies and mourns a being in whom George perceived physical and spiritual perfection so radiant that, to him, it could not be other than divine. "Traumdunkel" (Darkness of Dream) and "Lieder" retreat from emotional intensity to more remote, legendary worlds of artistry. The "Tafeln" (Tablets), finally, addressed to George's friends, associates, and adversaries, conduct the reader once more into the world of the present. Such careful design belies the fact that George wrote these poems during the better part of a decade. The sequence of sections has little to do with the time they were written. Throughout his life, George crafted poems and their larger settings to exert optimal aesthetic, emotional, and spiritual force upon the reader, not to reflect momentary moods. While acknowledging George's intent to represent and resolve inescapable human tensions within an aesthetic artifice, Claude David rightly judges *Der Siebente Ring* to be among the most "tormented, contradictory, and inscrutable" of the poet's works, but also the most moving (201–2).

Aside from "Carl August," all fourteen of the "Zeitgedichte" were published in the *Blätter* between 1899 and 1904 and appear, excepting the first two, in the order of their first printings. They share a common form: four strophes of eight lines each in blank verse. Some are "occasional" in the truest sense, George's responses to immediate, public events: the festivities commemorating Goethe's 150th birthday, the widely discussed deaths of Nietzsche (Hillebrand 68–84), Böcklin, Pope Leo XIII, and the assassination of the Empress Elisabeth of Austria as well as her sister's death by fire. Others mark more private concerns: George's struggle for artistic identity and his hopes for transforming Germany's cultural aspirations (initial and final "Zeitgedichte"), his choice of Dante as the model for his own poetic mission ("Dante und das Zeitgedicht"), heartfelt gratitude to France and her poets for delivering him from despair ("Franken"), outrage that Kaiser Wilhelm II had ordered the sepulchers of Germany's great medieval rulers be opened ("Die Gräber in Speier" [The Tombs in Speier]), sorrowful admiration for a younger friend killed in battle ("Pente Pigadia"), or paying tribute to his long association with Carl August Klein ("Carl August"). While the poems celebrate human virtues, they express, above all, contemptuous anger over Germany's failure to honor these qualities, whether revealed under heroic or humble circumstances. Dante declares that he lavished his greatest art and love on creating "Paradiso," and that the "Inferno" seems trivial by comparison (1: 229). Goethe, the stereotypical serene Olympian, is depicted in lifelong torment (1: 230). Nietzsche, "Donnerer" and "Erlöser," could never himself experience the freedom and vital joyousness he proclaimed because he stifled love and lost himself in solitude (1: 231). George assails the imperviousness of ordinary people to the spirit's higher claims: "Blöd trabt die menge drunten · scheucht sie nicht! / Was wäre stich der qualle · schnitt dem kraut!" (1: 231). Those at society's pinnacle are no better: "Trompetenstoss mag aus- und einbegleiten / Umflitterten popanz und feisten krämer" (1: 232). George included a poem in "Zeitgedichte" only if it balanced despair with hope. "Der Preusse," on Bismarck, failed that test and was excluded (Aurnhammer 195–96).

"Porta Nigra" and "Die tote Stadt" (The Dead City) convey the essential attitude of George and the *Kreis* towards modern Europe. The ghost of a boy prostitute from the first century visits the Porta Nigra, a monumental Roman gate in today's Trier, and recalls the glory of the city he had known. Despised himself in his time, he feels only contempt for modern humanity's "Gedunsne larven mit erloschnen blicken / Und frauen die ein sklav zu feil befände —" (1: 234). George dedicated the poem to Alfred Schuler's "ingenium," in whose spirit the boy condemns the Germans for losing their race's vitality and purity: "Das edelste ging euch verloren: blut . ." (1: 234). "Die tote Stadt" attacks technology, materialism, and mass urban civilization. Though their city sucks the land dry of sustenance, a nameless malady befalls the populace of the "new harbor": "uns mäht ein ödes weh und wir verderben [. . .] — im überflusse siech" (1: 243). They turn in desperation to the ancient, impoverished "mutterstadt." There, people walk in rags on streets overgrown with grass, but feel no hardship as they guard their sacred emblems, for they know their day shall dawn. When the inhabitants of the city below offer limitless rewards for "reinen odem eurer höhe / Und klaren quell" (1: 243), they receive a harsh reply: "Das gut das euch vor allem galt ist schutt. [. . .] Euch all trifft tod. Schon eure zahl ist frevel" (1: 244). The parable assumes that material wealth and modernity weaken a people and render it soulless, while those living in poverty and pursuing archaic ways are somehow sacred, noble, and entitled to be cruelly vindictive. These facile associations escape rebuttal, for they do not claim to be factual, but rather poetic, inspired, perhaps even prophetic to wishful thinkers. Increasingly, such ominous allegories that operate with vague, but powerfully allusive referents will come to characterize the tone and temper of George's writing. The close of the "Zeitgedichte," hopeful amidst history's fatal gloom, risks platitude in its vagueness and barely avoids nihilism despite a majestic faith in "something that has always been":

> Nacht kommt für helle — busse für das glück.
> Und schlingt das dunkel uns und unsre trauer:
> Eins das von je war (keiner kennt es) währet
> Und blum und jugend lacht und sang erklingt. (1: 245)

"Maximin" aside, the remaining cycles recall themes and forms found in George's six earlier volumes, often with greater intensity of feeling or more concentrated craftsmanship. The concluding "Tafeln" correspond to epigrammatic tributes or warnings in earlier books. Like *Der Teppich des Lebens,* "Gestalten" portrays exemplary archetypes in brilliantly wrought, almost sculptural figures that recall the colors and textures of Art Nouveau. "Sonnwendzug" (Summer Solstice), for instance, forcefully conveys the paradoxical fusion of creation and destruction, the rhythms of Bacchic abandon restrained and enhanced by meter:

> Ruf von lust und grausen hallt im haine
> Vom beginnenden jagen ·
> Zitternd tasten hände noch nach locken
> Da verdurstet schon manche
> Heiss von fang und flucht · besprizt vom safte
> Ausgequollener früchte ·
> Blut und speichel harter lippen trinken
> Und auf qualmigen garben
> Andre wechselnd beide blumen küssen
> Auf der brust den Gewählten. (1: 254)

Throughout *Der Siebente Ring*, vital urgency has displaced the detached languor of *décadence* that prevailed in George's poetry prior to *Der Teppich des Lebens*. "Gezeiten" expresses more spontaneously than ever before his impassioned joy over his friendships with younger men, subtle, intense fusions of spiritual and erotic energy. The cycle concludes with a tribute to Dionysus, the lord of intoxication, fertility, and abandonment of the self to life's fullness, whether it bring glory or suffering: "Kein ding das webt in deinem kreis ist schnöd. [. . .] In fahr und fron · wenn wir nur überdauern · / Hat jeder tag mit einem sieg sein ende" (1: 277).

As the name implies, "Traumdunkel" harbors many divergent impulses, most notably didactic, historical nostalgia in "Ursprünge" (Origins 1: 294–95), luminous representations of nature that express subjective states in "Landschaft I · II · III" (Landscape 1: 296–98) and elsewhere, and reverent meditation (1: 303–6) in "Feier" (Rites), "Empfängnis" (Conception), and "Litanei" (Litany). "Hehre Harfe" (Sacred Lyre), finally, argues that the natural world's glory demands amazed wonder, not analysis and exploitation:

> Hegt den wahn nicht: mehr zu lernen
> Als aus staunen überschwang
> Holden blumen hohen sternen
> Einen sonnigen lobgesang. (1: 307)

While many of the "Lieder" possess delicate, lyrical charm, others, especially towards the close, are more portentous and epic, ballads at best. The three concluding songs (1: 322–23) speak of the poet's faith in a spiritual "Du," distant and exalted, yet present everywhere, perhaps the Angel of the *Teppich*'s prologue, perhaps Maximin. The poet is serene in his devotion, craving peace even at the price of isolation: "Die hände die mienen / Erflehn von mir ruh nun · / Ich frieden vor ihnen . . / Und wach bleibest Du nur" (1: 323).

At the center of *Der Siebente Ring* stands the cycle "Maximin," at its heart the six poems "Auf das Leben und den Tod Maximins" (On the Life and Death of Maximin) that appeared in the *Gedenkbuch*. A work of mourning and of adoration, it claims unabashedly that Maximin not only possesses divine beauty of body and spirit, but that he is a god, *the* god governing the poet's destiny. "Ich seh in dir den Gott / Den schauernd ich erkannt / Dem meine andacht gilt" (1: 279). These poems celebrate Maximin chiefly as George's personal redeemer from the solitude of his despair over the tragic situation of humanity: "Du kamst am lezten tag / Da ich von harren siech / Da ich des betens müd / Mich in die nacht verlor" (1: 279). To George, the dead youth is at times a benevolent presence within nature ("Wie dank ich sonne" [How grateful am I, sun] 1: 290), at others the object of desirous longing ("Einverleibung" [Incarnation] 1: 291), to be fulfilled only in a vision crafted of words. In the life of the *Kreis*, Maximin represents salvation, "heil" from the chiliastic ecstasies that the

"Cosmics" propagated and a counterweight to the arguments of Klages and Schuler. The notion that the mortal Maximin could assume such spiritual and physical sublimity as to merit faith in his divinity later becomes central to George's ideology in leading his ever-younger disciples. Maximin is a postulation of a spiritual presence in a world from which it seemed to have fled entirely, a world whose gods were dead. That his earthly life ended in his youth hardly detracted from his power as a possible model and ideal:

> Ihr hattet augen trüb durch ferne träume
> Und sorgtet nicht mehr um das heilige lehn.
> Ihr fühltet endes-hauch durch alle räume —
> Nun hebt das haupt! denn euch ist heil geschehn.
> [. . .]
> Nun klagt nicht mehr — denn auch ihr wart erkoren —
> Dass eure tage unerfüllt entschwebt . . .
> Preist eure stadt die einen gott geboren!
> Preist eure zeit in der ein gott gelebt! (1: 284)

Der Stern des Bundes

Appearing in 1913, on the eve of the First World War, *Der Stern des Bundes* is consecrated to the memory of Maximin and to Stefan George's hopes that Germany might renew itself and come to pursue the ideals that the gods intended for humanity (Landmann 89–91; George, *Stern* 117–50).[11] George believed that a "heilige schar" recruited from the best of the nation's youth could bring this renewal about through a revolution that was in the first instance aesthetic and spiritual, but that would in the longer run require destroying the old, corrupt order of things to make way for "neues leben." The youthful disciples who were to usher in this radical change firmly believed that poetry could provide them with not only the spiritual impetus, but also with much of the doctrine to guide them. The ethos of George and his followers rejected analytical theories and manifestos in favor of intuitive, visionary decrees whose authority rested as much upon the poet's terse, oracular eloquence as upon the ideology that his words embodied. The closing axiom of the preface to the *Blätter's* final volume, published in 1919, following Germany's defeat, declares defiantly: "Nur den wenigen dürfte es einleuchten dass in der dichtung eines volkes sich seine lezten schicksale enthüllen" (*BfdK* 11/12: 6). In *Der Stern des Bundes,* intended initially only for his closest friends, George was widely considered to have diagnosed the spiritual perversity of modern Europe and to have prophesied the Great War that was its price. Selections appearing in volume 10 of the *Blätter* (1910) so intrigued readers that he chose to publish the entire volume: "nur die erwägung dass ein verborgen-halten von einmal ausgesprochenem heut kaum mehr möglich ist hat die öffentlichkeit vorgezogen als den sichersten schutz" (1: 347).

The volume, published without Melchior Lechter's elaborate ornamentation, contains one hundred poems, a reverent allusion to the number of cantos in Dante's *La Commedia* (1321). Three "Bücher" (Books) of thirty poems each are preceded by an "Eingang" (Introit) of nine poems and followed by a single "Schlusschor" (Closing Chorus). "Eingang," which — like the other parts — glorifies Maximin while never naming him, is also a subtle poetic tribute to Shakespeare, whose *Sonnets* to a beloved but unnamed young man George had translated. All of the poems contain fourteen lines in iambic pentameter. Though all but the last of these are unrhymed, they correspond to the sonnet's traditional patterns of disposition. They are no less a tribute, incidentally, to Dante, who recounted his quest for Beatrice in a sonnet cycle, the *Vita Nuova* (circa 1293). Essentially, however, the "Eingang" explicates Maximin's godhead. He is the "Herr der Wende" (1: 350), appearing to the poet when his despair over his own life and the crisis of faith pervading the culture was greatest. Above all, Maximin miraculously brings liberation from "qual der zweiheit"; he personifies "die verschmelzung fleischgeworden," revealing "Eines zugleich und Andres," the wondrous fusion of "Rausch und Helle," Nietzsche's opposition of Dionysian and Apollonian (1: 350). Maximin's very being implies for George reconciliation of the duality of Body and Soul, of the temporal and the eternal, that haunted Western theology and philosophy. George believed that Maximin, his god of unity and synthesis, "Den neue mitte aus dem geist gebar" (1: 354), answered needs beyond his own anxieties and those of the *Kreis*. "Neu" occurs with exceptional frequency in George's writings and clearly has a special semantic weight for him. In "neue mitte," it signifies that an unprecedented, radically different balance has been ordained between the hitherto incommensurable extremities of matter and spirit.

Nineteenth-century Europe had constantly experienced struggle between implacable adversaries as a principal force in history, and Hegel and Marx made dialectical opposition central to their philosophies. In modern thought, a transcendent notion of bipolar conflict achieved a decisive triumph over the old postulates of harmony stabilized by its Creator within a unitary universe. George lamented this change and sought to redress it. He believed that it had caused and made more extreme many inevitable conflicts of modern Germany. As a remedy, George favored return to an hierarchical social order akin to the "Christenheit" idealized by Novalis in *Die Christenheit oder Europa* (Christendom or Europe, 1799). A new, monistic worldview facilitating such a society could crystallize around a personal godhead that transcends polarity to embody archetypal unity. Maximin is ultimately a mystery for George, one that can only

be venerated. But we must not lose sight of how Germany's tormented ideology at the turn of the century shaped his image and his function. In the
"Eingang," Maximin speaks only once, and from a vast distance: "nun naht
das jahr / In dem ich meine neue form bestimme. / Ich wandle mich doch
wahre gleiches wesen / Ich werde nie wie ihr: schon fiel die wahl" (1: 351).

Although his style, both in his writing and in his life, strongly recalls
traditional religious usage (Linke 103–37), George's proofs for Maximin's
divinity are not theological arguments or philosophical propositions, but
arise from his own poetic intuition and passionate sensuality, ultimately
irrational, super-rational, and not accessible to argument. The second of
the "Gebete" (Prayers) in "Maximin" (1: 289–90) reveals that George
regarded human sensation and emotions as being of divine origin, their
intuitive guidance true, nearly beyond any doubt: "Wirbel uns aus niedrer
zelle / Sternenan entführt geschwind: / Deinesgleichen in der welle / In
der wolke in dem wind?" George states his readiness to grant subjective
perceptions precedence over the teachings of any church even more
emphatically in the last poem of the "Eingang":

> Wer ist dein Gott? All meines traums begehr ·
> Der nächste meinem urbild · schön und hehr.
> Was die gewalt gab unsrer dunklen schösse
> Was uns von jeher wert erwarb und grösse —
> Geheimste quelle innerlichster brand: (1: 354)

A poem in the Second Book expounds George's views in the style
of Socrates in the *Symposium,* echoing too Shakespeare's love of paradox, Hölderlin's gnomic compression, and Platen's sinuous ghazals. The
miraculous synthesis that is Maximin, Beauty manifest in a human form,
the symbol of Virtue and Truth, arouses the artist to desire and to create,
endowing it with permanence.

> Die einen lehren: irdisch da — dort ewig . .
> Und der: ich bin die notdurft du die fülle.
> Hier künde sich: wie ist ein irdisches ewig
> Und eines notdurft bei dem andern fülle.
> Sich selbst nicht wissend blüht und welkt das Schöne
> Der geist der bleibt reisst an sich was vergänglich
> Er denkt er mehrt und er erhält das Schöne
> Mit allgewalt macht er es unvergänglich.
> Ein leib der schön ist wirkt in meinem blut
> Geist der ich bin umfängt ihn mit entzücken:
> So wird er neu im werk von geist und blut
> So wird er mein und dauernd ein entzücken. (1: 380)

The thirty poems in each of the three Books at the core of *Der Stern
des Bundes* are divided yet again into groups of ten linked by shared themes.

The tenth poem in each group is rhymed to mark the boundaries between them. Otherwise they are unrhymed, mainly in iambic pentameter, and between seven and twelve lines long. The initial part of the First Book affirms poetry's sacred role and the poet's priestly office. The next, the most celebrated and controversial, condemns the blind materialism of the age and its failure to fulfill or even comprehend humanity's spiritual hunger, warning of dire consequences. Highly compressed, intricately worked clauses bristle with prophetic contempt: "Siech ist der geist! tot ist die tat!" (1: 360), "Des götzen eiter in den adern rinnt"; "Ihr baut verbrechende an maass und grenze" (1: 361). Metaphors representing modern humanity's transgressions appear to claim parabolic directness, yet admit so many possible meanings as to weaken the force of their vivid imagery:

> Alles habend alles wissend seufzen sie:
> 'Karges leben! drang und hunger überall!
> Fülle fehlt!'
> Speicher weiss ich über jedem haus
> Voll von korn das fliegt und neu sich häuft —
> Keiner nimmt . . (1: 360)

It is too late to repent; George seems to prophesy that the gods will send the punishment whose warning tremors many had felt in 1913:

> Zehntausend muss der heilige wahnsinn schlagen
> Zehntausend muss die heilige seuche raffen
> Zehntausende der heilige krieg. (1: 361)

The section closes with a promise that trauma inflicted by the cataclysm will be healed magically (1: 363). Ancient purity and beauty will flourish anew, inspired by a radical cleansing that Fate ordained. Over this world will reign a figure still shadowy: "Bringt kranz und krone für den Ungenannten!" Is it to be Dionysus as imagined by Hölderlin, Maximin as George saw him, or a more reckless actor on history's stage?

The ten remaining poems of the First Book speak to the "friends and helpers" of George's own age. Effectively, he bids them farewell; trapped in their own era, they are unable to profess a more compelling faith. He, on the other hand, feels bound to a new life and his duty to his younger disciples in the service of Maximin:

> So muss ich sehn wie ich ein eines fasse
> Wie ich im raum den du mir maassest hafte
> Bedingte arbeit meines tags vollbringe
> Und mit dem traum von morgen mich vermähle. (1: 358)

The Second Book reflects George's role as mentor to his younger disciples, whose deeds shall bring his dream to fruition. Their discourse suggests a powerful interplay of physical eros and all registers of the mind: soul, intellect, instinct, impulse, and irrational ecstasy. The Third Book propounds the ethos that is to govern their lives in the world, if they are to become the "herrn der welt" George envisions. "Neugestaltet umgeboren" (1: 382), they must hew to a mean between discipline and freedom, faithful in their allegiance to the "reich des Geistes." Many aspects of George's new ethos, however, partake undeniably of the idiomatic sexism, racism, and nationalism dominating Western ideology at the time. As males, for instance, they serve "geist / Der immer mann ist" (1: 387), which has shaped this epoch, respecting but excluding from influence the "female" principle, "stoff." "Der neue stand" (1: 386), as George defines it, is elitist, hierarchical, exclusive, ritualistic, and secretive. Though similar in this respect to other associations of the day, the young men inspired by George's words and actions were guided by precepts rooted in Stoical self-reliance and responsibility:

> Fleht nicht um schnellern zuwachs grössrer macht:
> Die krönungszahl birgt jede möglichkeit . .
> Das in ihr Tuende tut die allheit bald
> Und was ihr heut nicht leben könnt wird nie. (1: 390)

Das Neue Reich

To commemorate Stefan George's sixtieth birthday in 1928, Georg Bondi published the *Gesamt-Ausgabe der Werke: Endgültige Fassung* (Complete Works: Definitive Edition) in eighteen volumes (Landmann 128–30), the ninth being *Das Neue Reich*. It embraces the period from 1905, when "Goethes letzte Nacht in Italien" (Goethe's Last Night in Italy) was conceived, until shortly after the First World War (Landmann 129; George *Reich* 113–75).[12] The *Blätter* had published almost all of these poems in its regular issues, or, in the case of "Der Krieg" and the *Drei Gesänge* (Three Hymns), as separate printings. Though suggestive, the title, *Das Neue Reich,* has no political or geographic connotations, even where it appears in "Der Dichter in Zeiten der Wirren" (The Poet in Times of Turmoil, 1: 418). Rather, it names George's ideal of a utopian locus of humane balance between body and spirit envisioned in *Der Stern des Bundes* as "neue mitte" (1: 354), necessary to "neues leben" for the "neue stand" his disciples comprised. It demands of them courageous service to virtue, truth, and beauty if they are to endure. Like a chasm, the First World War separated the youths George celebrated in *Der Stern des Bundes* from the men, their number sorely diminished, who gathered often in the postwar years to hear "the Master's" ever darker warnings, observing but rarely engaging in the turbulent agony of the Weimar Republic. The volume's title conveys a bitter irony likely not intended by

George, for the Republic, near the end of its life in 1928, still appeared as "Deutsches Reich" on maps, the new state whose liberal and egalitarian values and evident tolerance for every kind of debauchery the *Kreis* despised.

The war and its aftermath also define a sharp thematic boundary within *Das Neue Reich*. "Goethes letzte Nacht in Italien" and "Hyperion I · II · III" — first printed in *Blätter* Eight (1908/09) and Ten (1914) respectively — still reflect George's hope that he might help to bring about a "deutsche geste" in the cultural life of Germany, a disciplined artistic diction appropriate to the creative passion that inspires it. For George, this conception of art and its greatest examples had originated in Greece, and it was still alive on the Mediterranean's shores among the heirs to the Greek tradition, particularly in Italy. Goethe and Hölderlin had best understood the essence of that tradition and sought to realize its ideals without slavishly imitating older models. Imagined at the end of his decisive Italian journey, Goethe is troubled, in large part because he has now confronted a culture essentially different from that of his homeland. He laments that Germany did not have a Promethean artist-seer present at its birth, "Der noch ein sohn war und nicht ein enkel der Gäa" (1: 402), who would have stolen for his people from the gods the fire of inspiration and the ambrosia of beauty, ennobling the entire nation's life. But Goethe still hopes to inspire his people with the Classical world's sublimity, though he fears that they will not understand his plea. Instead of analyzing all things and holding them to lifeless, intellectualized ideals, he urges his countrymen to bring about a harmonious synthesis between the world's multitude of phenomena and the ideal forms of thought that they embody:

> Nehmt diesen strahl in euch auf — o nennt ihn nicht kälte! —
> Und ich streu euch inzwischen im buntesten wechsel
> Steine und kräuter und erze: nun alles · nun nichts . .
> Bis sich verklebung der augen euch löst und ihr merket:
> Zauber des Dings — und des Leibes · der göttlichen norm.
>
> (1: 403)

"Hyperion I · II · III," a tribute to Hölderlin, elaborates on this theme. Sensual and sentimental, plaintive and awkward, the Germans exhaust their souls in music and self-reflection: "Ihr die in tönen verströmten [. . .] Ihr auch zu zweien allein: / Ihr mit dem spiegel" (1: 404). George was to praise Hölderlin in 1919 for discovering even before Nietzsche the Dionysian antipode to the Apollonian ideals revealed by Goethe (1: 518–21). Hyperion/George praises the Greek world's cultivation of beauty, grace, and wisdom: "Die ihr in fleisch und in erz muster dem menschtum geformt" (1: 405). Like Schiller in "Die Götter Griechenlands" (The Gods of Greece; Schiller 1: 142–51), he mourns

Christianity's triumph over the radiance of Hellas: "Weh! auf des Syrers
gebot stürzte die lichtwelt in nacht" (1: 405). Events in his homeland "ein
pochen [. . .] von schlafenden gewalten" (1: 405) offers hope that the
ancient ideals will once again bear fruit: "LIEBE / GEBAR DIE WELT · LIEBE
GEBIERT SIE NEU" (1: 406). He will not enter into this new realm: "der
im Reich nie wandeln darf: / Ich werde heldengrab · ich werde scholle"
(1: 405).

The First World War dispelled any hope for George that his ideas
might be more widely shared. "Der Krieg" (1: 410–15), written between
1914 and 1917 and issued as a brochure in July 1917, expresses deep
anger and pessimism at the ordeal he had long foretold. The visionary
"hermit" diagnoses the sickness of the age that has brought Europe (for
all are complicit) to this juncture. Far more than the people's hypocrisy
and false hopes, the wantonness of the slaughter appalls him, the degradation of war to orgies of blood-lust: "Blut-schmach" (Mommsen 4–9). The
war stems from a civilization that has suffocated its vitality by worshiping
the intellect and material ends: "Was ist IHM mord von hunderttausenden /
Vorm mord am Leben selbst?" (1: 411). The poet's unflinching verdict on
his age is: "Ein volk ist tot wenn seine götter tot sind" (1: 414). This
conflict, surely not the last, will end badly, but "Die jugend ruft die Götter
auf . ." (1: 414). New awareness of the sacredness of life itself will inspire
a fusion, the "marriage," emphatically excluding Christianity, of Hellenic
and Germanic cultures that George had once envisioned: "Apollo lehnt
geheim / An Baldur" (1: 415). The closing words exhort to faith, loyalty,
and the readiness to change: "Sieger / Bleibt wer das schutzbild birgt in
seinen marken / Und Herr der zukunft wer sich wandeln kann" (1: 415).

"Der Dichter in Zeiten der Wirren" also centers on the poet as bard
and seer, tolerated in quiet times for lending charm and beauty to life.
When his visions warn of impending catastrophe, he is ignored, even punished. The doom of disintegration he now foresees can only be avoided if
"alles / Was eine sprache spricht," whatever their nationality or politics,
who believe in salvation through the spirit, throw down the banners that
divide them and act as one. A new generation shall, by force of its high
ideals, "aus geweihtem träumen tun und dulden," bring forth "den
Mann," the leader, charismatic, radical, and very likely ruthless, who is to
rescue the nation. Like many Germans, George believed that rigorous
autocracy was the only alternative to the chaos that followed the collapse
of the Kaiser's state:

> Der sprengt die ketten fegt auf trümmerstätten
> Die ordnung · geisselt die verlaufnen heim
> Ins ewige recht wo grosses wiederum gross ist
> Herr wiederum herr · zucht wiederum zucht · er heftet
> Das wahre sinnbild auf das völkische banner

Er führt durch sturm und grausige signale
Des frührots seiner treuen schar zum werk
Des wachen tags und pflanzt das Neue Reich. (1: 418)

None of the poems that George wrote in the 1920s discuss Germany's current situation as directly as "Der Krieg" and "Der Dichter in Zeiten der Wirren." Rather, as their style suggests, they seek to address more universal questions as archetypal myths. In "Burg Falkenstein" (Falkenstein Castle), an excursion occasions a meditative dialogue on myth, magic, the Germans and their poetry, and a perspective on medieval history that carries the imagination beyond the Alps to glory in the deeds of legendary emperors: "Mär von blut und von lust mär von glut und von glanz: / Unserer kaiser gepräng unserer kämpfer gedröhn" (1: 424). In the terse, dense style of the oracle under a spell, "Geheimes Deutschland" (Secret Germany, 1: 425–28) conveys a grotesque vision of nature devastated by human greed, of a technology that spreads poison worldwide, provoking mythic spirits of the World Beneath and of the Heavens to employ their "lezt geheimnis," to turn back the laws of matter and create "Neuen raum in den raum. . . ." This notion represents a sanctuary for George, an Archimedean fulcrum for the vindication of the poetic imagination.

Magic and myth had always fascinated George, but especially so in his last years, as "Der Gehenkte" (He Who was Hanged, 1: 429) and "Der Mensch und der Drud" (Man and Faun, 1: 430–32) reveal; the latter's conclusion affirms his abiding faith in chthonic forces: "Nur durch den zauber bleibt das leben wach" (1: 432). Shortly after the war, George wrote *Der Brand des Tempels* (The Burning of the Temple, 1: 435–41), a brief drama that bespeaks at once tragic despair and hope for a future in which his ideals might become reality. But first, the "Geissel Gottes," a conqueror, ruthless, barbarously principled, but ominously attractive, must purge a culture steeped in corrupt self-indulgence, utterly destroying its monuments: "Der tempel brennt. Ein halbes tausend-jahr / Muss weiter-rollen bis er neu erstehe" (1: 441).

With the twelve songs of "Das Lied," George bids poetry farewell, closing with the exquisitely intense "Du schlank und rein wie eine flamme" (Thou pure and slender as a flame, 1: 469), at once a love song and a hymn. "Horch was die dumpfe erde spricht" (The brooding earth decrees, 1: 463) and "Die Becher" (The Cups, 1: 467) reflect George's fatalism regarding the legacy he leaves behind in an inscrutable world, where chance thwarts the human will, whose freedom is but an illusion: "Du frei wie vogel oder fisch — / Worin du hängst · das weisst du nicht" (1: 463). Finally, "Das Wort" (The Word, 1: 466–67) affirms the conviction underlying George's entire artistic achievement: that the magic of language alone mediates between men and the universe; the world we possess is language's gratuitous gift (Heidegger 275–77; Matt, "Anthropologie"

71–74). We disregard this maxim at our peril. The poet brings his trea-
sured dreams to the "norn," the symbol of his poetic power, who validates
their reality by finding their "names" in the spring she guards, the ultimate
trial of what the people of a language's community may conceive within its
structure and lexicon. However, since she can find no name for one especially precious dream, it is doomed to disappear, driving home the ultimate
truth of poetic art, but also of life itself:

> So lernt ich traurig den verzicht:
> Kein ding sei wo das wort gebricht. (1: 467)

Notes

[1] Unless otherwise stated, citations from works by Stefan George are indicated in
parentheses in the text by volume and page numbers, e.g. (1: 227), from George,
Werke. See also Marx and Morwitz. Translations of titles usually follow Marx and
Morwitz.

[2] See, for example, Hermand 156–73; Metzger and Metzger, *George* 23–38;
Winkler, *George* 43–53; Winkler, *Kreis* 11–54.

[3] "Das süssliche bürgertum der nachfahren wurde verdrängt durch das formlose
plebejertum der wirklichkeitsapostel und dieses durch die dichterische und schön-
heitliche wiedergeburt. [. . .] Blätter für die Kunst [. . .] waren [. . .] wie heute
noch in dem verworrenen getriebe der sonder-erscheinungen die einzige dichterische und künstlerische *Bewegung*." (*Auslese* 1904, 6).

[4] See on this, e.g., Metzger-Hirt 289–92.

[5] See Seekamp 97–390.

[6] "Kaum eines aber erkannte den gehalt: die anbetung vor der schönheit und den
glühenden verewigungsdrang. [. . .] im mittelpunkte [. . .] steht [. . .] die leidenschaftliche hingabe des dichters an seinen freund. Dies hat man hinzunehmen auch
wo man nicht versteht und es ist gleich töricht mit tadeln wie mit rettungen zu
beflecken was einer der grössten Irdischen für gut befand. Zumal verstofflichte und
verhirnlichte zeitalter [. . .] [können] [. . .] nicht etwas ahnen [. . .] von der weltschaffenden kraft der übergeschlechtlichen Liebe" (2: 149; Keilson-Lauritz 142–43).

[7] See Landmann 161–360 and Frank 35–320.

[8] While this list is by no means exhaustive, works by the following authors represent
recent critical efforts to understand George within the contexts of German artistic,
social, and political developments: Breuer, Heintz, Jost, Kahler, von Klemperer,
Kluncker, Kraft, Landfried, von Matt, Mohler, Norton, Raulff, Wuthenow.

[9] See Gugenberger 19–30; Reventlow 95–218; Boehringer 1: 96–109.

[10] For fuller discussions, see Morwitz 215–338; David 201–74; Metzger and
Metzger, *George* 116–56.

[11] For fuller discussions, see Morwitz 339–401; David 275–336; Metzger and
Metzger, *George* 157–71.

¹² For fuller discussions, see Morwitz 403–83; David 337–96; Metzger and Metzger, *George* 171–88.

Works Cited

Aurnhammer, Achim. "Zum Zeitbezug der 'Zeitgedichte' Stefan Georges im Spiegel der Bismarck-Lyrik." In Braungart, Oelmann, Böschenstein. 173–96.

Boehringer, Robert. *Mein Bild von Stefan George.* 2 vols. Düsseldorf: Küpper-Bondi, 1967.

Braungart, Wolfgang, Ute Oelmann, and Bernhard Böschenstein, eds. *Stefan George: Werk und Wirkung seit dem 'Siebenten Ring.'* Tübingen: Niemeyer, 2001.

Breuer, Stefan. *Ästhetischer Fundamentalismus: Stefan George und der deutsche Antimodernismus.* Darmstadt: Wissenschaftliche Buchgesellschaft, 1995.

Brodsky, Patricia Pollock. "Colored Glass and Mirrors: Life with Rilke." *A Companion to the Works of Rainer Maria Rilke.* Eds. Erika A. and Michael M. Metzger. Rochester, NY: Camden House, 2001. 19–39.

David, Claude. *Stefan George: Sein dichterisches Werk.* Munich: Hanser, 1967.

Frank, Lore, and Sabine Ribbeck, eds. *Stefan George-Bibliographie 1976–1997. Mit Nachträgen bis 1976.* Tübingen: Niemeyer, 2000.

George, Stefan. *Werke. Ausgabe in zwei Bänden.* Düsseldorf: Küpper-Bondi, 1968.

———, ed. *Blätter für die Kunst. Eine Auslese aus den Jahren 1898–1904.* Berlin: Bondi, 1904.

———. *Der Siebente Ring.* 1907; rpt. Stuttgart: Klett-Cotta, 1986.

———. *Der Stern des Bundes.* 1913; rpt. Stuttgart: Klett-Cotta, 1993.

———. *Das Neue Reich.* 1928; rpt. Stuttgart: Klett-Cotta, 2001.

George, Stefan, and Carl August Klein, eds. *Blätter für die Kunst.* 12 vols. 1892–1919; reprint, 6 vols. Düsseldorf: Küpper-Bondi, 1968.

George, Stefan, and Karl Wolfskehl, eds. *Deutsche Dichtung: Jean Paul, ein Stundenbuch für seine Verehrer.* Berlin: Blätter für die Kunst, 1900.

———, eds. *Deutsche Dichtung: Goethe.* Berlin: Blätter für die Kunst, 1901.

———, eds. *Deutsche Dichtung: Das Jahrhundert Goethes.* Berlin: Blätter für die Kunst, 1902.

Gugenberger, Eduard. *Hitlers Visionäre: Die okkulten Wegbereiter des Dritten Reichs.* Vienna: Ueberreuter, 2001.

Gundolf, Friedrich, ed. and trans. *Shakespeare in deutscher Sprache.* 10 vols. Berlin: Bondi, 1908–18.

———. *Shakespeare und der deutsche Geist.* Berlin: Bondi, 1911.

Gundolf, Friedrich, and Friedrich Wolters, eds. *Jahrbuch für die geistige Bewegung.* 3 vols. Berlin: Blätter für die Kunst, 1910–12.

Heidegger, Martin. "Dichten und Denken. Zu Stefan Georges Gedicht 'Das Wort.'" *Unterwegs zur Sprache.* Pfullingen: Neske, 1959. 275–82.

Heintz, Günter. *Stefan George: Studien zu seiner künstlerischen Wirkung.* Stuttgart: Hauswedell, 1986.

Hermand, Jost. *Die deutschen Dichterbünde: Von den Meistersingern bis zum PEN-Club.* Cologne: Böhlau, 1998.

Hillebrand, Bruno. *Nietzsche: Wie ihn die Dichter sahen.* Göttingen: Vandenhoeck & Ruprecht, 2000.

Jaime-Liebig, Edward. *Stefan George und die Weltliteratur.* Ulm: Aegis, 1949.

Jost, Dominik. *Blick auf Stefan George. Ein Essay.* Bern: Lang, 1991.

Kahler, Erich von, "Stefan George. Größe und Tragik." *Untergang und Übergang. Essays.* Munich: dtv, 1970. 228–49.

Keilson-Lauritz, Marita, "Übergeschlechtliche Liebe als Passion. Zur Codierung mannesmännlicher Intimität im Spätwerk Stefan Georges." In Braungart et al. 142–55.

Klages, Ludwig. *Stefan George.* Berlin: Bondi, 1902.

Klemperer, Klemens von. *German Incertitudes 1914–1945: The Stones and the Cathedral.* Westport, CT: Praeger, 2001.

Kluncker, Karlhans. *"Das geheime Deutschland": Über Stefan George und seinen Kreis.* Bonn: Bouvier, 1985.

Kraft, Werner. *Stefan George.* Munich: Text + Kritik, 1980.

Landfried, Klaus. *Stefan George: Politik des Unpolitischen.* Heidelberg: Stiehm, 1975.

Landmann, Georg Peter, ed. *Stefan George und sein Kreis.* 2nd ed. Hamburg: Hauswedell, 1976.

Linke, Hansjürgen. *Das Kultische in der Dichtung Stefan Georges und seiner Schule.* 2 vols. Munich: Küpper-Bondi, 1960.

Marx, Olga, and Ernst Morwitz, trans. *The Works of Stefan George Rendered into English.* Chapel Hill: U of North Carolina P, 1974.

Matt, Peter von. "Das Einhorn geht unter das Volk. Stefan George im Taschenbuch." *Die verdächtige Pracht: Über Dichter und Gedichte.* Munich: Hanser, 1998. 249–52.

———. "Zur Anthropologie des Gedichts und zum Ärgernis seiner Schönheit." *Die verdächtige Pracht: Über Dichter und Gedichte.* Munich: Hanser, 1998. 7–84.

Metzger, Erika A., and Michael M. Metzger. *Stefan George.* Boston: Twayne, 1972.

Metzger, Michael M. "Blätter für die Kunst." *Encyclopedia of German Literature.* Ed. Matthias Konzett. Chicago: Fitzroy Dearborn, 2000. 1: 117–18.

———. "Stefan George 1868–1933." *Encyclopedia of German Literature.* Ed. Matthias Konzett. Chicago: Fitzroy Dearborn, 2000. 1: 326–27.

Metzger, Michael M. "Der Teppich des Lebens und die Lieder von Traum und Tod mit einem Vorspiel." *Encyclopedia of German Literature*. Ed. Matthias Konzett. Chicago: Fitzroy Dearborn, 2000. 1: 328–29.

Metzger-Hirt, Erika. "Das Klopstockbild Stefan Georges und seines *Kreises*." *PMLA* 79 (1964). 289–96.

Mohler, Armin. *Die konservative Revolution in Deutschland 1918–1932: Ein Handbuch*. Darmstadt: Wissenschaftliche Buchgesellschaft, 1972.

Mommsen, Momme. " 'Ihr kennt eure Bibel nicht!' Bibel- und Horazanklänge in Stefan Georges Gedicht 'Der Krieg.' " *Lebendige Überlieferung: George · Hölderlin · Goethe*. Bern: Lang, 1999. 1–27.

Morwitz, Ernst. *Kommentar zu dem Werk Stefan Georges*. Munich: Küpper-Bondi, 1960.

Nietzsche, Friedrich. *Werke in drei Bänden*. Ed. Karl Schlechta. Munich: Hanser, 1966.

Norton, Robert E. *Secret Germany: Stefan George and His Circle*. Ithaca/London: Cornell UP, 2002.

Novalis [Hardenberg, Friedrich von]. *Die Christenheit oder Europa*. Novalis, *Schriften, Dritter Band*. Ed. Richard Samuel. Stuttgart: Kohlhammer, 1960. 497–524.

Raulff, Ulrich. "Stefan George-Biografie, Ihr wisst nicht, wer ich bin" (*Süddeutsche Zeitung*, 11 June 2002) www.sueddeutsche.de/kultur/literatur/rezensionen/45724/index.php (review of Norton).

Reventlow, Franziska zu. *Herrn Dames Aufzeichnungen oder Begebenheiten aus einem merkwürdigen Stadtteil*. Franziska zu Reventlow, *Drei Romane*. Munich: Biederstein, 1958. 95–218.

Schiller, Friedrich. *Sämtliche Gedichte*. 2 vols. Munich: dtv, 1965.

Seekamp, H[ans].-J[ürgen]., R[aymond]. C[urtis]. Ockenden, and M[arita]. Keilson[-Lauritz]. *Stefan George / Leben und Werk. Eine Zeittafel*. Amsterdam: Castrum Peregrini, 1972.

Shelley, Percy Bysshe. *Selected Poetry and Prose*. Ed. Carlos Baker. New York: Random House, 1951.

Winkler, Michael. *George-Kreis*. Stuttgart: Metzler, 1972.

———. *Stefan George*. Stuttgart: Metzler, 1970.

Wuthenow, Ralph-Rainer, ed. *Stefan George in seiner Zeit: Dokumente zur Wirkungsgeschichte*. 2 vols. Stuttgart: Klett-Cotta, 1980–81.

Contexts

Stefan George and Two Types of Aestheticism

Jeffrey D. Todd

*A*ESTHETICISM IS A CATCHWORD used to designate an attitude toward art that developed during the nineteenth century. Its central tenet is that art occupies its own autonomous realm independent of other spheres of life.[1] Although these other spheres may be represented by various names, they reduce in most cases to the spheres of traditional religion, ideology, morality, and politics — all sources of meaning that tend to determine the form and content of art. These spheres have influenced the style and content of literature as long as there has been literature and continue to do so to the present day. However, in the nineteenth century, historical conditions arose that were favorable to the development of a novel conception of art, one that sought to stake out a territory in which art would be entirely self-determining or autonomous and therefore free from the usual determination by any other sphere. Kant's *Kritik der Urteilskraft* (Critique of Judgment, 1790) laid the theoretical foundation for this development, while others, above all the French poet Théophile Gautier (1811–1872), worked not only to diffuse Kant's notions but also to reshape and simplify them.[2] Proponents of this emerging viewpoint saw in it the possibility for a new kind of artistic freedom.

Given the autonomy structure inherent in aestheticism, two types are conceivable. The first type, for which Bell-Villada has coined the apt term "aesthetic separatism," is characterized by a reciprocal separation between spheres (2). If an autonomous art conceives of the separation between spheres as reciprocal, that is to say, if it understands itself as being just as unable to encroach upon the domain of, say, morals as morals are to determine the content of art, its possibilities will be circumscribed by those boundaries, and consequently rather limited. In this case, the freedom from determination by other spheres won through autonomy exacts a rather high price: the separation of art from life. This kind of aestheticism, which accepts the restrictions imposed on art by other life-spheres can be called a "weak" aestheticism, its most representative group being probably the French Parnassians. However, another aestheticist attitude can be conceived, according to which art, while maintaining the autonomy of its own sphere, oversteps the boundaries of the other spheres, trespasses on their terrain, and proceeds to determine their content. Here art is less well behaved, less self-effacing, less observant of the boundaries between itself and the other domains. Such an aggressive aestheticism might be called a "strong" aestheticism, as opposed to the weak aestheticism outlined above. The finest description of the strong aesthetic position that I have found is Gottfried Benn's definition of *Artistik*. "Artistik," for Benn,

> ist der Versuch der Kunst, innerhalb des allgemeinen Verfalls der Inhalte sich selber als Inhalt zu erleben und aus diesem Erlebnis einen neuen Stil zu bilden, es ist der Versuch, gegen den allgemeinen Nihilismus der Werte eine neue Transzendenz zu setzen: die Transzendenz der schöpferischen Lust. (500)

In addition to outlining the intellectual structure of strong aestheticism, this definition also situates it historically as a response to nihilism, or to the "allgemeinen Verfall der Inhalte." Both types of aestheticism are to be found in George. The poetic program he and his associates laid out in the early issues of *Blätter für die Kunst* is of a weak aesthetic character, and much of his early poetry can be read in this light. A kernel of strong aestheticism is present in *Algabal,* but more significantly for his later work, at the very beginning of his *Hymnen,* and the main stream of his development moves clearly in this direction, for a strong aestheticism dominates his later work.

While some scholars, including Braungart, have considered that George's more activist later poetry cannot be classified as autonomous (78), I argue that it can and should be. But then it is crucial to keep in mind what the autonomy of art requires and what it does not. It does not require the autonomy of other spheres as well. It may exist under those conditions — that is the weak aesthetic alternative — but it may not. There is of course a distinction between George's early work and his late work. However, this lies not in the difference between autonomous and non-autonomous art, but between weak aestheticism and strong aestheticism, both being positions within the domain of autonomous art. I hope that it will also become obvious that the development of George's poetry has nothing whatever to do with a retreat from life, as some of his critics have maintained, or with a mere preoccupation with form, but has everything to do with life and the determining of its content through art.[3]

The purpose of this essay is to delineate more precisely George's relation to the two types of aestheticism just characterized. In the early programmatic statements of George and his associates, one finds a clear desire to inscribe their activity within the domain of an autonomous poetry. The programmatic statement in the first issue of the *Blätter* (1892) could not state this intention more emphatically:

> Der name dieser veröffentlichung sagt schon zum teil was sie soll: der kunst besonders der dichtung und dem schrifttum dienen, alles staatliche und gesellschaftliche ausscheidend. Sie will die GEISTIGE KUNST auf grund der neuen fühlweise und mache - eine kunst für die kunst - und steht

deshalb im gegensatz zu jener verbrauchten und minderwertigen schule die einer falschen auffassung der wirklichkeit entsprang. Sie kann sich auch nicht beschäftigen mit weltverbesserungen und allbeglückungsträumen in denen man gegenwärtig bei uns den keim zu allem neuen sieht, die ja sehr schön sein mögen aber in ein andres gebiet gehören als das der dichtung.

(BfdK 1,1: 1)

Through the coinage *kunst für die kunst,* George translates into German that staple slogan of French aestheticism, *l'art pour l'art.* In so doing, he places his work and that of his associates within the French tradition. In keeping with this tradition, the rest of the statement marks distinctions between poetry and other spheres of thought and endeavor. All questions of state and society, all efforts at improving the world do not belong in the realm of poetry, as we see above. The theoretical direction sketched out in this initial statement is confirmed and completed by many other statements published in later issues of the *Blätter* and elsewhere, written not only by George but by others as well. This distance from political and social matters was already anticipated in *Rosen und Disteln,* the publication George edited in 1887 while a gymnasial student. Its programmatic statement contained the phrase: "Artikel religiösen und politischen Inhalts streng ausscheidend."[4] Thus, the earlier publication also excluded religious concerns, an exclusion not repeated in the programmatic statement in *Blätter* 1,1. Not insignificantly, this difference calls attention to the religious domain.

The moral sphere is similarly declared distinct from artistic concerns in the *Blätter.* At the end of his essay "Geistige Kunst" in *Blätter* 2,4, the Belgian poet Paul Gérardy characterized the *Blätter*-poets as follows: "Sie sind keine sittenprediger und lieben nur die schönheit die schönheit die schönheit" (113). The exclusion of moral preaching is buttressed by George's own introductory statements to *Blätter* 2,2 from March 1894:

> Die älteren dichter schufen der mehrzahl nach ihre werke oder wollten sie wenigstens angesehen haben als stüze einer meinung: einer weltanschauung — wir sehen in jedem ereignis jedem zeitalter nur ein mittel künstlerischer erregung. auch die freisten der freien konnten ohne den sittlichen deckmantel nicht auskommen (man denke an die begriffe von schuld u.s.w.) der uns ganz wertlos geworden ist. (34)

Statements such as this bespeak a strong Nietzschean influence in the thinking of the new poets, and it would be difficult to reject morality and moralizing in stronger terms. The same passage claims that previous poets wanted their work to be seen as supportive of a meaning or a worldview. Hence, meaning takes first place, the work second. This primacy of meaning over work is then reversed by George and his fellows in *Blätter* 2,4 (October 1894):

> Den wert der dichtung entscheidet nicht der sinn (sonst wäre sie etwa weisheit gelahrtheit) sondern die form d. h. durchaus nichts äusserliches

> sondern jenes tief erregende in maass und klang wodurch zu allen zeiten
> die Ursprünglichen die Meister sich von den nachfahren den künstlern
> zweiter ordnung unterschieden haben. (122)

This statement does not deny that the poem has meaning, but rejects the
notion that meaning is where the value of the poem lies. Consequently, the
quotation above confirms this position by reproaching those who wish to
"say something" through their poetry: "In der dichtung — wie in aller
kunst-bethätigung ist jeder der noch von der sucht ergriffen ist etwas
'sagen' etwas 'wirken' zu wollen nicht einmal wert in den vorhof der kunst
einzutreten" (122). Thus, questions of state, society, social betterment,
and moral preaching are all banned from poetry. Meaning is secondary in
the poem, form primary. What is proper to the poem thus conceived is, as
Gérardy previously noted with triple emphasis, beauty, that is, the beauty
of form. Is this aestheticism? Yes, for art is staking out a territory of its own
independent of the encroachment of other spheres. However, this poetic
program seems to be a recipe for a weak aestheticism rather than a strong
one; art makes no attempt to impinge on those other spheres.

It should be noted in passing that the place of one important sphere
has not yet been determined: religion. According to the weak aesthetic
model, one would expect religion to be excluded. Of all the spheres, religion is traditionally the master sphere from which positions in morals, politics, social issues, and art have been determined. For this reason the
encroachment of religious morality was one of Gautier's chief targets.
Consequently, it is quite strange that religion should not be excluded from
a poetic program that seeks autonomy for art. It is important to bear this
in mind as we examine George's work for instances of the relation between
art and these spheres.

Much of George's early work from *Hymnen* to *Der Teppich des Lebens*
follows the weak aesthetic model prescribed in his poetic program. The
examples that follow are taken from *Hymnen* but numerous appropriate
examples exist in all of the works from this period. The early work is completely void of moralizing tendencies; such issues are often not even
broached, and allusions to state and society are infrequent. The positive
content of this poetry — the "reine freude am formen" mentioned by
George in the preface to his Baudelaire translations — is found in poems
like "Verwandlungen" (Transformation), "Nachmittag" (Afternoon), and
"Strand" (Shore); intellectual content is clearly secondary (but not absent).
"Im Park" is an important poem in which the poet reflects on his art. The
feeling between two persons comes to the fore in "Von einer Begegnung"
(An Encounter) and "Nachthymne" (Serenade), while one of the most
charming *études* of the early George, "Hochsommer" (Late Summer),
exquisitely captures a mood so uncharacteristic of German poetry that one
might well take it for a translation. And it is a translation of an expressive

possibility more characteristically French into German. "Der Infant" (The Infante) combines the impulse of artistic self-reflexivity with the discipline of descriptive portraiture. All of these poems fall within the confines of a weak aestheticism. Some of George's early work, however, does not remain within those boundaries. Instead, his art encounters, in an obvious and provocative way, other spheres that would have been avoided if he had strictly adhered to a weak aesthetic program. These apparent deviations, however, do not regress to a pre-autonomous state in which the artistic representation becomes subordinate to the influence of non-aesthetic considerations. Instead, art remains autonomous and makes at least incipient gestures of hegemony over other spheres, harbingers of a strong aestheticism that will be more fully developed in George's work after *Der Teppich des Lebens.*

Algabal, the cycle whose main figure is the youthful Roman emperor Heliogabalus, occupies a special place in George's early work, and so it is not surprising that it should serve as our principal early example of strong aesthetic gestures. The initial gesture is made in the first section of the collection entitled "Das Unterreich" (The Realm Below), where the preeminence of the imagination over nature is signaled in Algabal's preference for the landscape "im schoosse der flut" over "die landschaft am strande" (1: 45). Guided by the power of his imagination, Algabal has constructed a strange, artificial world of his own in the watery depths, a world he prefers to the natural landscape above. The mainstream view of artistic creation in the Western tradition holds that art is the product of cooperation between nature, which is given, and the human conception. George himself articulates this very position in later poems such as "Der Freund der Fluren" (The Friend of the Fields) and "Leo XIII." The symbol of the "schwarze blume" embodies the very antithesis of this traditional notion, the hubristic dream of a work of art that is wholly the creation of the artist. Algabal wishes to share no credit for his creation with nature, or ultimately, with God.

Algabal is also a political figure. For all the talk of distance from political issues in the early poetic program, two important figures in George's early work are explicitly political: Algabal and the unnamed Middle Eastern lord of the *Buch der hängenden Gärten.* On the face of it, this would seem to be a breach of the weak aesthetic doctrine, but this point merits more detailed analysis. The key question seems to be: what is the nature of the political here? Does Algabal's political attribute function politically, or is it merely a metaphor for art? In *Algabal,* the artist clearly predominates in the *Unterreich.* The political seems to assume some significance here insofar as Algabal has the power to carry out the dictates of his imagination. On the other hand this power could simply be a metaphor for the mastery of the artist over his medium with no political implications. In "Tage" (Days), however, Algabal the artist is left behind, while the ruler and secondarily the priest (in "Gegen osten ragt der bau" [Toward the east the walls are massed]) come to the fore. Algabal's will to rule is manifest when he warns his mother and brother not to attempt to shake his power ("O mutter meiner mutter und Erlauchte" [O mother of my mother, long revered]) in the entertaining of guests ("Becher am boden" [Cups on the ground]); in his cruelty toward the people ("So sprach ich nur in meinen schwersten tagen" [These words were said when living was a loss]); in his presence on the battlefield ("Graue rosse muss ich schirren" [I must saddle ashen horses]); in addressing the crowds ("Lärmen hör ich im schläfrigen frieden" [Somnolent peace, yet I cannot dispel]). So Algabal's political function does in fact feature in George's representation. It is not as if George focuses exclusively on the theme of artistry and leaves Algabal's rulership in the background.

Does this violate the law of autonomy? Let us recall the context of those questions of *staat* and *gesellschaft* mentioned in the *Blätter*. What was explicitly excluded from poetry was the consideration of politics with a view to the well-being of society, the weighing of political issues. Are politics being weighed here? Of course not. That could be accomplished easily enough with the figure of Algabal by pointing to his excesses and cruelty and adducing them as proof of the flawed nature of his form of government. But this is not George's way. While Algabal's cruelty and excesses are indicated, they are not a focus, and therefore a case against Algabal as a political leader is not made. Nor is Algabal the ruler glorified, for that matter, *pace* David's view that Algabal constitutes "Verherrlichung des Negativen und des Bösen" (121). George does not want us to despise Algabal, largely because he identifies with him: Algabal is one of George's masks. But it is obvious that George's concern in *Algabal* is neither to critique nor to glorify the late Roman empire as such. Therefore, in spite of what might seem an apparent breach of the principle of autonomy in the choice of a political figure, the line between politics and art as drawn in the poetological statements of the *Blätter* is not crossed, since the purpose of *Algabal* is not to make an argument for or against a form of government. Nonetheless, this strong reference to the political in the face of a poetic program that would seem to steer the artist away from it remains provocative, a kind of preliminary assault on the barricades.

The issue of morality is also broached in *Algabal*. Indeed, it would hardly be possible to avoid morality entirely and write literature of any interest. We might expect George to portray Algabal as a libertine, not only because this potential is inherent in the subject, but also since this is a tack taken by authors from the literature of the *décadence,* most notably Oscar Wilde in his *Picture of Dorian Gray.* Dorian's morality, which infringes upon traditional morality at many points, is based on the pursuit of exquisite sensation and is therefore intimately related to Walter Pater's (1839–94) conception of art as something that intensifies sensation (Wilde had been a student of Pater's).[5] Hence, this effort represents at least an effort to determine the content of morality by way of the artistic sensibility, and consequently an attempt at a strong aestheticism. The reality of George's *Algabal* is, however, that there is not nearly the emphasis on immorality that one might expect, given the various *topoi* of the historical material. To be sure, certain aspects are present, as we have seen: the emperor's cruelty; the vision of killing the brother who threatens the throne; the guests suffocating under a bath of roses. But George does not portray Algabal primarily as an immoral figure. One therefore has to agree with Gundolf that an immoralistic one-upmanship was not George's intention with this figure (80). The far more prominent theme is that of Algabal as artist, absolute ruler over the domain of art. This is not to imply that morality is irrelevant to *Algabal.* The emperor's immorality, in light of Christian morality, is significant not as immoralism, but shows instead that he operates outside Judeo-Christian moral categories altogether. Gundolf therefore aptly calls *Algabal* "nicht widersittliches Bekenntnis eines Genießers, sondern *außersittliches* Gesicht eines Frommen" (81, my emphasis). A number of factors enable him to escape those categories: first, he lives at a time when Christian morality has not yet become the norm; secondly, as emperor and high priest of the cult of the sun-god Heliogabalus, no one can challenge his power or his moral authority. As a moral agent, he is in principle restricted by no moral law save the one that he himself sets. So, in spite of the fact that George's treatment of the emperor does not place primary emphasis on the theme of immorality, *Algabal* nevertheless serves as a symbol of the autonomy of art with respect to traditional morality, and is much more effective in this respect than Wilde's Dorian Gray or Joris Karl Huysmans's (1848–1907) fictional character Des Esseintes from the decadent novel *À Rebours* (Against the Grain). These two characters act in a world governed by Christian moral values. Their behavior departs from given social norms, and they are ostracized to varying degrees as a result. Although both authors clearly sympathize and even identify with their protagonists, their behavior ultimately reveals itself to be not only socially unacceptable but to be untenable: Dorian kills himself in the attempt to destroy the portrait that reflects his true moral state; Des Esseintes, for reasons of mental and physical health, is prescribed a more normal lifestyle, and while he rails against the change, he is compelled to cooperate. The immorality of Dorian Gray and Des Esseintes is a compulsive but impotent protest against the restrictions of traditional morality. Algabal, on the other hand, emperor and high priest of a pagan cult in the pre-Constantinian, that is, pre-Christian empire, is not oppressed by social morality, and George shows himself to be far less affected by and far more detached from traditional morality than either Huysmans or even, in spite of all of his protestations, Wilde. Instead of attacking traditional morality, he transcends it through Algabal.

But even Algabal is not entirely beyond good and evil: he also recognizes sin, albeit not after the Christian manner. George uses the word "sündig" once in the work, in reference to Algabal's first experience with a woman which, as "erstes ungemach" destroyed his "schönster traum" (1: 57). This sin is not presented as the destruction of his personal integrity through licentiousness, but as a sin against his "schönster traum": as a sin against the imagination. To sin against the imagination is also to sin against the aesthetic: here we have a strong aesthetic gesture in which the aesthetic determines the content of morality by defining what sin is. There is much more to this "schönster traum" than art. How can he have sinned against the imagination by sleeping with a woman? Given what is known about George's homosexual leanings, one might want to explain this negative marking of heterosexual relations as a sin against his homosexual identity. However, this biographical answer is too simplistic, and does not allow us to grasp the complexities of George's symbolism.

Another theme related to gender difference is of relevance here: hermaphroditism. Norton recounts an historical anecdote that reveals a fascination with hermaphroditism on the part of the emperor (111). The theme appears in George's *Algabal* in the reference to the "Zwiegestalt" of Algabal's god (1: 49). Morwitz and Gundolf were the first to emphasize the theme of hermaphroditism in *Algabal*. Morwitz characterizes Algabal's god, whom he visits in the sanctum sanctorum, as "doppelgeschlechtlich," and comments on the poem "So sprach ich nur in meinen schwersten tagen": "Wenn er sich selbst als Frau im Spiegel sieht, wenn er sich dem Ziel der Doppelgeschlechtlichkeit und dadurch seinem Gott näher glaubt, gerät er in einen Zustand überklarer Ruhe und völliger Wunschlosigkeit, wie die letzte Strophe des Gedichtes darlegt" (*Kommentar zu dem Werk* 51).[6] For Morwitz, hermaphroditism is a goal (*Ziel*). Gundolf, on the other hand, differs significantly from Morwitz by speaking of it as an achieved reality, calling Algabal a "Weibjüngling" (80). In the same vein, he states: "und weil bei ihm alles Frucht und Same zugleich ist" (79). Symbolically, hermaphroditism is a state of many gods and holy beings. Since it contains the marks of both sexes, the hermaphrodite is at least symbolically fertile and signifies a self-sufficient wholeness (Chevalier and Gheerbrant 498). Hermaphroditism is also associated with special powers: Tiresias the seer is an example of a hermaphrodite who, despite his blindness, sees more acutely into the nature of things than Oedipus (Campbell 154).

Leaving aside for a moment the question whether Algabal is physically a hermaphrodite, there does seem to be an analogue to the special power of the hermaphrodite in Algabal's "schönster traum." This dream was still intact during those "Grosse tage wo im geist ich nur der herr / Der welten hiess" (Days of grandeur when in fancy worlds awaited my command, 1: 55). Perhaps this dream is Algabal's analogue to Tiresias's inner vision. But then the sinful intercourse with woman intervenes and destroys the dream. If Algabal is in fact a hermaphrodite, that intercourse would be irrational and self-contradictory, a denial of the fact of his own self-sufficiency. On the other hand, if Algabal is not a hermaphrodite, then the sex act with woman would be part of the normal course of nature, but it would have other symbolic consequences: he would thereby be leaving his hermaphroditic god and cleaving to another, constituting a kind of infidelity and a fall from that state in which, as a child, Algabal lived as priest in exclusive dedication to Heliogabalus. Moreover, intercourse with woman signifies that the young priest is a man like all others, firmly situated in the realm of duality with all its impurities, imperfections, and insufficiencies, requiring the female as a complement to himself. His initiation into this fact of life wrenches him from an ideal realm, introduces him to the real and destroys the ideal embodied in this "schönster traum." The normal way of dealing with a baptism into reality is certainly to mourn the loss of the ideal, but ultimately to realize that it is part of life's duality. Instead, Algabal remains in perpetual mourning for his lost state (see the second poem in "Andenken" [Memories], "Fern ist mir das blumenalter" [I have lost the days of bloom]), and laments the sin that severed him from that paradise. He is fixated on this primal state and therefore unfree. In light of this, Morwitz's interpretation of Algabal as a would-be hermaphrodite seems to render the most convincing reading because it allows for a more satisfying explanation of Algabal's sense of loss. If Algabal were in fact a hermaphrodite, he would be indissolubly similar to and linked with his god. We see that Algabal's sin is not merely a sin against the aesthetic realm, for the aesthetic here is intimately bound up with the religious. His "schönster traum" is a dream of unity with his god and his sin is therefore an act that destroys this dream and separates him from his god at the same time. So he sins against his god as much as against his imagination.

In our consideration of the various interrelations between George's art and the spheres of politics and morality, references to religion have been continually present. Algabal the political figure is at the same time a religious figure and even primarily so, since his true affections lie not with ruling, but with worship.[7] The loss of his virginity is sin because intercourse with woman removes him from the sphere of unity with his god and places him into the sphere of duality. That religion is central to George's work has been maintained notably by the recent works of Braungart and Breuer as well as by the earlier studies of Frommel and Linke. Furthermore, the centrality of religion is evident from the very first poem of George's published work, "Weihe" (Initiation). Thus, the answer to our earlier question — why George did not exclude religion from his poetic program — is evident: because he wishes to include it. What is the significance of these strong references to morals, politics, and to religion, seeming exceptions to the weak aesthetic program laid out in the *Blätter*? While George's divergence from a weak aesthetic program in his later work is well known, he seems uncomfortable within those boundaries even in his early work. I would argue a) that the germ of his later position is found in these early poetic gestures and b) that the most important sphere outside of art for George is that of religion. This predilection is anchored symbolically in Algabal's preference for his youthful priesthood over his later emperorship. This prominence of religion is not evidence of a lapse to a pre-autonomous state in which art is governed by religion. George has no intention whatever of placing his poetry at the service of religion, even though he does recognize the importance of the religious sphere and its proven power to determine the content of culture. His project rather is to reverse the hierarchy: instead of submitting his poetry to the power of religion, George seeks to found a new religion through the power of poetry. And through the religion thus founded, he means to radiate his influence throughout all other cultural spheres. George's project is the exceedingly ambitious one of furnishing Western culture with a new religion by means of art, thereby founding a new society and creating a new man. He thus moves from a weak aestheticism to the strongest of all aestheticisms.

While we might view this strong aestheticism as a phenomenon peculiar to the fin-de-siècle and early twentieth century, George saw it as the way in which religions have always been formed. As he put it in the so-called "Teuflische Stanze" (Diabolical Stanza): "Noch jeder Gott war menschliches Geschöpf" (2: 603). This statement, which George reportedly called a "Zynismus aus meiner Knabenzeit," is powerfully extreme in its atheism and expresses George's rejection of the Catholic faith in which he had been raised (Boehringer 1: 117). Nonetheless, George seems to have held fast to one of its central insights, namely that religion is not the work of the gods. It is the work of the poet-cum-priest who, in response to the powers that move him, is compelled to speak; in this speaking, these forces take on form, and religion, with all its rituals and symbols, is born. Therefore, for George, it is art that gives birth to religion and religion in turn, by obtaining the faith of the people, takes hold in all spheres of life and determines their content. Since art determines the content of religion, art, not religion, is ultimately the origin of all meaning.

To an observer thinking within a purely naturalistic metaphysics, the poet's religious function would constitute nothing more than a kind of cynical game whereby the poet employs his rhetorical skill to set up a kind of puppet deity and gain the confidence of the people in an attempt to exercise control over them. George, however, seems to have invested faith in something greater than himself, not a transcendent God in the Judaeo-Christian sense, but a sense that a force like fate (*Schicksal*) guides his existence. Perhaps it was his experience with the Munich *Kosmiker* that taught him once again to believe in certain forces (*Mächte, Kräfte,* he often even uses the terms *Gott* und *Götter*), but for George it is the artist, especially the poet, whose task is to give those forces form and reality for the world. This is one of the ramifications of the famous line from the late poem "Das Wort" (The Word): "Kein Ding sei, wo das Wort gebricht," which applies not merely to inanimate objects, but to any entity whatever, even the gods themselves (1: 466).

The basic core of this religion is present in the figure of the poet who is not just a poet but also a priest-in-the-making in "Weihe." He is initiated as a priest by a rite of ordination and blessing by a figure called "die Herrin" who is both muse and angel. This "Herrin" is one of several instances in George's work where a quasi-divine, angelic figure appears. The existence of such figures cannot be explained sufficiently by references to another part of the self, because they are consistently seen as being *other,* their coming as an unexpected gift. So while these forces are immanent in the world (they are not experienced as something radically beyond, to be sure), they are experienced as something from above. The seed of this religion — poet/priest, the muse/angel, and the rite of ordination — having been sown, the priest is now ordained and qualified to exercise the functions of his office, to worship and praise the deity, and to bring the blessings of the deity down to the community. At the time of the *Hymnen,* George had no deity. He had lost faith in the God of his youth, and had yet to find another. Such a priest can fulfill neither his priestly nor his poetic function. Perhaps this is why George's first published collection of poems is so strange with respect to its declared genre. Since poetry is ultimately praise for George, he calls those poems *Hymnen.*[8] But as many have noticed, there is scarcely anything hymnic in any traditional sense about them.[9] Since George had not yet found a new divinity to replace the God of his youth, the very essence of the hymnic — the praise of a deity — necessarily eludes him in the *Hymnen.* In the meantime, he must content himself with the "scheue reime" that can be written in the absence of the fulfillment that he awaits (1: 136), poems that fit the weak aesthetic profile outlined in the *Blätter.*

As anyone acquainted with George's work knows, he eventually finds his god in Maximin. With the appearance of his deity, George's poetry is able to realize the purpose implicit in his poetic intuition from the beginning: praise. But it is important to remember that the centrality of praise, which becomes more explicit in his later work, is not a novel, unprepared development: it is implicit in the image of the youthful priest in "Weihe," and in the religiously-tinged title of his first collection of poetry. Once George, the priest, finds his deity, he must worship him. Praise is the foremost aspect of this worship. George the poet will then adjust his poetics to this sacerdotal function. Praise of Maximin is perhaps the primary theme in George's late work: from *Der Siebente Ring,* where praise of Maximin occupies the center of the work, through the *Stern des Bundes,* wholly devoted to the Maximin-cult, to *Das neue Reich,* where the memory of the Bavarian youth persists in numerous poems. Also of great importance in this work of praise is the so-called "Maximin-Vorrede," first published in the memorial book to Maximin in 1906 (Morwitz, *Kommentar zu Prosa-Dichtungen* 54), and later in the second edition of the prose volume *Tage und Taten*. Here the very frame for the Maximin-legend is constructed with literary motifs taken from Dante's *Vita nuova* and *Divina Commedia*. Maximin thereby assumes the place in George's work that Beatrice occupies in Dante's, as many have noted, among them Klussmann in his essay "Dante und Stefan George."

The poetics of George's late work has other linguistic functions as well, and gives rise to various kinds of poems. The reverse of praise in epideictic rhetoric is censure, and both praise and censure, "lob und fem," as it is put in the wartime poem "Der Krieg," belong in George's later poetics. However, the two functions are not of equal weight. Censure shall not outweigh praise. Dante, the patron saint of George's later religious poetics, is invoked in the poem "Dante und das Zeitgedicht" (Dante and the Poem of His Times) to place his seal of approval on this poetic precept. George has Dante speak of the creation of his *Divine Comedy:*

> Ich nahm aus meinem herd ein scheit und blies -
> So ward die hölle · doch des vollen feuers
> Bedurft ich zur bestrahlung höchster liebe
> Und zur verkündigung von sonn und stern. (1: 229)

Only an ember, paradoxically enough, was sufficient to light the "Inferno"; but the "Paradiso" required the full fire of the poet. Censure is easy; it is praise that presents the most difficult challenge.

Moreover, there are other rhetorical modes in operation besides the epideictic in George's religious poetry. Praise establishes a relation between the worshipper and the deity, a relation on a vertical axis. The horizontal axis, where the relation between members of the worshipping community is established, is also important, as one can see in the "Schlusschor" (Closing Chorus) of the *Stern des Bundes*. The major poetic achievement in the *Stern des Bundes* is the poetic creation of this new religion, and the establishment of the relations and literary themes that compose and order it. But praise remains the highest function of this religious poetry. And in fact, the very phrase, "poetry is praise," which George seems to have borrowed from Ruskin's *Laws of Fésole* in slightly modified form, becomes a motto for George's later poetics (Ruskin 11–12).[10]

The strong aestheticism that establishes a new religion in George's late work determines the content of other life spheres as well, including that of morality. Epideictic rhetoric is operative here as well: praise and censure are used in complementary fashion to achieve George's moral purpose. In the "Zeitgedichte" (Poems of Our Times) of *Der Siebente Ring,* part of George's multifaceted project is to upbraid his contemporaries, and in so doing, to offer guidance. Is this still aestheticism? After all, is it not what Gérardy called "Sittenpredigung," the incursion of morals into art? It might seem so, but there is a difference. The preaching, if you will, that appears in the "Zeitgedichte" differs from the *Sittenpredigung* of previous generations insofar as the poet does not preach traditional morality, nor any particular moral doctrine. Instead, he indicates flaws, such as the lack of a sense of greatness of soul (in "Goethe-Tag" [Goethe Anniversary] and the last of the "Zeitgedichte"), the pale lifelessness of his contemporaries ("Porta nigra"), greed ("Die tote Stadt" [The Dead City]), and points out that a different way is possible. This is where praise comes in. This different path is not indicated by way of description, which would run the risk of establishing some kind of doctrine, but by holding up examples of greatness, *Vorbilder,* for our admiration and instruction. For George, this praise of famous men is the main purpose of the poem; criticism is secondary. Most of the examples cited in the "Zeitgedichte" are contemporary (Nietzsche, Böcklin, Leo XIII, Carl August) but some are historical (Dante, Goethe), and one, the Porta Nigra in Trier, is an inanimate object made to stand for the greatness of the entire Roman world. So even the preaching so clearly evident in the "Zeitgedichte" still does not constitute *Sittenpredigung* in the sense of a message based on a doctrine outlawing certain acts as evil and declaring others good. What we have instead is the exaltation of exemplars by means of art. It is not a moral doctrine that determines the content of art, but the artistic gestures of praise and censure that establish the content of morality. The ban, then, on *Sittenpredigung* has technically not been broken. This poetry does however run contrary to the spirit of the early poetic program in other ways. Certainly the relation between form and content is not the same. The form of the "Zeitgedichte" is looser, more relaxed and capacious than most of the measures used in George's early poetry; the poem's message has become clearer and figures more prominently. Moreover, nothing in that early program calls for an epideictic poetry.

One would expect this strong aestheticism to extend into the domain of politics as well. And indeed it does have a political reach. It advances a certain, admittedly very general, political agenda much in the same way as it praises exemplars: not by promulgating a certain doctrine, but by representing human relationships according to a certain Platonic vision. We encounter this Platonic political vision in *Der Siebente Ring.* In the section entitled "Gestalten" (Pageant), we are met with examples of what Friedrich Wolters called "Herrschaft und Dienst" in his famous essay of the same name. The *Herrscher* is presented in many different incarnations, some of which are positive ("Der Fürst und der Minner" [The Prince and the Lover], "Manuel und Menes"), some of which are not, such as the world-weary Algabal. In George's vision of human relationships, *Herrschaft* requires *Dienst,* and so the necessary complement to the prince also appears among these *Gestalten:* the servant who recognizes the legitimacy of authority. This submission to authority is more than an acknowledgment of the sheer power a ruler may have over the life or death of his subjects — it is rather a recognition of the virtue that makes him worthy to rule. Even though it does not constitute an exact representation of Plato's own politics, this vision of human relations is nevertheless Platonic insofar as it views *Herrschaft* and *Dienst* as the two essential forms, if you will, of human relations and hence of politics. *Herrschaft* is not merely a matter of tradition nor of power. In George's legitimist politics, it involves combining personal virtue with official dignity. *Dienst,* on the other hand, represents the proper relation to *Herrschaft.* An analysis focusing on this particular point without regard for additional data would have no difficulty making George out to be a proto-Fascist. But such an analysis would have to discount the notion that not all instances of *Herrschaft* are worthy. This point is amply exemplified not only in the sharp distinction between worthy and unworthy leaders in poems like "Leo XIII" and "Der Krieg," but also in George's own explicit rejection of Nazi honors and his self-imposed exile.

Democracy is excluded from this political vision, which operates like an allegory. On the one hand, there are the ideal forms of Herrschaft and Dienst; on the other, certain real political forms that represent it well, and certain others that do not. Democracy does not because of the paradoxical character of its ideology: the leader is chosen by the people, not so much to lead, as to do its bidding; the people do not serve, but command. It would seem therefore that democracy has yet another problem in addition to those leveling tendencies that are anathema to an elitist like George, a problem of a purely aesthetic nature. But that shouldn't surprise us: for as we've seen, everything for George, even religion, starts with the aesthetic.

Notes

[1] Scholarly consensus holds that aestheticism is to be seen as part and parcel of the development of aesthetic autonomy. This view is central to all of the following important studies of the subject: Bell-Villada, Cassagne, Egan, Horstmann, Jenkins, Žmegač. Implicit in this view is the notion that the term "aestheticism" refers to a concrete literary-historical phenomenon whose nature is knowable. Such an approach is analytical rather than polemical. As many writers have noted, however, the term has not always been used in such a circumspect and cautious manner. Indeed, Horstmann points out that some kind of polemical stigma almost inevitably attaches to the word (7). While this statement may be truer of the term's German than its Anglo-American usage, one can safely say that aestheticism and polemics are intimately related. In this study, I had to choose between the two, and have opted for an analytical approach. But it remains to study the polemics of aestheticism in connection with George — more specifically, the reception of George's work as aestheticist and the various positions he and his associates took in response to that "charge."

[2] See Jenkins and Wilcox for succinct explications of this development.

[3] A particularly egregious example of this position is to be found in Bartels's Nazi-era literary history, which characterizes George's work as "l'art pour l'art poésie" and as "reine Aestheten- oder wahre Artisten-kunst, die mit dem Leben gar nichts mehr zu tun hat, sondern nur noch Selbstberauschung ist" (590).

[4] Quoted in Durzak 35.

[5] Pater's own sensualism is apparent in these lines from the conclusion to *The Renaissance:* "How shall we pass most swiftly from point to point, and be present always at the focus where the greatest number of vital forces unite in their purest energy? To burn always with this hard, gem-like flame, to maintain this ecstasy, is success in life" (197).

[6] Oswald objects to Morwitz's interpretation of the "Gottes Zwiegestalt" as bisexual, citing Herodian's description, which he interprets as exclusively phallic: "ambivalence, indeed, but hardly bisexuality" (202). The form of statue described by Herodian is that of a lingam. It is, however, characteristic of the lingam that it is not exclusively phallic and male-gendered, but represents both the masculine and feminine principles (Chevalier and Gheerbrant 610–11).

[7] He calls the day he left the temple in Emesa for Rome an "arger tag" (1: 55).

[8] Morwitz and Marx translate the title into English as *Odes,* however German also has the term *Oden,* which George could have chosen to use, but he did not. Instead, he used the term *Hymnen,* with its specifically religious connotations.

[9] I would make an exception for the phrase "glorreich grosse tat," which is definitely hymnic in tone, used in reference to the work of the painter in "Ein Angelico" (1: 21).

[10] I expand upon the Ruskinian derivation of George's motto in my article " 'Poetry is Praise.' Beobachtungen zu Stefan Georges Dichtung," *Castrum Peregrini* 52 (2003): 45–66.

Works Cited

Bartels, Adolf. *Geschichte der deutschen Literatur.* Berlin: Westermann, 1943.

Bell-Villada, Gene H. *Art for Art's Sake and Literary Life: How Politics and Markets Helped Shape the Ideology and Culture of Aestheticsm 1790–1990.* Stages vol. 5. Lincoln: U of Nebraska P, 1996.

Benn, Gottfried. "Probleme der Lyrik." *Gesammelte Werke in vier Bänden.* Vol. 1. Wiesbaden: Limes, 1958–61.

Boehringer, Robert. *Mein Bild von Stefan George.* 2 vols. Munich: Küpper, 1951.

Braungart, Wolfgang. *Ästhetischer Katholizismus: Stefan Georges Rituale der Literatur.* Communicatio vol. 15. Tübingen: Niemeyer, 1997.

Breuer, Stefan. "Zur Religion Stefan Georges." *Stefan George: Werk und Wirkung seit dem* 'Siebenten Ring.' Ed. Wolfgang Braungart et al. Tübingen: Niemeyer, 2001.

Campbell, Joseph. *The Hero of a Thousand Faces.* New York: Meridian, 1956.

Cassagne, Albert. *La Théorie de l'art pour l'art en France chez les derniers romantiques et les premiers réalistes.* 1906. Collection dix-neuvième. Rpt. Seyssel: Champvallon, 1997.

Chevalier, Jean, and Alain Gheerbrant, eds. *The Penguin Dictionary of Symbols.* Trans. John Buchanan-Brown. London: Penguin, 1996.

David, Claude. "Stefan George und die Gesellschaft." *Deutschland-Frankreich. Ludwigsburger Beiträge zum Problem der deutsch-französischen Beziehungen* 2 (1957). 117–36.

Durzak, Manfred. *Der junge Stefan George.* Munich: Fink, 1968.

Egan, Rose Frances. *The Genesis of the Theory of "Art for Art's Sake" in Germany and in England.* Smith College Studies in Modern Languages vol. 2, no. 4. Northampton, MA: n.p., 1921.

Frommel, Wolfgang. *Templer und Rosenkreuz, ein Traktat zur Christologie Stefan Georges.* Amsterdam: Castrum Peregrini, 1991.

George, Stefan. *Werke.* 2 vols. 1958. Reprint. Stuttgart: Klett-Cotta, 1984.

George, Stefan, and Karl August Klein, eds. *Blätter für die Kunst.* 1892–1919. Rpt. (in 6 vols.). Düsseldorf: Küpper, 1967.

Gundolf, Friedrich. *George.* 3rd expanded ed. Berlin: Bondi, 1930.

Horstmann, Ulrich. *Ästhetizismus und Dekadenz: Zum Paradigmakonflikt in der englischen Literaturtheorie des späten 19. Jahrhunderts.* Munich: Fink, 1983.

Jenkins, Iredell. "Art for Art's Sake." *Dictionary of the History of Ideas.* 5 vols. New York: Scribner's, 1973.

Klussmann, Paul-Gerhard. "Dante und Stefan George. Zur Wirkung der Divina Commedia in Georges Dichtung." *Stefan George Kolloquium.* Ed. Eckhard Heftrich et al. Cologne: Wienand, 1971.

Linke, Hansjürgen. *Das kultische in der Dichtung Stefan Georges und seiner Schule.* 2 vols. Munich: Küpper, 1960.

L'Ormeau, F. W. [Wolfgang Frommel]. *Die Christologie Stefan Georges.* Amsterdam: Castrum Peregrini, 1953.

Marx, Olga, and Ernst Morwitz. *The Works of Stefan George.* 2nd rev. and enlarged ed. Chapel Hill: U of North Carolina P, 1974.

Morwitz, Ernst. *Kommentar zu dem Werk Stefan Georges.* Munich: Küpper, 1960.

———. *Kommentar zu den Prosa- Drama- und Jugend-Dichtungen Stefan Georges.* Munich: Küpper, 1962.

Norton, Robert. *Secret Germany: Stefan George and his Circle.* Ithaca/London: Cornell UP, 2002.

Oswald, Victor A. Jr. "The Historical Content of Stefan George's Algabal." *The Germanic Review* 23 (1948): 193–205.

Pater, Walter. Conclusion to *The Renaissance.* 1868. Rpt. New York: Modern Library, n.d.

Ruskin, John. *The laws of Fésole. A joy forever. Our fathers have told us. Inaugural address. Modern painters, v. 1.* Vol. 6 of *The Complete Works of John Ruskin.* New York: E. R. Dumont, n.d.

Wilcox, John. "The Beginnings of *l'Art pour l'Art.*" *Journal of Aesthetics and Art Criticism* 11 (1953): 360–77.

Žmegač, Viktor. "Ästhetizismus." *Moderne Literatur in Grundbegriffen.* Ed. Dieter Borchmeyer and Viktor Žmegač. 2nd rev. ed. Tübingen: Niemeyer, 1994.

Title page of Max Kommerell's Der Dichter als Führer in der deutschen Klassik, *1928.*
Courtesy of the Stefan George-Stiftung.

Master and Disciples: The George Circle

Michael Winkler

B Y THE TIME STEFAN GEORGE was thirty years old, his plans for the second major phase of his life had fully crystallized: he was to confront his
age with a poetic work of singular beauty, dignity and greatness, and he was
to be the spiritual leader of a carefully prepared group of disciples who would
form the vanguard in a fundamental renascence of German culture.
George's opposition to all aspects of modern life was radical and unremit-
ting, no matter how stylized and ambivalently non-specific the terms and
metaphors of his invectives may sound. His contempt for Wilhelmine society in particular was aroused most vehemently by the perception that the
inexorable domination of capitalist materialism over every facet of the social
and the private world had leveled, if not forever destroyed, all traditional
bonds and values. Dignity and individuality, for example, as the right of a
unique person to subjective autonomy — the educational ideal of Weimar
Classicism and the social goal of bourgeois humanism — had succumbed to
the necessity of disguising the self behind so many roles, personae, or
assumed identities. It is obvious that the terms of George's social criticism
do not express original thinking. Rather, they derive their animus from a
keen familiarity with some of the most advanced positions in contemporary
intellectual debates. But his philippics against the spirit of his age also were
not meant to be singled out as a separate segment of an oeuvre that otherwise eschews partisanship and shuns the open market place of ideas. George
never wavered in his conviction that his art would retain its aesthetic autonomy, even as its commercial availability, since 1899 in the public editions of
the Georg Bondi Verlag, made it also a shrewdly marketed commodity. If
anything, his books, for some ten years lavishly decorated with the *Jugendstil*
designs of Melchior Lechter, signaled their status as an art of extraordinary
beauty, as a poetic *Gesamtkunstwerk*. Its purpose was to announce a new
vision of life, "das schöne leben," and to proclaim, progressively, the exclusive terms under which this visionary perception could be transformed into
human reality and ultimately become a force with societal relevance.

For George this new mission meant the subordination of his personal
life to the self-created myth of the *poet*. Even in times of private sociability
such an existence evinced not only complete seriousness but also the creation
of a statuesque unity between the human and the artistic components of

his personality. The stylization of his life according to the demands of his art allowed no self-expression that did not serve or might threaten to subvert the consciously created aura of charismatic exceptionality.

With the renunciation of woman in *Das Jahr der Seele* and the subsequent abandonment of commemorative poetry, George also had given up any hope that he might yet form "die bedeutsame grosse geistige allianz" with Hugo von Hofmannsthal (letter of 10 January 1892; *Katalog* 109) that for years could have exerted "eine sehr heilsame diktatur" (letter to Hofmannsthal of May 1902; *Briefwechsel* 150) over German poetry. Instead, through his initiation by the Angel of the Prelude into a new realm of experience, into an emphatically intense and exalted *Lebensgefühl* and its commensurate activities, he entered a period both of self-aggrandizement and solitude. The "Gesellschaft der Blätter für die Kunst," until now primarily "ein loser zusammenhang künstlerischer und ästhetischer menschen" (according to an advertisement from the end of 1903; *Katalog* 88), was being transformed into a circle of disciples and loyal followers. This *Kreis* was to be constituted as a perfective double, as a complementary doppelgänger, so to speak, of George's identity as a poet, much as the Angel and the youthful god Maximin are "mythic" duplicates of his own persona.

George felt perfectly justified in affirming his preceptorial guidance of a new generation for two reasons: he had become convinced "dass unsre jugend jezt das leben nicht mehr niedrig sondern glühend anzusehen beginnt: dass sie im leiblichen und geistigen nach schönen maassen sucht" (1897; *Einleitungen,* 25). And he was confident that he had himself attained that perfection of his art which Gustav von Aschenbach in Thomas Mann's *Der Tod in Venedig* would achieve only at a much more advanced age, namely "ein so sinnfälliges, ja gewolltes Gepräge der Meisterlichkeit und Klassizität" (Mann, 362). The deliberately masterful quality of *Der Teppich des Lebens,* so he could claim, entitled him to the same deferential loyalty and trusting love he had always been willing to extend the authority of superior accomplishment himself. He deserved, in other words, the appellation of "Meister."

George probably adopted this form of address from its French equivalent as used by the cenacle of Symbolist poets around Mallarmé who gathered for discussions on Tuesday evenings in their *maître's* small apartment in the rue de Rome. Starting as early as May 1889 during his first stay in Paris, George frequently attended these meetings. He found *historical* vindication in Dante, the initiator of all new poetry (2: 7), and assigned primary significance to the fact that Dante had placed "den Repräsentanten der Antike, Vergil, als seinen Führer an den Anfang seiner Dichtung" (*Katalog* 202): Tu se' lo mio maestro e 'l mio autore — Du Meister mir und Stab um mich zu lenken (2: 12). Characteristically, it is an apostrophe of the classical author Virgil whom the pilgrim-poet Dante chose as his guide — tu duce, tu segnore e tu maestro (Inferno II, 140) / Du bist der Herr, der Führer und der Weise (2: 18) — that Friedrich Wolters inscribed in the copy of his *"Blättergeschichte"* which he presented to his Master and collaborator (Wolters 452).

But it is no less probable that George was well aware of the sanctimoniousness and turgid unction that had become a hallmark of epistolary salutations especially among German litterateurs. Rilke, for example, addressed not only Rodin as "Honoré Maître" (letter of 28 June 1902 among many others) but also flattered a writer like Richard Zoozmann as "Hochverehrter Meister" (25 September 1896) and older colleagues like Dehmel and Ganghofer (1855–1920) as "Verehrte Meister." In Nietzsche's letters to Wagner from the early 1870s, he frequently addresses Wagner with "Verehrtester Meister" and calls himself "treuergeben."

Do such ludicrous superlatives merely bespeak a certain youthful insecurity and its compensatory need for grandiose gestures, perhaps for adulation? Or do they point to a deeper cultural malaise and generational conflict, which might suggest that, across almost three decades, a more than superficial kinship existed, for example, between George and the (future) Master of Bayreuth? Given the fact that two of his close (older) friends, Lechter and Karl Wolfskehl, were devoted Wagnerians, it is hard to imagine that they did not talk with him about their enthusiasm and their experiences at the Bayreuth *Festspielhaus* with other devotees. It is not likely, at any rate, that George was altogether unaffected by the challenge of Wagner's "Selbstinszenierung als 'Deutscher Meister'" ("Leiden," 260).

It seems futile to attempt pinpointing specific congruences. What connections do exist are best described *ex negativo,* George's own persona being systematically constituted in deliberate contradistinction to any life that would combine aesthetic principles with elements of bourgeois comfort and surfeit. Yet George was not immune to a style of luxurious excess that would serve and indeed highlight the claim of his art to exceptional stature. Lechter's decorative craftsmanship, in other words, also satisfied a distinctly bourgeois desire for rarefied opulence that contained more than a touch of mystic sanctity. In all practical matters of life, however, a frugality bordering on asceticism in George contradicted such tendencies with uncompromising rigor. His often monastic habits of simplicity may have been part of a conscious effort to emphasize the otherworldliness of his spiritual mission. They are also a "natural" component of his family background in a rural environment in which the skills of the craftsman and of exacting manual labor predominated. George never broke with the world of his parents and frequently returned home to recuperate from illnesses and from the exertions of his many travels and to reaffirm his ties to a world of orderly traditions and dignified moderation.

This is the same aspect that Thomas Mann saw in Wagner — in his speech "Leiden und Größe Richard Wagners" of February 1933 — and singled out as complementing "die Dämonie" and the "Feuerflüssig-Vulkanische in dieser Produktion." He called it "das altdeutsch-kunstmeisterliche

Element" and the patiently and solidly "Handwerksfromme und Sinnig-Arbeitsame" that reveals a "bürgerliche Arbeitsakkuratesse, wie sie sich in seinen keineswegs hingewühlten, sondern höchst sorgfältig-reinlichen Partituren spiegelt, — derjenigen seines entrücktesten Werkes zumal, der Tristanpartitur, einem Musterbild klarer, penibler Kalligraphie" ("Leiden," 260–61).

Although George, of course, preferred the beret to Wagner's "Dürermütze," his sense of what makes a "Meister," far from requiring the conventional modifier "old," did indeed include associations usually evoked by synonyms like *fabricator* and *opifex:* perfect command over all the details of a craft. Such dedication to the ethos of the artificer is reflected in the forced and occasionally overstrained density of his most ambitious poems. It also recurs in his epistolary style even though his letters are mostly an expedient for the exchange of information. With the exception of some long and self-probing confessions in his early correspondence with Hofmannsthal, George was a highly reticent letter writer and avoided any locution that might sound casual or insinuate a special degree of familiarity. He very rarely — and consistently only with Friedrich Gundolf and Ernst Morwitz (1887–1971) — deviated from the formal "Sie" and from an attitude of distance and reserve.

Only Lechter, probably because he stood outside the circle of poet-friends, would sometimes address him as "LIEBER STEFAN" and even "mein lieber Stefano" and in return be called "lieber und verehrter freund" or "teurer Melchior." But even George's first and for a decade his most important disciple and deeply beloved friend, Gundolf, at first is addressed as "lieber Dichter" until a kind of internal code of abbreviations takes effect so that l. G. (or, lieber Gundel) can speak of George to others (and they among themselves of Him) as d. M. [= der Meister], as if names had become trademarks signifying grades of quality.

At any rate, George held all of his companions and especially those he selected for special duties to extremely high standards of technical proficiency. Such tasks primarily included work like fact checking and proof-reading of *Kreis* — publications, but the standards also extended to virtually any aspect of the group's activities that might be subject to expert or public scrutiny. At the same time, George did not involve himself in his followers' private affairs so long as they were conducted according to certain fundamental precepts, and he usually evaded what pleas for personal guidance may cast him in the role of father confessor. He was, however, directly concerned with the professional reputation, specifically with the academic success and indeed prominence of his followers.

Women were excluded from official *Kreis* activities; feminist issues had absolutely no place in its canon of cultural and social aspirations. George's interests in this respect ended with acknowledging the desirability of a harmonious family life and with cognizance of the human animal's drive to satisfy various physical needs, which, if done discreetly, will not interfere with his higher calling. George himself did little to promote a kind of communal sense of togetherness that might look like clubbish sociability. He had a generally cordial relationship especially with the wives and sisters of those among his friends in whose homes he would be a very undemanding guest. As a point of policy, however, he remained taciturn about his private circumstances and often maintained strict secrecy concerning his whereabouts. He was also careful to avoid any suggestion that he favored one or the other group. More than anything, a shifting constellation of small groups of friends in a few centers of German academic life constituted the core of the artistic-intellectual circles whose charismatic focus was George.

His virtual anonymity — sometimes for weeks and months — fostered the proselytizing independence of those of his adherents who had a particular pedagogical talent or an overpowering, magnetic personality. It was they who personally attracted, or who were approached by, older schoolboys and young students who were in thrall of George's poetry and satisfied the eligibility requirements for continuing education in the Master's spirit. First among these imperatives, of course, was a natural aptitude for appreciating high poetry, and the willingness to become inured in it through the disciplined exercise of recitations. A "candidate's" first evaluation was decided not so much by analytic intellectual comprehension as by almost spontaneous submission to the force of carefully modulated rhythms and sounds. A broad humanistic education along with an unobtrusive quickness of mind as well as an attractive physical appearance and the promise of psychological stability were additional, though not always indispensable prerequisites.

Personal mentorship in whatever form was limited by necessity to an extremely small and fairly homogeneous group that never exceeded a total of some fifteen to twenty special disciples. Consequently, it was through the publications of its prominent spokesmen that the *Kreis* expanded, sustaining by way of "unofficial" or imaginary affiliations its very considerable presence in German academic life especially during the 1920s. This presence was being established by a self-conscious elite, the highly gifted children of the educated and, at least during the pre-war years, economically secure bourgeoisie, the *Bildungsbürgertum*. They came to predominate George's "staat," his ideal state within society, as its "staatsstützen" (pillars of the state). But the distinctive talents and predispositions that seemed to "predestine" them for this role also stem from certain peculiarities, perhaps insufficiencies of the German educational system and its origins in the era of Weimar Classicism. The Gymnasium and the university as institutions provided almost no opportunities for the kind of elitist socialization of exceptional youth that distinguish the French *lycées* as well as British public schools and prestigious colleges. Classes were held on a half-day basis, their purpose being the authoritative transmission of information and of a cultural ethos saturated with an idealized vision of ancient Greece. Lectures were an opportunity for rapid note-taking. While teachers were for the most part competent in their specific disciplines, they provided little psychological guidance and, almost as a rule, were impervious to pedagogical subtleties and hostile to idiosyncrasies. Homework and studying were done largely in quiet isolation, often at a considerable distance from classrooms or lecture halls.

Equally relevant in this context is the function that the German concept of education and refinement (*Bildung*) allocated to poetic literature, though more as programmatic ideal than as customary practice. *Dichtung* was highly valued as a critical corrective that served to counterbalance the progressive domination of intellectual life by the methods and results of scientific research and of dispassionate scholarship (*Wissenschaft*). This is an orientation, to be sure, that itself had originally been perceived as autonomous. Its search for truth was expected to be guided by dedication to non-purposive knowledge so that its disciplined objectivity could become the intellectual prerequisite for success in any profession. But the rapid advances of industrial scientism in the later nineteenth century negated such expectations and reinforced the position of poets as social arbiters and specifically as critics of one-sided socio-cultural developments. Furthermore, their emotional-intuitive grasp of reality came to be seen as an alternative approach that cannot replace but, in terms of social values, supplement, or, culturally, neutralize the undeniably beneficial products and accomplishments of pragmatic positivism.

George was fully aware that any sustained engagement with the dominant principles and cognitive paradigms of his age would only provoke ridicule unless it included the ability to confront the enemy with his own weapons, with perfect *Arbeitsakkuratesse*. Only then could a convincing claim be made that the language of poetic imagery is not an arbitrary, uncontrolled emanation of inspirational genius: it is, rather, superior to the rational idioms of science because it is imbued with the creative power of synthesis. Moreover, high poetry, as the realization of beauty through language, was far from being, as all art, an essentially amoral phenomenon. It was equated with the good, and a life lived by aesthetic principles amounted to the ultimate fulfillment of the human spirit and thus also of humanistic *Bildung*.

The new interpretive method to vindicate this fundamental premise historically, and to dissociate it from identification with dandyish aestheticism, was called *Geistesgeschichte*. It sought to understand historical phenomena, especially those of cultural history, as emanations of the ideas (*geistige Kräfte*) said to be inherent in any particular movement, era, or nation. Whatever happens — in politics, philosophy, the arts —, that is, all *Geschehen*, is seen as the manifestation of an essential, unified attitude, a *Grundhaltung;* and as such it is the outcome of an epochal *Gesamtgeist*. The creative vitality of this "collective spirit" infuses all works with life and makes them part of an all-inclusive network of productive connections and developments. In contrast to the individualizing analyses typical of positivistic scholarship, the *geisteswissenschaftlich* mode offers speculative syntheses. It seeks to define the results of human activities through comprehensive descriptions of a core idea or problem that lives and unfolds beyond a narrowly designated time and place. As a "Kritik der historischen Vernunft" (Critique of Historical Reason) in Wilhelm Dilthey's anti-Kantian terms, the quest for historical and cultural knowledge when pursued in accordance with this life-oriented, vitalistic "nuova scienza" of the mind involves the total human being. It engages all his capacities for experience, including very prominently the faculties of volition, emotion, and imagination.

Dilthey (1833–1911; from 1883 until 1908 professor in Berlin) was the first philosopher to systematize the theoretical tenets of a methodology that had its own continuities in nineteenth-century thought, that is, in the history of the German mind since early Romanticism. He also wrote exemplary biographies that located a distinctive, great individual within the intellectual environment of a historical epoch. With equal attention he revealed the enduring relevance of a cultural hero through the ages by tracing how he continued to influence the thinking of posterity. Gundolf, who had met George as early as April 1899 at Wolfskehl's house in Munich and was also a doctoral student of Dilthey's in Berlin, became the first poet-scholar to develop *Geistesgeschichte* to its full potential. Under the impact of what George far more than what Dilthey taught him he introduced an epistemological reorientation to his chosen profession, *Literaturwissenschaft,* that became normative during the 1920s and beyond.

Shakespeare und der deutsche Geist (1911), the topic of Gundolf's *Habilitationsschrift,* is his first sustained attempt to describe "eine Geschichte lebendiger Wirkungen und Gegenwirkungen" as "die Gestaltung und geistige Durchdringung" not of past but of present things, "die unser eigenes Leben noch unmittelbar angehen" — as he outlines his intent in his "Vorwort" (vii–viii). It is a program he realizes again in *Caesar, Geschichte seines Ruhms* (Caesar, History of his Fame, 1924). The monograph compactly titled *George* (1920) applies the very same principles to that one heroic man who in his time embodies "das ewige Menschentum" as norm and idea, as "Einheit einer Person mit einer kosmischen Lage und einem geschichtlichen Augenblick." This "Gesamtmensch" opposes the dictatorship of the modern relativism of values and of what is being idolized as "progress" by positing the Eternal (*das Ewige*) against the "Verheutigung (*Aktualisierung*)" of values, by insisting on the Mystery (*das Geheime*) against their public display, by setting Magic (*Zauber*) up against exploitative utilization and pleasure, by holding *die Gestalt* against mass, the *Bund* against singularity (atomization). Against the raging flow of destructive change, George sets the permanence of the growing sphere

(*Kugel*), "die alles bewahrt und immer neues einbegreift mit der verborgen strahlenden, nie ertastbaren Mitte" — that contains everything and forever absorbs new things, its center unfathomable and radiant from a secret source. Five recent incarnations of the idea of *Gesamtmensch* above others testify to the potential resurrection of this figure in a new era: Goethe, Hölderlin, Napoleon, Nietzsche, George — according to his introductory chapter, "Zeitalter und Aufgabe."

Gundolf found the legitimacy of these maxims sustained by the essential qualities that live in George as "antikische Seelenkräfte": a sense of dignity as an intuitive ability to discern innate human gradations, a sense of destiny as an awareness of the inmost unity of being and happenstance, "von Tun und Leiden," and supra-sexual ("übergeschlechtige") love as a world-creating passion.

Gundolf's axioms demonstrate his continued attachment to George the great poet whom he revered as the incarnation of the divine, "des göttlichen." This reverence was based on the conviction that just as it is impossible to separate the mind from the body, so there can be no "trennung des göttlichen vom menschen." And it is the "grosse mensch" who personifies "die höchste form unter der wir das göttliche erleben." This entails the devotion to other great human beings, "die verehrung der grossen menschen," through a manner of adherence that is worthless unless it is religious. Such a bond holds within itself a mutually transformational power in that the great individuals *want* to exert their influence and effect by changing us, the recipients, by their "strahlen und samen." And in doing so, "bilden sie sich selber um, 'gestaltend umgestaltet.'" An analogous process takes place in history which he understands to be "die wechselwirkung der schöpferischen und der empfänglichen menschen." And it is also active in that process of historical mediation which recovers the exemplary documents (texts), monuments (deeds), and the *Gestalten* of a past come alive, of *erlebte Vergangenheit*. They have now been made visible and revitalized as forces that significantly affect our present *Lebenswelt*.

These ideas from the programmatic essay "Vorbilder," first published in the *Jahrbuch für die geistige Bewegung* 3, 1912; (quoted in *George-Kreis* 174–75), further specified the relevance that tradition holds in Gundolf's concept of *Bildung*. They also defined the role of the historian — social, political, cultural, literary — as that of a necessary mediator who first connects the manifestations of past greatness so as to establish a living continuity, and then relates its values to the needs of the present age.

The *Kreis* as a highly select community is, according to these premises, primarily an artistic-scholarly elite which, as a *Bildungsgemeinschaft*, is committed to activating cultural traditions in a new spirit. The function of this community as a "pedagogical province" is to exemplify the beneficial consequences of a worldview whose center is the Idea symbolized in the Master. To live in his image, as his "Gefolgschaft und Jüngertum" (to quote the title of apodictic statements Gundolf contributed to *Blätter* 8 [1909]) allowed a significant degree of individual freedom. The self-assurance and sense of self-worth it engendered constituted an enrichment of life in that it offered stringent guidance and values without, however, abrogating personal autonomy.

Gundolf's anti-ideological "individualism" gained him a good number of personal friends (among them Edgar Salin [1892–1974], Julius Landmann [1877–1931], Norbert von Hellingrath [1888–1916], Kurt Singer [1886–1962], and Wolfgang Heyer) and much intellectual admiration among the academic luminaries in Heidelberg where he had been appointed to a professorship in 1911. But it also meant that he would not proselytize directly and thus impart specific directives to a *Kreis* of his own. During the latter part of the First World War, moreover, he began to doubt that German culture could regenerate itself. And as he became pessimistic about the future of his country, he increasingly saw George's position itself in historical terms. Consequently, he found himself nearly isolated in the internal struggles that accompanied the reorganization of George's *Kreis* immediately after 1918.

Friedrich Wolters was the driving force in these maneuvers and George sided ever more emphatically with him. Wolters, even before the war, saw the *Kreis* in terms of national politics: it was to serve as the active vanguard of a movement yet to be initiated that would bring about a comprehensive rejuvenation of the German state. He based his hopes on the determined enthusiasm of an elite of young people which would be melded into a nearly homogeneous community by a singular interpretation of the poet's mission. Greatness in the poet, however, now goes beyond aesthetic autonomy. It includes creative activism which, as the emanation of a unique creativity, is not to be judged by ethical criteria or standards of evaluation it has not set for itself. Wolters, in other words, extends the authority of the poet beyond spiritual guidance (*geistige Führung*) into the realm of political leadership. His concept of Bildung, therefore, is characterized very prominently by the abdication of personal freedom in the interest of service to *one* idea that affects the whole people, *Gesamtheit*. It alone sets the standards for the reform of society *in toto*. Through "Herrschaft und Dienst" (Sovereignty and Service) of George's elite, to quote the title of Wolters's 1909 pamphlet, the German nation is to be reborn in the image of its culture.

Wolters was a historian specializing in economic and administrative issues during the Era of Absolutism. He stood at the beginning of a distinguished academic career when, in 1905, his teacher Kurt Breysig (1866–1940) introduced him to George. Breysig, an "Extraordinarius" (associate professor) at the Friedrich-Wilhelm-Universität in Berlin since 1896, taught *Universalgeschichte,* that is the comparative history of all human societies. It was his purpose to reveal, systematically and comprehensively, the grand underlying laws and anthropological consistencies that govern historical developments across the ages. His special focus was the relationship between the great individual and his world, specifically as it manifests itself in the interaction between the exceptional power of the genius and the malleable mass. Breysig, to be sure, remained an outsider in his scholarly discipline which was dominated by an ethos of objective, value-free research and was concerned above all, even in major projects, with the scrupulous attention to details that is required by specialization. But to an informal group of young scholars, the "Freier Bund bauender Forscher" (Free League of Constructive Scholars) he was an inspirational leader. They met socially and for intellectual discussions in the small towns on the northern periphery of Berlin where most of them lived, some in communal arrangements.

George personally found the capital of the German Reich distasteful and, quite in contrast to the ease with which he adopted Munich and later Heidelberg as temporary places of residence, he never felt comfortable there. But during the past decade he had established fruitful contacts among congenial Berlin artists and academic intellectuals — people like the painters Sabine and Reinhold Lepsius, like Georg Simmel (1858–1918), Karl Joël (1864–1934), Richard Moritz Meyer (1860–1914), and Max Dessoir (1867–1947) — whose prestige as the vanguard of the cultured class was essential to the dissemination of his message. George was shrewd enough to know that, at least as a cultural critic, he would be condemned to the status of a provincial celebrity if he failed to maintain a significant presence in Berlin.

That presence was represented most emphatically by the circle of friends around Wolters who had found each other in Schönhausen, a rural suburb near Pankow, and later moved to the charming suburb in southwest Berlin, Lichterfelde. The parks, gardens and woods there were more conducive than the metropolis to an enthusiastic lifestyle that included a good deal of festive carousing in addition to recitations of poetry, readings of Platonic dialogues, performances of plays, as well as impromptu discussions of their own literary efforts, and of any number of cultural issues and historical topics. When they met with George, it was usually at the studio (the "Pompeianum") of Ludwig Thormaehlen (1889–1956), a prospective art historian and sculptor. The forum of this group was the *Jahrbuch für die geistige Bewegung*. Its core, beside Wolters, included four intimate companions: Berthold Vallentin (1877–1933), the son of a prosperous merchant family who had studied history and law and later became a judge in Spremberg near Cottbus. His life-long intellectual obsession is reflected in his monograph *Napoleon* (1923), which he dedicated to George ("Hodierno Heroi"), and in its sequel, *Napoleon und die Deutschen* (Napoleon and the Germans, 1926). He also wrote a study of the enlightenment and its concept of education through classical art, *Winckelmann* (1933). Kurt Hildebrandt (1881–1966), whose paternal forebears were prominent Lutheran ministers, studied philosophy and medicine and, since

1906, worked as a physician and psychiatrist at an institution for mental patients in Berlin-Wittenau; in 1921 he wrote a philosophical dissertation on Nietzsche's struggle with Socrates and Plato under the direction of the neo-Kantian Paul Natorp (1854–1924) at Marburg (where Wolters had been appointed to an "Extraordinariat" in 1920 before advancing to a chair at Kiel in 1923). But it was not until 1928 that he became a lecturer (*Dozent*) in philosophy in Berlin; six years later he moved to Kiel as a full professor. Friedrich Andreae (1879–1939) taught history at Breslau since 1912; his brother Wilhelm (1888–1962) became an economist under Othmar Spann's aegis in Vienna (Habilitation 1925) and taught in Graz and Giessen and since 1937 at Marburg.

The Yearbook published twenty-one essays, five of them by authors (Robert Boehringer, Hugo Eick, Erich Kahler [1885–1970], Paul Thiersch [1879–1928]) without a "politically" motivated orientation. As the expression of an ideational group identity, these contributions were framed by two (constructive) programmatic discourses: Wolters's "Richtlinien" (1910), and Gundolf's "Vorbilder" (1912). The polemical intent of what is effectively Wolters's project is realized most aggressively in Vallentin's two critiques (of progress and of the collusion between the press and the theater) and in Hildebrandt's attack titled "Hellas und Wilamowitz" (*Jahrbuch* 1: 64–117). He chastises Ulrich von Wilamowitz-Moellendorff (1863–1941), the most prominent Greek scholar in Germany at the time, for debasing the high culture, and indeed the "sacred" greatness, of classical Athens by adapting their works to "der bürgerlichen bequemlichkeit und dem proletarischen geschmack" (quoted in Groppe 231). His anger is specifically directed against what he considers the blasphemy of translating the heroic-passionate language of Attic tragedy into the trivially moralizing idiom of contemporary disputations. Such a leveling of values is counteracted by an intuitive, almost visionary perception of ideas ("Schau der Ideen") leading to an experience of truth that is given only to "große Menschen." It comes as a kind of spiritual revelation at moments of the most heightened intensity ("im kairos"). As Hildebrandt states (in his contribution "Romantisch und Dionysisch," *Jahrbuch* 2: 91) with reference to Plato's manner of philosophizing, this visionary experience of Ideas is an all-enlivening, unifying process. It returns perfect beauty to our world, "gebannt in *eine* menschliche gestalt."

The exemplary one human being to embody this view of *Gestalt* and its will to exert a deep pedagogical impact was Plato. In a monograph titled *Plato: Seine Gestalt* (1914), Heinrich Friedemann (1888–1915), a teacher who had asked Gundolf to show his unpublished manuscript to George for approval, saw in Plato not the great metaphysician but the creator and ruler of a spiritual world, "den unvergänglichen Vater geistigen Reiches" (138). Using and shaping the best of what his time had to offer, Plato is seen to have lived the ideal of the "gotterfüllte Mensch." It is an existence in which, brought about by the power of Eros, mind and body, idea and material reality have been so perfectly fused as to be identical with what George spoke of as the "werk" of the "grosse Nährerin" who "Den leib vergottet und den gott verleibt" (1: 256) — who gives the body its divine and the divine its bodily nature. This concept of the man-god draws its principal inspiration from the *Symposium* and *Phaedrus*. Their central role among the dialogues informs two other works by friends of Gundolf that seek to show the contemporary relevance of the Platonic academy as a community that fosters critical self-education: Edgar Salin's *Platon und die griechische Utopie* (Plato and Greek Utopia, 1921) and Kurt Singer's *Platon der Gründer* (Plato the Founder, 1927).

Hildebrandt, by contrast and in close ideological proximity to Wolters, emphasized the importance of the Platonic "state" as a "political" entity, as the attempted realization of what George, in a letter to Gundolf of April 1911, praised as the "tat-mässige innerhalb des geistigen" (George-Gundolf 224). Its *locus classicus* is *The Republic* through its apparent legitimation of the "geistige Führer" — in the ideal personification of Plato's philosopher-ruler as well as now in George's action-oriented "Künstlertum" — for political leadership. In Wolters's program for the fundamental reform of society this entails the codification of aesthetic-spiritual principles as "Richtlinien" that are subject only to their own ethical considerations. In practical terms this meant the advocacy of a hierarchical absolutism with a strongly nationalistic bend. Hildebrandt saw it as "Der Kampf des Geistes um die Macht" — to quote the subtitle of his 1933 book on Plato.

Politics for most members of the circle was cultural politics, of course; it did not demand any form of direct involvement in the affairs of public life. Consequently, knowledge of the administrative organization of society and of the pragmatic mechanisms of industrial capitalism appears to have been minimal and did not go much beyond what insights into the practical world their artistic-academic positions afforded them. Their principal orientation continued to be communicated through the poetry of George who, however, did closely observe and keep himself informed about the events that made the news of his time. But he strictly opposed the participation of his friends in or affiliation of his "geistige Bewegung" with any other association, especially with a political party. Nor did he harbor any illusions about the First World War as the dawn of a new era, and when asked for personal reassurance, he advised his disciples to do their duty as their conscience demanded.

George himself attributed the war as much to the arrogant incompetence of German politicians as to any other single cause and was loath to be drawn into war propaganda that would equate his "geheimes Deutschland" with the "gesamtdeutschen Patriotismus" (George-Gundolf 265). The project of collecting a number of pronouncements by *Kreis* members in a small *Kriegsjahrbuch* was therefore abandoned. And there was no other internal directive or open manifesto that might have imposed a uniform position on them, or that would provoke acrimonious dissent among them. As could be expected, some of his intimates joined the pervasive war euphoria of the first few months, others refrained from any comment, for a few the war marked a crucial turning point in their movement.

Responding to an "Open Letter" by Romain Rolland (1866–1944) in the *Journal de Genève* of 29 August 1914 about the reasons for German intellectuals' hatred of France, Wolfskehl considered the war a god-willed necessity forced on Germany as a defense against the Russian moloch and motivated by a desire to preserve *"das Göttliche im Menschen"* (*Frankfurter Zeitung*, 12 September 1914); Gundolf defended Germany's obligation to go to war as the duty of the only people, "das mit einem Wort noch Jugend hat" to bring about the *"Wiedergeburt Europas"* (ibid., 11 October 1914). For him, this is what inspires "den heiligen Sinn der ungeheuren Opfer," not any redistribution of power. But it was Wolters, thirty-seven years old when he volunteered for service in the *Landsturm,* who most insistently saw the war as a demonstration of "grösse und heldentum," that is of a "geistig-leibliche haltung die nur aus göttlichem grunde erwachsen kann: aus einer welt von unsinn schein und frevel kann sie also nicht kommen" (George-Wolters 131, letter of 26 February 1917 from Felsö-Vissó, Romania). In the same letter, he expresses his faith in the "gesunden kräfte," in the "durchgeistigung eben jener guten und rein menschlichen kräfte in unserem volke," and the "bildmachung jener noch reinen blutskräfte im göttlichen" (132) found an ever stronger positive response from George. By the end of the war this shift in attitude had even dispelled his initial skepticism about the "welt die erst kommen soll und die den wirklichen feind + widerdämon besiegen soll" and that this force can as yet only be his own Circle: "da liegen seit UNSERN anfängen VOR ALLEM KRIEG alle unsre hoffnungen" (George-Gundolf 264).

It was most probably the unexpected length of the war with its unimaginably high casualties and the often chaotic and revolutionary convulsions of the early 1920s that persuaded George that "die Wirkung nach aussen überhaupt nur durch einen politischen Menschen, einen Täter zustande gebracht werden könne, der eines Tages die Gedanken der Bewegung politisch zu einem Körper zusammenstelle und damit die Nation bewege" — at least so Vallentin recorded George as saying in a conversation on 19 February 1928 (*Gespräche*, 102). George himself, who wrote no new poetry after the war and devoted nearly all of his diminishing energies to securing his posthumous reputation, withdrew from public life. Wolters, however, besides his commitment to writing the monumental history of the *Kreis,* expanded his public activities. It was most of all a severely disillusioned and disappointed academic youth whom he tried to reach through "patriotic" (*vaterländisch*) speeches and book publications.

One of his principal concerns now, intensified by a fear of Bolshevism and no less by hostile misgivings about liberal and democratic forms of socialization, was for the integrity of a distinctly German cultural sphere. But the vocabulary in which this apprehension expressed itself, especially such almost undefinable terms as "Volk," "Geist," "Volksgeist," or "Reich" remained open to various conceptualizations. It was never clarified, at any rate, to a point where suggestive vagueness might give way to delineations that actually have content. Wolters was, after all, not interested in concrete issues of political-economic organization but in a *geistiges Deutschtum*.

Such a Germany of the mind did not want to be confused with any emerging structures in the world of *Realpolitik*. As much as that of George's *Das Neue Reich,* the public appeal of Wolters's central concepts was grounded in semantic indeterminacy, which allowed a broad spectrum of expectations the assurance of at least some significant measure of consent. This openness to contiguous predispositions favored the broad camp of nationalist conservatism with which it shared an emotionally suggestive irrationalism. The force of personality, enhanced by some distinctive demeanor and by emblematic objects such as Wolters's tunic and chain, often left a strong initial impact and then helped to form a more enduring bond between student and mentor and among students themselves than did the cultural message.

By about 1925 this message had become well-established among those for whom it was meant. Even a certain proliferation with an attendant slide into routine and self-repetition was becoming noticeable. This observation is true especially of books from the smaller and, as it were, not fully sanctioned, peripheral circles. It does not apply to the two major works that, in complementary ways, consolidated the Georgean position vis-á-vis academia, both of them comprehensive attempts to define the idea of imperium/Reich historically. Ernst Kantorowicz (1895–1963) did this in his landmark biography, *Kaiser Friedrich der Zweite* (1927), and Max Kommerell in his study of the classical period in German literature, *Der Dichter als Führer in der deutschen Klassik* (The Poet as Leader in the Age of German Classicism, 1928).

Kantorowicz had replaced Gundolf in George's affection and, since 1922, was the Master's favorite companion during his stays in Heidelberg. He was a doctoral student of Eberhard Gothein's (1853–1923), when his friend Woldemar Graf von Uxkull-Gyllenband (1898–1939) — like his brother Bernhard Victor (1899–1918) and their cousins, the counts von Stauffenberg, he was close to Ernst Morwitz in Berlin — introduced him to George. The poet took an intense personal interest in Kantorowicz's work which interprets the great Hohenstaufen emperor as a "Weltmajestät" and as the last representative of a Germano-Latinate humanism with a Christian as well as a secular-cosmopolitan orientation. Kommerell had studied under Gundolf before he went to Marburg and, in the figure of "Maxim," became the poet's last intimate disciple, the youngest representative of his "staat." He frequently accompanied George on his travels and was chosen to become his legal heir, a special relationship that did not last, however, beyond the end of the decade. It was above all the coercive exclusiveness underlying Wolters's mythology of George's *geistige Bewegung* that motivated his decision, in 1930, to make Hofmannsthal the topic of his first public lecture as an *Ordinarius* in Marburg. But by this time the George-Kreis itself had become a historical phenomenon, not the least due to the fact that it had practically lost its charismatic center.

Works Cited

Blätter für die Kunst. 6 vols. Düsseldorf/Munich: Küpper, 1968.

Briefwechsel zwischen George und Hofmannsthal. Ed. Robert Boehringer. Berlin: Bondi, 1938.

Friedemann, Heinrich. *Plato: Seine Gestalt.* Berlin: Verlag der Blätter für die Kunst, 1914.

George, Stefan. *Werke.* Ausgabe in zwei Bänden. Munich/Düsseldorf: Küpper, 1958.

George, Stefan, and Friedrich Gundolf. *Briefwechsel.* Eds. Robert Boehringer and Georg Peter Landmann. Munich/Düsseldorf: Küpper, 1962.

George, Stefan, and Friedrich Wolters. *Briefwechsel 1904–1930.* Ed. Michael Philipp. Amsterdam: Castrum Peregrini Presse, 1998.

Groppe, Carola. *Die Macht der Bildung: Das deutsche Bürgertum und der George-Kreis 1890–1933.* Cologne/Weimar/Vienna: Böhlau, 1997.

Gundolf, Friedrich. *Shakespeare und der deutsche Geist.* Berlin: Bondi, 1911.

———. *George.* Berlin: Bondi, 1920.

Landmann, Georg Peter, ed. *Der George-Kreis: Eine Auswahl aus seinen Schriften.* Stuttgart: Klett-Cotta, 1980.

———. *Einleitungen und Merksprüche der Blätter für die Kunst.* Düsseldorf/Munich: Küpper, 1964.

Lechter, Melchior, and Stefan George. *Briefe.* Ed. Günter Heintz. Stuttgart: Hauswedell, 1991.

Mann, Thomas. "Der Tod in Venedig." *Sämtliche Erzählungen.* Frankfurt a.M.: Fischer, 1963.

———. "Leiden und Größe Richard Wagners." *Leiden und Größe der Meister.* Frankfurt a.M.: Fischer, 1957. 216–75.

Vallentin, Berthold. *Gespräche mit Stefan George, 1902–1931, Tagebuchaufzeichnungen.* Amsterdam: Castrum Peregrini Presse, 1961.

Wolters, Friedrich. *Stefan George und die Blätter für die Kunst: Deutsche Geistesgeschichte seit 1890.* Berlin: Bondi, 1930.

Zeller, Bernhard, et al., eds. *Stefan George 1868–1968: Der Dichter und sein Kreis.* Eine Ausstellung des Deutschen Literaturarchivs im Schiller-Nationalmuseum Marbach a.N. Katalog Nr. 19, 1968.

George, Verwey and the Cosmologists, Munich, April 1902.
From left to right: Wolfskehl, Schuler, Klages, George, Verwey.
Photograph by K. Bauer, Munich. Courtesy of the Stefan George-Stiftung.

Stefan George and the Munich Cosmologists

Paul Bishop

A RGUABLY THE GREATEST INFLUENCE on George's development as a poet was his first visit to Paris (June–August 1889), where he met the French symbolist Stéphane Mallarmé.[1] Arguably the greatest influence on George as a *person,* however, and on how he *presented* himself, were the months he spent in Munich, which he first visited in February 1891 and repeatedly thereafter. One aspect of fin-de-siècle Munich has been captured in the famous words of Thomas Mann in his 1902 short story "Gladius Dei": "München leuchtete [Munich gleamed]" (215). The fact that turn-of-the-century Munich its darker side as well did not escape Thomas Mann either, and would, in turn, be discovered by George. His four-line poem on the city, in the "Tafeln" section of *Der siebente Ring* (1907), is largely, but not entirely, positive in its evocation of "München":

> Mauern wo geister noch zu wandern wagen ·
> Boden vom doppelgift noch nicht verseucht:
> Du stadt von volk und jugend! heimat deucht
> Uns erst wo Unsrer Frauen türme ragen. (I, 336)

The "spirits" inhabiting the city are perhaps those cosmopolitan intellectuals George met in Munich, and whose relations with George are the subject of this essay; but there is also a hint of something "ghostly" in these lines. The "ground" has not been poisoned — not yet — by the unspecified "two-fold poison" (for Ernst Morwitz, these two "poisons" are *zerstreuung,* "entertainment," and the seductive sound of music [*dort in häusern / Bunte klänge laden schmeichelnd / Saugen süss die seele*]).[2] What is more, the final image of this brief poem looks up at the copper, onion-domed towers of the Frauenkirche, the imposing Late Gothic cathedral, dominating the Munich skyline as one of the city's greatest symbols.[3] Other poems, however, allude more precisely to George's experiences and acquaintances in Munich, particularly three figures — Ludwig Klages (1872–1956), Alfred Schuler (1865–1923), and Ludwig Derleth (1870–1948) — who were members of the so-called "Cosmic Circle" (*Kosmiker-Kreis, Kosmische Runde*) in Munich at the turn of the century.

Stefan George can be thought of as a member of two intersecting circles (although none of these groupings existed in any official sense). First, there is the "George Circle" (*George-Kreis*), consisting of, among others, Robert Boehringer (1884–1974) (one of George's literary executors and founder of the Stefan George Stiftung), the scholar Ernst Bertram (1884–1957), the writer Max Dauthendey (1867–1918), the calligrapher Ernst Glöckner (1885–1934), the biographer Friedrich Gundolf (1880–1931), and the historian Friedrich Wolters (1876–1930).[4] At the center of this circle stood George himself, "the Master." Second, George belonged, if more marginally, to the "Cosmic Circle," a much looser band of friends and associates centering around Klages and Schuler. Some members of this circle — including Derleth and the writer Karl Wolfskehl (1869–1948) — remained in the *George-Kreis* even as other members moved away from George. From one point of view, the "Cosmic Circle" was a subset of the "George Circle" which gradually moved out of it, but, rather than being a break-away group from the "George Circle," the "Cosmic Circle" was in fact formed prior to it. So the model of a close group of friends dedicated to a particular cause was adopted, at least in part, by George from his experiences with the *Kosmiker* (although the "George Circle" certainly had a greater consistency and unity of purpose than the *Kosmiker*).

Although George referred to Wolfskehl, Richard Perls (1873–1898), and Klages as "ein Kreis verschiedenster denker, künstler [. . .], und feinde der schmutzigen seelen,"[5] the actual name of the "Cosmic Circle" was practically invented, or at any rate lent currency, by a member of the *George-Kreis*, Friedrich Wolters.[6] (Within "cosmic" thought, the circle itself was a symbol of the pattern of the universe.)[7] So what, if anything, was "cosmic" about this circle to which Klages, Schuler, Wolfskehl, Derleth, and, for a time, it seems, George, belonged? What did the "Cosmic Circle" believe in?

There is no single statement of what the members of the "Cosmic Circle" believed (and they believed different things at different times). As the critic Gerhard Plumpe has suggested, if Derleth wanted a hierarchically organized religious state, Schuler the revival of Nero's Rome, and Wolfskehl a Zionist colony, then Klages was interested in the theoretical conception of a dualistic *Weltanschauung* which was critical of contemporary issues but ultimately resigned in its outlook.[8] Nevertheless, the "Kosmogoniae Fragmenta" (Fragments for a Cosmogony) (1895) from Schuler's *Nachlass* functions as a representative "cosmic" text, not least because of its fragmentary, even incoherent, nature. In "Lucernae dispersae" from the "Kosmogoniae Fragmenta," which George considered publishing in *Blätter für die Kunst* (but never did), we can read such lines as the following:[9]

> Siehe den Eros der Zeit, der mit grünen Fingern die Erze dämpft
> und mit gelben Küssen den Schnee des Marmors — Siehe wie um den

roten, spiegelgetrübten Porphyrschaft Unsterblichkeit sein weinblauer
Flügel haucht. In Säulenblut der Purpur des Kosmischen —

[. . .]

Kennt ihr den Dunst und braunen Fackelgeruch über den Feuern
kosmischer Nächte? Ahnt ihr, was die gereinigte Flamme ins Dunkel
empor und selige Vergessen wirbelt? Was ist uns Mann noch und Weib
und alles Hälftenhafte, das nicht im eigenen Kern erglüht —?

Was ist Freiheit im Werdedrang —? Eros in Pan.
Was ist Eros im Untergang —? Christenwahn.[10]

This text displays six characteristics which might be said to typify "cosmic"
thought in general. First, it was indebted to vitalist thought for the belief
in an irrational, organic life energy. Second, it was influenced by
Bachofen's conception of "matriarchy," the notion that our current,
"patriarchal" society was preceded by an ancient civilization based on
gynaecocracy. In 1897 Wolfskehl read the recently published second edition of Bachofen's *Das Mutterrecht* (1861), followed a couple of years later
by Klages, and both were struck by Bachofen's imaginative depiction of
woman in earlier societies as a "hetaira" (courtesan or concubine). Third,
it laid emphasis on the Dionysian aspect of life, as described by Nietzsche
in terms of *Rausch* (ecstasy) and the celebration of bodily drives. In fact,
Nietzsche was a key figure both for the "George Circle" and the
Kosmiker.[11] Fourth, it tended toward a blatantly, and sometimes brutally,
anti-intellectual stance; for example, Schuler is reported to have said: "Die
Intellektuellen wischt man mit dem Scheuerlappen weg" (*FuV* 54). Fifth,
it embraced a pagan view of life, appreciating in Christianity (particularly
Catholicism) the persistence of earlier rites and beliefs, and some of the
Kosmiker became increasingly committed to an anti-Semitic outlook.
Finally, this text, like so much "cosmic" thought, makes startling, occasionally alarming, use of imagery of heat, light, and blood. Elsewhere in
Schuler's *Nachlass,* we find the line "Rund, vollkommen und unfruchtbar
ist alles Kosmische" (*FuV* 138; *CA* 92), a phrase which was picked up and
developed in another direction by Stefan George in his introduction to the
ninth series of *Blätter für die Kunst:*

> Diese äusserste sorge bei der feilung der gefüge · dieses ringen nach der
> höchsten formalen vollendung im werke · diese liebe für das Runde · das
> in sich vollkommene · das nach allen seiten hin richtige · diese ablehnung
> des nur triebhaften skizzenhaften nicht-ganz-gekonnten · des halb über-
> schüssigen halb unzulänglichen · das so lange ein fehler heimischer lei-
> stung war: diese liebe und diese ablehnung setzen mehr voraus als eine
> formel — nämlich eine geistige haltung ja eine lebensführung.[12]

As it stands, with its emphasis on the exclusively formal in art as in life,
Schuler's maxim is an encomium of sterility. Later, George reportedly

remarked to Karl Wolfskehl that Schuler ultimately stood for nothing less than the elimination of beauty itself— "die Elimination alles Schönen, alles Lebendigen, aller Kräfte zugunsten eines blutleeren Gespensterwortes."[13] In George's hands, it is transformed into a rejection of dilettantism and failure ("des nicht-ganz-gekonnten"), and becomes not just an attitude towards life, but a core principle for leading one's own life. As the introduction to the ninth *Blätter für die Kunst* shows, George believed he could take up and transform "cosmic" formulae to express the aims of his own aesthetic project.

Before looking at the impact of the "Cosmic Circle" on George's life and work, let us examine more closely his relationship with three of its members, beginning with Ludwig Klages. In conversation with Edith Landmann in 1919, Stefan George reportedly recalled his first encounter with the *Kosmiker:*

> Zuerst fand ich Klages, der zufällig im selben Haus wohnte, dann Wolfskehl, dann einen Psychiater, der Schuler als einen Verrückten studierte, und Schuler war von jung an verbunden mit Derleth — ein brodelnder Hexenkessel. In Paris da, das bisschen schwarze Messe, das war Literatur. Hier waren Kräfte, alle einig im Wissen, dass es so nicht weitergeht, dass auf diese Weise Menschheit zugrunde gehe, und dass nicht soziale Utopien da helfen, sondern allein das Wunder, die Tat, das Lebendige. Aber sie wussten alle nicht zu zeugen. Sie hatten keinen einzigen Jünger, so wenig wie Nietzsche.[14]

Not surprisingly, when dealing with memories, there is some confusion about the actual date of the first meeting between George and Klages. According to Klages, for example, he and George met at lunch one day in the summer of 1893, in the Munich *Pension* where they were both staying, and discussed the current exhibition of the works of Dutch artist Jan Toorop (1858–1928).[15] Looking at his friendship with George six months on, Klages told Theodor Lessing (1872–1933):

> Ein merkwürdiges Schicksal ist mir widerfahren . . . Das kommt durch die Bekanntschaft mit einem hochmodernen und hochdekadenten Künstler sive Poeten . . . Er ist ein weit gereister Mann mit sehr exzentrischem Kopf; sehr blasiert . . . Seine sämtlichen bisherigen Werke sind schon im Äußern merkwürdig. Beim ersten Durchlesen habe ich nicht den fünften Teil verstanden; jetzt aber habe ich den Schlüssel zu dieser Art von Poesie.[16]

According to Wolters, on the other hand, George did not meet Klages until the last three months of 1893,[17] but what is certain is that George persuaded him to contribute to *Blätter für die Kunst,* as Klages told Lessing:

> Ich gab mich ihm schließlich als einen ehemaligen Poeten zu erkennen und brachte ihm ein Stück der "Desiderata." Das versetzte den sonst

zugeknöpften, im Verkehr vornehm förmlichen, mit verachtender Blasiertheit dreinschauenden Menschen in ein nicht zu verbergendes Feuer der Begeisterung. Er gestand mir anderthalb Monate später, daß er von der Turmszene mehrere Tage "gradezu krank" gewesen sei. Er ließ mich nun nicht wieder los, und ich mußte ihm diesen Fetzen eines Fetzens für sein Kunstblatt liefern . . . Ich hatte ein fast wehmütiges Gefühl . . . wie viel hätte ich wohl darum gegeben, wenn ich das vermocht hätte zur Zeit, wo "Desiderata" entstand. Und jetzt kostet es Überwindung, sie mir zum Zweck des Druckens abzulocken.[18]

In the January 1894 edition of *Blätter für die Kunst* there duly appeared the fragments from Klages's unfinished five-act drama, "Desiderata," a tragedy set at the time of the founding of the Carolingian Empire by Karl the Great, the defeat of the Langobards in 774, and the Saxon revolts in 782, at the heart of which lies the conflict between paganism and Christianity.[19] Later issues of *Blätter für die Kunst* contained additional works by Klages, and in 1895 he also sent George poems by his friend, Richard Perls, for inclusion in *Blätter für die Kunst*.[20] According to Ernst Morwitz, one of the poems from the "Preisgedichte" section of *Das Buch der Hirten- und Preisgedichte* (1895), "An Isokrates" (I, 79), whose title alludes to a rhetorically-gifted follower of Socrates, refers in fact to none other than Klages.[21] Within a matter of months, however, the relationship between George and Klages was to become fraught with difficulty.

In the meantime, what of Klages's close friend and associate, Alfred Schuler? Although Wolters claims that George met Schuler in October 1893,[22] and George told Edith Landmann he met Schuler at an unspecified date through a psychiatrist who was studying him, it is likely that they first met on 28 January 1897 in a Munich café.[23] The next day, Schuler wrote to Klages, asking him to tell George that he would be prepared to recite some of his work for George.[24] In the section "Überschriften und Widmungen" of the second edition (1898) of *Das Jahr der Seele* (1897), George inserted a poem dedicated to "A. S.," and it is not hard to guess to whom the initials refer:

> So war sie wirklich diese runde? da die fackeln
> Die bleichen angesichter hellten · dämpfe stiegen
> Aus schalen um den götterknaben und mit deinen worten
> In wahneswelten grell-gerötet uns erhoben?
> Dass wir der sinne kaum mehr mächtig · wie vergiftet
> Nach schlimmem prunkmahl taglang uns nicht fassten ·
> Stets um die stirn noch rosen brennen fühlten · leidend
> Für neugierblicke in die pracht verhängter himmel. (I, 151)

Whether this poem refers to a particular occasion in the "Cosmic Circle" and, if so, which, is a difficult question answer. That George's *Algabal*

(1892), a collection of poems about the notorious Roman emperor Heliogabalus, was one of the influences on Schuler's attempts to write a work set in Roman times, particularly the fragmentary drama *Elagabal* (1895), is very probable; and, were it not for the dating, the poem "A. S." could be read, as it has been by Klages and Edgar Salin,[25] as a response to the occasion of a "Roman party" at Schuler's flat on 29 April 1899.[26] Klages, Karl Wolfskehl and his wife, Hanna, and Schuler's mother were also invited to this party, which had a secret agenda, for it was also intended, as Klages later recalled, to be "eine[n] erschütternden und dadurch besitzer-greifenden Angriff" on George's soul. Klages's account of how Schuler recited his poetry, and how George reacted, has become as well-known as Franziska von Reventlow's parodistic description of such events:

> [I]m besten seiner nicht geräumigen Zimmer eine längliche Tafel, imgrunde bescheiden, für seine Verhältnisse üppig mit Speisen bedeckt; Licht von Kerzen und einem römischen Dreidochter; vor diesem auf metallenem Sockel eine Nachbildung des "Adoranten", dahinter Lorbeer und andres Grün; um jeden Teller ein Kranz leuchtender Blüten; Weihrauchduft. — Nach der Mahlzeit beginnt [Schuler] mit dem Vorlesen seiner stärksten Fragmente, mächtig schon einsetzend und zu immer mächtigerem Pathos fortgerissen. Es bildet sich, so möchte man meinen, ein magisches Feld, Verwandtes sich anähnelnd, alles Fremde fortstoßend und austreibend. Die alte Mutter ist in sich zusammenge-sunken; Wolfskehl, seelisch und geistig immun, saugt und assimiliert; [. . .] George gerät in wachsende, schließlich kaum noch beherrschte Erregung. Er hat sich hinter seinen Stuhl gestellt; fahler denn fahl scheint er im Begriff, die Fassung zu verlieren. Die seelenatmosphärische Spannung wird unerträglich. [. . .] Wann es vorbei ist, wie es vorbei ist, bleibt unerfaßlich, nur *daß* es vorbei ist, weiß unversehens ein jeder, indem er aufbruchsbereit einen Strauß in der Hand hält [. . .].

What did George himself make of all this? In his account, Klages portrays George as being severely discomfited by these proceedings:

> Auf der nächtlichen Straße stehe ich plötzlich mit George allein. Da fühle ich mich am Arm ergriffen: "Das ist Wahnsinn! Ich ertrage es nicht! Was haben Sie getan, mich dorthin zu locken! Das ist Wahnsinn! Führen Sie mich fort; führen Sie mich in ein Wirtshaus, wo biedere Bürger, wo ganz gewöhnliche Menschen Zigarren rauchen und Bier trinken! Ich ertrage es nicht!" — Nun, so geschah es. In einem ganz gewöhnlichen Wirtshaus voll biederer Bürger trank jeder sein Bier, George angegriffen, aufge-wühlt, innerlich ruhelos, ich nachdenklich, sehr nachdenklich.[27]

Yet we know that George carried on attending these "toga parties" in Munich, as the photographs of George in costume attest — in the Wolfskehls' flat in 1903 (the famous *Maskenzug* when George dressed as Caesar, Schuler as the Magna Mater, Klages as an Indian monk, Wolfskehl as Dionysus/Bacchus, and Anna Maria Derleth as Vestalin),[28] in Henry von Heiseler's flat in 1904,[29] and, in fact, George held a similar social event in his own flat in 1910.[30] Morwitz reads "A. S." as a text that anticipates and predicts precisely these future celebrations, particularly those held in honor of "Maximin" — a figure to whom we shall return.[31] So it is questionable whether Klages's account of Schuler's dinner-party in 1899, amusing as it is, is entirely accurate.

What neither the debate over the chronology of the event(s) referred to in "A. S." nor the doubt about the accuracy of Klages's memory can obscure, however, is the persistent difficulties in the relationship between George and Klages. According to Theodor Lessing, "Ludwig Klages, halb Phantast, halb Skeptiker und gänzlich Doktrinär, übte durch seine, uns allen weit überlegene Begriffsmeisterschaft auf George bängsten Druck."[32] And looking back in 1905 in conversation with Kurt Breysig (1866–1940), George admitted that Klages had been "der Führende," describing him as "ganz seherhaft," but: "Den Bruch habe George längst vorausgesehen."[33] In other words, it seems there were as many intellectual differences as affinities between George and Klages.[34] On 15 December 1895, Klages is reported to have written to George, saying he felt he had to withdraw from the circle of contributors to *Blätter für die Kunst* (*Zeittafel* 52). And a letter from George to Klages, dated 11 February 1896, hints at a vigorous ongoing debate between the two men:

> Wie es so gewöhnlich geht haben Sie in dem was Sie bejahen recht — in dem was Sie verneinen unrecht. Eine bildungswelt (Kultur) einmal erkannt lässt sich nicht wieder vergessen. wie könnten Sie sich Ihre lateinische und griechische wissenschaft aus dem sinn schlagen? versuchten Sie es so wäre das die künstliche rückzüchtung. Sie haben mit Ihrem geist unsre bildungswelt aufgenommen. Sie konnten sie jedoch — gemütlich unfähig — nicht geniessen. daher Ihre auflehnungen.
>
> Doch traue ich weiter auf Ihren geist. Geben Sie nur ganz ohne hintergedanken *Ihr* wesen so gehören Sie ganz zu denen von heute. Auch hat der grosse wesens-unterschied zwischen Ihnen und uns den zwischen uns selber viel zu gering anzunehmen verleitet.

George even felt able to give Klages some poetic advice, and Raymond Furness has spoken of George's attempt to assert "poetic hegemony" over Klages:[35]

> Was Ihre gedichte angeht so hören Sie was ein Dichter Ihnen rät: Nicht weicher zarter schwankender sollen Sie werden sondern reiner stärker und bestimmter. O gelänge es Ihnen nur uns die töne deutlich zu machen wenn "die winde durch die nadeln der tannen harfen." Seien Sie vor denen gewarnt die geistig weit unter Ihnen stehend doch durch die drückende gewohnheit einen einfluss üben könnten.[36]

So if Klages and Schuler were trying to turn George into a mouthpiece for their "cosmic" beliefs,[37] George, by contrast, was attempting to convert them to his poetic cause. What may have sustained the relationship with Klages at least in part was George's willingness to entertain belief in "character-ological" principles. Early in September 1897, about a year after Klages had visited him in his home town of Bingen, George sent Klages a letter containing samples of handwriting for him to analyze. (Following his study of chemistry, Klages had co-founded in 1896, together with the psychiatrist Georg Meyer (1869–1917) and the graphologist Hans Hinrich Busse (1871–1920), the "Deutsche Graphologische Gesellschaft," and had begun publishing extensively in the field of characterology. In 1905 he went on to found in Munich the "Psychodiagnostisches Seminar," and embarked upon as series of publications outlining what he called — to borrow the title of his published version of his lectures in 1910 — the "principles of characterology.")[38] In his reply, Klages responded with a brief analysis of the handwriting samples of some of George's closest poetic collaborators, including Albert Verwey, Carl August Klein, Melchior Lechter, Hugo von Hofmannsthal, Waclaw Rolicz-Lieder, and Paul Gérardy.[39] Later that year, when George's next collection of poetry, *Das Jahr der Seele,* appeared, Klages will have noticed that it included a poem dedicated to "L. K." (in fact, the text had been added to the final proofs sent to Bondi):

> Doch unser aller heimat bleibt das licht
> Zu dem wir kehren auf gewundnen stegen.
> Magst du dich einig nennen mit den recken
> Und trotzigen gewalten bracher ebnen:
> Sagt nicht bei jedem treffen die umschlingung
> Und dass ich oft dich suche wie du viel
> In mir erregst und mir gehörst? verrät nicht
> Dass du mich fliehst wie sehr ich in dir bin? (I, 151)

As Marita Keilson-Lauritz has pointed out, George's dedicatory poems should be read in tandem with the proviso of the preface to the second edition that "selten sind sosehr wie in diesem buch ich und du die selbe seele" (I, 119), but still, this poem reflects the intensity of the dialogue at this time between George and Klages.[40] And this intensity is further reflected in the dedication George inscribed in the copy of the luxury edition (1900) of *Der Teppich des Lebens und die Lieder von Traum und Tod* (1899) he presented to Klages:

> Eine kleine schar zieht stille bahnen.
> Stolz entfernt vom wirkenden getriebe
> Und als losung steht auf ihren fahnen:
> Hellas ewig unsre liebe.[41]

At this point in the story of George and the Munich Cosmologists Ludwig Derleth enters the scene.

According to George, people go to Paris for all sorts of reasons; in the case of Derleth, he thought, it was because of Ignatius Loyola, the founder of the Jesuits (who went to Paris in 1528 and stayed for seven years) or Napoleon (whose tomb is one of the city's most famous landmarks).[42] During George's visit to Paris in January 1898, Derleth, who happened to living in the French capital at the time, recorded seeing the poet almost every day, but not speaking to him;[43] in conversation with Berthold Vallentin (1877–1933) in 1928, however, George remembered meeting Derleth in a Parisian café, and it is likely they made contact in Paris.[44] Derleth had met Schuler in 1894,[45] and through him reportedly come into contact with Wolfskehl.[46] Dividing his time between teaching classics in grammar schools and establishing himself as a writer, Derleth had had some early poems published in the *Jugendstil* literary periodical *Pan* in 1896, and some of his work would later appear in *Blätter für die Kunst*.[47] Like Klages and Schuler, Derleth was also, as he told Harry Graf Kessler, deeply influenced by Nietzsche,[48] and while in Paris, he had met the Rosicrucian "great master," Sâr Joséphin Péladan (1858–1918).[49] The time was ripe, then, for Derleth to fall under the spell of another *Meister*, this time George, and at least one critic has commented upon the striking similarity of syntax, diction and vocabulary between George and Derleth.[50] In 1889, Derleth moved to Munich to begin studying philosophy and theology, and became a member — or at least an associate one — of the "Cosmic Circle."[51]

At the end of 1901, when Bondi published Klages's study of Stefan George (the book itself carried the publication date of 1902), it seemed as if George's investment in his relationship with Klages had been rewarded.[52] By and large, the book equally pleased George and those who wished to please him, although there were some doubts. Roderich Huch (1880–1944), for example, considered that Klages's book had "für die ersten Jahrzehnte das bedeutendste gesagt [. . .], was überhaupt über George gesagt werden kann." Even so, he remained uncertain whether George would agree with this statement, for the reason "dass kein grosser Künstler damit einverstanden ist, wenn man seine Kunst soweit zergliedert, dass am Schlusse nur verschiedene Seelen von verschiedenen Zeiten übrig bleiben — und nichts Neues, besonders keine neue Persönlichkeit anerkannt wird" (*Zeittafel*, 116). In a letter of December 1901, Gundolf told the Wolfskehls that Klages's book on George had been enthusiastically received in Berlin, that "bei allen geistesspitzen: M[elchior] L[echter] R[einhold] L[epsius] vor allen die grösste begeisterung erregt nur die Halben autschen etwas. die jugend ist in verzückung."[53] Writing to the Dutch poet Albert Verwey (1865–1937), even George expressed his pleasure at Verwey's approval of the book, and remarked: "wie wenig werke giebt es heute die uns über die tiefsten und geheimsten mächte etwas verraten können!"[54] As for Klages, the scope of his ambition was expressed to Gundolf in the following terms:

> Ich war in meinem Buch nur STIMME und redende Zunge eines ganzen KREISES, und was an Erkenntnis aus meinen Seiten spricht, ward nicht in MIR allein, sondern im Zusammenstoss der Geister bereitet, und wenn mir ein Verdienst gebührt, so ist es das: dem AUSDRUCK verliehen zu haben. Vor allem aber wollte mein Buch dem GEORGE ein Denkmal setzen, seiner WÜRDIG.[55]

In retrospect, however, Klages saw this work as marking the end of his collaboration with George, from whom he had begun to distance himself since the evening of 29 April 1899:

> Kommenden Tages entschied sich in mir, was im Stillen längst sich vorbereitet hatte. [. . .] So entstand 1900 die bekannte Broschüre, an deren weltanschaulichem Gehalt ich nach fast vierzig Jahren keine Silbe zu ändern wüßte und die gleichwohl gründlich mißlungen ist. [. . .] Meine Schrift ist unhaltbar, soweit sie von Anfang bis Ende am *falschen Objekt* erläutert; und sie ist verfehlt in der Form, weil der Geist dem Wesen anzubilden sich vermessen hatte, was von der Seele verworfen war.[56]

But this perspective still lay in the future. By February 1902, the relationship between the two men was still so close that Klages reportedly sent George two poems that no one else (with the exception of Wolfskehl) should see and which could not be published (*Zeittafel* 119). Things were, however, about to change.

In March 1902, Albert Verwey traveled to Munich to meet George, who introduced him in turn to Klages, Wolfskehl, and Schuler. Through Verwey's account of his stay in Munich, we have a source of information about the profound transformations that were to separate the "Cosmic Circle" from the "George Circle." On 4 April 1902, Verwey spent an evening at the Wolfskehls' in the company of George, Klages, and Schuler, and was treated to some typically "cosmic" behavior. His record gives a good impression of what an evening with the *Kosmiker* was like:

> Schuler und Klages haben eine Theorie über eine Urkraft, die sie das Dämonische nennen und die sich unmittelbar, auch durch den Menschen hin, offenbart. Nach einigen Fechtersprüngen war Klages zu der Erklärung genötigt, dass dieses Dämonische sich auf diese Weise bisher in keiner einzigen Kunst, mit Ausnahme allein von der Böcklin's,[57] offenbart habe, und dass er also jede frühere Kunst, sowohl holländische wie italienische, verwerfe. Ich für mich fand diese Erklärung entscheidend; aber hernach kamen die Sprecher erst recht ins Allgemeine. Aus ägyptischen Monumenten, kabbalistischen Zeichen, uralten Bräuchen wurde die Möglichkeit dargelegt, wider zu ursprünglichen Offenbarungen zu gelangen.[58]

Even when George and Verwey were walking back home to the Giselastrasse, Schuler remained "cosmic":

> Noch beim Nachhausegehen, um 12 Uhr nachts, in der Leopoldstrasse, versuchte Schuler Stefan und mich davon zu überzeugen, dass, wenn ein ägyptisches Grab völlig unversehrt geöffnet würde and der reine, ganz zur Andacht bereite Mensch allein hineinginge, er *dann* die Möglichkeit annähme, dass aus dem Mutterschoss der Erde und dem Dampf des Urlebens, das sich dort wirksam hält, Traumgesichte in diesem Bevorzugten aufsteigen würden, die ihm unmittelbare Offenbarung des Lebensgeheimnisses wären. Im allgemeinen *vor* den christlichen Zeiten [. . .] lag diese Kenntnis des Geheimnisses, wozu wir zurück müssen. [. . .] Und von diesem Geheimnis aus, sobald es gefunden ist, werden Leben und Welt auf eine wunderbare Weise regeneriert werden.[59]

Reportedly tiring of such "Lingualorgien," as he called them, the next day George placed on Wolfskehl's desk a short note:

> Setzet nicht für den priester den fakir
> für den vates den magus
> für die geister die gespenster.[60]

A few days later, George read Verwey two poems, later published in the "Zeitgedichte" section of *Der siebente Ring* (1907) — "Boecklin" (I, 232–33) (which shared, Verwey thought, Klages's admiration for the painter), and "Porta Nigra" (I, 233–34), which is actually dedicated to Schuler ("Ingenio Alf. Scolari").[61] That evening, neither Klages (who was ill) nor Schuler (who had not been informed) showed up at the Wolfskehls' flat, and George spent the whole evening in silence. Was George missing Klages and Schuler? Was he regretting the way they had behaved last time? Or was he missing someone else?

In February 1902 George had met Maximilian Kronberger — Maximin, as he called him — an attractive thirteen-year-old boy, who would, tragically for George, die two years later, on Good Friday of 1904. For George, Maximin would come to represent all that was beautiful, or even divine, on earth. Looking back on the moment he first saw Maximin, George recalled: "Er kam uns aus dem siegesbogen geschritten mit der unbeirrbaren festigkeit des jungen fechters und den mienen feldherrlicher obergewalt jedoch gemildert durch jene regbarkeit und schwermut die erst durch jahrhunderte christlicher bildung in die angesichter des volkes gekommen war" (I, 522–23). George's next collection of poetry, *Der siebente Ring,* was the fruit of "das Maximin-Erlebnis," and intended to commemorate it. (Despite the clearly erotic component of that experience,[62] George later told Ernst Glöckner of his battle against the spreading of pederasty (*Knabenliebe*) by Klages and Schuler.)[63] While the relationship with Maximin represented the resolution of George's mid-life crisis (I, 522), it also coincided with, and possibly contributed to, the dissolution of the "Cosmic Circle." Equally, according to Stefen Breuer, it marks the moment when the "George Circle" first defined itself fully, as a circle of individuals centered not around a publication (the *Blätter*) but around an individual (George), who was not just a person but the Master.[64]

Initially, the friendship with Maximin had minimal influence on relations between George and the *Kosmiker*. In 1902 the photographer Karl Bauer took one of the most famous literary historical snaps of twentieth-century modernity, the group photograph of Wolfskehl, Schuler, Klages, George, and Verwey; Verwey went for walks with George and sometimes Klages around Munich; and, on one occasion, went with Klages and George to see a wrestling-match — an event which may have inspired George's poem "Der Kampf" (I, 246). (What Morwitz sees in this poem as "den allen Sonnenreligionen zugrunde liegenden Sieg einer jüngeren, vaterrechtlichen Epoche über eine ältere, mutterrechtliche Weltzeit" has been interpreted by Marita Keilson-Lauritz as "eine Abrechnung mit der chtonischen Welt der Kosmiker," albeit a problematic one.)[65] Yet the correspondence of George's closest friends and *confidants* indicates that a change was on the way. For example, in a letter to Wolfskehl, Gundolf expressed his doubts about the value of "das Kosmische": "Das ist was mich an der Klages-Schulerischen Welt verwirrt dass sie jenseits ihrer selbst ein umwälzendes Wissen empfangen haben und davon Kunde geben müssen mit und für Organe in einem Diesseits."[66] In his correspondence with Hugo von Hofmannsthal (1874–1929), George, still smarting from his failure to win the Austrian poet over to his aesthetic cause, was forced to defend his association with the *Kosmiker*. In one of his letters to Hofmannsthal, George wrote:[67]

> Gar nicht zu reden von ausländern wie [Waclaw Rolicz-]Lieder · Verwey begreife ich nicht wie Sie an künstlern und denkern wie z.B. Wolfskehl und Klages vorüber gehen konnten. — die dunklen gluten des Einen wie die scharfe ebnenluft des andren sind so einzig urbedingt dass ich aus Ihrem kreis (soweit er sich geoffenbart hat) niemanden auch nur annähernd mit ihnen vergleichen dürfte . . .[68]

In his reply, Hofmannsthal elaborated on his reservations about Wolfskehl and Klages, mentioning two of Klages's essays, "aus einer Seelenlehre des Künstlers" and "vom Schaffenden," published in *Blätter für die Kunst*,[69] and criticizing his recently-published study of George:

> [I]ch habe die klugen scharfen Denker in Klages und Wolfskehl nicht verkannt; da hätte ich Klages Ausführungen über den Dichter in den "Blättern" nicht gelesen haben, mit Wolfskehl nie ein Gespräch geführt haben dürfen. Aber ich muß offen gestehen, daß mir in Klages' Schrift über Sie an unendlichen wichtigen Stellen der Ausdruck, also die Kraft das Innerlich-geschaute zu verleiblichen, peinlich zurückzubleiben schien. Es fanden sich da Metaphern, die ich zu vergessen trachte.[70]

In his reply to this, George was quick to defend Klages, although his support was not exactly unequivocal:

> Wegen K · und seinem buch lassen Sie mich heut nur sagen dass wir uns da auf würdigem streit-boden befinden. Er ist ein Edler der für höchste werte glüht · aber auch ein titan der blöcke entgegen wälzt. Um sich gegen ungeheuerliche bilder die dem nordmenschen minder anstössig sind zu wappnen rate ich Ihnen einmal in die Edda-folger einen blick zu werfen. — Ich begreife Ihre abneigung sehr gut · ich begreife sogar wie man K. als glühenden feind betrachtet . .[71]

On the surface, all was well — in January, George asked Klages to help him analyze Maximin's handwriting (*Zeittafel* 135). In February, he held a reading session for Hofmannsthal with "die drei Freunde des Kosmischen Rings" ("Schuler weise und wieder rollend in dröhnendem römischem Pathos, Klages, adlig und hoch und dahinjagend gleich einem schlanken kräftigen Hirsch, Karl [Wolfskehl] feurig und funkelnd," as Hanna Wolfskehl noted).[72] In May, he published the sixth volume of *Blätter für die Kunst,* which included works by Wolfskehl, Klages, and (for the first time) Derleth.[73] But 1903 was the year things began to go wrong. If, during 1902, within the group of *Kosmiker,* Schuler and Derleth had had their disagreements (Zeller 175), then now, in the winter of 1903–1904, the "George Circle" and the "Cosmic Circle" began to go their own, separate ways. There were at least two reasons for this split.

First, there was the falling-out between Wolfskehl, on the one hand, and Klages and Schuler on the other. The root of this dispute probably lay in the increasingly anti-Semitic attitude of Schuler and Klages,[74] which by the end of 1903 had grown so intense that Wolfskehl felt threatened and wrote to George, calling him back to Munich for help (*Zeittafel* 147). According to some accounts, Wolfskehl began carrying a pistol to fend off physical attack (and once accidentally shot himself).[75] Schuler's anti-Semitism is evident in, for example, his aphorism from 1899 which begins "Ans Herz des Lebens schlich der Marder Juda" (*FuV* 151; *CA* 139), and Klages's attitude towards Judaism is reflected in the remark reported by George: "Über die Unterstellung: er sei Jude: besser hätte Klages sich nicht selbst desavouieren können: 'Wäre ich Jude, so wäre das Judentum nicht mehr eine Frage.'" (Landmann 185). George's support for Wolfskehl should not, by the way, be read as an indication that he was vastly different in his attitude towards Jews; a flavor of which can be gleaned from such remarks as the following reported by Sabine Lepsius to the effect that Schuler and Klages had been right to see a danger in the "Rührigkeit" of the Jews,[76] or the comment recorded by Edith Landmann: "Dass man ihm vorgeworfen habe, dass er so viele Juden um sich habe: 'Solche Juden, wie ich habe, könnte ich noch zehn um mich haben, würde mir gar nichts schaden'" (Landmann 146). On 7 January

1904 Gundolf wrote to George, expressing no surprise at the demise of the "Cosmic Circle":

> Dass die Kosmische Welt früher oder später wie eine grosse schöne schillernde Seifenblase platze war auch unprofetischen Gemütern vorauszusehen. [. . .] Was jetzt noch übrig bleibt, ist hoffentlich die berüchtigte Nur-kunst, die als graues Aschenputtel der gedunsenen Semiramis-Kosmik die Schleppe tragen sollte und dabei den übelduftigen Staub zu schlucken bekam, den jene aufwirbelte.[77]

Second, the dispute between Klages and Wolfskehl turned into a larger, and litigious, disagreement between George and Klages.

The source of the conflict was Klages's accusation that George was including or rejecting work for *Blätter für die Kunst* on a whim (or, as George phrased the charge, because of "menschliche vorlieben und ausserkünstlerische gründe").[78] Subsequently, both George and Wolfskehl wrote to Klages offering reconciliation, but when Klages asked for a personal meeting with George, the latter turned down this request. In a letter to Klages, George wrote:

> Für wie richtig ich auch Ihren satz halte: die allgemein-übliche unterredung ist nach meiner ansicht dennoch zu vermeiden wenn die grundstimmungen der parteien so verschieden sind dass jedes wort nur die klüfte weiter öffnet — während beide ehrlich auf schliessung hoffen · was nur durch zeit und veränderte umstände geschieht [. . .] Tiefere innere sowol vorübergehende wie dauernde spaltungen machen sich nach aussen in verschiedenster weise luft.[79]

On 13 January 1904, Schuler wrote a conciliatory letter to George in the context of a discussion about the poem "Porta Nigra,"[80] but another letter from Klages to George was less so, and concluded that "es sei die persönliche Beziehung zwischen Ihnen und mir nicht etwa in unbestimmter Weise verändert, sondern *abgebrochen*, und sowohl dies als auch die Prämisse davon im Sinne einer Tatsache von uneingeschränkter Öffentlichkeit zu nehmen."[81] Talking with Maximin about the factions in the *Blätter* group, George believed that Schuler and Oskar A. H. Schmitz were taking sides against him.[82] The March 1904 publication of the seventh volume of *Blätter für die Kunst* confirmed the break. According to one of George's conversations with Edith Landmann, the first poem in it, "Das Zeitgedicht" (later published in *Der siebente Ring* [I, 244–45]), referred to "das kosmische Chaos, das später den Stern? — the George Circle? — "geboren hat, von Schuler, Derleth, Klages" (Landmann 77). This edition of the *Blätter* contained work by Derleth ("Widmungen" (I–III), "Venus Maria," "Der Weinberg")[83] and what was to be Schuler's only contribution to the *Blätter,* the "Sonett an Leopold Andrian,"[84] but none by Klages. Nevertheless, all three men were portrayed on the "Dichter-Tafel" collated by Melchior Lechter and, to Klages's great annoyance, four lines from his poem "Aus

Wildenroth" — "Pfadlos rauchend eine feuerzunge / Bist du angefacht über finsterem urstrom / Dunkle falterflügel in schwerer traumnacht / Trinkend schattend lohende flammenseele"[85] — were printed as a motto to three poems by Gundolf, published under the dedication "Für Ludwig Klages."[86] Having earlier complained that George was not publishing his work, Klages was now complaining that it *had* been, and without his permission; he went to court, taking legal action against Gundolf as writer and George as editor.

This was a difficult time for George. On 15 April 1904, Maximin died. At the same time, the spirit of comradeship also died between George, Klages, and Schuler. In conversation with Kurt Breysig in October 1905, George is reported to have said the following about Klages and the "cosmic" conception of art:

> [Klages] habe sich ganz ins Kosmische gesteigert — Pflanzen, Tiere, Blut, Gedanke. Er, George, habe auch daran mitgeholfen; [. . .]. Alle Kunst hätten Klages und seine Folger nach und nach abgetan als zu gross: Renaissance, Giotto, Byzanz, Pyramiden; zuletzt seien sie bei den Urzeitvölkern angekommen. Klages habe mit einigem Naserümpfen gesagt: das, was er, George, und die Seinen täten, sei auch nur Kunst: *sie* wollten Religion schaffen.[87]

"Aus allem leuchtet vor," wrote Breysig about George, "Leben ist ihm ebensosehr der Zweck wie Kunst, und all seine Kunst meint nur das Leben." George and the *Kosmiker,* however, had a very different conception of life.

In November 1905, Klages won his lawsuit against George and Gundolf, each of whom was fined 50 Marks; the defendants appealed, but lost. Along with the appeal, any chance of reconciliation between George and the two chief *Kosmiker* was lost as well. George's friendship with Derleth, however, had continued to develop, even if only up to a point. If Derleth's poetry owed much in terms of style to George,[88] George owed his sartorial preference for dark clothing and high collars to Derleth.[89] In his poem "Michael," Verwey gave artistic expression to his impressions of Derleth and his sister; translated by George (II, 394), it was published in *Blätter für die Kunst.*[90] In February 1904, George was granted the privilege of being the first person to hear Derleth's work *Die Proklamationen,* a sequence of intensely declamatory, prose-poetic statements.[91] (A subsequent, public reading was attended by Thomas Mann, who based his short story "Beim Propheten" [1904] and, years later, the figure of Daniel zur Höhe in *Doktor Faustus* [1947], on the event.) Not surprisingly, visiting him in Bingen in July 1904, Berthold Vallentin records George as saying that Derleth had taken the step from art (*Kunst*) to mysticism (*Mystik*).[92] Nevertheless, George remained in contact with Derleth, and published his writings in *Blätter für die Kunst,* on which Derleth worked as a

"Mitarbeiter" from the 6th to the 9th series. One of the "Tafeln" in *Der siebente Ring* was dedicated to Derleth (George sent a handwritten copy of the second strophe to the dedicatee):

> Du fälltest um dich her mit tapfrem hiebe
> Und stehst nun unerbittlicher verlanger.
> Wann aber führt dich heim vom totenanger
> Die täglich wirksame gewalt der liebe? . .
>
> In unsrer runde macht uns dies zum paare:
> Wir los von jedem band von gut und haus:
> Wir einzig können stets beim ersten saus
> Wo grad wir stehn nachfolgen der fanfare. (I, 330–31)

Another poem in this series was dedicated to Derleth's sister, Anna (I, 331). Other poems in the collection evoked the carnival parties and *Maskenzüge* at the Wolfskehls', such as "Maskenzug" (I, 340–41) and "Feste" (I, 341) and "Fest":

> Wenn ihr die hüllen warft und die gewinde
> Ums haupt euch schlanget und die fackeln rochen
> Dann habt ihr mit des tages zwang gebrochen:
> Nun seid ihr eines andren herrn gesinde.
>
> Sobald das dunkel die gemächer spreitet ·
> Farbige flammen schlagen aus den kesseln
> Und hall von horn und pfeife eint und weitet:
> Dann sprengt ihr eures eignen willens fesseln.
>
> Dann schwillt das fest in rasendem getobe
> Und in den brennenden und blutigen küssen
> Wo alle sich in eins verlieren müssen ·
> Voll eines atems bei des gottes probe.
>
> Doch lockern sich die knäuel und die tänze ·
> Befrein die glieder sich aus süsser pachtung:
> Dann werden seufzer wach durch die umnachtung ·
> Dann fallen tränen auf die welken kränze. (I, 320)

In 1908, thanking Derleth for his contribution to the *Blätter*, George wrote: "Dank Derleth für diese schönen Gedichte — sie haben: das höchste was man als lob sagen kann: den grossen lebens-odem" (Zeller 225). Two years later, however, Derleth seemed no longer interested in contributing to *Blätter für die Kunst,* and anyway, *Die Proklamationen* had signaled that Derleth and George were going in different directions. In Stefan Breuer's terms, Derleth embodied the prophecy of mission ("Sendungsprophetie") and George "exemplary prophecy";[93] in those of Friedrich Wolters,

Derleth was a "Glaubenseiferer" or "Ordensstifter," while George was a "Dichter" ("der erste will zu seinem Gott überreden und zwar jeden der guten Willens ist, der Dichter aber stellt nur ein Bild auf").[94] Or to put it another way, Derleth may have seen himself as "Generalissimus" and "Imperator maximus," but George was "der Meister." Later, George expressed his own doubts about Derleth in a conversation with the Landmanns in Basle in September 1916:

> Er schwankte. Erst wollte er mich für seine Zwecke benutzen, dann bot er sich an für meine, dann wurde er giftig. Er besprach seine Aktionen mit mir, aber meine erfuhr er nicht. Wenn Ihr erst fragt, tue ichs lieber selber, sage ich den Jüngeren, wenn sie fragen. Über Aktionen habe ich nie gesprochen. [. . .] Später hat er dann gesehen, dass auf ganz anderen Wegen, als er sich gedacht, eine Macht sich bilde, und dass es mit ihm selbst nichts wurde. Da wurde er grimmig. (Landmann 51)

As the "George Circle" separated out from the "Cosmic Circle" — or as the "Cosmic Circle" fell apart and the "George Circle" moved on while at the same time Klages, followed by Schuler and Derleth, moved away from George and he from them, so other friendships blossomed and decayed. For example, in 1902 George began corresponding with Rudolf Pannwitz (1881–1969), whose poem "Das totengedicht" appeared in the seventh volume of *Blätter für die Kunst*,[95] because, as George later told Edith Landmann, "das war ganz gut und wurde auch aus einem besonderen Grunde aufbewahrt, nämlich weil es auch all die kosmischen Geheimnisse aussprach, welche die Münchener Kosmiker allein für sich zu haben glaubten. Es war," he explained, "nach dem Bruch mit denen, da sollten sie sehen, dass wir das auch wissen . . ." (Landmann 99). Just a couple of years later, however, Pannwitz offered a devastating critique of George's poetry in *Kultur, Kraft, Kunst* (1906)[96] (which he later retracted).[97] His friendship with Hugo von Hofmannsthal came to an end in 1906; there was the split with Gundolf in 1926; with Glöckner in 1928; and in 1931 with Max Kommerell (1902–1944).

To reduce the history of George's life and work to a series of personality clashes would, of course, be to trivialize his poetic achievements, and to misunderstand how, in all these relationships, George sought to define and sustain his artistic project. Moreover, it is possible to detect the wider influences of the "Cosmic Circle" in George's extensive lyric output. For example, the image of the "sunchild," found in Schuler's lectures "Vom Wesen der ewigen Stadt" (*FuV* 216; *CA* 265), recurs in the imagery of the poems dedicated to Maximin in *Der siebente Ring* and *Der Stern des Bundes* (1914),[98] while the poem "Du hausgeist der um alte mauern wittert" refers specifically to Schuler (I, 367).[99] As Jürgen Egyptien has shown, more general "cosmic" themes inform George's poetry, and a text such as "Entrückung" from *Der siebente*

Ring captures much of the tone, style, and atmosphere of "cosmic" thought and writing:[100]

> Ich fühle luft von anderem planeten.
> Mir blassen durch das dunkel die gesichter
> Die freundlich eben noch sich zu mir drehten.
>
> [. . .]
>
> Ich löse mich in tönen · kreisend · webend ·
> Ungründigen danks und unbenamten lobes
> Dem grossen atem wunschlos mich ergebend.
>
> [. . .]
>
> Ich fühle wie ich über lezter wolke
>
> In einem meer kristallnen glanzes schwimme —
> Ich bin ein funke nur vom heiligen feuer
> Ich bin ein dröhnen nur der heiligen stimme. (I, 293)

Ultimately, to judge by his later remarks to Edith Landmann, the *Kosmiker* came to represent for George an example of what he was *not* about. In 1925, for example, he commented on such "Neokosmiker" as Wilhelm Stein (1886–1970) that "die wollen weder von alter noch von neuer Wissenschaft etwas wissen, nur von reiner Intuition." "Also nur von Dichtung?" asked Landmann. "Nein," came the reply, "da ist sie auch schon zu sehr herabgezogen. Sie wollen die frei herumlaufende Intuition" (Landmann 137). A year later, he related another anecdote about Stein, adding: "Ich sage immer wieder: es sind doch Kosmiker. Wenn Sie wüssten! Sie kennen die Kosmik nicht. Die schwingen ein Schwert und rennen wütend auf ein Gespenst los, und dabei durchrennen sie ihren Nebenmann, und das Gespenst bleibt am Leben [. . .] Eine Zeitlang stand Verrücktheit hoch im Kurs, jetzt ist sie wieder schwach notiert" (Landmann 158–59). And in a particularly insightful comment in 1929 (made *a propos* of Jean Paul's woodcuts of the Ten Commandments), George remarked:

> Kosmiker als versetzte Dichter: Kosmik, die alte wie die neue, ist ein karikiertes symbolisches Sehen. Man betont das Sehen und doch nicht das Sehen des Sichtbaren und erwartet alls von vereinzelten Fähigkeiten. Das Beschwören des Bluthaften hatte seinen Sinn, aber sie wussten nicht, dass man auch zum Zauber mancherlei braucht. (Landmann 199)

For all that George drew on the language of religion and ritual, played the part of prophet and priest, and formed around him *Kreise, Runden,* and *Bünde,* these aspects of his life and work were in the end, always subordinated to his aesthetic task.[101] As a result, George was well placed to understand the potential power of the *Kosmiker,* as well as the inevitability of their failure to realize it. Schuler died in 1924; Klages became an influential thinker in certain circles for a time, leaving behind his philosophical masterpiece, *Der Geist als Widersacher der Seele* (1929–1932), nowadays almost totally neglected; and Derleth dedicated more or less the whole of his literary life to writing *Der fränkische Koran,* which hardly anyone has ever read at all.[102] But George, speaking as someone who himself had been a *Kosmiker,* was also in a position to understand the attractiveness of these figures: "Man soll die Kosmiker nicht zu wichtig nehmen, aber auch nicht zu unwichtig," he told Landmann: "Sie müssen sein, so wie zum Apoll dem Lichtgott die dunklen Mysterien sein müssen. Ich verstehe sie besser als die ahnen. Ich bin auch so gewesen" (Landmann 207).

Notes

[1] For further discussion, see Manfred Durzak, *Der junge Stefan George* (Munich: Wilhelm Fink Verlag, 1968).

[2] Ernst Morwitz, *Kommentar zu dem Werk Stefan Georges,* 2nd ed. (Düsseldorf/Munich: Helmut Küpper vormals Georg Bondi, 1969), 329; see the sixth "Jahrhundertspruch" (I, 340) and "Durch die gärten lispeln zitternd" in Book 3 of *Der Stern des Bundes* (1914) (I, 384).

[3] The darker side of Munich is embodied by the Frauenkirche itself, which, according to legend, was constructed by an architect who made a pact with the devil. Jörg von Halsbach asked the devil to help him build the church, promising to construct it so no windows could be seen from inside. When the devil saw the high Gothic windows, he thought he had won; but when he was led by the architect to a point in the middle of the church from which none of the windows could be seen, the devil, realizing he had lost, stamped his foot in anger, leaving his footprint (a black mark by the entrance).

[4] See Michael Winkler, *George-Kreis* (Stuttgart: J. B. Metzler, 1972).

[5] Draft of letter to Hugo von Hofmannsthal, Summer 1897 (*Briefwechsel zwischen George und Hofmannsthal,* ed. Robert Boehringer, 2nd edition (Munich/Düsseldorf: Helmut Küpper vormals Georg Bondi, 1953), 260).

[6] Friedrich Wolters, *Stefan George und die Blätter für die Kunst: Deutsche Geistesgeschichte seit 1890* (Berlin: Georg Bondi, 1930), "Die Kosmische Runde," 258–74; see also "Die Kosmiker in München," 240–58.

[7] See Ludwig Klages, *Rhythmen und Runen: Nachlaß herausgegeben von ihm selbst* (Leipzig: Johann Ambrosius Barth, 1944), "Kosmischer Entwicklungsgang" 260. For further discussion, see Marita Keilson-Lauritz, "Stefan George, Alfred Schuler und die 'kosmische Runde': Zum Widmungsgedicht 'A. S.' im 'Jahr der Seele,'" *Castrum Peregrini* 168–69 (1985): 24–41; here 33–36.

[8] Gerhard Plumpe, "Alfred Schuler und die Kosmische Runde," in Manfred Frank, *Götter im Exil: Vorlesungen über die neue Mythologie, II. Teil* (Frankfurt a.M.: Suhrkamp, 1988), 213–56; here 226.

⁹ See Ludwig Klages, letter of 28 June 1899 to Stefan George; cited in Hans-Jürgen Seekamp, Raymond C. Ockenden, and Marita Keilson, *Stefan George: Leben und Werk: Eine Zeittafel* (Amsterdam: Castrum Peregrini Press, 1972), 89. Henceforth this work is cited as *Zeittafel*, followed by a page reference.

¹⁰ Alfred Schuler, *Fragmente und Vorträge,* edited by Ludwig Klages (Leipzig: Johann Ambrosius Barth, 1940), 137–38; *Cosmogonische Augen: Gesammelte Schriften,* edited by Baal Müller (Paderborn: Igel Verlag, 1997), 75–76. Henceforth these works are cited as *CA* and *FuV* respectively, followed by a page reference.

¹¹ See Heinz Raschel, *Das Nietzsche-Bild im George-Kreis* (Berlin/New York: Walter de Gruyter, 1983); and Raymond Furness, *Zarathustra's Children: A Study of a Lost Generation of German Writers* (Rochester, NY: Camden House, 2000).

¹² *Blätter für die Kunst* 9 (1910), 1.

¹³ See Edgar Salin, *Um Stefan George: Erinnerung und Zeugnis,* 2nd ed. (Munich and Düsseldorf: Helmut Küpper vormals Georg Bondi, 1954), 191.

¹⁴ Edith Landmann, *Gespräche mit Stefan George* (Düsseldorf/Munich: Helmut Küpper vormals Georg Bondi, 1963), 72. Henceforth this work is cited as Landmann, followed by a page reference.

¹⁵ Klages, "Einführung des Herausgebers," in *FuV* 35–36.

¹⁶ Ludwig Klages, letter of 25 January 1894; cited in Theodor Lessing, *Einmal und nie wieder* [1935] (Gütersloh: Bertelsmann Sachbuchverlag, 1969), 302.

¹⁷ Wolters, *Stefan George und die Blätter für die Kunst* 65.

¹⁸ Lessing, *Einmal und nie wieder* 302.

¹⁹ See Ludwig Klages, "Aus Desiderata," *Blätter für die Kunst* 2/1 (January 1894): 21–24; this and other fragments reprinted in Klages, *Rhythmen und Runen* 77–109.

²⁰ *Zeittafel,* 46; Bernhard Zeller, ed., *Stefen George 1868–1968: Der Dichter und sein Kreis: Eine Ausstellung des Deutschen Literaturarchives im Schiller-Nationalmuseum Marbach a.N.* (Munich: Kösel Verlag, 1968), 78. Henceforth this work is cited as Zeller, followed by a page reference.

²¹ Morwitz, *Kommentar zu dem Werk Stefan Georges* 74–75.

²² Wolters, *Stefan George und die Blätter für die Kunst* 65.

²³ See Schuler's letters to Klages of 27 and 29 January 1897 in the Schuler-Nachlass, DLA, Marbach am Neckar, cited in Gerhard Plumpe, *Alfred Schuler: Chaos und Neubeginn: Zur Funktion des Mythos in der Moderne* (Berlin: Agora Verlag, 1978), 162; and see Wolfskehl's letters to Herbert Steiner of 14 January and 21 May 1945 in Karl Wolfskehl, *Zehn Jahre Exil: Briefe aus Neuseeland,* ed. Margot Ruben (Heidelberg/Darmstadt: Verlag Lambert Schneider, 1959), 191 and 201.

²⁴ See Plumpe, *Alfred Schuler* 162.

²⁵ See Klages, "Einführung des Herausgebers," in *FuV* 74; Salin, *Um Stefan George* 192 and 334.

²⁶ See Plumpe, *Alfred Schuler* 162; and Keilson-Lauritz (1985).

²⁷ Klages, "Einführung des Herausgebers," in *FuV* 72–73.

[28] *Zeittafel* 137; for more detailed description, see Franziska Gräfin zu Reventlow, *Herrn Dames Aufzeichnungen,* in *Gesammelte Werke in einem Bande* (Munich: A. Langen, 1925), 779–89, and Oscar A. H. Schmitz, *Dämon Welt: Jahre der Entwicklung* (Munich: Müller, 1926), 292.

[29] The occasion for Karl Wolfskehl's dramatic poem "Maskenzug 1904," published in *Blätter für die Kunst* 7 (1904): 148–55.

[30] For photographic documentation, see, for example, Helmut Bauer, ed., *Schwabing: Kunst und Leben um 1900* (Munich: Münchner Stadtmuseum; Tucson, Arizona: Nazraeli Press, 1998), 70–73.

[31] Morwitz, *Kommentar zu dem Werk Stefan Georges* 139.

[32] Lessing, *Einmal und nie wieder* 310–11.

[33] Kurt Breysig, "Begegnungen mit Stefan George," *Castrum Peregrini* 42 (1960): 9–32; here 15.

[34] See Baal Müller, "Bildgeburten: George, Schuler und die 'Kosmische Runde,'" in Helmut Bauer and Elisabeth Tworek eds., *Schwabing: Kunst und Leben um 1900: Essays* (Munich: Münchner Stadtmuseum), 41–55; here 49–50; and Dietrich Jäger, "'Kein ding sei wo das wort gebricht': Der Umgang mit Sprache und phänomenaler Welt in Stefan Georges *Jahr der Seele* und im Denken von Ludwig Klages," *Hestia: Jahrbuch der Klages-Gesellschaft* 19 (1998/1999): 28–52.

[35] Furness, *Zarathustra's Children* 100. The poem alluded to here by George is "Die Wettertanne" (1895), first published in *Blätter für die Kunst* 5 (1900/1901): 57; reprinted in Klages, *Rhythmen und Runen* 224.

[36] Robert Boehringer, *Mein Bild von Stefan George,* 2nd ed., 2 vols (Düsseldorf/ Munich: Bei Helmut Küpper vormals Georg Bondi, 1967), I, 102.

[37] Plumpe, *Alfred Schuler* 162.

[38] Ludwig Klages, *Prinzipien der Charakterologie* (Leipzig: Johannes Ambrosius Barth, 1910). For further discussion, see Ursula Avé-Lallemant ed., *Die vier deutschen Schulen der Graphologie: Klages — Pophal — Heiß — Pulver* (Munich/Basle: Erinst Reinhardt, 1989).

[39] Ludwig Klages, letter to Stefan George of 15 September 1897, cited in Robert Boehringer, *Mein Bild von Stefan George,* 1st ed. (Munich/Düsseldorf: Bei Helmut Küpper vormals Georg Bondi, 1951), 104–6.

[40] Marita Keilson-Lauritz, "Stefan George: L(udwig) K(lages): Marginalien zum Widmungsgedicht im 'Jahr der Seele,'" *Castrum Peregrini* 121–22 (1976): 48–63 (58). See also Morwitz, *Kommentar zu dem Werk Stefan Georges* 139–40.

[41] Hans Eggert Schröder, *Ludwig Klages 1872–1956: Centenar-Ausstellung 1972* (Bonn: Bouvier Verlag Herbert Grundmann, 1972), 34.

[42] Conversation of 19 December 1928, recorded in Berthold Vallentin, *Gespräche mit Stefan George, 1902–1931* (Amsterdam: Castrum Peregrini Presse, 1961), 109–10.

[43] Ludwig Derleth, letter of 11 January 1898 to Anna Maria Derleth, in Derleth Archive, St. Gallen (cited in *Zeittafel* 75).

[44] Vallentin, *Gespräche mit Stefan George* 110.

[45] Plumpe, *Alfred Schuler* 160.

[46] Wolfskehl, letter of 29 August 1900 to George (cited in *Zeittafel*, 103).

[47] For a discussion of the relationship between *Jugendstil* and George, see Claude David, "Stefan George und der Jugendstil," in Jost Hermand, ed., *Jugendstil* [*Wege der Forschung*, vol. 110] (Darmstadt: Wissenschaftliche Buchgesellschaft, 1971), 382–401.

[48] Diary entry for 18 July 1896, in Zeller 174.

[49] See Dominik Jost, *Ludwig Derleth: Gestalt und Leistung* (Stuttgart: W. Kohlhammer, 1965), 31–32.

[50] Stefan Breuer, *Ästhetischer Fundamentalismus: Stefan George und der deutsche Antimodernismus* (Darmstadt: Primus Verlag, 1996), 119.

[51] See Wolters, *Stefan George und die Blätter für die Kunst* 238; cf. 352.

[52] Ludwig Klages, *Stefan George* (Berlin: Georg Bondi, 1902).

[53] Gundolf, letter of 6 December 1901 to Karl and Hanna Wolfskehl, in Gundolf Archive, Institute of German Studies, University of London (cited in *Zeittafel* 117).

[54] Stefan George, letter to Albert Verwey of [22] December 1901, cited in Mea Nijland-Verwey, ed., *Albert Verwey en Stefan George: De documenten van hun vriendschap* (Amsterdam: Polak & Van Gennep, 1965), 105.

[55] Ludwig Klages, letter to Friedrich Gundolf of 18 December 1901, cited in Stefan George/Friedrich Gundolf, *Briefwechsel* (Munich/Düsseldorf: Bei Helmut Küpper vormals Georg Bondi, 1962), 100.

[56] Klages, "Einführung des Herausgebers" in *FuV* 73–74.

[57] The great Swiss fin-de-siècle painter Arnold Böcklin (1827–1901) was greatly favored in "cosmic" circles (see, for example, Wolfskehl's poem "Der Meister und der Tod," one of his *Nänien*, in Karl Wolfskehl, *Gesammelte Werke*, eds. Margot Ruben and Claus Victor Bock, 2 vols (Hamburg: Claassen, 1960), I, 9). For further discussion, see Stefan Breuer, "Ferntiefenrausch: Ludwig Klages und Arnold Böcklin," and Robert Josef Kozljanič, "Böcklin und die daimonische Dimension der Natur," *Hestia: Jahrbuch der Klages-Gesellschaft* 19 (1998/1999): 91–103 and 104–28.

[58] Albert Verwey, *Mein Verhältnis zu Stefan George: Erinnerungen aus den Jahren 1895–1928* (Strasbourg: Heitz & Co., 1936), 36.

[59] Verwey, *Mein Verhältnis zu Stefan George* 36–37.

[60] Salin, *Um Stefan George* 192.

[61] Verwey, *Mein Verhältnis zu Stefan George* 40. "Porta Nigra" was first published in *Blätter für die Kunst* 6 (1902/1903): 7–8.

[62] For further discussion, see Marita Keilson-Lauritz, *Von der Liebe die Freundschaft heißt: Zur Homoerotik im Werk Stefan Georges* (Berlin: Verlag rosa Winkel, 1987).

[63] Glöckner's entry for 28 February 1916 in Ernst Glöckner, *Begegnung mit Stefan George: Auszüge aus Briefen und Tagebüchern, 1913–1934*, ed. Friedrich Adam (Heidelberg: Lothar Stiehm, 1972), 78.

[64] Salin, *Um Stefan George*, 169; Breuer, *Ästhetischer Fundamentalismus*, 44.

[65] See Morwitz, *Kommentar zu dem Werk Stefan Georges* 237; Keilson-Lauritz (1976), 60.

[66] Gundolf, letter to Karl Wolfskehl of 15 June 1902, in Gundolf Archive (cited in *Zeittafel* 126).

[67] For further discussion, see Jerry Glen, "Hofmannsthal, George, and Nietzsche: 'Herrn Stefan George / einem, der vorübergeht,'" *Modern Language Notes* 97 (1982): 770–73; and Jens Rieckmann, *Hugo von Hofmannsthal und Stefan George: Significanz einer "Episode" aus der Jahrhundertwende* (Tübingen: Francke, 1997).

[68] Stefan George, letter of c.22–23 July 1902 to Hugo von Hofmannsthal, cited in *Briefwechsel zwischen George und Hofmannsthal* 159.

[69] In *Blätter für die Kunst* 2/5 (February 1895): 137–44; and 4/2 (November 1897): 34–38.

[70] Hugo von Hofmannsthal, letter of 27 August 1902 to Stefan George, cited in *Briefwechsel zwischen George und Hofmannsthal* 169.

[71] *Briefwechsel zwischen George und Hofmannsthal* 171.

[72] Letter of Hanna Wolfskehl to Ernst Gundolf of 9 February 1903, cited in Boehringer, *Mein Bild von Stefan George*, 2nd edition, 228.

[73] Ludwig Derleth, "Vom wissen und wege," *Blätter für die Kunst* 6 (1902/1903): 43–47.

[74] See Klages, "Einführung des Herausgebers," in *FuV* 50–59.

[75] Klages, "Einführung des Herausgebers," in *FuV* 76.

[76] Sabine Lepsius, letter to Reinhold Lepsius of 30 September 1904 in DLA (cited in *Zeittafel* 160).

[77] George/Gundolf, *Briefwechsel,* 146.

[78] George, letter to Ludwig Klages of mid-January 1904; cited in Boehringer, *Mein Bild von Stefan George*, 2nd ed., I, 107.

[79] Ibid., cited in Boehringer, *Mein Bild von Stefan George*, 2nd ed., I, 106–7.

[80] Reprinted in Franz Schonauer, *Stefan George mit Selbstzeugnissen und Bilddokumenten dargestellt* (Reinbek bei Hamburg: Rowohlt, 1960), 83.

[81] Klages, letter to Stefan George of 15 January 1904; cited in Hans Eggert Schröder, *Ludwig Klages: Die Geschichte seines Lebens,* vol. 1, *Die Jugend* (Bonn: Bouvier Verlag, 1966), 357.

[82] According to a note in the Nachlass of Maximilian Kronberger, cited in *Zeittafel,* 153.

[83] *Blätter für die Kunst* 7 (1904): 67–69; reprinted in Ludwig Derleth, *Das Werk,* eds. Christine Derleth and Dominik Jost, 6 vols (Darmstadt: Verlag Hinder + Deelmann, 1971–1972), I, 24–26.

[84] *Blätter für die Kunst* 7 (1904): 66; reprinted in *CA* 141.

[85] See Gundolf/George, *Briefwechsel,* 152; Klages, *Rhythmen und Runen* 431.

[86] *Blätter für die Kunst* 7 (1904): 97–99.

[87] Breysig, "Begegnungen mit Stefan George" 15.

[88] Breuer, *Ästhetischer Fundamentalismus* 119. For discussion of Derleth's relation to George, Klages, and Schuler, see Jost, *Ludwig Derleth* 43–58.

[89] Verwey, *Mein Verhältnis zu Stefan George* 38.

[90] *Blätter für die Kunst* 7 (1904): 147.

[91] Jost, *Ludwig Derleth* 54. See Ludwig Derleth, *Die Proklamationen* (Leipzig: Insel-Verlag, 1904); reprinted in *Werke*, I, 43–89; revised version, 91–156.

[92] Conversation of 3 July 1904, recorded in Vallentin, *Gespräche mit Stefan George* 21.

[93] Breuer, *Ästhetischer Fundamentalismus* 121.

[94] Wolters, *Stefan George und die Blätter für die Kunst* 353.

[95] *Blätter für die Kunst* 7 (1904): 142–44; reprinted in Rudolf Pannwitz, *Wasser wird sich ballen: Gesammelte Gedichte* (Stuttgart: Ernst Klett Verlag, 1963), 9–11.

[96] "Wachsen und Formen ist ja in Wirklichkeit gar kein Unterschied. Auch beim Menschen nicht. Man darf nur *beides* nicht mechanisch nehmen. [. . .] [D]ieser Wahn, formen zu müssen, führt zum bewußt regulierten Formen, und das bewußt regulierte Formen führt zum mechanischen Formen. Das ist zugleich — in einem Satze — die traurige Lebensgeschichte Stefan George's und seiner Schule, wie aller klassisch-akademischen, Vorbilder aufstellenden, und vor Bild und Gebilde sich beugenden Kunst" (Rudolf Pannwitz, *Kultur, Kraft, Kunst: Charon-Briefe an Berthold Otto* [Leipzig: Charonverlag, K. G. Th. Scheffer, 1906], 121–22).

[97] Rudolf Pannwitz, "Was ich Nietzsche und George danke," *Castrum Peregrini* 189–190 (1989): 50–100. "Mein Bild von George war lange durch die falschen und halb falschen Gerüchte über ihn getrübt. Es wurde in mir klarer, je mehr ich das Wesentliche aussonderte, sodass es zusammenschoss" (98).

[98] Müller, in Bauer and Tworek, eds., *Schwabing: Kunst und Leben um 1900* 54–55.

[99] Morwitz, *Kommentar zu dem Werk Stefan Georges* 364.

[100] Jürgen Egyptien, "'Kosmische Elemente' in der Dichtung Stefan Georges," *Hestia: Jahrbuch der Klages-Gesellschaft* 19 (1998/1999): 11–27.

[101] See Melitta Gerhard, "Schillers Zielbild der ästhetischen Erziehung und das Wirken Stefan Georges," *Monatshefte für deutschen Unterricht, deutsche Sprache und Literatur* 51 (1959): 275–82.

[102] Part One, 1932; "Der Tod des Thanatos," 1946; "Die himmlische Basilie," 1947; "Poem der Magischen Natur," 1958; "Advent" posthumously published in 1968; and Part Two in its entirety in *Das Werk*, 1971–1972.

Works Cited

Avé-Lallemant, Ursula, ed. *Die vier deutschen Schulen der Graphologie: Klages — Pophal — Heiß — Pulver*. Munich and Basel: Ernst Reinhardt, 1989.

Bauer, Helmut, ed. *Schwabing: Kunst und Leben um 1900*. Munich: Münchner Stadtmuseum; Tucson, Arizona: Nazraeli P, 1998.

Bergel, Lienhard. *Voraussetzungen und Anfänge der Beziehungen zwischen Stefan George und Hugo von Hofmannsthal*. New York: New York UP, 1949.

Boehringer, Robert. *Mein Bild von Stefan George*. 1st ed. Munich/Düsseldorf: Helmut Küpper vormals Georg Bondi, 1951.

Boehringer, Robert. *Mein Bild von Stefan George*, 2nd ed. Vol. 1. Düsseldorf/ Munich: Bei Helmut Küpper vormals Georg Bondi, 1967.

Breuer, Stefan. *Ästhetischer Fundamentalismus: Stefan George und der deutsche Antimodernismus*. Darmstadt: Primus Verlag, 1996.

———. "Ferntiefrausch: Ludwig Klages und Arnold Böcklin." *Hestia: Jahrbuch der Klages-Gesellschaft* 19 (1998/1999). 91–103.

Breysig, Kurt. "Begegnungen mit Stefan George." *Castrum Peregrini* 42 (1960). 9–32.

Briefwechsel zwischen Stefan George und Hugo von Hofmannsthal. Ed. Robert Boehringer. 2nd edition. Munich/Düsseldorf: Helmut Küpper vormals Georg Bondi, 1953.

David, Claude. "Stefan George und der Jugendstil. *Jugendstil.* Wege der Forschung vol. 110. Ed. Jost Hermand. Darmstadt: Wissenschaftliche Buchgesellschaft, 1971. 382–401.

Derleth, Ludwig. *Das Werk*. Ed. Christine Derleth and Dominik Jost. 6 vols. Darmstadt: Verlag Hinder + Deelmann, 1971–1972.

Durzak, Manfred. *Der junge Stefan George*. Munich: Wilhelm Fink Verlag, 1968.

Egyptien, Jürgen. "'Kosmische Elemente' in der Dichtung Stefan Georges." *Hestia: Jahrbuch der Klages-Gesellschaft* 19 (1998/1999). 11–27.

Furness, Raymond. *Zarathustra's Children: A Study of a Lost Generation of Writers*. Rochester, NY: Camden House, 2000.

George, Stefan, and Friedrich Gundolf. *Briefwechsel*. Munich/Düsseldorf: Helmut Küpper vormals Georg Bondi, 1962.

Gerhard, Melitta. "Schillers Zielbild der ästhetischen Erziehung und das Wirken Stefan Georges." *Monatshefte für deutschen Unterricht, deutsche Sprache und Literatur* 51 (1959). 275–82.

Glen, Jerry. "Hofmannsthal, George, and Nietzsche: 'Herrn Stefan George / einem, der vorübergeht.'" *Modern Language Notes* 97 (1982). 770–73.

Glöckner, Ernst. *Begegnung mit Stefan George: Auszüge aus Briefen und Tagebüchern, 1913–1934*. Ed. Friedrich Adam. Heidelberg: Lothar Stiehm, 1972.

Jäger, Dietrich. "'Kein ding sei wo das wort gebricht': Der Umgang mit Sprache und phänomenaler Welt in Stefan Georges *Jahr der Seele* und im Denken von Ludwig Klages." *Hestia: Jahrbuch der Klages-Gesellschaft* 19 (1998/1999). 28–52.

Jost, Dominik. *Ludwig Derleth: Gestalt und Leistung*. Stuttgart: W. Kohlhammer, 1965.

Keilson-Lauritz, Marita. "Stefan George: L(udwig) K(lages): Marginalien zum Widmungsgedicht im 'Jahr der Seele.'" *Castrum Peregrini* 121–22 (1976). 48–63.

———. "Stefan George, Alfred Schuler und die 'kosmische Runde': Zum Widmungsgedicht 'A. S.' im 'Jahr der Seele.'" *Castrum Peregrini* 168–69 (1985). 24–41.

Keilson-Lauritz, Marita. *Von der Liebe die Freundschaft heißt: Zur Homoerotik im Werk Stefan Georges*. Berlin: Verlag rosa Winkel, 1987.

Klages, Ludwig. *Stefan George*. Berlin: Georg Bondi, 1902.

———. *Prinzipien der Charakterologie*. Leipzig: Johannes Ambrosius Barth, 1910.

———. "Einführung des Herausgebers." In Alfred Schuler. *Fragmente und Vorträge*. Ed. Ludwig Klages. Leipzig: Johann Ambrosius Barth, 1940.

———. *Rhythmen und Runen: Nachlaß herausgegeben von ihm selbst*. Leipzig: Johann Ambrosius Barth, 1944.

Kozljanič, Robert Josef. "Böcklin und die daimonische Dimension der Natur." *Hestia: Jahrbuch der Klages-Gesellschaft* 19 (1998/1999). 104–28.

Landmann, Edith. *Gespräche mit Stefan George*. Düsseldorf/Munich: Helmut Küpper vormals Georg Bondi, 1963.

Lessing, Theodor. *Einmal und nie wieder* [1935]. Gütersloh: Bertelsmann Sachbuchverlag, 1969.

Mann, Thomas. "Gladius Dei" (1902), *Die Erzählungen*. Frankfurt a.M.: Fischer, 1986. 215–35.

Morwitz, Ernst. *Kommentar zu dem Werk Stefan Georges*, 2nd ed. Düsseldorf/ Munich: Helmut Küpper vormals Georg Bondi, 1969.

Müller, Baal. "Bildgeburten: George, Schuler und die 'Kosmische Runde.'" In Helmut Bauer and Elisabeth Tworek, eds. *Schwabing: Kunst und Leben um 1900: Essays*. Munich: Münchner Stadtmuseum, 1998. 41–45.

Nijland-Verwey, Mea, ed. *Albert Verwey en Stefan George: De documenten van hun vriendschap*. Amsterdam: Polak & Van Gennep, 1965.

Norton, Robert E. *Secret Germany: Stefan George and his Circle*. Ithaca/ London: Cornell UP, 2002.

Pannwitz, Rudolf. *Kultur, Kraft, Kunst: Charon-Briefe an Berthold Otto*. Leipzig: Charonverlag, K. G. Th. Scheffer, 1906.

———. *Wasser wird sich ballen: Gesammelte Gedichte*. Stuttgart: Ernst Klett Verlag, 1963.

———. "Was ich Nietzsche und George danke." *Castrum Peregrini* 189–190 (1989). 50–100.

Plumpe, Gerhard. *Alfred Schuler: Chaos und Neubeginn: Zur Funktion des Mythos in der Moderne*. Berlin: Agora Verlag, 1978.

———. "Alfred Schuler und die Kosmische Runde." *Götter im Exil: Vorlesungen über die neue Mythologie, II. Teil*. Ed. Manfred Frank. Frankfurt a.M.: Suhrkamp, 1988. 213–56.

Raschel, Heinz. *Das Nietzsche-Bild im George-Kreis*. Berlin/New York: Walter de Gruyter, 1983.

Reventlow, Franziska Gräfin zu. *Herrn Dames Aufzeichnungen*. In *Gesammelte Werke in einem Bande*. Munich: A. Langen, 1925.

Salin, Edgar. *Um Stefan George: Erinnerung und Zeugnis.* 2nd ed. Munich/ Düsseldorf: Helmut Küpper vormals Georg Bondi, 1954.

Schmitz, Oscar A. H. *Dämon Welt: Jahre der Entwicklung.* Munich: Müller, 1926.

Schonauer, Franz. *Stefan George mit Selbstzeugnissen und Bilddokumenten dargestellt.* Reinbek bei Hamburg: Rowohlt, 1960.

Schröder, Hans Eggert. *Ludwig Klages: Die Geschichte seines Lebens.* Vol. 1. *Die Jugend.* Bonn: Bouvier Verlag, 1966.

———. *Ludwig Klages 1872–1956: Centenar-Ausstellung 1972.* Bonn: Bouvier Verlag Herbert Grundmann, 1972.

Schuler, Alfred. *Fragmente und Vorträge.* Ed. Ludwig Klages. Leipzig: Johann Ambrosius Barth, 1940.

———. *Cosmogonische Augen: Gesammelte Schriften.* Ed. Baal Müller. Paderborn: Igel Verlag, 1997.

Seekamp, Hans-Jürgen, Ockenden, Raymond C., and Keilson, Marita. *Stefan George: Leben und Werk: Eine Zeittafel.* Amsterdam: Castrum Peregrini P, 1972.

Vallentin, Berthold. *Gespräche mit Stefan George, 1902–1931.* Amsterdam: Castrum Peregrini P, 1961.

Verwey, Albert. *Mein Verhältnis zu Stefan George: Erinnerungen aus den Jahren 1895–1928.* Strasbourg: Heitz & Co., 1936.

Winkler, Michael. *George-Kreis.* Stuttgart: Metzler, 1972.

Wolfskehl, Karl. *Zehn Jahre Exil: Briefe aus Neuseeland.* Ed. Margot Ruben. Heidelberg/Darmstadt: Verlag Lambert Schneider, 1959.

———. *Gesammelte Werke.* Ed. Margot Ruben and Claus Victor Bock. 2 vols. Hamburg: Claassen, 1960.

Wolters, Friedrich. *Stefan George und die Blätter für die Kunst: Deutsche Geistesgeschichte seit 1890.* Berlin: Georg Bondi, 1930.

Zeller, Bernhard, ed. *Stefan George 1868–1968: Der Dichter und sein Kreis: Eine Ausstellung des Deutschen Literaturarchives im Schiller-Nationalmuseum Marbach a.N.* Munich: Kösel Verlag, 1968.

George, Nietzsche, and Nazism

Ritchie Robertson

MY TITLE NAMES A TRIANGLE. One side is the relationship between George and Nietzsche. Though they never met, George felt the effect of Nietzsche's writings, as did a whole generation of German writers and thinkers. More than that, as I shall argue, George saw himself as a prophet succeeding and surpassing Nietzsche, and I shall ask which elements of Nietzsche's prophecies George absorbed into his own prescriptions for the future of Germany. Another side of the triangle, though one that can receive only brief discussion here, is the controversial relation between Nietzsche and the Nazis. Was the Third Reich an attempt to put Nietzschean ideas into practice, or were the Nazis too ignorant to have picked up more than a few crude distortions of Nietzsche's thought? The third side represents the problem that worries all George scholars: what is the relationship between George and Nazism? Is there any evidence that the poet, who died in the first year of the Third Reich, approved of it or even supported it? Independently of such evidence, can or must George's prophetic poetry, his denunciations of Germany, and his authoritarian control over his circle be seen as anticipating aspects of the Third Reich?

For most of his life Nietzsche was a relatively obscure figure whose philosophical and aphoristic works found few readers. Ironically, his fame began to spread only around 1890, after he had suffered a complete mental collapse. Until his death in 1900 he lived in the care of his family, communicating only on a childish level and unaware that his works were being read avidly by the younger generation throughout Germany and soon throughout Europe. His appeal lay in his challenge to conventional ideas, the stimulus he offered to independent thought, and the sheer diversity of his reflections. As Steven Aschheim has shown, Nietzsche's writings are so multi-faceted, not to say self-contradictory, that they could be appropriated by virtually anyone with an urge for radical renewal.[1] Thus he was adopted as a hero by such opposed avant-gardes as the Expressionists (including those who, like Gottfried Benn, would later gravitate to the far right), the apocalyptic Munich "Kosmiker" dominated by Ludwig Klages, and the elitist circle that George would assemble. His legacy was claimed by the idealistic *Wandervogel* movement, which sent thousands of young people hiking across pre-1914 Germany, but also by the most brutal anti-Semites and

Social Darwinists. Despite Nietzsche's hostility to the Wilhelmine Empire, his work was exploited for propaganda in the First World War. He was alleged to have prophesied German world domination, and anthologies of his writings were distributed to front-line soldiers. He was appropriated by Socialists, despite his elitism; by radical feminists like Lily Braun (1865–1916), despite his misogyny; by anarchists like Gustav Landauer (1870–1919), despite his implicit authoritarianism; and by the revolutionary Right around Ernst Jünger, despite his individualism. The question of his influence was complicated by the fact that one of the most-read books circulating under his name, *Der Wille zur Macht* (The Will to Power, 1900), was not published by him but by his sister, who assembled it from her brother's voluminous notebooks in order to provide a systematic account of what she supposed to be his doctrines.

From the internal evidence of George's writings and the external evidence of recorded remarks, one can identify some broad aspects of Nietzsche's thought that particularly appealed to him. The first book by Nietzsche that he read, *Die Geburt der Tragödie* (The Birth of Tragedy, 1872), puts forward Greek tragedy and its modern counterpart, Wagnerian music drama, as the supreme form of art, and art in turn as the most satisfying way in which to apprehend the world: "nur als *ästhetisches Phänomen* ist das Dasein und die Welt ewig *gerechtfertigt*."[2] This bold elevation of aesthetic experience above all other modes is much more radical than the amoral devotion to aestheticism that George practiced through his *Blätter für die Kunst,* but it could serve as a legitimation for George's commitment to art above any utilitarian, moral, or political goals.

Next, George shared the criticism of the Wilhelmine Empire which Nietzsche began in *Die Geburt der Tragödie* and continued in his next book, *Unzeitgemäße Betrachtungen* (Untimely Meditations, 1873–76). He attacked the vulgar triumphalism which followed the Franco-Prussian War and which absurdly claimed Germany's victory as a triumph of German culture, the complacent philistinism of the educated classes based on a combination of watered-down Christianity and popular Darwinism, and the university curricula which crammed young men with tedious information about the past and prevented them from using it to illuminate the present. According to his main hagiographer, Friedrich Wolters, George considered the Reich primarily an economic association without the unified bureaucratic and military structures that a state required. He thought it was out of touch with the forces of German culture, and he regretted that Nietzsche's denunciations had had no effect.[3] In 1905, refusing to sign a petition opposing war between Germany and Britain, George told Hugo von Hofmannsthal that it would not be a bad thing if the Empire were humiliated: "Wer weiss ob man als echter freund der Deutschen ihnen nicht eine kräftige SEE-schlappe wünschen soll damit sie jene völkische bescheidenheit wieder erlangen die sie von neuem zur erzeugung geistiger werte befähigt."[4] In opposition to the Empire he knew, he cele-brates in some famous poems the Roman Empire with its civilizing influ-ence on Germany ("Porta Nigra"), the spiritual domain of the Pope ("Leo XIII"), and the medieval Holy Roman Empire ("Die Gräber in Speier").

One would expect the elitist George to absorb Nietzsche's distinction between master morality, the outlook of generous aristocrats, and slave morality, the resentful and hypocritical doctrines of the oppressed, in which Nietzsche claims to see the origins of Christian morality. Evidence that George did attend to this distinction, set out especially in *Zur Genealogie der Moral* (The Genealogy of Morals, 1887), comes from his fraught correspondence with the young Hofmannsthal, who disappointed George by rejecting his importunate, sexually charged, and no doubt frightening advances. Writing to Hofmannsthal on 31 May 1897, some years after the crisis, George says: "ich glaubte der satz von der edlen plötz-lichkeit an der grosse und vornehme menschen sich allzeit erkannt haben erleide keine ausnahme" (*Briefwechsel zwischen George und Hofmannsthal* 116–17). This is a reference to a passage in *Zur Genealogie* where Nietzsche says that aristocratic people, being spontaneous, have "jene schwärmerische Plötzlichkeit von Zorn, Liebe, Ehrfurcht, Dankbarkeit und Rache, an der sich zu allen Zeiten die vornehmen Seelen wieder-erkannt haben" (N VI. ii. 287). The elitism which made George assemble his Circle in defiance of a mindless mass public therefore found legitima-tion in Nietzsche.

Finally, George presents himself not only as a poet but, increasingly, as a prophet. From *Der siebente Ring* (The Seventh Ring, 1907) onwards he writes as judge of his times, as prophet of a more heroic future, and even as the man of destiny who will bring it to pass. His prophetic stance is undoubtedly modeled on *Also sprach Zarathustra* (Thus Spoke Zarathustra, 1883–85), the most literary and in many respects most acces-sible of Nietzsche's books. Zarathustra (a figure remotely modeled on the Persian prophet Zoroaster), mocked or ignored by his shallow contempo-raries, delivers a series of speeches in quasi-biblical poetic prose which express many of Nietzsche's leading ideas in memorable images. Robert E. Norton has recently argued that *Zarathustra* is a "distant cousin" of George's most prophetic book, *Der Stern des Bundes* (The Star of the Covenant, 1914).[5] George's disparagement of Nietzsche may be an indi-rect tribute to him, disclosing the ambition to oppose and surpass the achievement of Nietzsche's prophetic writings.

First, however, we need to see how Nietzsche figures in George's writ-ings of the 1890s. In the early years of his journal *Blätter für die Kunst,* George was still looking for distinguished allies in his campaign against German mediocrity. In 1892, an essay by George's collaborator Carl August Klein (1867–1952) lists as the representatives of new German art the composer Richard Wagner, the "orator" Nietzsche, the painter Arnold

Böcklin, and the draughtsman Max Klinger, and explains that they have now been joined by a fifth, the poet Stefan George.[6] We can be sure that George encouraged and perhaps dictated this piece of publicity. In the same article the "Nouvelle Poésie" (French Symbolism) is traced back to German sources, with quotations from Novalis and Nietzsche; the latter is from *Also sprach Zarathustra,* where the prophet disparages all poets with the words: "was wußten sie bisher von der Inbrunst der Töne!" (Klein 48; N VI i. 161). Other references to Nietzsche identify him with Zarathustra. In October 1894, Paul Gérardy's article "Geistige Kunst" explains that the poets of the *Blätter,* after escaping to France from German philistinism, have returned to reform Germany: "der magische fingerzeig Zarathustra's wies ihnen den harten ruhmreichen und einsamen weg."[7] In 1896 George advocated an art "die nach dem Zarathustraweisen zur höchsten aufgabe des lebens werden kann."[8]

By the turn of the century, however, Nietzsche's authority had declined. George's poem "Nietzsche" was probably occasioned by its subject's death on 24 August 1900.[9] The poem begins from a specific time and place which rapidly acquire symbolic overtones. It refers to the house in Weimar where Nietzsche died, but the wall that enclosed the Thunderer ("Also diese mauer | Umschloss den Donnerer") also suggests the limitations that denied Nietzsche's mission any effect.[10] After all, as we learn in the next stanza, the crowd is "blöd," and as insensitive as jellyfish or weeds, and those who praise Nietzsche are "getier" flourishing in the foul air that suffocated him. The time mentioned at the outset, where the cold gales are "halb des herbstes boten | Halb frühen frühlings," is transitional, not only between autumn and spring, but between the old age in which Nietzsche delivered "die lezten stumpfen blitze" and the new age to which George shows the way. Eventually Nietzsche will be recognized as a radiant figure, "Wie andre führer mit der blutigen krone": the reference to Christ's crown of thorns places Nietzsche among those who have suffered on behalf of humanity. His imitation of Christ is underlined when he is addressed as "Erlöser." Yet, we are told, he was the unhappiest of all redeemers: his work was only destructive ("Erschufst du götter nur um sie zu stürzen") and self-destructive, condemning him to suffering, solitude, and dismal wandering in the wilderness. In the last stanza George is presumably alluding to himself ("Der kam zu spät") as the one who, had he reached Nietzsche in time, would have warned him that the prophet should not go out into the wilderness but assemble around him a circle united by love ("den kreis den liebe schliesst"), as George was doing with his disciples; the "love" here is not Christian but homoerotic. The poem ends by criticizing Nietzsche once more, this time in his own words:

> sie hätte singen
> Nicht reden sollen diese neue seele![11]

The quotation is from the preface Nietzsche added to *Die Geburt der Tragödie* when it was reissued in 1886. There Nietzsche regretted that in his early book he had proclaimed a spiritual awakening in unsuitably prosaic language: "Sie hätte *singen* sollen, diese 'neue Seele' — und nicht reden!" (N III. i. 9). George now reapplies this criticism to Nietzsche's work as a whole. It rounds off a series of reservations qualifying this tribute to Nietzsche and making the author of *Zarathustra* appear an inferior precursor of George himself.

Many of these criticisms occur elsewhere in George's writings or in his recorded utterances. The view of Nietzsche as a transitional figure reappears in a short poem from *Der Stern des Bundes,* beginning:

> Einer stand auf der scharf wie blitz und strahl
> Die klüfte aufriss und die lager schied
> Ein Drüben schuf durch umkehr eures Hier . . (362)

Though unnamed, this figure is generally understood to be Nietzsche. Like a prophet commanding lightning, he is said to have defined the opposing forces in his time, and, by overturning the values of the world around him, to have created a counter-reality, a "Drüben." But this, by implication, was not a renewal. All he did was reverse the values of his contemporaries; he did not create new values, and he was ignored: "Der warner ging." In conversation, George condemned Nietzsche as ineffectual because too enmeshed in his own age. He told Edith Landmann that Nietzsche's opposition to Christianity proved his own dependence on it: "Wogegen man kämpft, da steckt man noch drin. Nicht Nietzsche war jenseits von Gut und Böse, sondern Algabal."[12] He said to Kurt Breysig about Nietzsche: "Er hat nichts bewirkt," "Er hat nichts durchgesetzt" (quoted in Raschel 40). As for Nietzsche's writing, George often criticized it, calling it noisy and exaggerated,[13] and disparaging *Also sprach Zarathustra* to Edith Landmann as "ein Zwischen- und Mittelding" (Landmann 100), which may mean not only midway between prose and poetry, but also midway between past and future. He also said to Kurt Hildebrandt (in April 1917) that in 25 years' time *Zarathustra* would no longer be considered a great book, because "ihm fehle die gestaltende Kraft."[14] "Ihm lag das eigentlich Dichterische fern," he declared roundly (Landmann 45). In stressing Nietzsche's failure to find a congenial circle, George is alluding to an event in Nietzsche's life that greatly annoyed him, namely the breach with Wagner. George considered this a betrayal of the loyalty that Nietzsche owed his Master: "Nietzsche hat Wagner verraten," he declared (Salin 271). In his study of Nietzsche, one of the mythopoetic works in which the George Circle specialized, Ernst Bertram accordingly treated this incident in a chapter entitled "Judas."

George regarded himself, and was regarded by his followers, as a prophet to whom Nietzsche was merely a precursor. Thus Friedrich Gundolf, in his study of the Master, was at pains to deny that George was in any sense the pupil of Nietzsche:

> Nietzsche stellte ein neues Ziel in die höchste Höhe: den Übermenschen, die Vision eines erhabenen Einsiedlers, die Umkehr der Wirklichkeit, eine eschatologische Wunschfigur . . er ersinnt das Andere, das weder er selbst noch seine Zeit schon füllt. George stellt ein gesteigertes Leben dar das er selbst schon verwirklicht, kein spannendes ziehendes Droben und Drüben, sondern ein bindendes, verbindendes Hier und Jetzt.[15]

Thus Nietzsche was the futile dreamer, George the leader who created a new way of living. Much was made of George's claim to have visited Turin early in 1889, soon after Nietzsche had suffered his final collapse there and had been taken by his friend Overbeck to recuperate at Basle. This was brought about by fate, so George informed Edith Landmann:

> Wir wissen um das, was die andern nicht ahnen. Darum ist uns der Anfang gewiß, und das Schicksal führte ihn herbei, indem es fast zur selben Zeit, da der irre, sich Dionysos wähnende Nietzsche das Tor Turins verläßt, Apollon zum Tore hereintreten läßt. (Landmann 115)

The unreliable Wolters makes George arrive in Turin at the very same time as Nietzsche leaves it, so that a rising star meets a falling one (Wolters 18). In fact Nietzsche's collapse, when he flung his arms round the neck of a cab-horse in a Turin street, occurred on 3 January 1889; Overbeck took him to Basle on 9 January, and apart from George's assertion reported by his commentator Ernst Morwitz there is no evidence that George ever visited Turin.[16] This is a case of myth-making. Alluding to the fact that Nietzsche, on the verge of incurable insanity, signed some of his letters "Dionysos," George says that Nietzsche merely thought he was Dionysos, but implies that he himself really was the incarnation of Apollo. In *Die Geburt der Tragödie* (The Birth of Tragedy), Nietzsche portrays Dionysos as the god of music and intoxication, while Apollo represents poetry, sculptural form, and radiant light. Thus, with George's entry into Turin, the turbid energies of Dionysos give way to the formal perfection of George's Apollonian poetry.

George himself was quite specific about how he surpassed Nietzsche. Nietzsche, he admitted in a letter to Gundolf of 11 June 1910, was right about many things, especially about the shortcomings of the nineteenth century, but failed to anticipate the new divinity who would appear in visible, "plastic" form:

> In Nietzsche steht doch ziemlich alles. Er hat die wesentlichen grossen dinge verstanden: nur hatte er den PLASTISCHEN GOTT nicht (daher sein missverstehen der Griechen besonders Platons).
>
> (George/Gundolf, *Briefwechsel* 202)

The "plastic god," of course, is Maximin. It is well known how George idolized the handsome and gifted young Maximilian Kronberger, who died on the eve of his sixteenth birthday, and how George then declared "Maximin" to be literally a god who must be worshipped. The central section of *Der siebente Ring* is devoted to the cult of Maximin, beginning with the poem entitled "Kunfttag," George's reformulation of the Christian term "Advent."

George distances himself from Nietzsche, finally, in the poem "Geheimes Deutschland," where Nietzsche figures as his ancestor ("der Vorfahr"), and where Nietzsche's mystical experience, described in the poem "Sils-Maria" at the end of *Die fröhliche Wissenschaft* (The Joyful Science, 1882–87; N V. ii. 333) is adapted:

> Einst lag ich am südmeer
> Tief-vergrämt wie der Vorfahr
> Auf geplattetem fels
> Als mich der Mittagschreck
> Vorbrechend durchs ölgebüsch
> Anstiess mit dem tierfuss. (426)

The "Mittagschreck," the god Pan who, in Greek belief, appeared in the hot stillness of noontide, tells the poet to return to Germany, where he will find territory still untouched by the poisonous spread of modernity. Thus George adapts Zarathustra's universal mission into a distinctly national one.

It is now time to ask about Nietzsche's relation to Nazism. Can he be seen as an intellectual precursor of Nazism? And if so, does George, in calling Nietzsche his "ancestor," become a spiritual father of the Third Reich? Hans Sluga has pointed out that Hitler showed little knowledge of Nietzsche, and that Alfred Rosenberg's official summation of National Socialist ideology, *Der Mythos des zwanzigsten Jahrhunderts* (The Myth of the Twentieth Century, 1930), rarely mentions him. The famous 1934 photograph by Heinrich Hoffmann showing Hitler contemplating a bust of Nietzsche in the Nietzsche Archive at Weimar was an attempt to establish a connection between the two, stage-managed by Elisabeth Förster-Nietzsche to serve her own ambitions, and by the better-educated Nazis to give themselves a respectable genealogy. In *Nietzsche und der Nationalsozialismus* (1937), issued by the Party's own publishing house, Heinrich Haertle argued that to associate Nietzsche too closely with Nazism denigrated the latter's originality, and that Nietzsche had contributed less to the Nazi movement than had the more accessible anti-modern polemicists Paul de Lagarde and Houston Stewart Chamberlain.[17] The latter judgment is probably more accurate. Yet it is difficult to dismiss the feeling expressed by many exiles that Nietzsche's ideas did help pave the way for National Socialism in some diffuse form. Writing in 1940 in Japanese exile, the Nietzsche scholar Karl Löwith remarked that although a gulf separated Nietzsche from his Nazi propagators, he had prepared the way from them, and that his work and influence represented the bridge from the old to the new Germany.[18]

The unavoidable questions about Nietzsche, George, and the Third Reich cannot be answered within metaphors of ancestry and forerunners, with their implications of temporal, causal and narrative sequentiality and necessity. These metaphors trap us into the illegitimate intellectual procedure that Michael André Bernstein has called "backshadowing" and defined as follows: "Backshadowing is a kind of retroactive foreshadowing in which the shared knowledge of the outcome of a series of events by narrator and listener is used to judge the participants in those events *as though they too should have known what was to come*."[19] Backshadowing abuses the hindsight which is ours simply because we happen to live later. It imputes to historical events the inevitability of events in a completed novel. It forgets that at any given time the future is more or less open, that no event is absolutely inevitable, still less foreseeable. If we look at the past without foreshadowing, we will see that at any time there are many swirling currents of thought, that ideas spread in diffuse ripple effects, and that their influence exceeds what can be reconstructed by historical research.

Any attempt to place the George Circle within a linear narrative leading to the Third Reich is in any case frustrated by George's hospitality to Jews. Circle members of Jewish descent included Gundolf, Ernst Morwitz, Karl Wolfskehl, Berthold Vallentin, and numerous others. Wolfskehl, an important poet, managed to combine a fascination with Germanic mythology and membership in the neo-pagan Cosmic group with sympathy for Zionism and an interest in Jewish history that finds expression in his poems "An den alten Wassern" (originally published in the *Blätter für die Kunst*) and his Biblical drama *Saul* (1905). When reproached for having Jewish friends, George replied: "Solche Juden, wie ich habe, könnte ich noch zehn um mich haben, würde mir gar nichts schaden" (Landmann 146). A poem in *Der Stern des Bundes*, "Ihr Äusserste von windumsauster klippe" (365), asserts a deep affinity between Jews and Germans. Yet even George's defense of his Jewish friends may sound patronizing, and he was increasingly open to anti-Semitic clichés about Jewish over-rationality and the danger of Germany becoming swamped by Eastern Jewish immigrants.[20] *Das Neue Reich* demonstrates a concern with blood and its corruption by racial degeneration or miscegenation. "Krankes blut" makes some disciples unreliable (454). Nations guilty of "Blut-schmach" (presumably the British and French, who introduced African and Indian troops into Europe) are said to merit extermination (411; see Norton 547).

"Blood" is one of several images and concepts linking George and his Circle with many figures on the German Right in what may be described as an anti-modern mentality.[21] One is the search for a new religion, such as George aimed to found with his cult of Maximin. This aspiration sharply distinguishes him from Nietzsche, who declared in his autobiographical book *Ecce Homo:* "in mir ist nichts von einem Religionsstifter" (N VI. iii. 363). Yet Nietzsche and George are both deeply indebted to the versions of Christianity in which they were brought up. Nietzsche, the son of a Protestant clergyman, adopts the solitary stance of a prophet and preacher. George, raised in the Catholic Rhineland, seeks much more to found a group of believers with their own rituals. Many of his poems describe or enact rituals, and while some are clearly inspired by the paganism of the Munich Cosmics (for example, "Sonnwendzug" 253), others mix pagan and Christian imagery ("Ursprünge" 294–95) or openly adapt Christian rituals, the boldest example being "Einverleibung" (291), George's calque on "incarnation."[22]

As the founder of a religion, George seeks also to be a legislator. This task was foreshadowed in the section of Nietzsche's *Der Wille zur Macht* headed "Der höchste Mensch als Gesetzgeber der Zukunft." Precedents included the laws of ancient Sparta ascribed to Lycurgus and the Indian Laws of Manu which the late Nietzsche praised for establishing the caste system (N VI. iii. 238). Wolters reports that George said of Bismarck: "Er war rein Politiker, nicht Gesetzgeber, und so ist auch sein Werk ein rein politisches geblieben, ein Kern ohne geistigen Gehalt."[23] The poems in *Der Stern des Bundes* lay down laws for a new nobility ("Neuen adel" 383) recognizable not by traditional hallmarks of aristocracy ("schild und krone") but by their burning eyes ("der augen wahrer glut"). These people are to be reshaped and reborn ("Neugeboren umgestaltet") as the poet's sons ("sohnschaft") from whom he will choose the lords of the world. As members of a sacred order, they are not to pollute themselves by intercourse with foreign women (383). They are to renounce luxury, reject what is decayed, and arm themselves with daggers in preparation for the imminent war ("der nahen Wal" 386).

Such fantasies have nothing to do with the Third Reich as an economic and political entity, but they are not wholly removed from its imaginative and even religious dimensions. Recently it has been argued that National Socialism, like some other totalitarian ideologies, was a substitute for organized religion which adapted its predecessor's methods to satisfy otherwise unfulfilled emotional needs.[24] Admittedly, though Hitler often talked about God and Providence, his outlook was largely a vulgar Darwinian, scientific one, and he established neither a Church nor a theology.[25] But the National Socialist movement did create a liturgical calendar based on festivals, from the anniversary of its seizure of power on 30 January to the commemoration of its martyrs on 9 November, with choreographed rituals and hymns of praise to Hitler.

A political religion required a strong leader who might well have messianic attributes. Even before the First World War, the Pan-German League wanted democracy to be dismantled and government to be done by an elite of Imperial advisers. "Wenn heute der Führer ersteht, wird er sich wundern, wieviele Getreue er hat — und wie wertvolle, selbstlose Männer sich um ihn scharen," wrote their spokesman Heinrich Class in

1912.[26] Opponents of Weimar democracy longed for such a charismatic figure.[27] Spengler maintained in *Der Untergang des Abendlandes* (The Decline of the West, 1918–22) that Western civilization, like all others, would presently come under the dominion of Caesars who would put an end to politics based on money and intellect. On the eve of Hitler's accession to power, Ernst Jünger, in *Der Arbeiter: Herrschaft und Gestalt* (1932), foretold a new aristocracy of battle-hardened technocrats. Such fantasies often sought support in Nietzsche, whether in his conception of the *Übermensch,* in his contrast of master and slave morality, or in his prophecies of a new aristocracy which would ruthlessly reshape humanity like sculptors or surgeons. Within the George circle, both Gundolf and Wolters celebrated domination and disciplehood. The leader, according to Gundolf, is driven by destiny to reshape people's souls: "Umbildung der seelen aber ist wunsch oder sinn jedes gewaltigen sagers und tuers — mit oder ohne sein eigenes wissen."[28] Gundolf's heroic biographies included the best-selling *Caesar,* which announces "das Bedürfnis nach dem starken Mann" in its opening sentence.[29] And in *Das Neue Reich* George himself foretells a heroic leader who at the head of his loyal band will found the New Empire:

> Er führt durch sturm und grausige signale
> Des frührots seiner [sic] treuen schar zum werk
> Des wachen tags und pflanzt das Neue Reich.[30]

The idea of the "Reich" was also common coin among opponents of the Weimar Republic. They dismissed the Wilhelmine Empire as a mere rump. Looking back to the Holy Roman Empire and to the "großdeutsch" ideals of 1848, like the Pan-Germans they wanted a single state comprehending everyone who spoke German and had German blood. Advocates of the Imperial idea (*Reichsidee*) ranged from conservative Catholics who wanted a divinely ordered polity to imperialists who aimed at Germany's territorial and economic supremacy. Some Georgeans asserted that George's kingdom was not of this world, but "ein Geistiges Reich."[31] However, George was particularly attached to the Emperor Frederick II (1194–1250), "der Grösste Friedrich" as he called him in "Die Gräber in Speier" (238), and was closely involved in Ernst Kantorowicz's scholarly work on him. In a very Georgean spirit, Kantorowicz praises Frederick for giving Germany a cultural unity based on Latin civilization: "Denn noch gab es keinen deutschen, sondern nur einen römischen Grist, der die Germanen bildete, und noch war es keine deutsche, sondern römische Form, welche die Nordländer einte und einander anglich, und nur das Blut hatten die Stämme an Deutschem gemein."[32] Frederick II was a hero of Nietzsche's (N VI. iii. 338). A restored Empire like Frederick's would have been very remote from anything Hitler planned, yet Hitler's abolition of democracy, his territorial ambitions, and his aggressive nationalism could be interpreted, if one were optimistic enough, as the prerequisite for such a restoration.

George's *Das Neue Reich* contains a number of somberly impressive poems denouncing modern civilization and foretelling its apocalyptic overthrow and renewal under an autocratic leader. The modern world's greed has spread its poison into the remotest deserts and "Von dem pol bis zum gletscher" (425). Both sides in the First World War are equally bad: even a German victory (as George thought when he wrote "Der Krieg" in 1917) will not save the world. Redemption may come from secret Germany (425); from the Germans, who, like the Jews at the time of Christ, are regarded as "Ein 'Hass und Abscheu menschlichen geschlechtes'" (414);[33] and from a conjunction of Greek and Norse gods. Odin, who hung "an dem Baum des Heiles," will replace Christ; the swastika (a symbol used by the Circle quite independently of the Nazis) will replace the cross (429). But this redemption can only follow destruction: "Der welt erlösung kommt nur aus entflammtem blut" (433). The agent of redemption will be a merciless conqueror like the heroic leader mentioned above or the ruthless young warrior "JLI," suggesting Attila the Hun, who in "Der Brand des Tempels" destroys the center of an ancient civilization to liberate people from a useless past. As Claude David says, in what is still an outstandingly judicious discussion of these matters, it was no wonder if an ill-informed public saw in such a poem a prophecy of Hitler.[34] After all, the eminent professor Julius Petersen, in his time-serving study of the Third Reich legend, quoted George's poem about the New Empire and declared flatly: "Das neue Reich ist gepflanzt."[35]

What about the attitude of George and his Circle to the actual National Socialist movement? Since about 1906, the Master had abandoned his lofty contempt for politics. He called the Circle his "state," and seems to have considered it the nucleus from which a new Germany might develop. In 1916 he told Breysig that he was prepared to become Imperial Chancellor (*Reichskanzler*), and claimed to have influential support (Norton 543). He deplored the Versailles Treaty and regretted that Germany had not attacked France in the 1890s and Russia when it was weakened by the Russo-Japanese War (Landmann 193). The apocalyptic poems published in *Das Neue Reich* (1928), though written ten or more years earlier, pronounce the modern world ripe for destruction and renewal at the hands of ruthless conquerors. George had no first-hand knowledge of the Nazis, though Joseph Goebbels had attended Gundolf's lectures in Heidelberg in 1920 and had tried unsuccessfully to secure him as doctoral supervisor.[36] Claims that Hitler went drinking in Munich with George's one-time associate Alfred Schuler, who denigrated George to him, may be discarded.[37] But though Jewish members of the Circle were obliged to emigrate, according to the sculptor Ludwig Thormaehlen the general attitude of its younger Gentile members was that the new regime had at least stopped Communism, that anti-Semitism would blow over (and anyway only affected Jews), and that the loutish Nazis would be replaced by more competent and respectable leaders (Thormaehlen 283). Kurt Hildebrandt joined the Party opportunistically in April 1933, thus securing a long-sought chair of philosophy at Kiel from which a Jewish academic had been dismissed.[38] Some of George's admirers thought the Third Reich the embodiment of his aims. A professor of German at Bonn, Hans Naumann, dedicated the 1933 reprint of his book *Die Dichtung der Gegenwart* jointly to George and Hitler as "Unsere Führer."[39] Speaking at a book burning organized by students on the market-place at Bonn on 10 May 1933, Naumann cited George and Bertram as great poets, educators, and legislators who embodied the conscience of the nation.[40] A week earlier, Bertram had introduced his lecture course at Cologne with a speech, "Deutscher Aufbruch," hailing George as the prophet of national reawakening. When the University of Berlin celebrated the founding of the new Reich, a chorus recited George's poem "An die Toten" from *Das Neue Reich* (Hildebrandt 231). A Circle member, Woldemar Count Uxkull-Gyllenband, marked George's sixty-fifth birthday by telling an audience of Tübingen students, some of whom he expected to be leaders of the new Reich, that George, one of the greatest poets who ever lived (alongside Homer and Dante), was the sharpest critic of a corrupt, over-rational civilization and the proclaimer of new, revolutionary values focused on leadership and community and formulated in the sacred book *Der Stern des Bundes*.[41] Many other cultural spokesmen claimed George as the herald of National Socialism.[42]

George himself was cautiously positive about the Nazis (Hildebrandt 228). He spoke most unequivocally to Edith Landmann, saying they were at last echoing his ideas: "es sei doch immerhin das erste Mal, dass Auffassungen, die er vertreten habe, ihm von aussen wiederklängen" (Landmann 209). Their brutality, he added, was simply part of politics, while, in view of Germany's future, the fate of the Jews was of minimal importance. The new Prussian Minister for Science, Art and Education, Bernhard Rust, was not only a long-standing Nazi but an admirer of George's work. Through Ernst Morwitz he put out feelers to learn whether George might join the reconstituted Writers' Academy, from which the Mann brothers and many other distinguished liberal and/or Jewish writers had resigned under pressure. George, replying to Morwitz on 10 May, refused even an honorary association with the academy, but did welcome its reorganization under "a national sign" and acknowledged himself as the "forefather" of the new national movement (quoted in translation by Norton 728–29). And although George normally shunned all public recognition, on 12 July he did, unusually, travel to Berlin for his sixty-fifth birthday, so that, if a public ceremony had been planned (as rumors claimed), he could hardly have avoided it.

It was also rumored after George's death that his move to Switzerland was a voluntary exile. For that reason, Thomas Mann charitably told Bertram in a letter of 9 January 1934, George did not quite deserve the huge wreath that the new German government had sent to adorn his grave.[43] However, George was simply continuing his normal habit of visiting Switzerland in the autumn, and in any case he considered Switzerland to be part of Germany.

Yet, though George passively supported the Third Reich, and did not live to discover his mistake, it was one of his disciples, Claus von Stauffenberg, who came close to killing Hitler. A conservative aristocrat, Stauffenberg sympathized with the expansionist aims of the new Reich but was repelled by the thuggery practiced against Ernst Röhm's followers in 1934 and against the Jews in November 1938. What turned him against Hitler, however, was the pointlessly brutal treatment of civilians on the Russian front and the unrealistic instructions given to the army which rendered a catastrophic defeat increasingly likely. With his fellow-conspirators, Stauffenberg managed on 20 July 1944 to smuggle a suitcase containing a bomb into Hitler's headquarters. Unfortunately Hitler survived the explosion, and the conspirators were caught and executed. Stauffenberg's last words before being shot were either "Long live sacred Germany," or possibly "Long live secret Germany," the watchword of the George Circle.

If the conspiracy had succeeded, might Germany have been remodeled along Georgean lines? Claus von Stauffenberg and his brother Berthold drafted a manifesto calling for a new order that guaranteed law and justice but rejected equality ("die Gleichheitslüge"), reverenced natural hierarchy, and rested on "ein Volk, das in der Erde der Heimat verwurzelt den natürlichen Mächten nahebleibt" without aspiring to social mobility.[44] This sounds like a nostalgic fantasy. Even if the Allies had been prepared to negotiate with Stauffenberg, the German people, who a few years later, with tremendous effort, built up two industrial states on opposing political lines, would hardly have accepted the fixed, hierarchical, agrarian society that was envisaged. George's greatness as a poet did not make him reliable as a political visionary.

Notes

[1] Steven E. Aschheim, *The Nietzsche Legacy in Germany 1890–1990* (Berkeley/ Los Angeles/London: U of California P, 1992).

[2] Friedrich Nietzsche, *Werke*, ed. Giorgio Colli and Mazzino Montinari, 8 divisions (Berlin/New York, 1972-), III. i. 43. Further quotations will be identified by N with division, volume, and page numbers. For a fully detailed account of George's reading of and response to Nietzsche, see Heinz Raschel, *Das Nietzsche-Bild im George-Kreis: Ein Beitrag zur Geschichte der deutschen Mythologeme* (Berlin/ New York: de Gruyter, 1984).

[3] Friedrich Wolters, *Stefan George und die Blätter für die Kunst: Deutsche Geistesgeschichte seit 1890* (Berlin: Bondi, 1930), 434.

[4] Letter (unsent), 4 December 1905, in *Briefwechsel zwischen George und Hofmannsthal,* 2nd, enlarged edn. (Munich/Düsseldorf: Küpper, 1953), 227.

[5] Robert E. Norton, *Secret Germany: Stefan George and his Circle* (Ithaca/London: Cornell UP, 2002), 491.

[6] Carl August Klein, "Über Stefan George, eine neue kunst," *Blätter für die Kunst,* 1. Folge, II. Band (Dezember 1892), 47–50; here 50.

[7] *Blätter für die Kunst,* 2. Folge, IV. Band (October [sic] 1894), 111.

[8] *Blätter für die Kunst,* 3. Folge, I. Band (Jänner 1896), 2.

[9] Stefan George, *Werke,* 2 vols (Düsseldorf/Munich: Küpper, 1976), vol. 1, 231–32. All further quotations from George's poetry will be taken from volume 1 of this edition and identified parenthetically by page number.

[10] It is not clear when, or even whether, George visited Weimar. Friedrich Gundolf saw Nietzsche's house in December 1900 in weather like that of the poem; George may have borrowed his description. See Stefan George and Friedrich Gundolf, *Briefwechsel,* ed. Robert Boehringer and Georg Peter Landmann (Munich/ Düsseldorf: Küpper, 1962), 65. Raschel 39 notes also the similarity to the stormy atmosphere in Nietzsche's own poem "Ruhm und Ewigkeit" (N VI. iii. 400–401).

[11] On its first publication, in the *Blätter für die Kunst,* 5. Folge (1900/01), 5–6, the poem ended with a full stop instead of an exclamation mark.

[12] Edith Landmann, *Gespräche mit Stefan George* (Düsseldorf/Munich: Küpper, 1962), 100.

[13] Edgar Salin, *Um Stefan George: Erinnerung und Zeugnis* (Munich/Düsseldorf: Küpper, 1954), 271.

[14] Kurt Hildebrandt, *Erinnerungen an Stefan George und seinen Kreis* (Bonn: Bouvier, 1965), 108.

[15] Friedrich Gundolf, *George* (Berlin: Bondi, 1920), 49.

[16] See Ernst Morwitz, *Kommentar zu dem Werke Stefan Georges* (Munich/Düsseldorf: Küpper, 1960), 222; H.-J. Seekamp, R. C. Ockenden and M. Keilson, *Stefan George — Leben und Werk. Eine Zeittafel* (Amsterdam: Castrum Peregrini, 1972), 10.

[17] Hans Sluga, *Heidegger's Crisis: Philosophy and Politics in Nazi Germany* (Cambridge, MA: Harvard UP, 1993), 179–86.

[18] Karl Löwith, *Mein Leben in Deutschland vor und nach 1933* (Frankfurt a.M.: Fischer, 1989), 5–6.

[19] Michael André Bernstein, *Foregone Conclusions: Against Apocalyptic History* (Berkeley/Los Angeles: U of California P, 1994), 16. Emphasis in original.

[20] See Jürgen Egyptien, "Georges Haltung zum Judentum," in Gert Mattenklott, Michael Philipp and Julius H. Schoeps, eds., *"Verkannte brüder"? Stefan George und das deutsch-jüdische Bürgertum zwischen Jahrhundertwende und Emigration* (Hildesheim: Olms, 2001), 15–27.

[21] See Ritchie Robertson, *The "Jewish Question" in German Literature, 1749–1939* (Oxford: Oxford UP, 1999), 182–87.

[22] See Wolfgang Braungart, *Ästhetischer Katholizismus: Stefan Georges Rituale der Literatur* (Tübingen, 1997).

[23] Quoted in Achim Aurnhammer, "'Der Preusse.' Zum Zeitbezug der 'Zeitgedichte' Stefan Georges im Spiegel der Bismarck-Lyrik," in Wolfgang Braungart, Ute Oelmann and Bernhard Böschenstein, eds., *Stefan George: Werk und Wirkung seit dem "Siebenten Ring"* (Tübingen: Niemeyer, 2001), 173–96 (184–85).

[24] See Michael Burleigh, *The Third Reich: A New History* (London: Macmillan, 2000), 9–13.

[25] See Michael Rissmann, *Hitlers Gott: Vorsehungsglaube und Sendungsbewußtsein des deutschen Diktators* (Zurich/Munich: Pendo, 2001).

[26] Quoted in Jost Hermand, *Der alte Traum vom neuen Reich: Völkische Utopien und Nationalsozialismus* (Frankfurt a.M.: Athenäum, 1988), 63.

[27] See Kurt Sontheimer, *Antidemokratisches Denken in der Weimarer Republik: Die politischen Ideen des deutschen Nationalismus zwischen 1918 und 1933* (Munich: Nymphenburger Verlagsbuchhandlung, 1962).

[28] Gundolf, "Gefolgschaft und Jüngertum," *Blätter für die Kunst,* 8. Folge (1908/09), 106–12 (106).

[29] Gundolf, *Caesar. Geschichte seines Ruhms* (Berlin: Bondi, 1924), 7.

[30] The sense seems to require "seine treue schar."

[31] Friedrich Wolters, "Herrschaft und dienst," *Blätter für die Kunst,* 8. Folge (1908/09), 133–38 (133).

[32] Ernst Kantorowicz, *Kaiser Friedrich der Zweite* (Berlin: Bondi, 1927), 74–75.

[33] George is here quoting the description of Christians by the Roman historian Tacitus: see *The Annals of Imperial Rome,* tr. Michael Grant, revised ed. (London: Penguin, 1996), 365.

[34] Claude David, *Stefan George: son œuvre poétique* (Lyon/Paris: IAC, 1952), 369.

[35] Julius Petersen, *Die Sehnsucht nach dem Dritten Reich in deutscher Sage und Dichtung* (Stuttgart: Metzler, 1934), 61.

[36] See Ralf Georg Reuth, *Goebbels,* tr. Krishna Winston (London: Constable, 1993), 37.

[37] Ludwig Thormaehlen, *Erinnerungen an Stefan George* (Hamburg: Hauswedell, 1962), 282–83.

[38] On the Circle's behavior in 1933, see Carola Groppe, *Die Macht der Bildung: Das deutsche Bürgertum und der George-Kreis 1890–1933* (Cologne/Weimar/Vienna: Böhlau, 1997), 651–76.

[39] Hans Kohn, *The Mind of Germany* (London: Macmillan, 1961), 242.

[40] Naumann's speech is reproduced in Hermann Haarmann et al., *"Das war ein Vorspiel nur..." Bücherverbrennung Deutschland 1933: Voraussetzungen und Folgen,* Ausstellung der Akademie der Künste vom 8. Mai bis 3. Juli 1983 (Berlin and Vienna: Medusa, 1983), 202–4.

[41] Woldemar Graf Uxkull-Gyllenband, *Das revolutionäre Ethos bei Stefan George.* Vortrag gehalten zum 65. Geburtstag des Dichters vor der Studentenschaft der Universität Tübingen (Tübingen: Mohr, 1933).

[42] See Joseph Wulf, *Literatur und Dichtung im Dritten Reich: Eine Dokumentation* (Gütersloh: Mohn, 1963), 30–31.

[43] *Thomas Mann an Ernst Bertram: Briefe aus den Jahren 1910–1955*, ed. Inge Jens (Pfullingen: Neske, 1960), 180.

[44] The full text is in Peter Hoffmann, *Claus Schenk Graf von Stauffenberg und seine Brüder* (Stuttgart: Deutsche Verlags-Anstalt, 1992), 396–97.

Works Cited

Aschheim, Steven E. *The Nietzsche Legacy in Germany 1890–1990*. Berkeley/ Los Angeles/London: U of California P, 1992.

Aurnhammer, Achim. "'Der Preusse.' Zum Zeitbezug der 'Zeitgedichte' Stefan Georges im Spiegel der Bismarck-Lyrik." *Stefan George: Werk und Wirkung seit dem "Siebenten Ring."* Eds. Wolfgang Braungart, Ute Oelmann, Bernhard Böschenstein. Tübingen: Niemeyer, 2001. 173–96.

Bernstein, Michael André. *Foregone Conclusions: Against Apocalyptic History*. Berkeley/Los Angeles/London: U of California P, 1994.

Briefwechsel zwischen George und Hofmannsthal. Ed. Robert Boehringer. 2nd enlarged edn. Munich/Düsseldorf: Küpper, 1953.

Burleigh, Michael. *The Third Reich: A New History*. London: Macmillan, 2000.

David, Claude. *Stefan George: son oeuvre poétique*. Lyon/Paris: IAC, 1952.

Egyptien, Jürgen. "Georges Haltung zum Judentum." *"Verkannte brüder"? Stefan George und das deutsch-jüdische Bürgertum zwischen Jahrhundertwende und Emigration*. Eds. Gert Mattenklott, Michael Philipp, Julius H. Schoeps. Hildesheim: Olms, 2001. 15–27.

Groppe, Carola. *Die Macht der Bildung. Das deutsche Bürgertum und der George-Kreis 1890–1933*. Cologne/Weimar/Vienna: Böhlau, 1997.

Gundolf, Friedrich. "Gefolgschaft und Jüngertum." *Blätter für die Kunst*, 8. Folge (1908/09). 106–12.

———. *George*. Berlin: Bondi, 1920.

———. *Cäsar. Geschichte seines Ruhms*. Berlin: Bondi, 1924.

Haarmann, Hermann, et.al. *"Das war ein Vorspiel nur . . ." Bücherverbrennung Deutschland 1933: Voraussetzungen und Folgen*. Ausstellung der Akademie der Künste vom 8. Mai bis 3. Juli 1983. Berlin/Vienna: Medusa, 1983.

Hermand, Jost. *Der alte Traum vom neuen Reich. Völkische Utopien und Nationalsozialismus*. Frankfurt a.M.: Athenäum, 1988.

Jens, Inge, ed. *Thomas Mann und Ernst Bertram: Briefe aus den Jahren 1910–1955*. Pfullingen: Neske, 1960.

Kantorowicz, Ernst. *Kaiser Friedrich der Zweite*. Berlin: Bondi, 1927.

Klein, Carl August. "über Stefan George, eine neue kunst." *Blätter für die Kunst*, 1,2 (December 1892). 47–50.

Kohn, Hans. *The Mind of Germany*. London: Macmillan, 1961.

Landmann, Edith. *Gespräche mit Stefan George*. Düsseldorf/Munich: Küpper, 1963.

Landmann, Georg Peter, ed. *Stefan George–Friedrich Gundolf. Briefwechsel*. Munich: Küpper, 1962.

Löwith, Karl. *Mein Leben in Deutschland vor und nach 1933*. Frankfurt a.M.: S. Fischer, 1989.

Morwitz, Ernst. *Kommentar zu dem Werke Stefan Georges*. Düsseldorf/Munich: Küpper, 1960.

Norton, Robert E. *Secret Germany: Stefan George and his Circle*. Ithaca/London: Cornell UP, 2002.

Petersen, Julius. *Die Sehnsucht nach dem Dritten Reich in deutscher Sage und Dichtung*. Stuttgart: Metzler, 1934.

Raschel, Heinz. *Das Nietzsche-Bild im George-Kreis. Ein Beitrag zur Geschichte der deutschen Mythologeme*. Berlin/New York: de Gruyter, 1984.

Reuth, Ralf Georg. *Goebbels*. Trans. Krishna Winston. London: Constable, 1993.

Rissmann, Michael. *Hitlers Gott. Vorsehungsglaube und Sendungsbewußtsein des deutschen Diktators*. Zurich/Munich: Pendo, 2001.

Robertson, Ritchie. *The "Jewish Question" in German Literature, 1749–1939*. Oxford: Oxford UP, 1999.

Salin, Edgar. *Um Stefan George. Erinnerung und Zeugnis*. Munich/Düsseldorf: Küpper, 1954.

Seekamp, H. J., Ockenden, R. C., Keilson, M. *Stefan George. Leben und Werk. Eine Zeittafel*. Amsterdam: Castrum Peregrini, 1972.

Sluga, Hans. *Heidegger's Crisis: Philosophy and Politics in Nazi Germany*. Cambridge, Mass.: Harvard UP, 1995.

Sontheimer, Kurt. *Antidemokratisches Denken in der Weimarer Republik. Die politischen Ideen des deutschen Nationalsozialismus zwischen 1918 und 1933*. Munich: Nymphenburger Verlagsbuchhandlung, 1962.

Stern, J. P. *The Dear Purchase: A Theme in German Modernism*. Cambridge: Cambridge UP, 1995.

Thormaehlen, Ludwig. *Erinnerungen an Stefan George*. Hamburg: Hauswedell, 1962.

Wolters, Friedrich. *Stefan George und die Blätter für die Kunst. Deutsche Geistesgeschichte seit 1890*. Berlin: Bondi, 1930.

Wulf, Joseph. *Literatur und Dichtung im Dritten Reich. Eine Dokumentation*. Gütersloh: Mohn, 1963.

George and a friend, 1896. The friend is presumably "Ugolino,"
that is Hugo Zernik.
Courtesy of the Stefan George-Stiftung.

Stefan George's Concept of Love and the Gay Emancipation Movement

Marita Keilson-Lauritz

Such is my love

Shakespeare, Sonnet LXXXVIII

THERE IS NO DOUBT that the concept of love in the texts of Stefan George is a homoerotic one. That is to say, even if George never would have called himself "a homosexual," the main subject of his texts is love of men and boys.[1] There are so many love poems to a male addressee that — even if critics have paid little attention to this central subject of his work — it was (and still is) quite easy to claim George for a history of gay literature.[2] This is what the gay emancipation movement did at the latest in 1914, when the sexologist Magnus Hirschfeld published Peter Hamecher's (1879–1938) article "Der männliche Eros im Werke Stefan Georges" in his *Jahrbuch für sexuelle Zwischenstufen,* edited since 1899 on behalf of the "Wissenschaftlich-humanitäres Komitee," the first organization of the gay emancipation movement, founded in 1897.[3] The newsletter of the "Gemeinschaft der Eigenen" (another gay emancipation group, founded in 1903), published in 1924 an annotated list ("Flüchtiger Ueberblick über die Schöne Literatur, soweit sie Freundesliebe zum Inhalt hat") recommending to gay readers George's *Maximin-Gedenkbuch, Der Stern des Bundes, Der Siebente Ring, Der Teppich des Lebens, Das Jahr der Seele,* and the anthologies *Deutsche Dichtung I–III* (1900–1902) as well as George's translations in *Zeitgenössische Dichter* (1905). In the early 1930s Hans Dietrich Hellbach wrote in his thesis *Die Freundesliebe in der deutschen Literatur* that the triumph of Eros in modern German literature was achieved by George, who gave a new social-ethical dimension to what Hellbach called "Freundesliebe," a term used by the early German gay emancipation movement to stress the cultural impact of male-male relationships.[4] Modern gay anthologies such as *The Penguin Book of Homosexual Verse* (1983) also include George; there are articles on George in the *Encyclopedia of Homosexuality,* edited by Wayne R. Dynes (1990) and *Who's Who in Gay and Lesbian History,* edited by Robert Aldrich and Garry Wotherspoon (2001), in Claude J. Summers's *The Gay and Lesbian Literary Heritage* (1995), and in *Frauenliebe Männerliebe: Eine lesbisch-schwule Literaturgeschichte in Porträts* (1997). George is alluded to in the works of modern — mostly German — gay writers, for example Hubert Fichte (1935–1986), Detlev Meyer (1950–1999), and Thomas Böhme (1955–).[5]

Hamecher's 1914 article may seem perhaps a late reaction to George's poetry, which had been in print since 1890; even if we keep in mind that the first allusion to same sex love in *Algabal* (first printed privately in 1892) in the "Aufschrift" (Dedication) addressed to the homosexual Bavarian king Ludwig II was added only in the 1898 edition. But some hints about George's sexual orientation and the homoerotic connotations of his texts on same sex love pre-date Hamecher. In 1897, one of the advertisements placed by the publishing house Max Spohr in Leipzig — which since 1893 had been publishing many early homosexual books, and from 1899 on published the *Jahrbuch für sexuelle Zwischenstufen* (the most outstanding periodical of the early emancipation movement) — named Stefan George as one of its authors. Obviously, Spohr or Franz Evers, editor of "Kreisende Ringe," Spohr's literary division, had put out feelers to George, who at the time was in the market for a publisher. George asked the literary critic Richard M. Meyer for information about Spohr, and was told in a letter dated 19 October 1897 about the publishing house's sexuality-centered program. Meyer finished his letter with a negative recommendation and the rather enigmatic sentence: "An author has no sexe [*sic*]."[6] In 1898 George opted for the publishing house of Georg Bondi.[7] In 1903 Erich Mühsam (1878–1934) in his pamphlet *Die Homosexualität* referred to George explicitly and said that his poems testified to his homosexuality ("Urningtum").[8] In 1909/10 a homophobic attack was launched by a fellow writer and poet, Rudolf Borchardt (1877–1945), in his reaction to the publication of George's *Der Siebente Ring*.[9]

In 1912 the third *Jahrbuch für die geistige Bewegung*, edited by two close friends of George, Friedrich Gundolf and Friedrich Wolters, published what may be read as a reaction to such attacks. The text, probably written by the editors and sanctioned by George, is a defense of the cult of friendship between men. Citing examples such as Don Carlos's devotion ("hingabe") to Posa, Ferdinand's to Egmont in Goethe's drama, and Shakespeare's to his friend, Gundolf and Wolters deny that such passionate friendships have anything to do with the witch hunting paragraph 175 of the German penal code or with the medicalization of homosexuality by sexologists.[10] They further maintain that such friendships are an integral and essential element of education and cultural achievements. They do not deny that sexual excesses are possible in such relationships but stress that any lawyer or doctor could name unnatural sexual conduct practiced within the holy institution of marriage.[11] Finally they point out that the most virulent attacks against George and his Circle were launched by those pleading for the abolition of paragraph 175.

Hamecher cited this text — which takes a negative view of the "läppische medizinische Einreihung" by Hirschfeld and other doctors — in his article, in full and affirmatively.[12] Considering Hirschfeld's acceptance of the article for his journal this may seem curious, but it fits perfectly with Hamecher's position: he was one of the main contributors to Adolf Brand's *Der Eigene,* where he came out (making his literary début *and* disclosing his homosexuality) at the age of nineteen in 1899.[13] Presumably he would have published his article on George in *Der Eigene* — if there had been an issue in 1914. However, production was suspended in 1907 after Brand was convicted of defamation for calling the *Reichskanzler* von Bülow a homosexual and was jailed for eighteen months. It was only in 1919 that Brand succeeded in relaunching his journal.[14]

The editors of the *Jahrbuch für die geistige Bewegung* take a detached view of the medicalization of homosexuality, the "Zwischenstufen-Theorie," and the strategy of Hirschfeld and his followers; in a way they seem closer to the ideas represented by Brand's "Gemeinschaft der Eigenen," stressing the "manly" qualities of the homosexual, whom they called the "Freundliebende[r]" (friend-lover). But one wonders whether George really does fit into this alternative concept of gayness of the early emancipation movement which started in Germany at the turn of the century. Even if the argumentation of Brand and others stresses manliness and man-man or man-boy relationships, opposing Hirschfeld's concept of inborn homosexuality — there is also the strongly individualistic and anarchistic base of the "Gemeinschaft der Eigenen" pleading for every man to have the freedom to live his own sexuality. And of course Brand's sometimes provocative actions are quite un-George-like.[15] Brand would never have submitted to the boys he loved. George did.

So it may be useful to look for George's own concept of love, his concept of intimate human relationships, including eroticism and sexuality, called George's "Liebeslehre" by Hans Dietrich Hellbach (163). When in the 1980s I examined George's use of the word "love" in his poetry, I concluded that love on the one hand meant the search for the only, real *Traumliebe* (culminating in the "Maximin-Erlebnis") but also the repeatability of the experience of love (based on the finitude of the "Maximin-Erlebnis," marked by the early death of Maximin at the age of sixteen); love is meant to include somatic and sexual aspects, dominated by pain, soreness, and by submission and service; love is danger; to love is to expose oneself to danger; love is powerful, moving, constructive; love frequently connotes renunciation and sometimes sublimation. And of course, at least since *Der Teppich des Lebens,* love in George's texts refers exclusively to love for males.[16]

This brief description of George's use of the term love of course is *not* what we may call George's normative "concept of love." Unfortunately, George himself never explicated his concept of love. As far as we know, George did not write the text in the *Jahrbuch für die geistige Bewegung.* Moreover, the text reflects the point of view of the George *Kreis* concerning "friendship" (whatever this may mean — even if we decide it means "die Liebe die Freundschaft heißt"), not "love." So a text written by George about a fellow poet — Shakespeare — and the latter's concept of love may provide a better starting point.

In 1909 appeared Stefan George's translation of Shakespeare's sonnets, which form the core of the gay canon,[17] at least since Oscar Wilde quoted them at his trials in 1895, along with the sonnets of Michelangelo. George added a short preface informing the reader why — in his opinion — the sonnets were not appreciated: (1) poetical hermeticism, (2) lack of romanticism, and (3) the subject matter ("der gegenstand"). George spends more than three-quarters of his preface discussing this point: at the center of — and thus *the* subject of the sonnets, according to George — is the poet's "leidenschaftliche hingabe" (passionate devotion) to his friend. In his view, Shakespeare should neither be blamed for this passion nor is there any need to vindicate the poet's honor. Especially materialistic, rationalistic generations are in no position to discuss this point because they know nothing about the cosmogonic power of this "übergeschlechtliche Liebe." Implicitly this is to say: "But I, Stefan George, I know." So we may perhaps conclude that there is something like his own concept of love hidden in this term. In the following, I will try to unfold this concept from the term "übergeschlechtliche Liebe" as used by George in this short preface, and especially from its concluding section which reads:

> Unsrer tage haben sich menschen und dichter unverhohlen ausgesprochen: im mittelpunkte der sonnettenfolge steht in allen lagen und stufen die leidenschaftliche hingabe des dichters an seinen freund. Dies hat man hinzunehmen auch wo man nicht versteht und es ist gleich töricht mit tadeln wie mit rettungen zu beflecken was einer der grössten Irdischen für gut befand. Zumal verstofflichte und verhirnlichte zeitalter haben kein recht an diesem punkt worte zu machen da sie nicht einmal etwas ahnen können von der weltschaffenden kraft der übergeschlechtlichen Liebe. (2: 149)

Let us start with the two last words — "übergeschlechtliche Liebe." Regarding George's use of the word "Liebe," we have to bear in mind what was pointed out above. But there are some special points to notice here. First of all, according to the *Wort-Konkordanz,* "liebe/lieben" is one of the most frequent words in George's poetry, with about 150 occurrences in nine volumes comprising over 1,000 pages.[18] In George's translation of Shakespeare's sonnets (approximately 160 pages), "liebe/lieben" appears about 240 times.[19] This of course reflects Shakespeare's own use of the word "love" but is nevertheless quite remarkable. Secondly, capital letters in George's poetry are exceptionally rare and used mostly for emphasis. Even "liebe," a word so central to George's poetry, is almost never capitalized.[20] So the upper case "L" in "Liebe" here constitutes a relevant exception. In fact there is only one other place where George capitalized "Liebe": in a letter to his friend, the Dutch poet Albert Verwey (1865–1937), dated 5 December 1895, where he translates Verwey's *Van de liefde die vriendschap heet* as "Von der freundschaft die Liebe heist." It is rather telling that George reversed the order of the nouns.[21] We may therefore conclude that (a) George is emphasizing the term here in a special way, and (b) the term is connected in a special way to "Freundschaft."

As to "übergeschlechtlich," at first glance the term seems to mean "sex-transcending" and has been interpreted as such; "übergeschlechtliche Liebe" then refers to a love that is more than sex/sexuality, higher than sex/sexuality, of a higher value than sex/sexuality, surpassing sex/sexuality.[22] Since George more than once introduced German "trans-lations" of current terms in order to alienate them, we may look at "übergeschlechtliche Liebe" as a "translation" for the notion of "platonic love." In the context of the early gay emancipation movement, "platonic love" is by no means synonymous with "asexuality" — the term is vehe-mently discussed and claimed as meaning male-male love.

According to George, Plato's *Symposium* was the text which, in Rudolf Kassner's translation, first directed his attention to Plato.[23] Here, a distinc-tion is made between the "earthly," vulgar love of Aphrodite Pandemos and the "heavenly" love of men, Aphrodite Uranios:

> Der Eros der irdischen Aphrodite ist nun wirklich irdisch und überall und gemein und zufällig. [. . .] Der Gemeine liebt wahllos Weiber und Knaben, und er liebt immer nur den Leib, er liebt vor allem die geistig noch unentwickelten Knaben, da er eben nur den Zweck will und die Art ihn nicht kümmert. [. . .] Die hohe Liebe stammt von der himmlischen Aphrodite, und die himmlische Aphrodite war aus dem Manne frei geschaffen und ist die Ältere und voll Maß und gebändigt. Und darum also streben sehnend alle Jünglinge und Männer, welche diese Liebe begeistert, zum männlichen, zum eigenen Geschlechte hin: sie lieben die stärkere Natur und den höheren Sinn.[24]

The term "Uranian" love was in wide circulation by the turn of the century and mostly understood to mean "Greek Love," homosexuality, pederasty.[25] In Germany homosexuals occasionally were called "Uranier."[26] Another related term was introduced by Benedict Friedlaender: "Eros Uranios," similarly borrowed from Plato and connected by Friedlaender to the term "physiologische Freundschaft."[27] There is also another connection with the contemporary gay emancipation discourse: in this discourse, a platonic interpretation was applied to the love David felt for Jonathan "surpassing the love of women" — with all possible connotations.[28]

If we therefore take "übergeschlechtliche Liebe" as a "translation" of platonic or Uranian love, the connotations are not as asexual as they may seem at first blush. Moreover, it should perhaps be noted that George obviously considered "die leidenschaftliche hingabe des dichters an seinen freund" as representative of this sex-transcending love; "hingeben" in German, however, means "to give oneself to somebody" and includes sexual connotations. It would be quite interesting to know, if, while writing the preface to his Shakespeare translation, George remembered the letter Ida Coblenz had written him in the summer of 1895, three months after her marriage to Leopold Auerbach. In her letter Coblenz asked why George had not warned her that the consummation of the marriage ("dieses Grässliche") would be unbearable for her (George/Coblenz 54).

George in his answer adopted the term "das grässliche."[29] His use of "hingeben" in his poetry is nevertheless positively charged with erotic/sexual connotations. See for instance "Der Spiegel" (The Mirror, 1: 269): "Ich habe endlich ganz in wildem lodern / Emporgeglüht und ganz mich hingegeben."[30] The poem's persona here is giving himself to "Das Glück" (fortune); but George's erotic language is very often encoded (and, at the same time, articulated) in metaphors and/or allegories. Who, for instance, is addressed in *Lobgesang* (Encomium, 1: 276–77), the last poem of the cycle *Gezeiten* (Tides) in *Der Siebente Ring* (directly followed by the cycle *Maximin*)? The poem begins:

> Du bist mein herr! wenn du auf meinem weg,
> Viel-wechselnder gestalt doch gleich erkennbar
> Und schön, erscheinst beug ich vor dir den nacken.

No doubt: this is about "hingabe," but to whom is the persona giving himself? Perhaps it is indeed "Eros."[31] But even if this "herr" is Eros, Mister Love Himself: what the poem is about is a series of *incarnations* of Eros to whom the persona (the poet?) bows and submits, and by whom the persona even enjoys being beaten ("Und jede fiber zuckt von deinem schlag") and being treated badly ("Auch wenn du kommst mit deiner schar von tieren / Die mit den scharfen klauen mäler brennen / Mit ihren hauern wunden reissen, seufzer / Erpressend und unnennbares gestöhn."). It is essential to keep this in mind when talking about George's "übergeschlechtliche Liebe." And, of course, at this point Shakespeare's love is by no means more "intellectual" than George's. See for instance sonnet LVII, which starts:

> Being your slave what should I do but tend
> Upon the hours and times of your desire?

In George's translation:

> Ich bin dein sklave der nur auf die stunden
> Und zeiten deiner lust zu harren weiss. (2: 179)

There are some further points to consider if we take Shakespeare's sonnets into account.[32] Perhaps we should read "übergeschlechtlich" also in light of the "master-mistress" in sonnet XX (translated by George as "Herr-Herrin meiner minne"; see below), but most of all with regard to the famous sonnet CXLIV:

> Two loves I have of comfort and despair,
> Which like two spirits do suggest me still,
> The better angel is a man right fair:
> The worser spirit a woman coloured ill.

The poem "Two Loves" by Alfred Douglas, which contains the even more famous line concerning "The love that dare not speak its name," refers to this sonnet (explicitly by taking the first four lines as a motto).[33] It is noteworthy, however, that in Douglas's poem the love "that dare not speak its name" is the "dark" one of the two, called "Shame" by "true Love."[34] In Shakespeare's sonnet, according with Plato's vision, the manly love is the "fair" one (in George's translation: "ein mann hell fein," 2: 222). Contrasting "übergeschlechtliche Liebe" with "geschlechtliche liebe," George sees the representation of the latter in the Dark Lady ("ein weib von düstrem glanz").

As Jens Rieckman points out in the last chapter of his study on Hugo von Hofmannsthal and Stefan George, entitled "Übergeschlechtliche Liebe," we may assume that George knew of Oscar Wilde's famous speech at the court in London in April 1895, answering the question concerning "The love that dare not speak its name":

> "The love that dare not speak its name" in this century is such a great affection of an elder for a younger man as there was between David and Jonathan, such as Plato made the very basis of his philosophy, and such as you find in the sonnets of Michelangelo and Shakespeare. It is that deep spiritual affection that is as pure as it is perfect.[35]

It is indeed likely that George's short preface hints at this answer, translating Wilde's "perfect," "spiritual affection" — also called "intellectual" by Wilde — as "übergeschlechtliche Liebe."[36] Moreover, George alludes here to Wilde by referring to some "menschen und dichter" who have "[sich] unverhohlen ausgesprochen," concerning Shakespeare and the problem of the sonnets.[37]

And, of course, there *is* something "intellectual" and "spiritual" in the concept of love in Shakespeare's sonnets. A central subject is the immortality of the beloved/friend, to be realized in sonnets I–XVII by physical procreation, but further on by "spiritual" procreation by means of poetry. In fact, the shift to the latter begins in the last line of XVII: "You should live twice in it, and in my rhyme"; "it" here refers to a child/son to be begotten by the beloved, who "spiritually" is "THE ONLIE BEGETTER OF THESE INSVING SONNETS," the mysterious "Mr. W. H." to whom the sonnets were dedicated in their first printing. George's translation, "So lebst du zwier: in ihm und meinem lied" (2: 159) echoes in lines of his own poetry like "mein gram / Spricht nur mit mir und diesem armen lied" (1: 313, addressing a boy, presumably "Ugolino," that is Hugo Zernik). George's version of this "spiritual" concept of love is explicitly shown in *Der Stern des Bundes:*[38]

> Die einen lehren: irdisch da — dort ewig . .
> Und der: ich bin die notdurft du die fülle.
> Hier künde sich: wie ist ein irdisches ewig
> Und eines notdurft bei dem andern fülle.
> Sich selbst nicht wissend blüht und welkt das Schöne
> Der geist der bleibt reisst an sich was vergänglich
> Er denkt er mehrt und er erhält das Schöne
> Mit allgewalt macht er es unvergänglich.
> Ein leib der schön ist wirkt in meinem blut
> Geist der ich bin umfängt ihn mit entzücken:
> So wird er neu im werk von geist und blut
> So wird er mein und dauernd ein entzücken. (1: 380)

That is to say: the "spiritual" persona/poet, lacking beauty, embraces Beauty ("das Schöne"), which lacks self-consciousness and permanence, takes possession of it and gives duration/immortality to it "im werk." But it is also conspicuous that there is an effect/reaction in the poet's *blood* and that even the result is one of "geist *und blut*" (my emphasis).[39] Here, something like the spiritualization of sexuality — or perhaps the sexualization of spirituality — seems to be at work.

This poem contains at least two striking allusions to Hölderlin. The first is in the neuter "das Schöne" — which is reminiscent of the famous Hölderlin-poem often cited by gay anthologists, "Sokrates und Alkibiades." A second allusion is in the phrase "der geist der bleibt," repeated in "dauernd" in the last line which hints at the famous last line of Hölderlin's "Andenken" (Remembrance): "Was bleibet aber, stiften die Dichter."[40] The preface to the Shakespeare translations also contains an allusion to Hölderlin: the "weltschaffende kraft" of sex-transcending love echoes a quotation from Hölderlin in one of George's poems, the third in George's cycle "Hyperion" in *Das Neue Reich*. There we read in capital letters: "LIEBE / GEBAR DIE WELT · LIEBE GEBIERT SIE NEU" (1: 406), words that in Hölderlin's novel originally read: "Die Liebe gebahr die Welt, die Freundschaft wird sie wieder gebähren."[41] So here once more George relates friendship, love, and "spiritual," sex-transcending procreation/rebirth.

There is yet another possibility for re-translating "weltschaffende kraft der übergeschlechtlichen Liebe." The most openly homosexual member of George's circle was Alfred Schuler, who co-founded the Munich section of Hirschfeld's "Wissenschaftlich-humanitäres Komitee" in 1902.[42] His expressionist poetry mingles "spirituality" with intense sexual connotations. Some of his poems, containing the central concept of "Cosmogonischer

Eros," he read and handed over to George as early as 1897 and 1899.[43] A preliminary conclusion then may be: "übergeschlechtliche Liebe" does not imply that there is no sex or sexual connotation, but that there is something more.[44] "Transcending sex" does not mean ignoring sex altogether; it assigns, rather, socio-cultural meaning to (homo)sexuality.

Another possible interpretation may be "transcending the medicalization of love by sexologists."[45] In this interpretation "übergeschlechtlich" may mark the shift from the discourse of sexuality to the discourse of the cultural impact of male-male love, well known as the alternative early gay emancipation discourse, familiar primarily in Adolf Brand and his "Gemeinschaft der Eigenen" which included authors like Elisar von Kupffer (1872–1942) and Peter Hamecher and fitted perfectly into this branch of the early gay emancipation discourse.[46]

But there are at least two further interpretations of "übergeschlechtlich" with a very different impact, and similarly related to Plato, Shakespeare, and the emerging gay emancipation movement. One of them is "transcending sex/gender," along with transcending contemporary gender definitions and social norms concerning these definitions. "Übergeschlechtliche Liebe," in the first place, can be read as love transcending the limitations of social gender norms; that is to say: it does not matter whether the beloved is a woman or a man/boy. If this is what George wanted to say, he is once more remarkably close to Adolf Brand, who in a 1906 polemic passionately defended "die Liebe, die Heilige und Hochgeweihte, die *keinen Unterschied des Geschlechts* und keine Grenzen kennt."[47]

But there is more: arguing that "an author has no sexe," R. M. Meyer presumably did not mean that poets do not have sexual intercourse, but that, in his opinion, they transcend biological sex and the limitations of gender. But if George is supposed to have no biological sex, does this mean that he is something like Hirschfeld's "sexuelle Zwischenstufe"? The option of Teiresias, a comparison offered by Ernst Morwitz (144), was equally subjected to medicalization at the turn of the century; therefore this does not seem a plausible option for George. Nevertheless, in addition to the model of male-male erotic relationships that George called "liebe," a concept of a human condition, of transcending biological sex and/or gender can be discerned in George's poetry, starting with Algabal, who sees himself in the looking-glass as "beinah einer schwester angesicht" (1: 52).[48]

Along with re-translating George's "übergeschlechtliche Liebe" as "platonic/Uranian love" and placing it thus within the gay emancipation discourse, "übergeschlechtlich" in the sense of "sex/gender-transcending" can be paralleled to the German term "Urning/urnisch" which until the 1920s was used as a synonym for "homosexual."[49] This term, also derived from Plato's "Uranian" love, was coined by Karl Heinrich Ulrichs (1825–1895) in the 1860s.[50] According to Ulrichs's definition, "Urning" refers to a male with a female soul, longing for sexual intercourse with a man.

This sex/gender-transcending "Zwischenstufen"-model of the "third sex," adopted and medicalized by Hirschfeld, refers to a human condition, not to a human relationship, and of course not to a concept of love, because "loving a man" here is a symptom of the "urnisch"/homosexual condition and thus involves having a female soul and being feminine or even effeminate. George — like Brand, Kupffer, Hamecher and many others (even from the so-called Hirschfeld camp) — desperately rejected the image of the feminine/effeminate homosexual and would never have allowed himself to be identified with it.[51] At least, that is what it looks like at first glance.

Looking at Shakespeare's sonnets from this point of view, what comes to mind is not the famous "Two loves I have . . ." (sonnet CXLIV), but sonnet XX, which addresses the beloved friend as "master-mistress," translated by George as:

> Ein frauenantlitz das Natur selbsthändig
> Gemalt — hast du · Herr-Herrin meiner minne (2: 160)

But while this man ("a man in hue") with "a woman's face" was first "created" as a woman (George translated: "als frau gedacht"), nature also gave him "one thing to my purpose nothing," translated by George with unexpected candor as: "ein ding [. . .] — nicht für meine zwecke." That is why the poet asks for his friend's "love," while his "love's use" he may give to women.

In addition to the fact that the ranking of "love" between men and "love's use" for procreative purposes brings us back to the familiar sex-transcending concept of love, three observations may be added here: (1) obviously the beloved man/boy with "a woman's face" is the beloved, not the lover; (2) the woman-faced beloved is nevertheless "master-mistress"; and (3) there is a remarkable shift from "a woman's face" to the manliness of the beloved. This very shift can also be found in George's own poetry, especially after the "Eintritt des Engels" and — above all — after the "Maximin-Erlebnis."[52] See for instance in *Der Stern des Bundes:*

> Ist dies der knabe längster sage
> Der seither kam mit schmeichler-augen
> Mit rosig weichen mädchengliedern
> Mit üppigen binden im gelock?
> Sein leib ward schlank und straff. Er greift,
> Er lockt nicht mehr, ist ohne schmuck.
> Von mut und lust des kampfes leuchtet
> Sein blick . . sein kuss ist kurz und brennend.
> Hat er besämt aus heiligem schoosse
> Drängt er in mühe und gefahr. (1: 378)

There is a similar shift in George's *Lobgesang.* The addressee — "mein herr" — is deprived of "waffe" and "fittich," that is to say: Eros/Amor, deprived of bow, arrow, and wings, became a "real" man. But the shift here is also one of reception by the poet/persona:

> Der früher nur den Sänftiger dich *hiess*
> Ge*dachte* nicht dass deine rosige ferse
> Dein schlanker finger so zermalmen könne. (1: 276, my emphasis)

So Eros along with the beloved became "a man"; Eros is experienced and even literally received as a man. Both the lover and the beloved then are shifting in their gender roles. And so it is Maximin (or the experience of/with Maximin) who liberated George from "der qual der zweiheit" by "verschmelzung fleischgeworden" (also a rather ambiguous term!) and represents "doppel-schöne" (1: 350), culminating in metaphoric pornography:

> Ich bin der Eine und bin Beide
> Ich bin der zeuger bin der schooss
> Ich bin der degen und die scheide
> Ich bin das opfer bin der stoss (1: 359)

In Claus Victor Bock's *Wort-Konkordanz* we find only one combination "über" + "geschlecht"; it is from George's *Vorrede zu Maximin* (Prologue to Maximin 1: 522–28), the only prose text included by Bock: it is Maximin's destiny to be "nach oben entrückt [. . .] und unvergänglichen namens *über allen geschlechtern* zu thronen"[53] — transcending sex/gender.

In fact it is not Maximin himself who is "transcending" sex and gender: George refers to *youth* as "gipfel und vollendung," the culmination of life, and especially to the "Lenzbegnadeten," those who die at the "zenith of life" like Maximin. George introduces himself in this text by saying that he had transcended "die mittägliche Höhe" (the zenith) of his life. And so "über allen geschlechtern thronen[d]" may even refer to a third possibility to re-translate "übergeschlechliche Liebe": love transcending generations. In a way, this brings us back to the concept of "Uranian love," "the love that dare not speak its name," the "great affection of an elder for a younger man," such as — according to Wilde — we find in Shakespeare's sonnets.

George's concept of love is indeed strongly determined by this "great affection of an elder for a younger man" and — as we read in *Lobgesang* ("viel-wechselnder gestalt") — is not reserved for *one* young man alone. Moreover, there are at least two allusions to generation-transcending love in George's *Vorrede zu Maximin:* those, who "in dunkler welle versanken um nach oben entrückt zu werden und unvergänglichen namens über allen geschlechtern zu thronen" (1: 525) are Antinous and his kind (the loving one here is Hadrian). The second allusion is to Ganymede and Zeus: "so lass mich einmal auf deine höhe treten und dann von deinem adler schnell entrissen werden!"(1: 527).[54] Antinous/Hadrian, as well as Ganymede/Zeus, are well-known icons of the early gay emancipation movement — alluding to transgenerational relationship.[55]

According to Ernst Morwitz, two poems in George's *Teppich des Lebens*— "Der Jünger" (The Disciple) and "Schmerzbrüder" (Brothers in Sorrow, 1: 196–97) — represent "Formen der menschlichen Verbindung und Bindung [. . .] die der Dichter [. . .] vor dem Maximinerlebnis als die engsten, die überhaupt möglich seien, erachtet" (185). Both poems involve transgenerational relationships. "Der Jünger" describes the dedicated but foolish love of the younger man for his master/teacher. "Schmerzbrüder" (a neologism of George's) refers to those "brothers" who love their younger "geleit" passionately, desperately, but hopelessly, because "euer geleit hat vom morgen geträumt."

Maximilian Kronberger could have been supposed to fit the model of the "Jünger" (George being the Socratic master); but if we look closely at Maximin's diary, he did not. He could have been the "gespiel," George being the "Schmerzbruder," a role he presumably did not like at all. But in a way Maximin also was not. Dying young, he provided George with the model of an everlasting relationship, called "übergeschlechtliche Liebe," that is to say with love transcending sex, gender, and generations. By deifying Maximin, eroticism/sexuality are transfigured onto a higher plane laden with religious meanings. Now the attitude of the "Schmerzbruder" is changed into the passionate submission ("hingabe") as written in "Lobgesang":

> Du rührest an — ein duftiger taumeltrank
> Befängt den sinn der deinen odem spürt
> Und jede fiber zuckt von deinem schlag.
> [. . .]
> Auch wenn du kommst mit deiner schar von tieren
> Die mit den scharfen klauen mälern brennen
> Mit ihren hauern wunden reissen · seufzer
> Erpressend und unnennbares gestöhn,
> Wie dir entströmt geruch von weicher frucht
> Und saftigem grün: so ihnen dunst der wildnis.
> Nicht widert staub und feuchte die sie führen ·
> Kein ding das webt in deinem kreis ist schnöd.
> Du reinigst die befleckung · heilst die risse
> Und wischst die tränen durch dein süsses wehn.
> In fahr und fron · wenn wir nur überdauern ·
> Hat jeder tag mit einem sieg sein ende —
> So auch dein dienst: erneute huldigung
> Vergessnes lächeln ins gestirnte blau. (1: 276–77)

The version of love described in these lines is a painful, submissive one. However, it is important to note that it is the poet/persona himself who is submissive and zealous. But in the end he will overcome everything, ending up victorious.[56]

"Sieg des Sommers" (Triumph of Summer) was the title George gave to his first cycle about a male-male relationship (however carefully masked) in *Das Jahr der Seele* (1: 131–35).[57] "Sieg des Eros" is the title Hans Dietrich Hellbach gave to the final chapter of his dissertation *Die Freundesliebe in der deutschen Literatur.* According to Hellbach, George conquered the scruples August von Platen had about living his love for men and overcame the medicalization of his love by the doctors. Victories like these are gained day by day.

My interpretation of this line begins by linking the "erneute Huldigung" to the "vielwechselnde gestalt" in the second line of the poem. Then "erneute hulding" refers to just another representation of the addressee ("mein herr"), for instance the reunion with "Ugolino." One of the poems George wrote about this boy (who was twelve when they first met and fourteen by the time of their reunion in October 1905) is the well-known "Mein kind kam heim" (1: 312), which has been translated many times, among others by Stephen Spender ("My boy came home").[58] Hugo Zernik — "Ugolino" — came to Berlin with his parents from Argentina.[59] Only eighteen months after Maximin's death, and more than a year before the *Maximin-Gedenkbuch* was edited in December 1906, George wrote three poems in reaction to the October 1906 reunion with Zernik, and published them in *Der Siebente Ring* in 1907 with the neutral title "Lieder I · II · III" (1: 311–13). "Mein kind kam heim" is the second of these. The first, "Fern von des hafens lärm" (Far from the noisy wharves), connects feelings of expectation (hope, passion, love) with ecstatic images of nature ("Lautere brandung rauscht · / Zischend zur dünenhöh / Schlägt sie den dunklen schaum . . . / Wie nun die liebe stöhnt"). The third poem, "Liebe nennt den nicht wert der je vermisst" (Love does not value one who feels a lack), which completes the Ugolino-cycle, addresses the boy as "Teurer" and "Süsser" (so here at least it is absolutely clear that a male is being addressed), but at the same time expresses resignation/sacrifice: "damit kein hauch / Dein holdes spielen stört bleib ich verbannt / Und doppelt duldend scheid ich und mein gram / Spricht nur mit mir und diesem armen lied." Here — as in "Sieh mein kind ich gehe" (See, my child, I leave; 1: 95), another poem of renunciation from *Sänge eines fahrenden Spielmanns* — much more is going on than doing without the possibility of a physical act. And it is by no means pure chance that the last line — "Spricht nur mit mir und diesem armen lied" — is echoed in George's translation of Shakespeare: "So lebst du zwier: in ihm und meinem lied" (2: 159).

Particularly noteworthy in this context is that it is George himself whose love, desire, and sacrifice/resignation is verbalized here. The biographical background is supported by documentary evidence. Edith Landmann in her *Gespräche mit Stefan George* noted down a conversation about Ugolino. George, with a deep, heartfelt sigh of remembrance and looking very serious, sad, and longing, said: "Er war ein Süsser . . ."[60] Longing for Ugolino and resigning may be seen *together* as representing the submission to Eros and the final victory.

At virtually the same time (January 1929), in another conversation with Edith Landmann, George stated about eroticism: "Erotisch, wissen Sie, das ist ein Wort wenn ich das sage, dann heisst das nicht nur Hingebung, sondern auch Selbstbewahrung." Eroticism, then, implies both giving oneself away and keeping oneself, as a way of guarding against "nicht mehr loskommen" (*Zeittafel* 361). Here, George explicitly refers to the fate of Oscar Wilde, and so we are back to the love "that dare not speak its name," to the spiritual, intellectual affection "of an elder for a younger man," to the love of those called the "third sex" desperately in search of a new gender role, and therefore looking back to Plato, David and Jonathan, Michelangelo, and Shakespeare. George's concept of love encompasses all of this. He was not the first to try to give a new name to this love, calling it "übergeschlechtliche Liebe." According to Wilde, this love is "the very basis" of philosophy and poetry; according to George this love has "weltschaffende kraft," it is able to create a new world, outlined to a certain degree in George's poetry. This world, as I hope to have shown, is not a world without sex, without gender trouble, without longing and responsibility. It is a world of permanent reflection and questioning. Perhaps the answer is like the complaint of the dreams and desires, looking into a lake's mirror in George's poem "Der Spiegel": "wir sind es nicht! wir sind es nicht!" ("those are not we — we are not those!" 1: 269). But perhaps they are — to a certain degree.

Notes

[1] See my study *Von der Liebe die Freundschaft heisst: Zur Homoerotik im Werk Stefan Georges* (Berlin: rosa Winkel, 1987).

[2] See *Von der Liebe die Freundschaft heisst*, 19–24; more recently see Jens Rieckmann, *Hugo von Hofmannsthal und Stefan George: Signifikanz einer 'Episode' aus der Jahrhundertwende* (Tübingen/Basle: Francke, 1997), especially the final chapter "Übergeschlechtliche Liebe," 158–92.

[3] Peter Hamecher, "Der männliche Eros im Werke Stefan Georges," *Jahrbuch für sexuelle Zwischenstufen* 14.1 (1914): 10–23. On the early German gay emancipation movement and especially on the use of literature for strategic aims, see Marita Keilson-Lauritz, *Die Geschichte der eigenen Geschichte. Literatur und Literaturkritik in den Anfängen der Schwulenbewegung am Beispiel des Jahrbuchs für sexuelle Zwischenstufen und der Zeitschrift Der Eigene* (Berlin: rosa Winkel, 1997).

[4] Hellbach published his thesis in 1931 under the name "Hans Dietrich" in order to spare his parents any potential embarrassment. See my preface in Hans Dietrich

[Hans Dietrich Hellbach], *Die Freundesliebe in der deutschen Literatur.* Nachdruck der Ausgabe Leipzig 1931 (Berlin: rosa Winkel, 1996).

[5] On Hubert Fichte, see Marita Keilson-Lauritz, " 'Durch die goldene Harfe gelispelt': Zur George-Rezeption bei Hubert Fichte," *Forum Homosexualität und Literatur* 2 (1987): 27–51. Similarly, George figures in some of Detlev Meyer's poems ("Brief des Mundart-Dichters K. an Friedrich Gundolf"; "Obdach für Jussuf"; see Detlev Meyer, *Heute Nacht im Dschungel. 50 Gedichte* (Berlin: Oberbaumverlag, 1981), 48, 62; there is also a very George-minded, boy-loving German professor in Meyer's charming little novel *Im Dampfbad greift nach mir ein Engel* (Düsseldorf: Eremiten-Presse, 1985). See some of Thomas Böhme's poems and his novel *Die Einübung der Innenspur* (Berlin/Weimar: Aufbau-Verlag, 1990).

[6] The letter cited earlier in *Von der Liebe die Freundschaft heisst* and in "Übergeschlechtliche Liebe als Passion" is part of the collection in the Stefan George Archiv at the Württembergische Staatsbibliothek, Stuttgart; I am grateful to the late Professor Wilhelm Hoffmann for allowing me to see the unpublished letter in the 1980s, and to Dr. Ute Oelmann for verifying the quotation.

[7] Bondi first heard about the poet in a lecture given by Richard M. Meyer early in 1897 (*Zeittafel* 66–67).

[8] See Erich Mühsam, *Die Homosexualität: Eine Streitschrift.* Mit einer Einführung von Walter Fähnders und einem Dossier (Munich: belleville, 1996), 52. For the term "Urning" see below; for the dilemma of "outing" by claiming a living author as a homosexual see Marita Keilson-Lauritz, "Muss das Private öffentlich werden? Erkenntniswunsch und Diskretion als Dilemma der literarischen Homostudien," in Gerhard Härle, Maria Kalveram, Wolfgang Popp, eds. *Erkenntniswunsch und Diskretion. Erotik in biographischer Literatur. 3. Siegener Kolloquium Homosexualität und Literatur* (Berlin: rosa Winkel, 1992), 69–82.

[9] See Borchardt's review of *Der Siebente Ring* in *Hesperus: Ein Jahrbuch* (Leipzig: Insel, 1909), 49–82; Rudolf Borchardt, "Intermezzo," *Süddeutsche Monatshefte* 7.12 (1910): 694–716. On Borchardt's *Aufzeichnung Stefan George betreffend,* posthumously published in 1998 by Ernst Osterkamp, see my review in *Forum Homosexualität und Literatur* 32 (1998): 116–25.

[10] Paragraph 175 of the German Penal Code punished with a prison term the so-called "vice against nature" (i.e., homosexual acts); the early German homosexual emancipation movement had been fighting for abolition/revision of this paragraph since 1897, when Magnus Hirschfeld founded the "Wissenschaftlich-humanitäres Komitee."

[11] For George's own view of conjugal sexuality, see his letter to Ida Auerbach-Coblenz, dated 18 July 1895. In reaction to her letter from Berlin, dated 16 July 1895, concerning the sexual intercourse with her husband Leopold Auerbach, whom she married in April 1895, he adopts her term "dieses Gräßliche": "Haben Sie denn in meinem gesicht nie geraten dass es (mit ganz kleinen äusserlichen verän-derungen) das nämliche 'grässliche' war was meines lebens ganze qual gewesen ist und möglicherweise sein wird." Georg Peter Landmann and Elisabeth Höpker-Herberg, eds. *Stefan George–Ida Coblenz: Briefwechsel* (Stuttgart: Klett-Cotta, 1983), 54–55.

[12] Hamecher, see note 3, 13–14.

[13] See Hamecher's review of the first volume of Hirschfeld's *Jahrbuch für sexuelle Zwischenstufen* published in the review section "Liebe" of *Der Eigene*. Neue Folge 1 [later counted as vol. 3], 6/7 (1899): 236–38.

[14] Hamecher's article "Die Tragik des Andersseins," published in *Die Aktion* in 1914, never appeared in *Der Eigene;* however, Hamecher published an article of the same title in Brand's short-lived journal *Freundschaft und Freiheit* in 1919 (no. 6, 41–42). Rieckmann, 183n59, is misled by vague information in Harry Oosterhuis, ed. *Homosexuality and Male Bonding in Pre-Nazi Germany: The Youth Movement, the Gay Movement, and Male Bonding Before Hitler's Rise: Original Transcripts from Der Eigene. Journal of Homosexuality* 22.1/2 (1991).

[15] But perhaps we have to reconsider this since Robert E. Norton shows us a young George as an anarchist along with his growing awareness "about the nature and direction of his physical desire." *Secret Germany: Stefan George and His Circle.* (Ithaca/London: Cornell UP, 2002), 33–34.

[16] See Keilson-Lauritz, *Von der Liebe die Freundschaft heisst,* 60–61; as I point out there the term "Freundschaft" is not found in George's poetry, except once in the early poem "Prinz Indra."

[17] See Eve Kosofsky Sedgwick, *Epistemology of the Closet* (Berkeley/Los Angeles: U of California P, 1990), 49–54; see also Keilson-Lauritz, *Die Geschichte der eigenen Geschichte,* 269–360; Keilson-Lauritz, "The Making of the Gay Canon," in Gebhard Rusch, ed. *Empirical Approaches to Literature: Proceedings of the Fourth Conference of the International Society for the Empirical Study of Literature, IGEL, Budapest 1994.* LUMIS Publications Special Issue Vol. 6 (Siegen, 1995), 206–13.

[18] Claus Victor Bock, *Wort-Konkordanz zur Dichtung Stefan Georges* (Amsterdam: Castrum Peregrini Presse, 1964); only "sehen," "kommen" and "tag" are more frequent.

[19] According to my own count, since the translations are not included in Bock's *Wort-Konkordanz.*

[20] Except where a whole word or phrase is capitalized or where the word is at the beginning of a line. In the translation of the sonnets, "Liebe" is sometimes capitalized.

[21] See Keilson-Lauritz, *Von der Liebe die Freundschaft heisst* 61.

[22] See for example Manfred Herzer, "Asexuality as an Element in the Selfrepresentation of the Right Wing of the German Gay Movement before 1933," in *Among Men, Among Women: Sociological and Historical Recognition of Homosocial Arrangements.* [Papers of the] *Gay Studies and Women's Studies, University of Amsterdam Conference 22–26 June* (Amsterdam 1983), 315–21. Elisar von Kuppfer is, as far as I can see, the only member of the early German gay emancipation movement to adopt the term "übergeschlechtliche Liebe" — without referring to George.

[23] See *Zeittafel* 228–29 (Oktober 1911); Herbert Steiner reported that there was an edition of Kassner's translation of Plato's *Phaidros* in George's small private library at Munich (*Zeittafel* 210). The second edition of Kassner's translation of the *Symposium* was published by Eugen Diederichs in 1906.

[24] *Platons Gastmahl. Phaidros/Phaidon.* Ins Deutsche übertragen von Rudolf Kassner. (Jena: Eugen Diedrichs, 1914), 15–16.

[25] See Timothy d'Arch-Smith, *Love in Earnest. Some Notes on the Lives and Writings of English 'Uranian' Poets from 1889 to 1930* (London: Routledge & Kegan Paul, 1970). See also: Edward Perry Warren (pseud. Arthur Lyon Raile): *A Defense of Uranian Love* (London: Cayme Press, 1928–1930). For a comparison of Warren and George, see Rieckmann 183–84; for a strange reference to Warren (called Peter Warren there), see Claus Victor Bock, Manuel R. Goldschmidt, eds. *Wolfgang Frommel / Renata von Scheliha: Briefwechsel 1930–1967* (Amsterdam: Castrum Peregrini Presse, 2002), 54, 60, 125–26; the biography, "nicht ermittelt" (126), sent to Frommel by Scheliha, obviously is Osbert Burdett, E. H. Goddard, *Edward Perry Warren: The Biography of a Connoisseur* (London: Christophers, 1941).

[26] See e.g. Kurt Kliemcke, "Uranier aller Länder vereinigt euch," *Die Gemeinschaft der Eigenen. Bund für Freundschaft und Freiheit. Ein Nachrichten- und Werbeblatt* 5.7 (1920): 7, 41–42.

[27] See Benedict Friedlaender, *Die Renaissance des Eros Uranios. Die physiologische Freundschaft, ein normaler Grundtrieb des Menschen und eine Frage der männlichen Gesellungsfreiheit. In naturwissenschaftlicher, naturrechtlicher, culturgeschichtlicher und sittenkritischer Beleuchtung* (Schmargendorf-Berlin: "Renaissance" [Otto Lehmann], 1904). According to Friedlaender, attraction between human beings is based on chemotaxis. So when Friedlaender chooses the neologistic term "physiologische Freundschaft" for a highly erotic (but not necessarily sexual) attraction and relationship, we have to realize that "physiological" here just means something happening in a test tube, looked at through a microscope.

[28] See for example the tale of Ludmilla von Rehren entitled "Sonderlicher, denn Frauenliebe ist . . .," *Der Eigene* 4.4 (1903): 233–36. For more references see Wolfgang Popp, "Der biblische David als schwule Ikone der Kunst und Literatur." Gerhard Härle, Wolfgang Popp, Annette Runte, eds. *Ikonen des Begehrens: Bildsprachen der männlichen und weiblichen Homosexualität in Literatur und Kunst* (Stuttgart: M & P [Metzler], 1997), 67–100.

[29] Landmann and Höpker-Herberg, eds. *Stefan George–Ida Coblenz: Briefwechsel* (Stuttgart: Klett-Cotta, 1983), 54–55.

[30] See also "sich geben": "Wo das heilige bild entschleiert / Nur sich gibt dem einen gast" (1: 49); "Es waren tage gross wo ihr euch gabet" (1: 147); "Für viele zier gibst du dich keinem ganz" (1: 325); "Und warst zugleich der freund der frühlingswelle / Der schlank und blank sich ihrem schmeicheln gab" (1: 350); "sein gesetz ist dass sich der erfüllt / Der sich und allen sich zum opfer gibt" (1: 353); "Ich selbst ein freier gab mich frei zu eigen" (1: 374); "Seitdem ich ganz mich gab hab ich mich ganz" (1: 375); "Im kern ergriffen an ein all euch gabet" (1: 384); "Willig gaben wir uns der verwandelnden kraft hin" (1: 524–25). See also "preisgeben": 1: 192, 234 ("Und gab mich preis den söldnern der Cäsaren!").

[31] See Ernst Morwitz, *Kommentar zu dem Werk Stefan Georges* (Düsseldorf/Munich: Helmut Küpper vormals Georg Bondi, 1969), 265–66.

[32] An examination of the concept of love as it relates to George's Shakespeare translations exceeds the scope of this study, but clearly merits further consideration.

[33] I don't think it impossible that George himself refers to this line in the last line of the poem *Das Wort:* "Kein ding sei wo das wort gebricht" (1: 466). That is to say: there is no love without a name.

[34] Quoted in *The Penguin Book of Homosexual Verse.* Ed. Stephan Coote (Harmondsworth: Penguin, 1983), 262–64.

[35] Rieckmann 171. There was a publication in German concerning the Wilde trials, which Alfred Schuler in November 1899 sent to George: O. Sero, *Der Fall Wilde und das Problem der Homosexualität: Ein Prozess und ein Interview* (Leipzig: Max Spohr, 1896); see Keilson-Lauritz, "Alfred Schulers Utopie des offenen Lebens," *Forum Homosexualität und Literatur* 30 (1997): 37–58, 50n. Perhaps it was this book that Leopold Andrian mentioned to Hofmannsthal in March 1896: "ich [habe] eben die ganze so wunderbare Verteidigung Wilde's und seine freche Keckheit in einem hier [in Berlin] gekauften Buch bewundert" (quoted in Rieckmann 175).

[36] Both "spiritual" and "intellectual" are translated as "geistig" in Sero, *Der Fall Wilde,* 54.

[37] See Wilde's *The Portrait of Mr. W. H.,* published in German as *Das Sonetten-Problem des Herrn W. H.* (Leipzig: Max Spohr, 1902). The reference may also be to Shelley: Albert Verwey, George's Dutch fellow poet, noted down some lines of Shelley, reading: "If any should be curious to discover / Whether to you I am a friend or lover, / Let them read Shakespeare's Sonnets, taking thence / A whetstone for their dull intelligence. —" "Fragments connected with Epipsychidon"; see Albert Verwey, *Dichtspel. Oorspronkelijke en vertaalde gedichten* (Amsterdam: De Arbeiderspers, 1983), 100, 642.

[38] Of course there is a lot of Plato in this poem; George draws heavily from *Symposium,* especially from Socrates citing Diotima.

[39] See also: "Wir sind nicht wahr, solang wir uns bewahren, / Und nur der Blitz, von dem wir ganz entbrennen, / Läßt Blut im Geist und Geist im Blut sich kennen." Stefan Zweig, *Verwirrung der Gefühle: Drei Novellen* (Leipzig: Insel, 1927), 7. Meanwhile Zweig's novella "Verwirrung der Gefühle" (153–74) has also become part of the gay canon; see Keilson-Lauritz, *Die Geschichte der eigenen Geschichte,* 197–98.

[40] Friedrich Hölderlin, *Sämtliche Werke* [Grosse Stuttgarter Ausgabe] (Stuttgart: Kohlhammer, 1951 and 1957), 2: 189.

[41] Hölderlin 3: 64.

[42] See Marita Keilson-Lauritz, Friedemann Pfäfflin, eds., *100 Jahre Schwulenbewegung an der Isar I: Die Sitzungsberichte des Wissenschaftlich-Humanitären Komitees München 1902–1908* (Möckmühl: Verlag Martin Kick, 2002), 12n39.

[43] See Keilson-Lauritz, "Stefan George, Alfred Schuler und die 'Kosmische Runde.' Zum Widmungsgedicht 'A. S.' im 'Jahr der Seele,'" *Castrum Peregrini* 168/9 (1985): 24–41; see also Keilson-Lauritz, "Alfred Schulers Utopie" for Schuler's special way of using the term "urnisch" (55–56).

[44] Otto Weininger in his famous/infamous *Geschlecht und Charakter,* published in 1903, stated: "W[eib] ist nichts als Sexualität, M[ann] ist sexuell und noch *etwas darüber.*" *Geschlecht und Charakter: Eine prinzipielle Untersuchung.* 4th unrev. ed. (Vienna/Leipzig: Wilhelm Braumüller, 1905), 113; my emphasis). This might be another source of George's "Übergeschlechtlichkeit."

[45] See Marita Keilson-Lauritz, "Übergeschlechtliche Liebe als Passion. Zur Codierung mannmännlicher Intimität im Spätwerk Georges," in Wolfgang Braungart, Ute Oelmann, Bernhard Böschenstein, eds. *Stefan George: Werk und Wirkung seit dem 'Siebenten Ring'* (Tübingen: Max Niemeyer Verlag, 2001), 142–56.

[46] See Carola Groppe, *Die Macht der Bildung: Das deutsche Bürgertum und der George-Kreis 1890–1933* (Cologne/Weimar/Vienna: Böhlau, 1997), 422, and my explanation in Keilson-Lauritz, "Übergeschlechtliche Liebe als Passion," 142–43n 3.

[47] Adolf Brand, "Afterkultur und Homosexualität." *Die Gemeinschaft der Eigenen. Flugschrift für Sittenverbesserung und Lebenskunst* 6 (1906): 3, 29–33, 30; my emphasis.

[48] See Keilson-Lauritz, *Von der Freundschaft die Liebe heisst* 132–35.

[49] See Magnus Hirschfeld, *Der urnische Mensch* (Leipzig: Spohr, 1903); also entitled "Ursache und Wesen des Uranismus," *Jahrbuch für sexuelle Zwischenstufen* 5 (1903): 1–193.

[50] See Hubert Kennedy, *Ulrichs: The Life and Works of Karl Heinrich Ulrichs. Pioneer of the Modern Gay Movement* (Boston: Alyson Publications, 1988).

[51] There are few suggestions of feminine traits in characterizations of George by his contemporaries. However, a striking one is reported as an anecdote: on seeing Melchior Lechter's painting *Die Weihe am Mystischen Quell* — which features George as a priest in an art nouveau gown — one of Wolfskehl's young daughters exclaimed: "Tante Meister!"

[52] On the shift from the female "himmelsbild" in George's early poem "Ich wandelte auf öden düstren bahnen" (I walked along bleak dark paths) to the male angel in the "Vorspiel," see Keilson-Lauritz, *Von der Liebe die Freundschaft heisst* 39–40.

[53] Bock, *Wort-Konkordanz* 216 (see: GESCHLECHT); 1: 525; my emphasis.

[54] The image reminds us of Fidus, and indeed there is an illustration from his hand: Ganymede standing on a rock, reaching out for the eagle, printed in *Der Eigene* 4.4 (1903): 265.

[55] See Keilson-Lauritz, "Ganymed trifft Tadzio. Überlegungen zu einem 'Kanon der Gestalten,'" in *Ikonen des Begehrens* 23–39.

[56] For a more detailed interpretation, see Keilson-Lauritz, "Übergeschlechtliche Liebe als Passion."

[57] See Keilson-Lauritz, *Von der Liebe die Freundschaft heisst* 36–39.

[58] See *Stefan George in fremden Sprachen: Übersetzungen seiner Gedichte in die europäischen Sprachen ausser den slawischen.* Ed. Georg Peter Landmann (Düsseldorf/Munich: Küpper, vormals Georg Bondi, 1973), 448–55l; here 449–50.

[59] For biographical details, see Morwitz 321; Lothar Helbing (= Wolfgang Frommel), Claus Victor Bock, Karlhans Kluncker, eds. *Stefan George: Dokumente seiner Wirkung. Aus dem Friedrich Gundolf Archiv der Universität London* (Amsterdam: Castrum Peregrini Presse, 1974), 286–91; for the dates of the reunion and George's reaction, see also *Zeittafel* 171.

[60] Edith Landmann, *Gespräche mit Stefan George* (Düsseldorf/Munich: Küpper, vormals Georg Bondi, 1963), 199, quoted in Helbing/Bock, *Dokumente* 291.

Works Cited

Bock, Claus Victor. *Wort-Konkordanz zur Dichtung Stefan Georges.* Amsterdam: Castrum Peregrini, 1964.

Bock, Claus Victor, and Manuel R. Goldschmidt, eds. *Wolfgang Frommel / Renata von Scheliha: Briefwechsel 1930–1967.* Amsterdam: Castrum Peregrini, 2002.

Böhme, Thomas. *Die Einübung der Innenspur.* Berlin/Weimar: Aufbau-Verlag, 1990.

Borchardt, Rudolf. Review of *Der Siebente Ring. Hesperus: Ein Jahrbuch.* Leipzig: Insel, 1909. 49–82.

———. "Intermezzo." *Süddeutsche Monatshefte* 7.12 (1910): 694–716.

Brand, Adolf. "Afterkultur und Homosexualität." *Die Gemeinschaft der Eigenen. Flugschrift für Sittenverbesserung und Lebenskunst* 6 (1906): 29–33.

Braungart, Wolfgang, Ute Oelmann and Bernhard Böschenstein, eds. *Stefan George: Werk und Wirkung seit dem 'Siebenten Ring.'* Tübingen: Niemeyer, 2001.

Burdett, D., and E. H. Goddard, *Edward Perry Warren: The Biography of a Connoisseur.* London: Christophers, 1941.

Coote, Stephan, ed. *The Penguin Book of Homosexual Verse.* Harmondsworth: Penguin, 1983.

d'Arch-Smith, Timothy. *Love in Earnest: Some Notes on the Lives and Writings of English 'Uranian' Poets from 1889 to 1930.* London: Routledge & Kegan Paul, 1970.

Friedlaender, Benedict. *Die Renaissance des Eros Uranios. Die physiologische Freundschaft, ein normaler Grundtrieb des Menschen und eine Frage der männlichen Gesellungsfreiheit. In naturwissenschaftlicher, naturrechtlicher, culturgeschichtlicher und sittenkritischer Beleuchtung.* Schmargendorf-Berlin: "Renaissance" [Otto Lehmann], 1904.

Groppe, Carola. *Die Macht der Bildung: Das deutsche Bürgertum und der George-Kreis 1890–1933.* Cologne/Weimar/Vienna: Böhlau, 1997.

Hamecher, Peter. "Der männliche Eros im Werke Stefan Georges." *Jahrbuch für sexuelle Zwischenstufen* 14.1 (1914): 10–23.

Hamecher, Peter. Review of *Jahrbuch für sexuelle Zwischenstufen* by Magnus Hirschfeld. *Der Eigene.* Neue Folge 1 [later counted as vol. 3], 6/7 (1899): 236–38.

———. "Die Tragik des Andersseins." *Freundschaft und Freiheit* 6 (1919): 41–42.

Helbing, Lothar (= Wolfgang Frommel), Claus Victor Bock, Karlhans Kluncker, eds. *Stefan George: Dokumente seiner Wirkung. Aus dem Friedrich Gundolf Archiv der Universität London.* Amsterdam: Castrum Peregrini Presse, 1974.

Hellbach, Hans-Dietrich. *Die Freundesliebe in der deutschen Literatur.* [1931] Berlin: rosa Winkel, 1996.

Herzer, Manfred. "Asexuality as an Element in the Selfrepresentation of the Right Wing of the German Gay Movement before 1933." *Among Men, Among Women: Sociological and Historical Recognition of Homosocial Arrangements.* [Papers of the] *Gay Studies and Women's Studies, University of Amsterdam Conference 22–26 June.* Amsterdam 1983. 315–21.

Hirschfeld, Magnus. *Der urnische Mensch.* Leipzig: Spohr, 1903; also entitled "Ursache und Wesen des Uranismus." *Jahrbuch für sexuelle Zwischenstufen* 5 (1903): 1–193.

Hölderlin, Friedrich. *Sämtliche Werke* [Grosse Stuttgarter Ausgabe]. Stuttgart: Kohlhammer, 1951 and 1957.

Keilson-Lauritz, Marita. "Stefan George, Alfred Schuler und die 'kosmische Runde': Zum Widmungsgedicht 'A. S.' im 'Jahr der Seele.'" *Castrum Peregrini* 168–69 (1985): 24–41.

———. *Von der Liebe die Freundschaft heißt: Zur Homoerotik im Werk Stefan Georges.* Berlin: Verlag rosa Winkel, 1987.

———. "'Durch die goldene Harfe gelispelt': Zur George-Rezeption bei Hubert Fichte," *Forum Homosexualität und Literatur* 2 (1987): 27–51.

———. "Muss das Private öffentlich werden? Erkenntniswunsch und Diskretion als Dilemma der literarischen Homostudien." Gerhard Härle, Maria Kalveram, Wolfgang Popp, eds. *Erkenntniswunsch und Diskretion. Erotik in biographischer Literatur. 3. Siegener Kolloquium Homosexualität und Literatur.* Berlin: rosa Winkel, 1992: 69–82.

———. "The Making of the Gay Canon." Gebhard Rusch, ed. *Empirical Approaches to Literature: Proceedings of the Fourth conference of the International Society for the Empirical Study of Literature, IGEL, Budapest 1994.* LUMIS Publications Special Issue Vol. 6. Siegen, 1995. 206–13.

———. *Die Geschichte der eigenen Geschichte. Literatur und Literaturkritik in den Anfängen der Schwulenbewegung am Beispiel des Jahrbuchs für sexuelle Zwischenstufen und der Zeitschrift Der Eigene.* Berlin: rosa Winkel, 1997.

———. "Alfred Schulers Utopie des offenen Lebens." *Forum Homosexualität und Literatur* 30 (1997): 37–58.

———. "Ganymed trifft Tadzio. Überlegungen zu einem 'Kanon der Gestalten.'" Popp, et al, eds. *Ikonen des Begehrens* 23–39.

Keilson-Lauritz, Marita. Review of *Aufzeichnung Stefan George betreffend* by Rudolf Borchardt. *Forum Homosexualität und Literatur* 32 (1998): 116–25.

———. "Übergeschlechtliche Liebe als Passion. Zur Codierung mann-männlicher Intimität im Spätwerk Stefan Georges." *Stefan George: Werk und Wirkung seit dem "Siebenten Ring."* Eds. Wolfgang Braungart et al. Tübingen: Niemeyer, 2001. 142–55.

Keilson-Lauritz, Marita, and Friedemann Pfäfflin, eds. *100 Jahre Schwulenbewegung an der Isar I: Die Sitzungsberichte des Wissenschaftlich-Humanitären Komitees München 1902–1908.* Möckmühl: Verlag Martin Kick, 2002.

Kennedy, Hubert. *Ulrichs: The Life and Works of Karl Heinrich Ulrichs. Pioneer of the Modern Gay Movement.* Boston: Alyson Publications, 1988.

Kliemcke, Kurt. "Uranier aller Länder vereinigt euch." *Die Gemeinschaft der Eigenen. Bund für Freundschaft und Freiheit. Ein Nachrichten- und Werbeblatt* 5.7 (1920): 41–42.

Landmann, Edith. *Gespräche mit Stefan George.* Düsseldorf/Munich: Küpper, vormals Georg Bondi, 1963.

Landmann, Georg Peter, ed. *Stefan George in fremden Sprachen: Übersetzungen seiner Gedichte in die europäischen Sprachen ausser den slawischen.* Düsseldorf/Munich: Küpper, vormals Georg Bondi, 1973.

Landmann, Georg Peter, and Elisabeth Höpker-Herberg, ed. *Stefan George–Ida Coblenz: Briefwechsel* (Stuttgart: Klett-Cotta, 1983), 54–55.

Meyer, Detlev. *Heute Nacht im Dschungel. 50 Gedichte.* Berlin: Oberbaumverlag, 1981.

———. *Im Dampfbad greift nach mir ein Engel.* Düsseldorf: Eremiten-Presse, 1985.

Morwitz, Ernst. *Kommentar zu dem Werk Stefan Georges.* Düsseldorf/Munich: Helmut Küpper vormals Georg Bondi, 1969.

Mühsam, Erich. *Die Homosexualität: Eine Streitschrift.* Mit einer Einführung von Walter Fähnders und einem Dossier. Munich: belleville, 1996.

Norton, Robert E. *Secret Germany: Stefan George and His Circle.* Ithaca/London: Cornell UP, 2002.

Oosterhuis, Harry, ed. *Homosexuality and Male Bonding in Pre-Nazi Germany: The Youth Movement, the Gay Movement, and Male Bonding Before Hitler's Rise: Original Transcripts from Der Eigene. Journal of Homosexuality* 22.1/2 (1991).

Platons Gastmahl. Phaidros/Phaidon. Ins Deutsche übertragen von Rudolf Kassner. Jena: Eugen Diederichs, 1914.

Popp, Wolfgang. "Der biblische David als schwule Ikone der Kunst und Literatur." Gerhard Härle, Wolfgang Popp, Annette Runte, eds. *Ikonen des Begehrens: Bildsprachen der männlichen und weiblichen Homosexualität in Literatur und Kunst.* Stuttgart: M & P [Metzler], 1997. 67–100.

Rehren, Ludmilla von. "Sonderlicher, denn Frauenliebe ist. . . ." *Der Eigene* 4.4 (1903): 233–36.

Rieckmann, Jens. *Hugo von Hofmannsthal und Stefan George: Signifikanz einer "Episode" aus der Jahrhundertwende.* Tübingen/Basle: Francke, 1997.

Sedgwick, Eve Kosofsky. *Epistemology of the Closet.* Berkeley/Los Angeles: U of California P, 1990.

Seekamp, H[ans].-J[ürgen]., R[aymond]. C[urtis]. Ockenden and M[arita]. Keilson[-Lauritz]. *Stefan George / Leben und Werk. Eine Zeittafel.* Amsterdam: Castrum Peregrini, 1972.

Sero, O. *Der Fall Wilde und das Problem der Homosexualität: Ein Prozess und ein Interview.* Leipzig: Max Spohr, 1896.

Verwey, Albert. *Dichtspel. Oorspronkelijke en vertaalde gedichten.* Amsterdam: De Arbeiderspers, 1983.

Warren, Edward Perry. Pseud. Arthur Lyon Raile. *A Defense of Uranian Love.* London: Cayme Press, 1928–1930.

Weininger, Otto. *Geschlecht und Charakter: Eine prinzipielle Untersuchung.* 4th unrev. ed. Vienna/Leipzig: Wilhelm Braumüller, 1905.

Wilde, Oscar. *Das Sonetten-Problem des Herrn W. H.* Trans. Johannes Gaulke. Leipzig: Max Spohr, 1902.

Zweig, Stefan. *Verwirrung der Gefühle: Drei Novellen.* Leipzig: Insel, 1927.

Works Cited

Adorno, Theodor W. *Gesammelte Schriften*. 20 Volumes. Ed. Rolf Tiedemann. Frankfurt a.M.: Suhrkamp, 1973–86.

———. *Kompositionen 1*. Ed. Heinz-Klaus Metzger and Rainer Riehn. Munich: edition text+kritik, 1980.

Aler, Jan. *Symbol und Verkündung: Studien um Stefan George*. Düsseldorf/ Munich: Helmut Küpper vormals Georg Bondi, 1976.

Arbogast, Hubert. *Versuche über George*. Stuttgart: Akademie für gesprochenes Wort, 1998.

Aschheim, Steven E. *The Nietzsche Legacy in Germany 1890–1990*. Berkeley/ Los Angeles/London: U of California P, 1992.

Aurnhammer, Achim. " 'Der Preusse.' Zum Zeitbezug der 'Zeitgedichte' Stefan Georges im Spiegel der Bismarck-Lyrik." *Stefan George: Werk und Wirkung seit dem 'Siebenten Ring.'* Eds. Wolfgang Braungart, Ute Oelmann, Bernhard Böschenstein. Tübingen: Niemeyer, 2001. 173–96.

Avé-Lallemant, Ursula, ed. *Die vier deutschen Schulen der Graphologie: Klages — Pophal — Heiß — Pulver*. Munich/Basel: Ernst Reinhardt, 1989.

Bartels, Adolf. *Geschichte der deutschen Literatur*. Berlin: Westermann, 1943.

Baudelaire, Charles. *Œuvres complètes*. Ed. Claude Pichois, Bibliothèque de la Pléiade. Paris: Gallimard, 1975.

Bauer, Helmut and Elisabeth Tworek, eds. *Schwabing: Kunst und Leben um 1900: Essays*. Munich: Münchner Stadtmuseum; Tucson, Arizona: Nazraeli P, 1998.

Beck, Claus Victor. *Wort-Konkordanz zur Dichtung Stefan Georges*. Amsterdam: Castrum Peregrini, 1964.

Bell-Villada, Gene H. *Art for Art's Sake and Literary Life: How Politics and Markets Helped Shape the Ideology and Culture of Aestheticism 1790–1990*. Stages, vol. 5. Lincoln: U of Nebraska P, 1996.

Benjamin, Walter. *Ursprung des deutschen Trauerspiels*. Frankfurt a.M.: Suhrkamp, 1978.

Benn, Gottfried. "Probleme der Lyrik." *Gesammelte Werke in vier Bänden*. Vol. 1. Wiesbaden: Limes, 1958–61.

Bergel, Lienhard. *Voraussetzungen und Anfänge der Beziehungen zwischen Stefan George und Hugo von Hofmannsthal*. New York: New York UP, 1949.

Bernstein, Michael André. *Foregone Conclusions: Against Apocalyptic History*. Berkeley/Los Angeles/London: U of California P, 1994.

232 ♦ Works Cited

Bock, Claus Victor. *Wort-Konkordanz zur Dichtung Stefan Georges.* Amsterdam: Castrum Peregrini Presse, 1964.

Bock, Claus Victor, and Manuel R. Goldschmidt, eds. *Wolfgang Frommel / Renata von Scheliha: Briefwechsel 1930–1967.* Amsterdam: Castrum Peregrini Presse, 2002.

Boehringer, Robert. *Mein Bild von Stefan George.* 1st ed. Munich/Düsseldorf: Helmut Küpper vormals Georg Bondi, 1951.

———. *Mein Bild von Stefan George.* 2 vols. Düsseldorf: Helmut Küpper vormals Bondi, 1967.

Böhme, Thomas. *Die Einübung der Innenspur.* Berlin/Weimar: Aufbau-Verlag, 1990.

Borchardt, Rudolf. Review of *Der Siebente Ring. Hesperus: Ein Jahrbuch.* Leipzig: Insel, 1909. 49–82.

———. "Intermezzo." *Süddeutsche Monatshefte* 7.12 (1910): 694–716.

Brand, Adolf. "Afterkultur und Homosexualität." *Die Gemeinschaft der Eigenen. Flugschrift für Sittenverbesserung und Lebenskunst* 6 (1906): 29–33.

Braungart, Wolfgang, *Ästhetischer Katholizismus: Stefan Georges Rituale der Literatur.* Tübingen: Niemeyer, 1997.

Braungart, Wolfgang, Ute Oelmann, and Bernhard Böschenstein, eds. *Stefan George. Werk und Wirkung seit dem 'Siebenten Ring.'* Tübingen: Niemeyer, 2001.

Breuer, Stefan. *Ästhetischer Fundamentalismus: Stefan George und der deutsche Antimodernismus.* Darmstadt: Wissenschaftliche Buchgesellschaft, 1995.

———. "Ferntiefrausch: Ludwig Klages und Arnold Böcklin." *Hestia: Jahrbuch der Klages-Gesellschaft* 19 (1998/1999): 91–103.

———. "Zur Religion Stefan Georges." *Stefan George: Werk und Wirkung seit dem 'Siebenten Ring.'* Eds. Wolfgang Braungart et al. Tübingen: Niemeyer, 2001.

Breysig, Kurt. "Begegnungen mit Stefan George." *Castrum Peregrini* 42 (1960): 9–32.

Briefwechsel zwischen George und Hofmannsthal. Ed. Robert Boehringer. Berlin: Bondi, 1938.

Briefwechsel zwischen George und Hofmannsthal. 2nd edition. Ed. Robert Boehringer. Munich/Düsseldorf: Helmut Küpper vormals Georg Bondi, 1953.

Brodsky, Patricia Pollock. "Colored Glass and Mirrors: Life with Rilke." *A Companion to the Works of Rainer Maria Rilke.* Eds. Erika A. and Michael M. Metzger. Rochester, NY: Camden House, 2001. 19–39.

Burleigh, Michael. *The Third Reich: A New History.* London: Macmillan, 2000.

Campbell, Joseph. *The Hero of a Thousand Faces.* New York: Meridian, 1956.

Cassagne, Albert. *La Théorie de l'art pour l'art en France chez les derniers romantiques et les premiers réalistes.* 1906. Collection dix-neuvième. Reprint. Seyssel: Champvallon, 1997.

Chevalier, Jean, and Alain Gheerbrant, eds. *The Penguin Dictionary of Symbols.* Trans. John Buchanan-Brown. London: Penguin, 1996.

Coote, Stephan, ed. *The Penguin Book of Homosexual Verse.* Harmondsworth: Penguin, 1983.

Cross, Charlotte M., and Russell A. Berman, eds. *Schoenberg and Words: The Modernist Years.* New York/London: Garland, 2000.

Curtius, Ernst Robert. *Kritische Essays zur europäischen Literatur.* Bern: Francke, 1950.

d'Arch-Smith, Timothy. *Love in Earnest: Some Notes on the Lives and Writings of English 'Uranian' Poets from 1889 to 1930.* London: Routledge & Kegan Paul, 1970.

David, Claude. *Stefan George: son oeuvre poétique.* Lyon/Paris: IAC, 1952.

———. "Stefan George und die Gesellschaft." *Deutschland-Frankreich. Ludwigsburger Beiträge zum Problem der deutsch-französischen Beziehungen* 2 (1957): 117–36.

———. "Stefan George und der Jugendstil." *Formkräfte der deutschen Dichtung vom Barock bis zur Gegenwart. Vorträge gehalten im Deutschen Haus, Paris 1961/1962.* Göttingen: Vandenhoeck & Ruprecht, 1963.

———. *Stefan George. Sein dichterisches Werk.* Trans. Alexa Remmen and Karl Thimer. Munich: Hanser, 1967; originally *Stefan George. Son Œuvre poétique* (Lyon/Paris: IAC, 1952).

———. "Stefan George und der Jugendstil." *Jugendstil.* Wege der Forschung vol. 110. Ed. Jost Hermand. Darmstadt: Wissenschaftliche Buchgesellschaft, 1971. 382–401.

Derleth, Ludwig. *Das Werk.* Ed. Christine Derleth and Dominik Jost. 6 vols. Darmstadt: Verlag Hinder + Deelmann, 1971–72.

Durzak, Manfred. *Der junge Stefan George.* Munich: Wilhelm Fink Verlag, 1968.

———. *Zwischen Symbolismus und Expressionismus: Stefan George.* Stuttgart: Kohlhammer, 1974.

Egan, Rose Frances. *The Genesis of the Theory of "Art for Art's Sake" in Germany and in England.* Smith College Studies in Modern Languages vol. 2, no. 4. Northampton, MA: n.p., 1921.

Egyptien, Jürgen. "'Kosmische Elemente' in der Dichtung Stefan Georges." *Hestia: Jahrbuch der Klages-Gesellschaft* 19 (1998/1999): 11–27.

———. "Georges Haltung zum Judentum." *"Verkannte brüder"? Stefan George und das deutsch-jüdische Bürgertum zwischen Jahrhundertwende und Emigration.* Eds. Gert Mattenklott, Michael Philipp, Julius H. Schoeps. Hildesheim: Olms, 2001. 15–27.

Faletti, Heidi E. *Die Jahreszeiten des Fin de siècle: Eine Studie über Stefan Georges Das Jahr der Seele.* Bern/Munich: Francke, 1983.

Frank, Lore, and Sabine Ribbeck, eds. *Stefan George-Bibliographie 1976–1997. Mit Nachträgen bis 1976.* Tübingen: Niemeyer, 2000.

Friedemann, Heinrich. *Plato. Seine Gestalt.* Berlin: Verlag der Blätter für die Kunst, 1914.

Friedlaender, Benedict. *Die Renaissance des Eros Uranios. Die physiologische Freundschaft, ein normaler Grundtrieb des Menschen und eine Frage der männlichen Gesellungsfreiheit. In naturwissenschaftlicher, naturrechtlicher, culturgeschichtlicher und sittenkritischer Beleuchtung.* Schmargendorf-Berlin: "Renaissance" [Otto Lehmann], 1904.

Frommel, Wolfgang. *Templer und Rosenkreuz, ein Traktat zur Christologie Stefan Georges.* Amsterdam: Castrum Peregrini, 1991.

Furness, Raymond. *Zarathustra's Children: A Study of a Lost Generation of German Writers.* Rochester, NY: Camden House, 2000.

George, Stefan. *Werke. Ausgabe in zwei Bänden.* Ed. Robert Boehringer and Georg Peter Landmann. Stuttgart: Klett-Cotta, 1984.

———. *Sämtliche Werke in 18 Bänden.* Eds. Georg Peter Landmann and Ute Oelmann. Stuttgart: Klett-Cotta, 1982–.

———, ed. *Blätter für die Kunst. Eine Auslese aus den Jahren 1892–1898.* Berlin: Bondi, 1899.

———, ed. *Blätter für die Kunst. Eine Auslese aus den Jahren 1898–1904.* Berlin: Bondi, 1904.

———, ed. *Blätter für die Kunst. Eine Auslese aus den Jahren 1904–1909.* Berlin: Bondi, 1909.

———. *Einleitungen und Merksprüche der Blätter für die Kunst.* Ed. G. P. Landmann. Düsseldorf: Küpper vormals Bondi, 1964.

George, Stefan, and Carl August Klein, eds. *Blätter für die Kunst.* 12 vols. 1892–1919; reprint, 6 vols. Düsseldorf: Helmut Küpper vormals Bondi, 1968.

George, Stefan, and Karl Wolfskehl, eds. *Deutsche Dichtung: Jean Paul, ein Stundenbuch für seine Verehrer.* Berlin: Blätter für die Kunst, 1900.

———, eds. *Deutsche Dichtung: Goethe.* Berlin: Blätter für die Kunst, 1901.

———, eds. *Deutsche Dichtung: Das Jahrhundert Goethes.* Berlin: Blätter für die Kunst, 1902.

George, Stefan, and Friedrich Gundolf. *Briefwechsel.* Eds. Robert Boehringer and Georg Peter Landmann. Munich/Düsseldorf: Helmut Küpper vormals Georg Bondi, 1962.

George, Stefan, and Ida Coblenz. *Briefwechsel.* Eds. Georg Peter Landmann and Elisabeth Höpker-Herberg. Stuttgart: Klett-Cotta, 1983.

George, Stefan, and Friedrich Wolters. *Briefwechsel 1904–1930.* Ed. Michael Philipp. Amsterdam: Castrum Peregrini Presse, 1998.

Gerhard, Melitta. "Schillers Zielbild der ästhetischen Erziehung und das Wirken Stefan Georges." *Monatshefte für deutschen Unterricht* 51 (1959): 275–82.

Gibbons, Reginald, ed. *The Poet's Work.* Chicago: U of Chicago P, 1979.

Glen, Jerry. "Hofmannsthal, George, and Nietzsche: 'Herrn Stefan George / einem, der vorübergeht.'" *Modern Language Notes* 97 (1982): 770–73.

Glöckner, Ernst. *Begegnung mit Stefan George: Auszüge aus Briefen und Tagebüchern, 1913–1934.* Ed. Friedrich Adam. Heidelberg: Lothar Stiehm, 1972.

Goddard, E. H. *Edward Perry Warren. The Biography of a Connoisseur.* London: Christophers, 1941.

Goethe, Johann Wolfgang von. *Goethes Werke.* Ed. Erich Trunz. 11th ed. Hamburger Ausgabe. Munich: Beck, 1978.

Groppe, Carola. *Die Macht der Bildung: Das deutsche Bürgertum und der George-Kreis 1890–1933.* Cologne, Weimar, Vienna: Böhlau, 1997.

Gugenberger, Eduard. *Hitlers Visionäre: Die okkulten Wegbereiter des Dritten Reichs.* Vienna: Ueberreuter, 2001.

Gundolf, Friedrich, ed. and trans. *Shakespeare in deutscher Sprache.* 10 vols. Berlin: Bondi, 1908–18.

———. "Gefolgschaft und Jüngertum." *Blätter für die Kunst,* 8. Folge (1908/09). 106–12.

———. *Shakespeare und der deutsche Geist.* Berlin: Bondi, 1911.

———. *George.* Berlin: Bondi, 1920.

———. *Cäsar. Geschichte seines Ruhms.* Berlin: Bondi, 1924.

———. *George.* 3rd expanded ed. Berlin: Bondi, 1930.

Gundolf, Friedrich, and Friedrich Wolters, eds. *Jahrbuch für die geistige Bewegung.* 3 vols. Berlin: Blätter für die Kunst, 1910–12.

Haarmann, Hermann, et. al. *"Das war ein Vorspiel nur . . ." Bücherverbrennung Deutschland 1933: Voraussetzungen und Folgen.* Ausstellung der Akademie der Künste vom 8. Mai bis 3. Juli 1983. Berlin/Vienna: Medusa, 1983.

Hamecher, Peter. "Der männliche Eros im Werke Stefan Georges." *Jahrbuch für sexuelle Zwischenstufen* 14.1 (1914): 10–23.

———. Review of *Jahrbuch für sexuelle Zwischenstufen* by Magnus Hirschfeld. *Der Eigene.* Neue Folge 1 [later counted as vol. 3], 6/7 (1899): 236–38.

———. "Die Tragik des Andersseins." *Freundschaft und Freiheit* 6 (1919): 41–42.

Heidegger, Martin. "Dichten und Denken. Zu Stefan Georges Gedicht 'Das Wort.'" *Unterwegs zur Sprache.* Pfullingen: Neske, 1959. 275–82.

Heintz, Günter. *Stefan George: Studien zu seiner künstlerischen Wirkung.* Stuttgart: Hauswedell, 1986.

Helbing, Lothar (= Wolfgang Frommel), Claus Victor Bock, Karlhans Kluncker, eds. *Stefan George. Dokumente seiner Wirkung: Aus dem Friedrich Gundolf Archiv der Universität London.* Amsterdam: Castrum Peregrini Presse, 1974.

Hellbach, Hans-Dietrich. *Die Freundesliebe in der deutschen Literatur.* [1931] Berlin: rosa Winkel, 1996.

Hermand, Jost. *Der alte Traum vom neuen Reich: Völkische Utopien und Nationalsozialismus.* Frankfurt a.M.: Athenäum, 1988.

Hermand, Jost. *Die deutschen Dichterbünde: Von den Meistersingern bis zum PEN-Club.* Cologne: Böhlau, 1998.

Herzer, Manfred. "Asexuality as an Element in the Selfrepresentation of the Right Wing of the German Gay Movement before 1933." *Among Men, Among Women. Sociological and Historical Recognition of Homosocial Arrangements.* [Papers of the] *Gay Studies and Women's Studies, University of Amsterdam Conference 22–26 June.* Amsterdam 1983. 315–21.

Hillebrand, Bruno. *Nietzsche: Wie ihn die Dichter sahen.* Göttingen: Vandenhoeck & Ruprecht, 2000.

Hirschfeld, Magnus. *Der urnische Mensch.* Leipzig: Spohr, 1903; also entitled "Ursache und Wesen des Uranismus." *Jahrbuch für sexuelle Zwischenstufen* 5 (1903): 1–193.

Hofmannsthal, Hugo von. "Gedichte von Stefan George" in *Reden und Aufsätze.* Vol. 1, *1891–1913.* Frankfurt a.M.: Fischer, 1979.

———. *Sämtliche Werke.* Vol. 31. Ed. Ellen Ritter. Frankfurt a.M.: S. Fischer, 1991.

Hofmannsthal, Hugo von, and Richard Beer-Hofmann. *Briefwechsel.* Ed. Eugene Weber. Frankfurt a.M.: Fischer, 1972.

Hofmannsthal, Hugo von, und Rudolf Pannwitz. *Briefwechsel 1907–1926.* Ed. Gerhard Schuster. Frankfurt a.M.: S. Fischer, 1994.

Hölderlin, Friedrich. *Sämtliche Werke.* Grosse Stuttgarter Ausgabe. Stuttgart: Kohlhammer, 1951 and 1957.

———. *Sämtliche Werke und Briefe 1.* Ed. Michael Knaupp. Munich: Carl Hanser, 1992.

Horstmann, Ulrich. *Ästhetizismus und Dekadenz: Zum Paradigmakonflikt in der englischen Literaturtheorie des späten 19. Jahrhunderts.* Munich: Fink, 1983.

Jäger, Dietrich. " 'Kein ding sei wo das wort gebricht': Der Umgang mit Sprache und phänomenaler Welt in Stefan Georges *Jahr der Seele* und im Denken von Ludwig Klages." *Hestia: Jahrbuch der Klages-Gesellschaft* 19 (1998/1999): 28–52.

Jaime-Liebig, Edward. *Stefan George und die Weltliteratur.* Ulm: Aegis, 1949.

Jenkins, Iredell. "Art for Art's Sake." *Dictionary of the History of Ideas.* 5 vols. New York: Scribner's, 1973.

Jens, Inge, ed. *Thomas Mann und Ernst Bertram: Briefe aus den Jahren 1910–1955.* Pfullingen: Neske, 1960.

Jost, Dominik. *Ludwig Derleth: Gestalt und Leistung.* Stuttgart: W. Kohlhammer, 1965.

———. *Blick auf Stefan George: Ein Essay.* Bern: Lang, 1991.

Kahler, Erich von. "Stefan George. Größe und Tragik." *Untergang und Übergang. Essays.* Munich: dtv, 1970. 228–49.

Kaiser, Gerhard. *Die deutsche Lyrik von Heine bis zur Gegenwart.* Frankfurt a.M.: Suhrkamp, 1991.

Kantorowicz, Ernst. *Kaiser Friedrich der Zweite.* Berlin: Bondi, 1927.

Keilson-Lauritz, Marita. "Stefan George: L(udwig) K(lages): Marginalien zum Widmungsgedicht im 'Jahr der Seele.'" *Castrum Peregrini* 121–22 (1976): 48–63.

———. "Stefan George, Alfred Schuler und die 'kosmische Runde': Zum Widmungsgedicht 'A. S.' im 'Jahr der Seele.'" *Castrum Peregrini* 168–69 (1985): 24–41.

———. *Von der Liebe die Freundschaft heißt: Zur Homoerotik im Werk Stefan Georges.* Berlin: Verlag rosa Winkel, 1987.

———. "'Durch die goldene Harfe gelispelt': Zur George-Rezeption bei Hubert Fichte," *Forum Homosexualität und Literatur* 2 (1987): 27–51.

———. "Muss das Private öffentlich werden? Erkenntniswunsch und Diskretion als Dilemma der literarischen Homostudien." Gerhard Härle, Maria Kalveram, Wolfgang Popp, eds. *Erkenntniswunsch und Diskretion: Erotik in biographischer Literatur. 3. Siegener Kolloquium Homosexualität und Literatur.* Berlin: rosa Winkel, 1992. 69–82.

———. "The Making of the Gay Canon." Gebhard Rusch, ed. *Empirical Approaches to Literature: Proceedings of the Fourth Conference of the International Society for the Empirical Study of Literature, IGEL, Budapest 1994.* LUMIS Publications Special Issue Vol. 6. Siegen, 1995. 206–13.

———. *Die Geschichte der eigenen Geschichte. Literatur und Literaturkritik in den Anfängen der Schwulenbewegung am Beispiel des Jahrbuchs für sexuelle Zwischenstufen und der Zeitschrift Der Eigene.* Berlin: rosa Winkel, 1997.

———. "Alfred Schulers Utopie des offenen Lebens." *Forum Homosexualität und Literatur* 30 (1997): 37–58.

———. "Ganymed trifft Tadzio. Überlegungen zu einem 'Kanon der Gestalten.'" Gerhard Härle, Wolfgang Popp, Annette Runte, eds. *Ikonen des Begehrens: Bildsprachen der männlichen und weiblichen Homosexualität in Literatur und Kunst.* Stuttgart: M & P [Metzler], 1997. 23–39.

———. Review of *Aufzeichnung Stefan George betreffend* by Rudolf Borchardt. *Forum Homosexualität und Literatur* 32 (1998): 116–25.

———. "Übergeschlechtliche Liebe als Passion. Zur Codierung mannesmännlicher Intimität im Spätwerk Stefan Georges." *Stefan George: Werk und Wirkung seit dem "Siebenten Ring."* Eds. Wolfgang Braungart et al. Tübingen: Niemeyer, 2001. 142–55.

Keilson-Lauritz, Marita, and Friedemann Pfäfflin, eds. *100 Jahre Schwulenbewegung an der Isar I: Die Sitzungsberichte des Wissenschaftlich-Humanitären Komitees München 1902–1908.* Möckmühl: Verlag Martin Kick, 2002.

Kennedy, Hubert. *Ulrichs: The Life and Works of Karl Heinrich Ulrichs. Pioneer of the Modern Gay Movement.* Boston: Alyson Publications, 1988.

Klages, Ludwig. *Stefan George.* Berlin: Georg Bondi, 1902.

———. *Prinzipien der Charakterologie.* Leipzig: Johannes Ambrosius Barth, 1910.

———. "Einführung des Herausgebers." *Alfred Schuler. Fragmente und Vorträge.* Ed. Ludwig Klages. Leipzig: Johann Ambrosius Barth, 1940.

Klages, Ludwig. *Rhythmen und Runen: Nachlaß herausgegeben von ihm selbst.* Leipzig: Johann Ambrosius Barth, 1944.

Klein, Carl August. "Über Stefan George, eine neue kunst." *Blätter für die Kunst,* 1. Folge, II. Band (December 1892): 47–50.

Klemperer, Klemens von. *German Incertitudes 1914–1945: The Stones and the Cathedral.* Westport, CT: Praeger, 2001.

Kliemcke, Kurt. "Uranier aller Länder vereinigt euch." *Die Gemeinschaft der Eigenen. Bund für Freundschaft und Freiheit. Ein Nachrichten- und Werbeblatt* 5.7 (1920): 41–42.

Kluncker, Karlhans. *"Das geheime Deutschland": Über Stefan George und seinen Kreis.* Bonn: Bouvier, 1985.

Klussmann, Paul-Gerhard. "Dante und Stefan George. Zur Wirkung der Divina Commedia in Georges Dichtung." *Stefan George Kolloquium.* Ed. Eckhard Heftrich et al. Cologne: Wienand, 1971.

Kohn, Hans. *The Mind of Germany.* London: Macmillan, 1961.

Kozljanič, Robert Josef. "Böcklin und die daimonische Dimension der Natur." *Hestia: Jahrbuch der Klages-Gesellschaft* 19 (1998/1999): 104–28.

Kraft, Werner. *Stefan George.* Munich: Text+Kritik, 1980.

Kristeva, Julia. *Revolution in Poetic Language.* Trans. Margaret Waller. New York: Columbia UP, 1984.

L'Ormeau, F. W. [Wolfgang Frommel]. *Die Christologie Stefan Georges.* Amsterdam: Castrum Peregrini, 1953.

Landfried, Klaus. *Stefan George — Politik des Unpolitischen.* Heidelberg: Lothar Stiehm, 1975.

Landmann, Edith. *Gespräche mit Stefan George.* Düsseldorf/Munich: Helmut Küpper vormals Georg Bondi, 1963.

Landmann, Georg Peter. *Vorträge über Stefan George.* Düsseldorf/Munich: Helmut Küpper vormals Georg Bondi, 1974.

———, ed. *Stefan George in fremden Sprachen: Übersetzungen seiner Gedichte in die europäischen Sprachen ausser den slawischen.* Düsseldorf/Munich: Küpper, vormals Georg Bondi, 1973.

———, ed. *Stefan George und sein Kreis.* 2nd ed. Hamburg: Hauswedell, 1976.

———, ed. *Der George-Kreis. Eine Auswahl aus seinen Schriften.* Stuttgart: Klett-Cotta, 1980.

Lechter, Melchior, and Stefan George. *Briefe. Kritische Ausgabe.* Ed. Günter Heinz. Stuttgart: Hauswedell, 1991.

Lessing, Theodor. *Einmal und nie wieder* [1935]. Gütersloh: Bertelsmann Sachbuchverlag, 1969.

Linke, Hansjürgen. *Das Kultische in der Dichtung Stefan Georges und seiner Schule.* 2 vols. Munich: Helmut Küpper vormals Georg Bondi, 1960.

Löwith, Karl. *Mein Leben in Deutschland vor und nach 1933.* Frankfurt a.M.: S. Fischer, 1989.

Lukács, Georg. *Die Zerstörung der Vernunft. Vol. 1 Irrationalismus zwischen den Revolutionen.* Darmstadt/Neuwied: Luchterhand,1983.

Mallarmé, Stéphane. *Oeuvres complètes.* Ed. Henri Mondor and G. Jean-Aubry. Paris, 1945.

Mann, Thomas. "Leiden und Größe Richard Wagners." *Leiden und Größe der Meister.* Frankfurt a.M.: S. Fischer, 1957. 216–75.

———. "Der Tod in Venedig." *Sämtliche Erzählungen.* Frankfurt a.M.: S. Fischer, 1963.

———. "Gladius Dei," *Die Erzählungen.* Frankfurt a.M.: S. Fischer, 1986. 215–35.

Marx, Olga, and Ernst Morwitz. *The Works of Stefan George.* 2nd rev. and enlarged ed. Chapel Hill: U of North Carolina P, 1974.

Matt, Peter von. "Der geliebte Doppelgänger. Die Struktur des Narzißmus bei Stefan George." *Das Schicksal der Phantasie, Studien zur deutschen Literatur.* Munich/Vienna: Carl Hanser, 1994. 257–76.

———. "Das Einhorn geht unter das Volk. Stefan George im Taschenbuch." *Die verdächtige Pracht: Über Dichter und Gedichte.* Munich: Hanser, 1998. 249–52.

———. "Zur Anthropologie des Gedichts und zum Ärgernis seiner Schönheit." *Die verdächtige Pracht: Über Dichter und Gedichte.* Munich: Hanser, 1998. 7–84.

Mattenklott, Gert. *Bilderdienst: Ästhetische Opposition bei Beardsley und George.* 2nd ed. Frankfurt a.M.: Syndikat, 1985.

Meesen, H. J. "Stefan Georges *Algabal* und die französische *décadence.*" *Monatshefte für deutschen Unterricht* 39 (1947): 304–21.

Mettler, Dieter. *Stefan Georges Publikationspolitik: Buchkonzeption und verlegerisches Engagement.* Munich/New York/London/Paris: Saur, 1979.

Metzger, Erika A., and Michael M. Metzger. *Stefan George.* New York: Twayne, 1972.

Metzger, Michael M. "Blätter für die Kunst." *Encyclopedia of German Literature.* Ed. Matthias Konzett. Chicago: Fitzroy Dearborn, 2000. 1: 117–18.

———. "Der Teppich des Lebens und die Lieder von Traum und Tod mit einem Vorspiel." *Encyclopedia of German Literature.* Ed. Matthias Konzett. Chicago: Fitzroy Dearborn, 2000. 1: 328–29.

———. "Stefan George 1868–1933." *Encyclopedia of German Literature.* Ed. Matthias Konzett. Chicago: Fitzroy Dearborn, 2000. 1: 326–27.

Metzger-Hirt, Erika. "Das Klopstockbild Stefan Georges und seines *Kreises,*" *PMLA* 79 (1964): 289–96.

Meyer, Detlev. *Heute Nacht im Dschungel. 50 Gedichte.* Berlin: Oberbaumverlag, 1981.

———. *Im Dampfbad greift nach mir ein Engel.* Düsseldorf: Eremiten-Presse, 1985.

Mohler, Armin. *Die konservative Revolution in Deutschland 1918–1932: Ein Handbuch*. Darmstadt: Wissenschaftliche Buchgesellschaft, 1972.

Mommsen, Momme. "'Ihr kennt eure Bibel nicht!' Bibel- und Horazanklänge in Stefan Georges Gedicht 'Der Krieg.'" In Mommsen, *Lebendige Überlieferung: George · Hölderlin · Goethe*. Bern: Lang, 1999. 1–27.

Morwitz, Ernst. *Kommentar zu dem Werk Stefan Georges*. Munich/Düsseldorf: Helmut Küpper vormals Georg Bondi, 1960.

———. *Kommentar zu den Prosa- Drama- und Jugend-Dichtungen Stefan Georges*. Düsseldorf/Munich: Helmut Küpper vormals Georg Bondi, 1962.

Mühsam, Erich. *Die Homosexualität: Eine Streitschrift*. Mit einer Einführung von Walter Fähnders und einem Dossier. Munich: belleville, 1996.

Müller, Baal. "Bildgeburten: George, Schuler und die 'Kosmische Runde.'" In Helmut Bauer and Elisabeth Tworek, eds. *Schwabing: Kunst und Leben um 1900: Essays*. Munich: Münchner Stadtmuseum; Tucson, Arizona: Nazraeli P, 1998. 41–45.

Nietzsche, Friedrich. *Werke in drei Bänden*. Ed. Karl Schlechta. Munich: Hanser, 1966.

Nijland-Verwey, Mea, ed. *Albert Verwey en Stefan George: De documenten van hun vriendschap*. Amsterdam: Polak & Van Gennep, 1965.

Norton, Robert E. *Secret Germany: Stefan George and His Circle*. Ithaca/London: Cornell UP, 2002.

Novalis [Hardenberg, Friedrich von]. *Die Christenheit oder Europa*. Novalis. *Schriften, Dritter Band*. Ed. Richard Samuel. Stuttgart: Kohlhammer, 1960. 497–524.

Oosterhuis, Harry, ed. *Homosexuality and Male Bonding in Pre-Nazi Germany: The Youth Movement, the Gay Movement, and Male Bonding Before Hitler's Rise: Original Transcripts from Der Eigene. Journal of Homosexuality* 22.1/2 (1991).

Oswald, Victor A. "The Historical Content of Stefan George's Algabal." *Germanic Review* 23 (1948): 193–205.

———. "Oscar Wilde, Stefan George, Heliogabalus." *Modern Language Quarterly* 10 (1949): 517–25.

Pannwitz, Rudolf. *Kultur, Kraft, Kunst: Charon-Briefe an Berthold Otto*. Leipzig: Charonverlag, K. G. Th. Scheffer, 1906.

———. *Wasser wird sich ballen: Gesammelte Gedichte*. Stuttgart: Ernst Klett Verlag, 1963.

———. "Was ich Nietzsche und George danke." *Castrum Peregrini* 189–190 (1989): 50–100.

Pascal, Blaise. *Pensées. Oeuvres complètes*. Ed. Louis Lafuma. Paris, 1963.

Pater, Walter. Conclusion to *The Renaissance* [1868]. Rpt. New York: Modern Library, n.d.

Petersen, Julius. *Die Sehnsucht nach dem Dritten Reich in deutscher Sage und Dichtung*. Stuttgart: Metzler, 1934.

Petrow, Michael. *Der Dichter als Führer? Zur Wirkung Stefan Georges im 'Dritten Reich.'* Marburg: Tectum, 1995.

Platons Gastmahl. Phaidros/Phaidon. Ins Deutsche übertragen von Rudolf Kassner. Jena: Eugen Diederichs, 1914.

Plumpe, Gerhard. *Alfred Schuler: Chaos und Neubeginn: Zur Funktion des Mythos in der Moderne.* Berlin: Agora Verlag, 1978.

———. "Alfred Schuler und die Kosmische Runde." *Götter im Exil: Vorlesungen über die neue Mythologie, II. Teil.* Ed. Manfred Frank. Frankfurt a.M.: Suhrkamp, 1988. 213–56.

Popp, Wolfgang. "Der biblische David als schwule Ikone der Kunst und Literatur." Gerhard Härle, Wolfgang Popp, Annette Runte, eds. *Ikonen des Begehrens: Bildsprachen der männlichen und weiblichen Homosexualität in Literatur und Kunst.* Stuttgart: M & P [Metzler], 1997. 67–100.

Prawer, S. S. *German Lyric Poetry: A Critical Analysis of Selected Poems from Klopstock to Rilke.* London: Routledge & Kegan Paul, 1952.

Raschel, Heinz. *Das Nietzsche-Bild im George-Kreis. Ein Beitrag zur Geschichte der deutschen Mythologeme.* Berlin/New York: de Gruyter, 1984.

Raulff, Ulrich. "Stefan George-Biografie, Ihr wisst nicht, wer ich bin" (*Süddeutsche Zeitung,* 11 June 2002) www.sueddeutsche.de/kultur/literatur/rezensionen/45724/index.php.

Rehren, Ludmilla von. "Sonderlicher, denn Frauenliebe ist . . . ." *Der Eigene* 4.4 (1903): 233–36.

Reuth, Ralf Georg. *Goebbels.* Trans. Krishna Winston. London: Constable, 1993.

Reventlow, Franziska Gräfin zu. *Herrn Dames Aufzeichnungen: Gesammelte Werke in einem Bande.* Munich: A. Langen, 1925.

———. *Herrn Dames Aufzeichnungen oder Begebenheiten aus einem merkwürdigen Stadtteil.* Franziska zu Reventlow. *Drei Romane.* Munich: Biederstein, 1958. 95–218.

Rieckmann, Jens. *Hugo von Hofmannsthal und Stefan George: Signifikanz einer "Episode" aus der Jahrhundertwende.* Tübingen/Basle: Francke, 1997.

Rissmann, Michael. *Hitlers Gott: Vorsehungsglaube und Sendungsbewußtsein des deutschen Diktators.* Zurich/Munich: Pendo, 2001.

Robertson, Ritchie. *The "Jewish Question" in German Literature, 1749–1939.* Oxford: Oxford UP, 1999.

Roos, Martin. *Stefan Georges Rhetorik der Selbstinszenierung.* Düsseldorf: Grupello Verlag, 2000.

Ruskin, John. *The laws of Fésole. A joy forever. Our fathers have told us. Inaugural address. Modern painters, v. 1.* Vol. 6 of *The Complete Works of John Ruskin.* New York: E. R. Dumont, n.d.

Salin, Edgar. *Um Stefan George: Erinnerung und Zeugnis.* 2nd ed. Munich/Düsseldorf: Helmut Küpper vormals Georg Bondi, 1954.

Schefold, Karl. *Hugo von Hofmannsthals Bild von Stefan George: Visionen des Endes, Grundsteine neuer Kultur.* Basle: Schwabe, 1998.

Schiller, Friedrich. *Sämtliche Gedichte.* 2 vols. Munich: dtv, 1965.

Schmitz, Oscar A. H. *Dämon Welt: Jahre der Entwicklung.* Munich: Müller, 1926.

Schonauer, Franz. *Stefan George mit Selbstzeugnissen und Bilddokumenten dargestellt.* Reinbek bei Hamburg: Rowohlt, 1960.

Schönberg, Arnold, and Wassily Kandinsky. *Briefe, Bilder, Dokumente einer außergewöhnlichen Begegnung.* Ed. Jelena Hahl-Koch. Salzburg: Residenz, 1980.

Schönberg, Arnold. *Brettllieder, Lieder op. 2, Lieder op. 15 (15 Gedichte aus Das Buch der Hängenden Gärten von Stefan George).* Compact disk. Berkeley: Music and Arts Programs of America, 1991.

Schröder, Hans Eggert. *Ludwig Klages 1872–1956: Centenar-Ausstellung 1972.* Bonn: Bouvier, 1972.

———. *Ludwig Klages: Die Geschichte seines Lebens.* Vol. 1. *Die Jugend.* Bonn: Bouvier, 1966.

Schuler, Alfred. *Fragmente und Vorträge.* Ed. Ludwig Klages. Leipzig: Johann Ambrosius Barth, 1940.

———. *Cosmogonische Augen: Gesammelte Schriften.* Ed. Baal Müller. Paderborn: Igel Verlag, 1997.

Schulz, H. Stefan. *Studien zur Dichtung Stefan Georges.* Heidelberg: Lothar Stiehm, 1967.

Sedgwick, Eve Kosofsky. *Epistemology of the Closet.* Berkeley/Los Angeles: U of California P, 1990.

Seekamp, H[ans].-J[ürgen]., R[aymond]. C[urtis]. Ockenden and M[arita]. Keilson [-Lauritz]. *Stefan George / Leben und Werk. Eine Zeittafel.* Amsterdam: Castrum Peregrini, 1972.

Sero, O. *Der Fall Wilde und das Problem der Homosexualität: Ein Prozess und ein Interview.* Leipzig: Max Spohr, 1896.

Shelley, Percy Bysshe. *Selected Poetry and Prose.* Ed. Carlos Baker. New York: Random House, 1951.

Sluga, Hans. *Heidegger's Crisis: Philosophy and Politics in Nazi Germany.* Cambridge, MA: Harvard UP, 1995.

Sontheimer, Kurt. *Antidemokratisches Denken in der Weimarer Republik: Die politischen Ideen des deutschen Nationalsozialismus zwischen 1918 und 1933.* Munich: Nymphenburger Verlagsbuchhandlung, 1962.

Stern, J. P. *The Dear Purchase: A Theme in German Modernism.* Cambridge: Cambridge UP, 1995.

Thiel, Friedrich. *Vier sonntägliche Straßen: A Study of the Ida Coblenz Problem in the Works of Stefan George.* New York: Lang, 1988.

Thormaehlen, Ludwig. *Erinnerungen an Stefan George.* Hamburg: Hauswedell, 1962.

Tiedemann-Bartels, Hella. *Versuch über das artistische Gedicht: Baudelaire, Mallarmé, George.* Munich: Edition text+kritik, 1990.

Vallentin, Berthold. *Gespräche mit Stefan George, 1902–1931, Tagebuchaufzeichnungen.* Amsterdam: Castrum Peregrini Presse, 1961.

Verwey, Albert. *Mein Verhältnis zu Stefan George: Erinnerungen aus den Jahren 1895–1928.* Strasbourg: Heitz & Co., 1936.

———. *Dichtspel. Oorspronkelijke en vertaalde gedichten.* Amsterdam: De Arbeiderspers, 1983.

Vilain, Robert. "Schoenberg and German Poetry." *Schoenberg and Words: The Modernist Years.* Eds. Charlotte M. Cross and Russell A. Berman. New York/London: Garland, 2000. 1–29.

Warren, Edward Perry. Pseud. Arthur Lyon Raile. *A Defense of Uranian Love.* London: Cayme Press, 1928–1930.

Weber, Marianne. *Max Weber. Ein Lebensbild.* Heidelberg: L. Schneider, 1950.

Weininger, Otto. *Geschlecht und Charakter: Eine prinzipielle Untersuchung.* 4th unrev. ed. Vienna/Leipzig: Wilhelm Braumüller, 1905.

Wilcox, John. "The Beginnings of *l'Art Pour l'Art.*" *Journal of Aesthetics and Art Criticism* 11 (1953): 360–77.

Wilde, Oscar. *Das Sonetten-Problem des Herrn W. H.* Trans. Johannes Gaulke. Leipzig: Max Spohr, 1902.

Winkler, Michael. *Stefan George.* Stuttgart: Metzler, 1970.

———. *George-Kreis.* Stuttgart: Metzler, 1972.

Wolfskehl, Karl. *Gesammelte Werke.* Ed. Margot Ruben and Claus Victor Bock. 2 vols. Hamburg: Claassen, 1960.

———. *Zehn Jahre Exil: Briefe aus Neuseeland.* Ed. Margot Ruben. Heidelberg and Darmstadt: Verlag Lambert Schneider, 1959.

Wolters, Friedrich. *Stefan George und die Blätter für die Kunst: Deutsche Geistesgeschichte seit 1890.* Berlin: Bondi, 1930.

Woods, Gregory. *A History of Gay Literature: The Male Tradition.* New Haven/London: Yale UP, 1998.

Wulf, Joseph. *Literatur und Dichtung im Dritten Reich: Eine Dokumentation.* Gütersloh: Mohn, 1963.

Wuthenow, Ralph-Rainer, ed. *Stefan George in seiner Zeit: Dokumente zur Wirkungsgeschichte.* 2 vols. Stuttgart: Klett-Cotta, 1980–81.

Zeller, Bernhard, ed. *Stefan George 1868–1968: Der Dichter und sein Kreis: Eine Ausstellung des Deutschen Literaturarchives im Schiller-Nationalmuseum Marbach a.N.* Munich: Kösel Verlag, 1968.

Zweig, Stefan. *Verwirrung der Gefühle: Drei Novellen.* Leipzig: Insel, 1927.

Žmegač, Viktor. "Ästhetizismus." *Moderne Literatur in Grundbegriffen.* Eds. Dieter Borchmeyer and Viktor Zmegac. 2nd rev. ed. Tübingen: Niemeyer, 1994.

Contributors

PAUL BISHOP is Professor of German at the University of Glasgow. He has published various articles on C. G. Jung, Ludwig Klages, Ernst Cassirer, and Friedrich Nietzsche, and has edited *A Companion to Goethe's Faust: Parts I and II* (2001) and *Nietzsche and Antiquity: His Reaction and Response to the Classical Tradition* (2004).

MARITA KEILSON-LAURITZ has published widely on Stefan George, including *Stefan George: Leben und Werk. Eine Zeittafel* (with H. J. Seekamp and R. C. Ockenden, 1972), *Von der Liebe die Freundschaft heißt: Zur Homoerotik im Werk Stefan Georges* (1987), and on the role of literature in the gay emancipation movement. She is a co-editor and co-founder of the journal *Forum Homosexualität und Literatur*.

MICHAEL M. METZGER is emeritus Professor of German at the University at Buffalo. He is the author of *Lessing and the Language of Comedy* (1966) and numerous articles and editions. Together with Erika A. Metzger, his wife, he has published books on Stefan George (1972), Andreas Gryphius (1994), collaborated on volumes 3–7 of the critical edition *Herrn von Hoffmannswaldau und andrer Deutschen Gedichte* (1970–91), and edited *A Companion to the Works of Rainer Maria Rilke* (Camden House, 2002; paperback 2004).

JENS RIECKMANN is Professor Emeritus at the University of California, Irvine. He has published widely on turn-of-the-century and twentieth century literature and culture, including *Hugo von Hofmannsthal und Stefan George: Signifikanz einer "Episode" aus der Jahrhundertwende* (1997).

RITCHIE ROBERTSON is Professor of German at Oxford University and a Fellow of St. John's College, Oxford. His books include *Kafka: Judaism, Politics, and Literature* (1985), *The "Jewish Question" in German Literature, 1749–1939* (1999), *Kafka: A Very Short Introduction* (2004), and, as editor, *The Cambridge Companion to Thomas Mann* (2002). He has also edited and partly translated *The German-Jewish Dialogue: An Anthology of Literary Texts, 1749–1993* (1999).

KARLA SCHULTZ, Professor Emerita at the University of Oregon, has written numerous articles on the interface of modernism, critical theory, poetry, and gender, as well as *Mimesis on the Move: Theodor W. Adorno's Concept of Imitation* (1990). She also edited *The Idea of the Forest: German and American Perspectives on the Culture and Politics of Trees* (1996), and produced and directed seven theatrical plays in German.

JEFFREY D. TODD is Associate Professor of German and French at Texas Christian University. Some of his most recent work on George has been published in the *Germanisch-Romanische Monatsschrift* and *Castrum Peregrini*. He is also co-author, with Jerry Glenn, of *Paul Celan: Die zweite Bibliographie* (1998), accessible via the Internet at http://polyglot.lss.wisc.edu/german/celan/, as well as of updates to the bibliography published in the *Celan-Jahrbuch*. He is currently working on a critical overview of George criticism for Camden House.

ROBERT VILAIN is Professor of German and Comparative Literature at Royal Holloway, University of London. He is the author of *The Poetry of Hugo von Hofmannsthal and French Symbolism* (2000) and has published numerous scholarly articles on German and French literature, particularly poetry, of the nineteenth and twentieth centuries. He has edited volumes on *Yvan Goll – Claire Goll: Texts and Contexts* (1997) and *The Art of Detective Fiction* (2000), and with Judith Beniston edits the journal *Austrian Studies*. The Leverhulme Trust is currently funding a major research project on Franco-German literature circa 1870–1936.

WILLIAM WATERS is Associate Professor of German at Boston University. He is the author of *Poetry's Touch: On Lyric Address* (2003) and of other scholarly publications on lyric poetry and poetics generally, on Rilke, and on English and American poets. He is at work on a study of Rilke's *Neue Gedichte*.

MICHAEL WINKLER, Professor Emeritus of German Studies at Rice University, has published scholarly studies on a variety of topics and authors. His areas of special concentration are fin-de-siècle and exile literature. He has also translated three novels as well as Rilke's *Diaries* and his correspondence with Lou Andreas-Salomé (with E. Snow), and edited two volumes in the annotated edition of Gustav Regler's works.

Index

Adorno, Theodor W., 18, 92–97
Adorno, Theodor W., works by:
  Dialektik der Aufklärung, 93–94;
  "George," 93, 96; "George und
  Hofmannsthal. Zum Briefwechsel:
  1891–1906," 92–93; *Vier George-
  Lieder, op. 7,* 94
aestheticism, 1, 18, 32, 127–40, 150.
  See also l'art pour l'art; décadence
Aldrich, Robert, 207
Allgemeine Kunstchronik, 7
Andreae, Friedrich, 155
Andreae, Wilhelm, 155
Angelico, Fra, works by: *Coronation
  of the Virgin,* 56
anti-Semitism, 11, 104, 173, 189,
  196, 200
Arabian Nights Entertainments, 65
Art Nouveau, 84–90, 102–3, 110
l'art pour l'art, 1, 10, 129. *See also*
  aestheticism
Aschheim, Steven, 189
Attila, 199
Auerbach, Leopold, 212
Aurnhammer, Achim, 109

Bachofen, Johann Jakob, 104, 163
Bachofen, Johann Jakob, works by:
  Das Mutterrecht, 163
Bartels, Adolf, 17
Baudelaire, Charles, 3, 8, 9, 102
Baudelaire, Charles, works by:
  "L'albatros," 32, 65;
  "Correspondances," 60; "Le
  peintre de la vie moderne," 28;
  "Rêve parisien," 60
Bauer, Karl, 172
Bechtold, Ferdinand, 16

Beck, Claus Victor, 39
Bell-Villada, Gene H., 127
Benjamin, Walter, works by:
  *Ursprung des deutschen
  Trauerspiels,* 96–97
Benn, Gottfried, 189
Benn, Gottfried, works by:
  "Probleme der Lyrik," 128
Bernstein, Michael André, 196
Bertram, Ernst, 18, 162, 200
Bertram, Ernst, works by:
  "Deutscher Aufbruch," 200;
  *Nietzsche. Versuch einer
  Mythologie,* 193
Bildungsbürgertum, 10, 106–7,
  149
Bismarck, Otto von, 197
Blätter für die Kunst, 4, 6–7, 8, 9,
  10, 11, 18, 25, 30, 51, 53, 63,
  81, 83, 92, 100, 101, 103,
  104–6, 107, 109, 112, 116, 117,
  128–30, 132, 135, 137, 146,
  162, 163, 164, 165, 167, 169,
  172, 174, 175, 176, 177, 190,
  191, 192, 196
Blavatsky, Helena Petrovna, 104
Bock, Claus Victor, 217
Böcklin, Arnold, 191–92
Bodenstedt, Friedrich, 1
Boehringer, Robert, 136, 155, 162
Böhme, Thomas, 208
Bondi, Georg, 6, 11, 53, 116, 168,
  169, 208
Borchardt, Rudolf, 208
Brand, Adolf, 209, 215, 216
Brand, Adolf, works by: "Afterkultur
  und Homosexualität," 215
Braun, Lily, 190

Braungart, Wolfgang, 128, 135
Brentano, Clemens, 100
Breuer, Stefan, 135, 176
Breysig, Kurt, 153–54, 175
Brodsky, Patricia P., 99
Bülow, Bernhard Heinrich von, 209
Bunsen, Marie von, 10, 11
Busse, Hans Hinrich, 168

Campbell, Joseph, 134
Castrum Peregrini, 1
Celan, Paul, 96–97
Chamberlain, Houston Stewart, 104, 195
Chevalier, Jean, 134
Class, Heinrich, 197
Classicism, 102, 105
Clemenceau, Georges, 15
Coblenz, Ida, 10, 63, 66, 69, 80, 81, 212
Crane, Hart, 39

d'Annunzio, Gabriele, 100
Dante Alighieri, 3, 101, 107, 109, 146, 200
Dante Alighieri, works by: *La Commedia*, 113, 138; *Vita Nuova*, 113, 138
Darwin, Charles, 190, 197
Dauthendey, Max, 162
David, Claude, 1, 81, 90, 92, 108, 132, 199
décadence, 59, 102, 111, 132
Dehmel, Richard, 10, 69, 80, 147
de Lagarde, Paul, 195
de Régnier, Henri, 100
Derleth, Anna Maria, 166, 176
Derleth, Ludwig, 161, 162, 168–69, 173, 175–77
Derleth, Ludwig, works by: *Der fränkische Koran*, 179; "Die Proklamationen," 175, 176; "Venus Maria," 174; "Der Weinberg," 174; "Widmungen," 174
Dessoir, Max, 154

Deutsche Dichtung I–III, 100, 207
"Deutsche Graphologische Gesellschaft," 168
Dilthey, Wilhelm, 151
Douglas, Lord Alfred, works by: "Two Loves," 213
Dowson, Ernest, 100
Dynes, Wayne R., 207

Egyptien, Jürgen, 177
Eichendorff, Joseph von, 100
Eick, Hugo, 155
Der Eigene, 209
L'Ermitage, 10
Evers, Franz, 208

Faletti, Heidi E., 83
Fichte, Hubert, 208
fin de siècle, 35, 95, 135
First World War, 13, 14–15, 112, 116, 118, 156–57, 190, 197, 199
Floréal, 10
Förster-Nietzsche, Elisabeth, 195
Frauenlob, 67
Freie Bühne für den Entwicklungskampf der Zeit, 7
"Freier Bund bauender Forscher," 154
French Symbolists, 6, 14, 69, 95–96, 146
Friedemann, Heinrich, works by: *Plato: Seine Gestalt*, 155–56
Friedlaender, Benedict, 211
Friedrich II, 198
Frommel, Wolfgang, 135
Furness, Raymond, 167

Gandhi, Mohandas K., 15
Ganghofer, Ludwig, 147
Gautier, Théophile, 59, 127
Gay Emancipation Movement, 2, 8, 207–9, 211, 215, 217–18
Geibel, Emanuel, 1
"Gemeinschaft der Eigenen," 207, 209, 215
George, Anna Maria Ottilie, 10, 80

George, Eva (née Smitt), 3
George-Jahrbuch, 2
George-Kreis (Circle), 1, 4, 11–13,
  14, 15, 17, 18, 51, 101, 102,
  103, 104, 108, 109, 112, 113,
  115, 117, 145–59, 162, 170,
  173, 189, 192, 196, 198, 199,
  201, 208, 209–10
George, Stefan, works by:
"A. S.," 165–67
"Abend des Festes," 65
Algabal, 6, 8, 28–32, 33, 34, 45,
  57, 58, 59–63, 67, 69, 70,
  108, 128, 131–36, 139,
  165–66, 208, 215
"Alles habend alles wissend," 115
"Als neuling trat ich ein," 71
"Als wir hinter dem beblümten
  tore," 72
"Am markte sah ich erst," 61–62
"An Antinous," 66
"An Damon," 55
"An Derleth," 176
"An die Toten," 200
"Angst und hoffen wechselnd,"
  72
"An Isokrates," 66, 165
"An Kallimachus," 66
"An Kotytto," 66
"An Menippa," 66
"An Phaon," 66
"An Sidonia," 66
"Auf das Leben und den Tod
  Maximins," 111–12, 114
"Auf neue tafeln schreibt," 197
"Aus Purpurgluten sprach," 115
"Der Auszug der Erstlinge," 65
"Bangt nicht vor rissen," 115
*Baudelaire · Die Blumen des
  Bösen · Umdichtungen,* 3, 8,
  51–53, 101, 130
"Die Becher," 119
"Becher am boden," 30, 132
"Das Bild," 67
"Bilder," 56
"Boecklin," 109, 139

"Der Brand des Tempels," 119,
  199
*Die Bücher der Hirten- und
  Preisgedichte · der Sagen und
  Sänge und der hängenden
  Gärten,* 6, 32, 34, 63–74, 94,
  108, 131, 165, 219
"Burg Falkenstein," 119
"Carl August," 109, 139
"Da auf dem seidenen lager," 61
"Da meine lippen reglos sind," 71
*Dante · Die Göttliche Komödie ·
  Übertragungen,* 3, 15, 101
"Dante und das Zeitgedicht,"
  109, 138, 139
"Dass er auf fernem felsenpfade,"
  59
"Des ruhmes leere dränge," 73
"Der Dichter in Zeiten der
  Wirren," 43–46, 47, 116,
  118–19
"Dies ist reich des Geistes," 116
"Dies leid und diese last," 84
"Die du in glück vermehrst," 10
"Der du uns aus der qual," 113,
  217
"Du hausgeist der um alte
  mauern," 77
"Du schlank und rein wie eine
  flamme," 119
"Du stets noch Anfang uns," 113
"Du willst am mauerbrunnen," 81
"Du willst mit mir ein reich der
  sonne stiften," 82
"Ein Angelico," 56
"Ein edelkind sah vom balkon,"
  68–69
"Ein Hingang," 55, 56
"Die einen lehren," 114, 214
"Einer stand auf der scharf wie
  blitz," 193
"Einladung," 55
"Der Einsiedel," 68
"Einverleibung," 197
"Empfängnis," 111
"Das Ende des Siegers," 65

George, Stefan, works by:
(continued)
"Entrückung," 177
"Er liess sich einsam hin," 73
"Erinna," 65
"Erkenntag," 64
"Das Erste," 13
"Erwachen der Braut," 68–69
"Erwiderungen: Die
   Verkennung," 13
"Es heulet der Dezemberwind," 3
"Feier," 111
"Fern ist mir das blumenalter,"
   135
"Fern von des hafens lärm," 219
"Fest," 176
"Feste," 176
Die Fibel: Auswahl erster Verse,
   3, 101
"Flurgottes Trauer," 64
"Franken," 6, 109
"Der Freund der Fluren," 103,
   131
"Friedensabend," 71
"Fühl ich noch dies erste
   ungemach," 134
"Der Fürst und der Minner," 139
"Die Gärten schliessen," 54–55
"Gegen osten ragt der bau,"
   131–32, 134
"Geheimes Deutschland," 119,
   199
"Das Geheimopfer," 65
"Der Gehenkte," 119
"Gemahnt dich noch das schöne
   bildnis," 82
"Goethes letzte Nacht in Italien,
   116, 117, 139
"Goethe-Tag," 109, 139
"Gespräch des Herrn mit dem
   römischen Hauptmann," 199
"Gezeiten," 111
"Gräber," 3
"Die Gräber in Speier," 109, 191,
   198
Graf Bothwell, 3

"Graue rosse muss ich schirren,"
   132
"Grosse tage wo im geist," 61,
   134
"Hain in diesen paradiesen," 71,
   73
"Halte die purpur- und goldenen
   gedanken," 71
"Hehre Harfe," 41–43, 45, 47,
   111
"Helfer von damals," 9
"Der Herr der Insel," 32–34, 38,
   43, 45, 64–65
"Hochsommer," 130
"Horch was die dumpfe erde
   spricht," 119
Hymnen, 6, 7, 53–56, 61, 62, 63,
   103, 108, 128, 130–31, 137
"Hyperion I · II · III," 117–18
"Ich bin der Eine," 217
"Ich bin freund und führer dir,"
   12, 91
"Ich forschte bleichen eifers,"
   86
"Ich kam zur heimat," 214
"Ich schrieb es auf," 82
"Ich trat vor dich mit einem
   segenspruche," 81–82
"ich wandelte auf öden düstren
   bahnen," 3
"Ich warf das stirnband," 73
"ich will mir jener stunden lauf
   erzählen," 30
"Ihr alten bilder," 58, 59
"Ihr Äusserste von windumsauster
   klippe," 196
"Ihr baut verbrechende," 115
"Die ihr die wilden dunklen
   zeiten," 115
"Ihr hallen prahlend," 60, 131
"Ihr seid die Gründung," 116
"Ihr wisset nicht wer ich bin,"
   114
"Im Park," 55, 56, 130
"Im unglücklichen Tone dessen,"
   67

"In alte lande laden bogenhallen,"
57
"In hohen palästen," 70
"In meinem leben rannen
schlimme tage," 86
"In stillste ruh," 16
"Indes deine mutter dich stillt," 83
"Indes in träumen," 73
"Der Infant," 131
"Irrende Schar," 68
"Ist dies der knabe längster sage,"
216
"Ist es neu dir was vermocht," 68
Das Jahr der Seele, 10, 34, 35, 36,
47, 63, 79–85, 103, 108, 146,
165, 168, 207, 219
"Jahrestag," 64
"Jedem werke bin ich fürder tot,"
72
"Der Jünger," 218
"Der Kampf," 172
"Kaum deuten dir gehorsam," 70
"Kindliches Königtum," 4, 70
"Komm in den totgesagten Park,"
35–36, 39, 45, 47, 79–80
"Kreuz der Strasse," 94
"Der Krieg," 14, 15, 103, 116,
118–19, 138, 140, 196, 199
"L. K.," 168
"Landschaft I · II · III," 111
"Lärmen hör ich," 132
"Lass deine tränen," 57
"Lass der trauer kleid und miene,"
58
"Leo XIII," 131, 140, 191
"Das Licht," 16
"Liebe nennt den nicht wert,"
214, 219
"Lied des Zwergen," 67
"Lieder wie ich gern sie sänge,"
83, 137
"Lilie der auen," 65
"Litanei," 111
"Lobgesang," 111, 212, 216–17,
218–19
"Lostag," 64

"M. L.," 83–84
"Mächtiger traum dem ich
zugetraut," 58
"Mahnung," 57, 58, 70
Manuel, 3, 69
"Manuel und Menes," 139
"Dem markt und ufer," 38–40,
41, 43, 86
"Maskenzug," 176
Maximin, Ein Gedenkbuch, 13,
107, 138, 207, 219
"Mein garten bedarf nicht," 29,
31–32, 34, 45, 47, 60
"Mein kind kam heim," 219
"Meine weissen ara," 34, 43
"Der Mensch und der Drud," 2,
119
"Mit den frauen fremder
ordnung," 197
"Mühle lass die arme still," 57
"München," 161
"Nach der Lese," 82
"Nachmittag," 55, 130
"Nachthymne," 55, 56, 130
Das Neue Reich, 2, 16, 17, 43,
46, 99, 116–20, 137, 198,
199, 200, 214
"Neuen adel den ihr suchet,"
197
"Neuländische Liebesmahle," 53
"Nicht ohnmacht rät mir ab,"
60–61
"Nietzsche," 109, 139, 192–93
"O mutter meiner mutter," 30,
132
"Pente Pigadia," 109
Phraortes, 3
Pilgerfahrten, 6, 7, 8, 55, 56–59,
61, 62, 63, 67, 70, 73, 108
"Porta Nigra," 107, 139, 171,
174, 191
"Der Preusse," 109
"Prinz Indra," 3, 69
"Der redende Kopf," 96
"Die reichsten schätze lernet frei
verschwenden," 83

George, Stefan, works by:
(continued)
"Saget mir auf welchem pfade,"
71
"Der Schleier," 90–91
"Schlusschor," 138
"Schmerzbrüder," 218
"Das schöne beet betracht ich
mir," 72
"Der Schüler," 5
"Schweige die klage!" 58
"Des sehers wort," 36–38, 39,
41, 42, 43, 45, 46
Shakespeare Sonnette · Umdichtung,
3, 13, 15, 113, 210, 211–14,
216, 219
Der Siebente Ring, 13, 15, 41,
84, 94, 99, 101, 102, 108–12,
127, 139, 161, 171, 177–78,
191, 207, 208, 212, 219
"Siedlergang," 56–57
"Sieh mein kind ich gehe," 68,
219
"So sprach ich nur," 61, 132
"So werd ich immer harren," 91
"Sonnwendzug," 110, 197
"Die Spange," 25–30, 36, 47,
59, 74
"Der Spiegel," 212, 220
"Sporenwache," 67
"Sprich nicht immer," 73
Der Stern des Bundes, 15, 17, 99,
106, 112–16, 137, 138, 177,
191, 193, 196, 197, 200, 207,
214, 216
"Stimmen im Strom," 74
"Strand," 130
"Streng ist uns das glück," 72
"Der Tag des Hirten," 64
"Tage," 131
Tage und Taten, 9, 25, 101, 103,
138
"Tagelied," 67
"Tag-Gesang," 91
"Die Tat," 67
"Templer," 156

"Der Teppich," 39–41, 45, 87,
88–90
Der Teppich des Lebens und die
Lieder von Traum und Tod ·
Mit einem Vorspiel, 9, 11, 34,
38, 39, 47, 85–92, 100, 103,
108, 110, 111, 130, 131, 146,
168, 207, 218
"Teuflische Stanze," 136
"Die tote Stadt," 109–10, 139
"Traum und Tod," 87–88
"Trauer I," 13
"Uns du durch viele jahre," 88
"Die Untergehenden," 9
"Ursprünge," 4, 111, 197
"Vernunft! Du legtest deine
kalten hände," 3
"Verschollen des traumes," 111
"Verwandlungen," 55, 130
"Verweilst du in den traurigsten
bezirken," 86
"Der Verworfene," 9
"Vogelschau," 62
"Von einer Begegnung," 56, 130
"Vorbereitungen," 70
"Vorrede zu Maximin," 217
"Waller im Schnee," 82
"Weihe," 54, 55, 56, 135, 137
"Die weltzeit die wir kennen," 116
"Wem du dein licht gabst," 115
"Wenn ich heut nicht deinen leib
berühre," 72
"Wenn sich bei heilger ruh," 72
"Wenn solch ein sausen," 83
"Wenn um der zinnen," 30
"Wer ist dein Gott?" 114
"Willst du noch länger auf den
kahlen böden," 80, 85
"Wir bevölkerten die abend-
düstern," 73
"Wir werden noch einmal zum
lande fliegen," 69
"Das Wort," 46–47, 119–20, 137
"Worte trügen worte · fliehen," 68
"Das Zeitgedicht," 14, 102, 110,
174

"Zeitgedichte," 13–14, 102, 108
"Zweifel der Jünger," 196
"Das Zweite: Wallfahrt," 13
"Zwiegespräch im Schilf," 64
George, Stephan, 3
Gérardy, Paul, 10, 66, 130, 139, 168
Gérardy, Paul, works by: "Geistige
   Kunst," 129, 192
Gheerbrant, Alain, 134
Glöckner, Ernst, 1, 162, 177
Goebbels, Joseph, 17, 199
Goethe, Johann Wolfgang von, 87,
   91, 100, 105–6, 117, 152
Goethe, Johann Wolfgang von,
   works by: *Egmont*, 208; "Selige
   Sehnsucht," 42, 55; *West-Östlicher
   Divan*, 42
Gothein, Eberhard, 158
Groppe, Carola, 155
Gundolf, Friedrich, 5, 11, 12, 79,
   84, 87, 100, 134, 148, 151–53,
   156, 158, 162, 169, 172, 174,
   175, 177, 193–94, 196, 199, 208
Gundolf, Friedrich, works by:
   Caesar, Geschichte seines Ruhms,
   151, 198; "Gefolgschaft und
   Jüngertum," 152–53, 198;
   George, 133, 151–52, 194;
   Goethe, 12; *Shakespeare in
   deutscher Sprache*, 101;
   Shakespeare und der deutsche Geist,
   101, 151; "Vorbilder," 155

Haertle, Heinrich, works by:
   *Nietzsche und der
   Nationalsozialismus*, 195
Hallwachs, Karl, 68
Hamecher, Peter, 215, 216
Hamecher, Peter, works by: "Der
   männliche Eros im Werke Stefan
   Georges," 207–9
Hart, Julius, 7
Hebbel, Friedrich, 100
Hegel, Georg Wilhelm Friedrich,
   113
Heidegger, Martin, 119
Heidegger, Martin, works by: "Das
   Wesen der Sprache," 46; "Das
   Wort," 46
Heine, Heinrich, 100
Heiseler, Henry von, 166–67
Heliogabalus, 8, 59–60, 131, 133,
   135, 166
Hellbach, Hans Dietrich, 207, 209,
   219
Hellingrath, Norbert von, 153
Herzfeld, Marie, 9
Heyer, Wolfgang, 153
Heyse, Paul, 1
Hildebrandt, Kurt, 154–56, 200
Hildebrandt, Kurt, works by:
   "Hellas und Wilamowitz," 155;
   *Platon. Der Kampf des Geistes um
   die Macht*, 156; "Romantisch und
   Dionysisch," 155
Hindenburg, Paul, 15
Hirschfeld, Magnus, 207, 208, 209,
   215, 216
Hitler, Adolf, 17, 115, 195,
   198–99, 200, 201
Hoffmann, Heinrich, 195
Hofmannsthal, Hugo von, 1, 2, 5,
   8–9, 10, 59, 60, 62–63, 93, 146,
   148, 159, 168, 172, 173, 177,
   191
Hofmannsthal, Hugo von, works
   by: *Andreas*, 9; "Gedichte von
   Stefan George," 63–64; *Das
   gerettete Venedig*, 9; "Das
   Schrifttum als geistiger Raum der
   Nation," 9
Holbein, Hans, 91
Hölderlin, Johann Christian
   Friedrich, 36, 100, 117, 152
Hölderlin, Johann Christian
   Friedrich, works by: "Andenken,"
   214; *Hyperion*, 214; *Menons
   Klagen um Diotima*, 79;
   "Sokrates und Alkibiades," 214
Homer, 200
Hopkins, Gerard Manley, works by:
   "To A. B.," 46

Huch, Roderich, 169
Husman, August, 12
Huysmans, Joris Karl, 59
Huysmans, Joris Karl, works by:
À rebours, 30

Ibsen, Henrik, 3
Impressionists, 80
innere Emigration, 13

Jacobsen, Jens Peter, 100
Jahrbuch für die geistige Bewegung,
   12–13, 100, 152, 154, 155, 298,
   209
Jahrbuch für sexuelle Zwischenstufen,
   207, 208
Joël, Karl, 154
Journal de Genève, 157
Jugendstil, 83, 85, 93, 95, 97, 145,
   169
Jünger, Ernst, 190
Jünger, Ernst, works by: Der
   Arbeiter: Herrschaft und Gestalt,
   198

Kafka, Franz, works by: "Eine
   kaiserliche Botschaft," 33
Kahler, Erich, 155
Kandinsky, Vasily, 95
Kant, Emanuel, works by: Kritik
   der Urteilskraft, 127
Kantorowicz, Ernst, works by: Kaiser
   Friedrich der Zweite, 158, 198
Kassner, Rudolf, 211
Keilson-Lauritz, Marita, 2, 7, 168,
   172
Klages, Ludwig, 11, 66, 104, 112,
   161, 162, 163, 164, 165, 166,
   167, 168, 170, 171, 172, 173,
   174, 175, 177, 189
Klages, Ludwig, works by: "Aus
   einer Seelenlehre des Künstlers,
   172; "Aus Wildenroth," 174–75;
   "Desiderata," 165; Der Geist als
   Widersacher der Seele, 179;
   Prinzipien der Charakterologie,

168; Stefan George, 169–70;
   "Vom Schaffenden," 172
Klein, Carl August, 8, 51, 53,
   168
Klein, Carl August, works by:
   "Über Stefan George, eine neue
   kunst," 191–92
Klinger, Max, 192
Kloos, Willem, 100
Klopstock, Friedrich Gottlieb, 36,
   100
Klussmann, Paul-Gerhard, 138
Kommerell, Max, 158–59, 177
Kommerell, Max, works by: Der
   Dichter als Führer in der deutschen
   Klassik, 12, 158
Kristeva, Julia, 95
Kronberger, Maximilian, 5, 13, 94,
   107–8, 115, 137–38, 171–72,
   175, 194–95, 209, 218, 219
Kupffer, Elisar von, 215, 216

Landauer, Gustav, 190
Landmann, Georg Peter, 18, 106,
   112, 116
Landmann, Julius, 153
Lechter, Melchior, 51, 69, 81,
   83–84, 87, 113, 145, 147, 148,
   168, 174
Lenau, Nikolaus, 100
Lenin, Vladimir Ilyich, 15
Lepsius, Richard, 11, 154
Lepsius, Sabine, 11, 154
Lessing, Theodor, 167
Linke, Hansjürgen, 114, 135
Löwith, Karl, 195
Loyola, Ignatius, 169
Ludwig II, 8, 59, 208
Lukács, Georg, 17, 94
Luxemburg, Rosa, 18

Maeterlinck, Maurice, 57
Mallarmé, Stéphane, 6, 8, 9, 55, 69,
   100, 102, 103, 146, 161
Mann, Heinrich, 200
Mann, Klaus, 18

Mann, Klaus, works by: "Das Schweigen Stefan Georges," 17
Mann, Thomas, 200, 201
Mann, Thomas, works by: "Beim Propheten," 175; *Doktor Faustus,* 175; "Gladius Dei," 161; "Leiden und Grösse Richard Wagners," 147–48; *Der Tod in Venedig,* 156; "Von deutscher Republik," 12; *Der Zauberberg,* 108
Marx, Karl, 104, 113
Marx, Olga (Carol North Valhope), 2
Matt, Peter von, 4–5, 119
Le Mercure de France, 10
Mettler, Dieter, 7, 11
Metzger, Erika A., 13, 59
Metzger, Michael M., 13, 59, 92
Meyer, Conrad Ferdinand, 100
Meyer, Detlev, 208
Meyer, Georg, 168
Meyer, Richard M., 11, 154, 208, 215
Michelangelo, 210, 220
Mockel, Albert, 6
modernism, 8, 16
modernity, 109–10, 112, 113, 115, 196
Mommsen, Momme, 118
Morwitz, Ernst, 2, 72, 134, 135, 148, 158, 161, 165, 167, 172, 194, 196, 200, 215, 218
Mühsam, Erich, 18
Mühsam, Erich, works by: *Die Homosexualität. Eine Streitschrift,* 208
Munich cosmologists, 11, 18, 104, 111–12, 136, 161–79, 189, 197

Napoleon Bonaparte, 152, 169
National Socialism, 16–18, 19, 95, 103, 140, 189, 195–201
Natorp, Paul, 155
Naturalism, 7, 8, 100, 104
Naumann, Hans, 18, 200
Nebuchadnezzar II, 69

New Hellenism, 12, 17, 106
Nietzsche, Friedrich, 19, 86, 99, 100, 104, 105, 113, 117, 129, 147, 152, 163, 169, 189–98
Nietzsche, Friedrich, works by: *Also sprach Zarathustra,* 19, 192, 193, 195; *Ecce Homo,* 196; *Die fröhliche Wissenschaft,* 195; *Die Geburt der Tragödie,* 190, 192–93, 194; "Sils-Maria," 195; *Unzeitgemäße Betrachtungen,* 190; "Vom Nutzen und Nachteil der Historie für das Leben," 99; *Der Wille zur Macht,* 197; *Zur Genealogie der Moral,* 191
Norton, Robert E., 2, 5, 14, 17, 134, 196, 199, 200
Novalis (Friedrich von Hardenberg), 100, 192
Novalis (Friedrich von Hardenberg), works by: *Die Christenheit oder Europa,* 113; *Heinrich von Ofterdingen,* 31

Overbeck, Franz, 194

Pan, 169
Pan-German League, 197, 198
Panizza, Oskar, 7
Pannwitz, Rudolf, works by: *Kultur, Kraft, Kunst,* 177; "Das totengedicht," 177
Parnassians, 127
Pascal, Blaise, 73
Pater, Walter, 132
Péladan, Sâr Joséphin, 169
Perls, Richard, 162, 165
Petersen, Julius, 199
Petrow, Michael, 15, 16–17
Pindar, 105
Platen, August von, 100, 114, 219
Plato, 99, 102, 140, 211, 213, 215, 220
Plato, works by: *Phaedrus,* 156; *The Republic,* 156; *Symposium,* 114, 156, 211

La Plume, 10
Plumpe, Gerhard, 162
Poe, Edgar Allan, 9
Preußische Jahrbücher, 11
"Psychodiagnostisches Seminar," 168

Raschel, Heinz, 193
Rassenfosse, Edmond, 66, 82
Raulff, Ulrich, 17–18
Renaissance, 102
Réveil, 63
Reventlow, Franziska von, 166
Richter, Johann Paul Friedrich
  (pseud. Jean Paul), 91, 100, 178
Rieckmann, Jens, 213
Rilke, Rainer Maria, 1, 2, 99, 100,
  147
Rilke, Rainer Maria, works by:
  "Archaïscher Torso Apollos," 40;
  *Die Aufzeichnungen des Malte
  Laurids Brigge,* 99; *Duineser
  Elegien,* 99; *Neue Gedichte,* 99;
  Sonnette an Orpheus, 99
Rimbaud, Arthur, 102
Rodin, Auguste, 147
Röhm, Ernst, 201
Rolicz-Lieder, Waclaw, 66, 100, 168
Rolland, Romain, 157
Romanticism, 90, 102
Roos, Martin, 17
Rosen und Disteln, 3–4, 10, 129
Rosenberg, Alfred, works by: *Der
  Mythos des zwanzigsten
  Jahrhunderts,* 195
Rossetti, Dante Gabriel, 9, 100
Rouge, Carl, 4, 10
Ruskin, John, works by: *The Laws of
  Fésole,* 138
Rust, Bernhard, 16, 200

Saint-Paul, Albert, 3, 6, 66
Salin, Edgar, 153, 166
Salin, Edgar, works by: *Platon und
  die griechische Utopie,* 156
Schack, Adolf von, 1
Scheler, Max, 12

Schiller, Friedrich, 100
Schiller, Friedrich, works by: *Don
  Carlos,* 208; "Die Götter
  Griechenlands," 117–18; "Die
  Sänger der Vorwelt," 102; "Die
  Teilung der Erde," 102
Schmitz, Oskar A. H., 174
Schoenberg, Arnold, 69, 94
Schoenberg, Arnold, works by:
  Opus 15, 71
Schuler, Alfred, 11, 104, 109, 112,
  161, 162, 163, 165, 167, 169,
  170–71, 172, 173, 174, 175,
  177, 179, 199, 214
Schuler, Alfred, works by: *Elagabal,*
  166; "Kosmogoniae Fragmenta,"
  162–63; "Sonett an Leopold
  Andrian," 174; "Vom Wesen der
  ewigen Stadt," 177
Schulz, H. Stefan, 63, 66
Scott, Cyril M., 2, 82
Semiramis, 69
Shakespeare, William, 3, 101, 210,
  213, 215, 216, 220
Shakespeare, William, works by:
  Sonnets, 210, 212–13, 217
Shelley, Percy B., 9
Shelley, Percy B., works by:
  "A Defence of Poetry," 102
Simmel, Georg, 92, 154
Singer, Kurt, 153
Singer, Kurt, works by: *Platon der
  Gründer,* 156
Sluga, Hans, 195
Spann, Othmar, 155
Spengler, Oswald, works by: *Der
  Untergang des Abendlandes,* 198
Spohr, Max, 208
Stahl, Arthur, 3
Stauffenberg, Berthold von, 158,
  201
Stauffenberg, Claus von, 158, 201
Stein, Wilhelm, 178
Summers, Claude J., 207
Swinburne, Algernon Charles, 9,
  100

Symbolism/Symbolists, 6, 7, 10, 54, 59, 69, 102–3, 192

Thiersch, Paul, 155
Third Reich, 13, 16, 200. *See also* National Socialism
Thormaehlen, Ludwig, 154, 199–200
Toorop, Jan, 164

Ulrichs, Karl Heinrich, 215–16
Uxkull-Gyllenband, Bernhard Victor, 158
Uxkull-Gyllenband, Woldemar, Graf von, 158, 200

Vallentin, Berthold, 154, 155, 196
Vallentin, Berthold, works by: *Napoleon*, 164; *Napoleon und die Deutschen*, 154; *Winckelmann*, 154
Verhaeren, Emile, 100
Verlaine, Paul, 6, 9, 59, 100, 102
Verwey, Albert, 100, 168, 169, 170–71, 172
Verwey, Albert, works by: "Michael," 175; *Van de liefde die vriendschap heet*, 211
Virgil, 36, 146
Vordtriede, Werner, 16

Wagner, Richard, 95, 147, 148, 190, 191, 193
La Wallonie, 6
Wandervogel movement, 189
Weber, Max, 11

Wilamowitz-Moellendorff, Ulrich von, 155
Wilde, Oscar, 210, 213, 217, 220
Wilde, Oscar, works by: "The Decay of Lying," 30; *The Picture of Dorian Gray*, 30, 132, 133
Wilhelmine Germany, 1, 7, 13–14, 48, 103–5, 145, 190–91, 198
Wilson, Woodrow, 15
Winkler, Michael, 13, 94
"Wissenschaftlich-humanitäres Komitee," 207, 214
Wolfskehl, Hanna, 11, 166, 173
Wolfskehl, Karl, 11, 100, 104, 147, 151, 157, 162, 163, 164, 166, 169, 170, 172, 173, 174, 196
Wolfskehl, Karl, works by: "An den alten Wassern," 196; *Saul*, 196
Wolters, Friedrich, 12, 100, 153, 154, 155, 156, 157–58, 162, 165, 176–77, 190, 194, 198, 208
Wolters, Friedrich, works by: "Herrschaft und Dienst," 4, 139, 153, 198; "Richtlinien," 155, 156; *Stefan George und die Blätter für die Kunst: Deutsche Geistesgeschichte seit 1890*, 15–16, 146–47, 157
Woods, Gregory, 2
Wotherspoon, Garry, 207

Zeitgenösische Dichter, 100, 207
Zeller, Bernhard, 173
Zernik, Hugo, 214, 219–20
Zimmer-Zerny, Frieda, 66
Zoozmann, Richard, 147
Zoroaster, 191

Stefan George (1868–1933) is, along with Hugo von Hofmannsthal and Rainer Maria Rilke, one of the pre-eminent German poets of the twentieth century. He also had an important, albeit controversial and provocative, role in German cultural history. It is generally agreed that he played a significant part in the transition of German literature to Modernism, particularly in poetry. At the same time he was an outspoken critic of modernity. He believed that only an all-encompassing cultural renewal could save modern man. Although George is often linked with the *l'art pour l'art* movement, and although his artistic consciousness was formed by European aestheticism, his poetry and the writings that emerged from the poets and intellectuals he gathered around him in the George Circle are above all a scathing commentary on the political, social, and cultural situation in Germany at the turn of the century.

George, who was imbued with the idea of the poet as a prophet and priest, saw himself as the Messiah of a New Hellenism and a New Reich led by an intellectual and aesthetic elite consisting of men who were bonded together through their allegiance to a charismatic leader. Some of the values that George proclaimed, among them a glorification of power, of heroism and self-sacrifice, were seized upon by the National Socialists, and subsequently his writings and those of his circle were considered by some to be proto-fascist. It did not help his reputation that after the Second World War much of the criticism of his works was practiced by uncritical, hagiographic George worshippers. In recent years, however, there has been a renewed and unbiased interest among scholars and critics in George and his circle. The wide-ranging and original essays in this volume explore anew George's poetry and his contribution to Modernism, the relation between his vision of a New Reich and fascist ideology, and his importance as a cultural critic.

JENS RIECKMANN is emeritus professor of German at the University of California, Irvine.

The wise plan of the book is well realized: those who would like to be introduced to the world of Stefan George — and not just in the Anglo-Saxon realm — will find in the *Companion* a well-versed guide.

CASTRUM PEREGRINI

This collection of nine essays is a rare addition to George scholarship in English. The editor's introduction gives welcome attention to George's early years . . . as well as an account of the *George-Kreis,* the troubled relationship with Hofmannsthal, and the poet's encounter with Maximin.

GERMAN STUDIES REVIEW

The *Companion* provides an accessible, intelligent, and wide-ranging introduction to George's works for Anglo-American readers.

MLR, 2006

An accessible, intelligent, and wide-ranging introduction to George's works. . . .

MODERN HUMANITIES RESEARCH

. . . provides an accessible, intelligent, and wide-ranging introduction to George's work for Anglo-American readers.

MODERN LANGUAGE REVIEW